CULTURE AND SOCIETY IN BRITAIN 1850–1890

A Source Book of Contemporary Writings

Edited by
J. M. GOLBY
at the Open University

OXFORD UNIVERSITY PRESS
in association with
THE OPEN UNIVERSITY

*This book has been printed digitally and produced in a standard specification
in order to ensure its continuing availability*

OXFORD
UNIVERSITY PRESS

Great Clarendon Street, Oxford OX2 6DP

Oxford University Press is a department of the University of Oxford.
It furthers the University̓ objective of excellence in research, scholarship,
and education by publishing worldwide in

Oxford New York

Auckland Bangkok Buenos Aires Cape Town Chennai
Dar es Salaam Delhi Hong Kong Istanbul Karachi Kolkata
Kuala Lumpur Madrid Melbourne Mexico City Mumbai Nairobi
S‹o Paulo Shanghai Taipei Tokyo Toronto

Oxford is a registered trade mark of Oxford University Press
in the UK and in certain other countries

Published in the United States
by Oxford University Press Inc., New York

ISBN 0-19-871112-3

Printed in Great Britain by

Antony Rowe Ltd., Eastbourne

Preface

THIS collection of contemporary writings from the period 1850–1890 has been assembled by the course team members of the third Arts Foundation Course (A102). All the extracts in the book are central to the debates and discussions which are raised in the Foundation Course, especially in the second part of the course, which consists of an interdisciplinary study of Culture and Society in Britain, 1850–1890. It is a set book for the course and one which is intended to be used throughout, from the opening history units to the concluding unit, which discusses change in later Victorian Britain.

Although this book has been designed particularly for Open University students, it is hoped that it will attract general readers who are interested in the period. But to them I must emphasize that the course team members had a number of particular and specific contemporary debates in mind when selecting the documents and, as a result, some issues are dealt with extensively whilst others are not touched upon. Hence there are, for example, no writings on imperialism or foreign affairs. Nevertheless, although, of necessity, there are gaps and a few writers who made valuable contributions to the period are omitted, it is hoped that readers will find a wide variety of informative, thought-provoking, and occasionally amusing, writings of the period.

The book is divided into six sections: (I) Historical and Social Background; (II) Religion: Conformity and Controversy; (III) Moral Values and the Social Order; (IV) Culture: Production, Consumption, and Status; (V) The Representation of the People; (VI) Town and Country. Unlike many other books containing collections of documents, there are no introductions to the extracts and we have not given the individual extracts titles other than quoting their source or the chapter-heading or title of the article from which they are taken. This was a deliberate decision taken on the grounds that such introductions only serve to convey our own views and opinions and we wish readers to reach their own conclusions from their readings of the various texts.

There is just one further point concerning the organization of the reader. In order that students may quickly identify particular sections in some of the longer extracts, we have numbered the paragraphs of these extracts. We have done this by indenting each paragraph with square brackets [ ] containing the number of the paragraph.

Finally, my thanks to all the members of the course team who have been so helpful at all the stages of the preparation of this book. Unfortunately, the course team is far too large to mention all by name but I should like, in particular, to thank Briony Fer for the time and trouble she spent in helping me select the illustrations and Sabine Phillips, who most efficiently typed large sections of this book.

J.M.G.

Acknowledgements

The editor and publisher gratefully acknowledge permission to reproduce copyright material.

Hannah Cullwick: *Diary, January 1871*. From *The Diaries of Hannah Cullwick* edited and introduced by Liz Stanley. Copyright © 1984 by Liz Stanley. Reprinted by permission of Virago Press Limited.

Majority Report of the Royal Commission on Trade Unions (1867–1869). Reprinted from *English Historical Documents 1833–1874* by G. M. Young and W. D. Hancock (1956). By permission of Eyre and Spottiswoode Publishers Limited.

Karl Marx: *Introduction to the Critique of Political Economy 1857*. From *Karl Marx, Friedrich Engels on Literature and Art*, Lee Baxandall and Stefan Morawski, eds. (1974). Reprinted by permission of Lawrence and Wishart Limited.

William Plomer, ed.: Extract from *Kilvert's Diary*. Reprinted by permission of Jonathan Cape Limited on behalf of the editor, Mrs Sheila Hooper.

George Bernard Shaw: Extracts from *The Star* (31 Jan. 1889, 21 Feb. 1889, 6 Dec. 1889), *The World* (21 Jan. 1891), and *The Hornet* (28 Feb. 1877, 4 July 1877). Reprinted by permission of The Society of Authors on behalf of the Bernard Shaw Estate.

Every reasonable effort has been made to obtain permission to quote extracts still in copyright, where these extracts are in excess of the amount covered by 'fair dealing'.

Contents

CONTENTS

II Religion: Conformity and Controversy

III Moral Values and the Social Order

List of Illustrations

I

Historical and Social Background

'A speech by Prince Albert in 1850 at a Banquet at the Mansion House
given by the Lord Mayor of London to Her Majesty's Ministers,
Foreign Ambassadors, Royal Commissioners of the Exhibition of 1851
and the Mayors of one hundred and eighty towns'

My Lord Mayor,

I am sincerely grateful for the kindness with which you have proposed my
health, and to you, gentlemen, for the cordiality with which you have
received this proposal.

It must indeed be most gratifying to me to find that a suggestion which I had
thrown out, as appearing to me of unimportance at this time, should have met
with such universal concurrence and approbation; for this has proved to me
that the view I took of the peculiar character and claims of the time we live in
was in accordance with the feelings and opinions of the country.

Gentlemen—I conceive it to be the duty of every educated person closely
to watch and study the time in which he lives, and, as far as in him lies, to
add his humble mite of individual exertion to further the accomplishment
of what he believes providence to have ordained. Nobody, however, who
has paid any attention to the peculiar features of our present era, will doubt
for a moment that we are living at a period of most wonderful transition,
which tends rapidly to accomplish that great end, to which, indeed, all history points—the realization of the unity of mankind. Not a unity which
breaks down the limits and levels the peculiar characteristics of the different nations of the earth, but rather a unity, the result and product of those
very national varieties and antagonistic qualities.

The distances which separated the different nations and parts of the
globe are rapidly vanishing before the achievements of modern invention,
and we can traverse them with incredible ease; the languages of all nations
are known, and their acquirement placed within the reach of everybody;
thought is communicated with the rapidity, and even by the power, of
lightning. On the other hand, the great principle of division of labour,
which may be called the moving power of civilisation, is being extended to
all branches of science, industry, and art.

Whilst formerly the greatest mental energies strove at universal know-ledge, and that knowledge was confined to the few, now they are directed on specialities, and in these, again, even to the minutest points; but the know-ledge acquired becomes at once the property of the community at large; for, whilst formerly discovery was wrapped in secrecy, the publicity of the pres-ent day causes that no sooner is a discovery or invention made than it is already improved upon and surpassed by competing efforts. The products of all quarters of the globe are placed at our disposal, and we have only to choose which is the best and the cheapest for our purposes, and the powers of production are intrusted to the stimulus of competition and capital.

So man is approaching a more complete fulfilment of that great and sacred mission which he has to perform in this world. His reason being created after the image of God, he has to use it to discover the laws by which the Almighty governs His creation, and, by making these laws his standard of action, to conquer nature to his use; himself a divine instrument.

Science discovers these laws of power, motion, and transformation; industry applies them to the raw matter, which the earth yields us in abun-dance, but which becomes valuable only by knowledge. Art teaches us the immutable laws of beauty and symmetry, and gives to our productions forms in accordance to them.

Gentlemen—the Exhibition of 1851 is to give us a true test and a living picture of the point of development at which the whole of mankind has arrived in this great task, and a new starting-point from which all nations will be able to direct their further exertions.

I confidently hope that the first impression which the view of this vast collection will produce upon the spectator will be that of deep thankfulness to the Almighty for the blessings which he has bestowed upon us already here below; and the second, the conviction that they can only be realized in proportion to the help which we are prepared to render each other; there-fore, only by peace, love, and ready assistance, not only between individ-uals, but between the nations of the earth.

This being *my* conviction, I must be highly gratified to see here assem-bled the magistrates of all the important towns of this realm, sinking all their local and possibly political differences, the representatives of the dif-ferent political opinions of the country, and the representatives of the dif-ferent Foreign Nations—today representing only *one interest*!

(*Principal Speeches and Addresses of H.R.H. the Prince Consort*, 1862, pp. 110–12.)

1.2 Thomas Babington Macaulay's Diary (1 May 1851)

Thursday, May 1, 1851.
A fine day for the opening of the Exhibition. A little cloudy in the morning, but generally sunny and pleasant. I was struck by the number of foreigners

in the streets. All, however, were respectable and decent people. I saw none of the men of action with whom the Socialists were threatening us. I went to the Park, and along the Serpentine. There were immense crowds on both sides of the water. I should think that there must have been near three hundred thousand people in Hyde Park at once. The sight among the green boughs was delightful. The boats, and little frigates, darting across the lake; the flags; the music; the guns;—everything was exhilarating, and the temper of the multitude the best possible. I fell in with Punch Greville, and walked with him for an hour. He, like me, thought the outside spectacle better worth seeing than the pageant under cover. He showed me a letter from Madame de Lieven, foolish, with an affectation of cleverness and profundity, just like herself. She calls this Exhibition a bold, a rash, experiment. She apprehends a horrible explosion. 'You may get through it safe; and, if you do, you will give yourselves more airs than ever.' And this woman is thought a political oracle in some circles! There is just as much chance of a revolution in England as of the falling of the moon. . . .

(The Life and Letters of Lord Macaulay, ed. Sir G. O. Trevelyan, 1889,
pp. 550–1.)

Letter from the Duchess of Gloucester to Queen Victoria (2 May 1851) 1.3

Gloucester House, 2nd May 1851.

My Dearest Victoria,

It is impossible to tell you how warmly I do participate in all you must have felt yesterday, as well as dear Albert, at everything having gone off so beautifully. After so much anxiety and the trouble he has had, the joy *must* be the greater.

The sight from my window was the gayest and the most gratifying to witness, and to me who loves you so dearly as *I do*, made it the more delightful. The good humour of all around, the fineness of the day, the manner you were received in both going and coming from the Exhibition, was quite perfect. Therefore what must it have been in the inside of the building!

Mary and George came away in perfect *enchantment*, and every soul I have seen describes it as the fairest sight that ever was seen and the best-conducted *fête!* Why, G. Bathurst told me it far surpassed the *Coronation* as to magnificence, and we all agreed in rejoicing that the *Foreigners should* have witnessed the affection of the *People to you* and *your Family*, and how the *English people* do *love* and respect the *Crown*. As to Mary, she was in *perfect enchantment*, and full of how pretty your dear little Victoria looked, and how nicely she was dressed, and so grateful to your Mother for all her kindness to her. I should have written to you last night, but I thought I would not plague you with a letter until to-day, as I think you must have been tired last night with the *excitement* of the day. I shall ever lament the having missed such a sight, but I comfort myself in feeling sure I could not have followed you (as I ought) when you walked round. Therefore I was *better* out of the way. We drank your health at dinner and *congratulation* on the *complete success* of *Albert's plans* and *arrangements*, and also dear little Arthur's health. Many thanks for kind note received last night. Love to Albert.

Yours,
Mary

(*The Letters of Queen Victoria, 1837–61*, ed. A. C. Benson and Viscount
Esher, 1908, vol. 2, p. 317.)

1.4 Letter from Queen Victoria to the King of the Belgians (3 May 1851)

Buckingham Palace, 3rd May 1851

My dearest Uncle,

. . . I wish you *could* have witnessed the *1st May* 1851, the *greatest* day in our history, the *most beautiful* and *imposing* and *touching* spectacle ever seen, and the triumph of my beloved Albert. Truly it was astonishing, a fairy scene. Many cried, and all felt touched and impressed with devotional feelings. It was the *happiest, proudest* day in my life, and I can think of nothing else. Albert's dearest name is immortalised with this *great* conception, *his* own, and my *own* dear country *showed* she was *worthy* of it. The triumph is *immense*, for up to the *last hour* the difficulties, the opposition, and the ill-natured attempts to annoy and frighten, of a certain set of. fashionables and Protectionists, were immense; but Albert's temper, patience, firmness, and energy surmounted all, and the feeling is universal. *You* will be astounded at this great work when you see it!—the beauty of the building and the vastness of it all. I can never thank God enough. I feel *so* happy, so proud. Our dear guests were much pleased and impressed. You are right to like the dear Princess, for she is a noble-minded, warm-hearted, distinguished person, much attached to you, and who revered dearest Louise. Oh! *how* I thought of *her* on that great day, how kindly she would have rejoiced in our success! Now good-bye, dearest Uncle.

Ever your devoted Niece,

Victoria R.

(*The Letters of Queen Victoria, 1837–61*, ed. A. C. Benson and Viscount
Esher, 1908, vol. 2, pp. 317–18.)

The Great Exhibition (17 May 1851)

For the nonce, and until further orders and new arrangements, London is not simply the capital of a great nation, but the metropolis of the world. The Exhibition has deprived it of its local character, and rendered it no longer English merely, but cosmopolitan.

The English are great travellers. Ever since the peace of Waterloo let loose the swarms of our sight-seeing countrymen to visit every nook and corner of Europe—to admire fine scenery—to pry into collections of pictures and curiosities, and to cultivate the national taste for the foreign, the nations of the Continent have been familiar with the long purses, the eccentricities, and the polyglot accomplishments of the restless English of the upper and middle classes. But our Continental friends have not returned our visits. They have seen us abroad, and not at home; and have, for the most part, been slow to understand what inducements we could have to travel. While it has been rare to find an educated Englishman who did not speak French, or perhaps German and Italian, more or less perfectly, and who did not know by personal inspection the main features of the most celebrated of the Continental cities; it has been still more rare, among the same classes in France or Germany, to find a man who personally knew anything about London or who could speak, or even read, the English language. But what with the Crystal Palace and the facilities afforded by the railway system, without which the Exhibition would not have been possible, the people of the Continent have, for the first time, been smitten with the love of seeing strange parts. Already this intercourse has produced a good effect: the columns of the French press bear pleasant testimony to the more kindly feeling consequent upon more intimate knowledge which the Exhibition has been the means of producing: and a whole host of errors, misconceptions, and prejudices bid fair to be driven for ever out of the heads of our nearest neighbours. John Bull is no longer an ogre, but a genial and courteous gentleman. The old joke about the gloom, smoke and dirt of London, and the austerity, inhospitality, and semi-lunacy of the English character, has been dissipated, and our Parisian friends confess that the 'sombre' city has produced the gayest, most fairy-like, most beautiful and original building in the world, and that these gloomy English people are positively well dressed, as pleasure-loving, as agreeable, and as polite as the French themselves. They joke us a little about our public statues and buildings, but they forgive much for the sake of the Crystal Palace.

There was at one time a fear that London would suffer in the estimation of strangers, for all time to come, by the extortionate prices demanded for lodgings and food during the period of the Exhibition. But this fear has blown aside. The lodging-house keepers and the *exploiteurs* of furnished houses, though at one time inclined to be exorbitant in their demands, have come to their senses, and foreigners in London may be lodged almost, if not quite, as reasonably as usual. The price of food has remained the same, and the only extortion that has really taken root and flourished, and served to give us a bad character in the eyes of our visitors, is the vile attempt of the omnibus proprietors to raise their fares twenty-five per cent. But we rejoice to see that the omnibus people are likely to be losers by their impudent rapacity, and that the fourpenny fares will not pay . . .

Until the present time, the upper and middle classes, both of Great Britain and the Continent, are the only classes who have come to London. The multitudes have not yet made their appearance; but when the price of admission shall be reduced to a shilling, the excursionists will rush in by the cheap trains from every part of the United Kingdom, as well as from the Continent. Paris will land its thousands per day upon our shores; and the workers of Sheffield and Birmingham, of Manchester and the West Riding, of Glasgow and Belfast, and of countless other industrial towns and districts, will pour their teeming myriads into the great cosmopolitan metropolis, to carry away with them, there cannot be a doubt, a remembrance of pleasure and instruction to last them for the remainder of their lives. For six months or more, the intelligent mechanics of our distant towns have been clubbing their weekly shillings and pence for this rational purpose; and among the many interesting spectacles which London will shortly offer to foreigners, none will be more interesting than the visits of these hordes of working-men—the men who made the Exhibition what it is, and who, we fervently hope, will derive the greatest advantage from it . . .

(*Illustrated London News*, 17 May 1851.)

1.6 Henry Mayhew

(a) 'Of the Earnings of Costermongers' (1851)

Some costers, I am told, make upwards of 30s. a week all the year round; but allowing for cessations in the street trade, through bad weather, neglect, ill-health, or casualty of any kind, and taking the more prosperous costers with the less successful—the English with the Irish—the men with the women—perhaps 10s. a week may be a fair average of the earnings of the entire body the year through.

These earnings, I am assured, were five years ago at least 25 per cent. higher; some said they made half as much again: 'I can't make it out how it is,' said one man, 'but I remember that I could go out and sell twelve bushel of fruit in a day, when sugar was dear, and now, when sugar's cheap, I can't sell three bushel on the same round. Perhaps we want thinning.'

Such is the state of the working-classes, say all the costers, they have little or no money to spend. 'Why, I can assure you,' declared one of the parties from whom I obtained much important information, 'there's my missus—she sits at the corner of the street with fruit. Eight years ago she would have taken 8s. out of that street on a Saturday, and last Saturday week she had one bushel of apples, which cost 1s. 6d. She was out from ten in the morning till ten at night, and all she took that day was 1s. 7½d. Go to whoever you will you will hear much upon the same thing.' Another told me, 'The costers are often obliged to sell the things for what they gave for them. The people haven't got money to lay out with them—they tell us so; and if they are poor we must be poor too. If we can't get a profit upon what goods we buy with our stock-money, let it be our own or anybody's else, we are compelled to live upon it, and, when that's broken into, we must either go to the workhouse or starve. If we go to the workhouse, they'll give us a piece of dry bread, and abuse us worse than dogs.' Indeed, the whole course of my narratives shows how the costers generally—though far from universally—complain of the depressed state of their trade.

(H. Mayhew, *London Labour and the London Poor*, 1851; reprinted 1968, vol. 4, p. 54.)

(b) 'Prostitution among Needlewomen' (1849)

During the course of my investigation into the condition of those who are dependent upon their needle for their support, I had been so repeatedly assured that the young girls were mostly compelled to resort to prostitution to eke out their subsistence, that I was anxious to test the truth of the statement. I had seen much want, but I had no idea of the intensity of the privations suffered by the needlewomen of London until I came to inquire into this part of the subject. But the poor creatures shall speak for themselves. I should inform the reader, however, that I have made inquiries into the truth of the almost incredible statements here given, and I can in most of the particulars at least vouch for the truth of the statement. Indeed, in one instance—that of the last case here recorded—I travelled nearly ten miles in order to obtain the character of the young woman. The first case is that of a good-looking girl. Her story is as follows:

'I make moleskin trowsers. I get 7d. and 8d. per pair. I can do two pairs in a day, and twelve when there is full employment, in a week. But some weeks I have no work at all. I work from six in the morning to ten at night; that is what I call my day's work. When I am fully employed I get from 7s. to 8s. a week. My expenses out of that for twist, thread, and candles are about 1s. 6d. a week, leaving me about 6s. per week clear. But there's coals to pay for out of this, and that's at the least 6d. more; so 5s. 6d. is the very outside of what I earn when I'm in full work. Lately I have been dreadfully slack; so we are every winter, all of us "sloppers", and that's the time when we wants the most money. The week before last I had but two pair to make all the week; so that I only earnt 1s. clear. For this last month I'm sure I haven't done any more than that each week. Taking one week with another, all the year round I don't make above 3s. clear money each week. I don't work at any other kind of slop-work. The trowsers work is held to be the best paid of all. I give 1s. a week rent.

'My father died when I was five years of age. My mother is a widow, upwards of 66 years of age, and seldom has a day's work. Generally once in the week she is employed pot-scouring—that is, cleaning publicans' pots. She is paid 4d. a dozen for that, and does about four dozen and a half, so that she gets about 1s. 6d. in the day by it. For the rest she is dependent upon me. I am 20 years of age the 25th of this month. We earn together, to keep the two of us, from 4s. 6d. to 5s. each week. Out of this we have to pay 1s. rent, and there remains 3s. 6d. to 4s. to find us both in food and clothing. It is of course impossible for us to live upon it, and the consequence is I am obliged to go a bad way. I have been three years working at slop-work.

'I was virtuous when I first went to work, and I remained so till this last twelvemonth. I struggled very hard to keep myself chaste, but I found that I couldn't get food and clothing for myself and mother, so I took to live with a young man. He is turned 20. He is a tinman. He did promise to marry me, but his sister made mischief between me and him, so that parted us. I have not seen him now for about six months, and I can't say whether he will keep his promise or not. I am now pregnant by him, and expect to be confined in two months' time. He knows of my situation, and so does my mother. My mother believed me to be married to him. She knows otherwise now. I was very fond of him, and had known him for two years before he seduced me. He could make 14s. a week. He told me if I came to live with him he'd take care I shouldn't want, and both mother and me had been very bad off before. He said, too, he'd make me his lawful wife, but I hardly cared so long as I could get food for myself and mother.

'Many young girls at the shop advised me to go wrong. They told me how comfortable they was off; they said they could get plenty to eat and drink, and good clothes. There isn't one young girl as can get her living by slop-work. The masters all know this, but they wouldn't own to it of course. It stands to reason that no one can live and pay rent, and find clothes, upon 3s. a week, which is the most they can make clear, even the best hands, at the moleskin and cord trowsers work. There's poor people moved out of our house that was making $\frac{3}{4}$d. shirts. I am satisfied there is not one young girl that works at slop-work that is virtuous, and there are some thousands in the trade. They may do very well if they have got mothers and fathers to find them a home and food, and to let them have what they earn for clothes; then they may be virtuous, but not without. I've heard of numbers who have gone from slop-work to the streets altogether for a living, and I shall be obliged to do the same thing myself unless something better turns up for me.

'If I was never allowed to speak no more, it was the little money I got by my labour that led me to go wrong. Could I have honestly earnt enough to have subsisted upon, to find me in proper food and clothing, such as is necessary, I should not have gone astray; no, never—As it was I fought against it as long as I could—that I did—to the last. I hope to be able to get a ticket for a midwife; a party has promised me as much, and, he says, if possible, he'll get me an order for a box of linen. My child will only increase my burdens, and if my young man won't support my child I must go on the streets altogether. I know how horrible all this is. It would have been much better for me to have subsisted upon a dry crust and water rather than be as I am now. But no one knows the temptations of us poor girls in want. Gentlefolks can never understand it. If I had been born a lady it wouldn't have been very hard to have acted like one. To be poor and to be honest, especially with young girls, is the hardest struggle of all. There isn't one in a thousand that can get the better of it. I am ready to say again, that it was want, and nothing more, that made me transgress. If I had been better paid I should have done better. Young as I am, my life is a curse to me. If the Almighty would please to take me before my child is born, I should die happy.'

(The Unknown Mayhew: Selections from the Morning Chronicle,
ed. E. P. Thompson and E. Yeo, 1971, pp. 147–9.)

From the Report of Leonard Horner, Factory Inspector, to Lord Palmerston, Home Secretary (1852)   1.7

At no period during the last seventeen years that I have been officially acquainted with the manufacturing districts in Lancashire have I known such general prosperity; the activity in every branch is extraordinary. In my last report I gave on [*sic*] account of the vast increase of factories during the two preceding years, and there is no cessation, for new mills are going up everywhere. It is not to be wondered at, therefore, that I should hear of a great scarcity of hands, of much machinery standing idle from the want of people to work it, and of a rise of wages. This scarcity of hands has led to a considerable increase in the number of children employed in my district, which indeed has been going on, happily, for a long time; I say 'happily' without hesitation, for now that children are restricted to half a day's work, and are required to attend school, I know no description of work so advantageous for them as that in a factory. . . .

If those who in 1833 predicted (and there were some of great authority among our political economists who did so) the ruin of our manufacturers if the then proposed restrictions on factory labour were adopted, will now fairly and candidly look at the results of this great practical experiment in legislation, whether in relation to the improved condition of the factory workers, or to the increase of mills and to the fortunes since made in every department of manufacture subject to the law, they must, I think, admit, that they have seen grounds to make them pause before they, in future, condemn measures for elevating the moral and social condition of the humbler classes by the regulation of their labour, as being opposed to principle; for the factory legislation has been proved to be in entire accordance with principle, even with that of the production of wealth, when the term principle is understood in an enlarged and comprehensive sense.

I believe the workpeople never were so well off as they are at present; constant employment, good wages, cheap food, and cheap clothing; many cheap, innocent, and elevating amusements brought within their reach; and thanks to the last Factory Act, the greater proportion of all the operatives in mills have at length time for some mental improvement, healthful recreation, and enjoyment of their families and friends.

(*British Parliamentary Papers, Factories*, 1852–6, vol. 9, pp. 19–21.)

1.8 Karl Marx, Speech on the fourth anniversary of the *People's Paper*, London (14 Apr. 1856)

The so-called revolutions of 1848 were but poor incidents—small fractures and fissures in the dry crust of European society. However, they denounced the abyss. Beneath the apparently solid surface they betrayed oceans of liquid matter, only needing expansion to rend into fragments continents of hard rock. Noisily and confusedly they proclaimed the emancipation of the proletarian, i.e. the secret of the nineteenth century, and of the revolution of that century. That social revolution, it is true, was no novelty invented in 1848. Steam, electricity, and the self-acting mule were revolutionists of a rather more dangerous character than even citizens Barbès, Raspail and Blanqui. But, although the atmosphere in which we live weighs upon every one with a 20,000 lb. force, do you feel it? No more than European society before 1848 felt the revolutionary atmosphere enveloping and pressing it from all sides. There is one great fact, characteristic of this our nineteenth century, a fact which no party dares deny. On the one hand, there have started into life industrial and scientific forces which no epoch of former human history had ever suspected. On the other hand, there exist symptoms of decay, far surpassing the horrors recorded of the latter times of the Roman empire. In our days everything seems pregnant with its contrary. Machinery, gifted with the wonderful power of shortening and fructifying human labour, we behold starving and overworking it. The new-fangled sources of wealth, by some strange weird spell, are turned into sources of want. The victories of art seem bought by the loss of character. At the same pace that mankind masters nature, man seems to become enslaved to other men or to his own infamy. Even the pure light of science seems unable to shine but on the dark background of ignorance. All our invention and progress seem to result in endowing material forces with intellectual life, and in stultifying human life into a material force. This antagonism between modern industry and science on the one hand, modern misery and dissolution on the other hand; this antagonism between the productive powers and the social relations of our epoch is a fact, palpable, overwhelming, and not to be controverted. Some parties may wail over it; others may wish to get rid of modern arts, in order to get rid of modern conflicts. Or they may imagine that so signal a progress in industry wants to be completed by as signal a regress in politics. On our part, we do not mistake the shape of the shrewd spirit that continues to mark all these contradictions. We know that to work well the new-fangled forces of society, they only want to be mastered by new-fangled men—and such are the working men. They are as much the invention of modern time as machinery itself. In the signs that bewilder the middle class, the aristocracy and the poor prophets of regression, we do recognize our brave friend, Robin Goodfellow, the old mole that can work in the earth so fast, that worthy pioneer—the Revolution. The English working men are the first-born sons of modern industry. They will then, certainly, not be the last in aiding the social revolution produced by that industry, a revolution which means the emancipation of their own class all over the world, which is as universal as capital-rule and wages-slavery. I know the heroic struggles the English working class have gone through since the middle of the last century—struggles [no] less glorious because they are shrouded in obscurity, and burked by the middle-class historian. To revenge the misdeeds of the ruling class, there existed in the Middle Ages, in Germany, a secret tribunal called the 'Vehmgericht'. If a red cross was seen marked on a house, people knew that its owner was doomed by the 'Vehm'. All the houses of Europe are now marked with the mysterious red cross. History is the judge—its executioner, the proletarian.

(*Surveys from Exile*, ed. D. Fernbach, 1973, vol. 2, pp. 299–300.)

J. D. Milne, from *The Industrial and Social Position of Women* (1857)   1.9

The situation of a domestic servant . . . is attended with considerable comfort. With abundant work it combines a wonderful degree of liberty, discipline, health, physical comfort, good example, regularity, room for advancement, encouragement to acquire saving habits. The most numerous class of depositors in the Savings Banks is that of domestic servants. The situation frequently involves much responsibility, and calls forth the best features of character. Kind attachment in return for honest service is not uncommon with the master or mistress; and an honest pride in the relation springs up on both sides and lasts throughout life.

(*Women in Public 1850–1900*, ed. P. Hollis, 1979, p. 60.)

1.10 Notes by the Chief Constable of Staffordshire of a Meeting of Colliers held at Horsley Heath, Staffordshire (30 Aug. 1858)

Present, in the open-air 800 Colliers; with Col. Hogg, Chief Constable of Staffordshire, with a strong body of police assisted by Capt. Seagrave Chief Constable of Wolverhampton, and a detachment of men under him.— Time, from 10 a.m. till 1.20.

Joseph Linney was called to the chair. He gave out a Hymn. When it had been sung he said that their employers compelled them to strike. Before the strike the work they had would not support their wives and their children, and now their masters wanted to reduce one shilling. He had looked at it in all its various shapes and forms, and a more barbarous action never could be acted, than was now attempted by the masters. From Xmas last to the time that the strike took place, the average wages of the coal miners was not more than 15/– a week. (Voices: It was not so much as that.) Out of the 15/– they had to pay 1s for drink and 6d for 'sick' money before they left the 'field'; and when they got home there was the rent to pay, and also the taxes. After that how much had they got to support their families? In general not more that 11s a week; and yet their employers were so 'hard hearted' as to treat them in the way they had. He did not wish to injure their employers, but it was the duty of their masters to give them a fair day's wages for a fair day's work; and he thought they would all agree with him when he said with the auctioneer—'We ask no more and we will take no less'. (*Ld. app.*) The speaker said he was a teetotaller and a Sunday School teacher. Because he would not drink he had been turned out of a pit. . . . When the policemen saw the dangers that the miners worked in they said—'Why we would not work in such places for a pound a day'. (*Ap.*) And the colliers might get a pound a day if they liked—for the coal was the spring of all commerce and industry, and a pound of it was worth more than a pound of gold. They had to sell their labour, and it was their duty to sell it at the highest price. If all the colliers in the Kingdom were to lay down their tools and demand a high price for their labour they could get it. It was because of the extravagance of their masters in a time of prosperity that they now that trade was bad wanted to reduce their wages. They wanted even now to spend on themselves what they got out of the wages of their workmen. But should they reduce their wages? (*Cries of No!!*) He was glad to hear them say so. They had gone on comfortably till Oldbury Wake; and if the meeting intended to go on till West Bromwich Wake, which was held at the end of November, they would then take a fresh start and remain on strike till Christmas. (*Laughter and applause*) In this great struggle colliers had been working with their brains and had turned poets. They had been asking other districts to join them. He held a letter in his hand from one of these districts. It was from Brierley Hill and Kingswinford. That letter asked the miners of that (the Tipton, Oldbury and West Bromwich) district to come amongst them and have a good meeting, and then the writer said—'We will lay down our tools to a man and will work no more till you have got your wages and we have got ours'. (*Ld. applause.*) [The letter was dated from Brierley Hill, incorrectly spelled, and signed 'A Miner'.] The agitation was spreading far and wide. He told them (the meeting) that they would do it, and they were doing it. (*Applause.*) In a fortnight they should get their money. . . .

Job Radford, a brickmaker, of Oldbury, then spoke at some length encouraging the miners to form a trades association, similar to that of the brickmakers of Manchester—in consequence of which association the brickmaker now got twice the wages that he used to get. . . .

Job Radford again spoke inculcating temperance; after which it was determined that a meeting should be held at Brierley Hill on that day week at 11 o'clock; and on that evening (Monday) at Tipton; after which the proceedings terminated.

(Documents in English Economic History: England since 1760, ed. B. W.
Clapp, 1976, pp. 359–61.)

Karl Marx, from the Preface to *A Contribution to the Critique of Political Economy* (1859)

In the social production of their life, men enter into definite relations that are indispensable and independent of their will, relations of production which correspond to a definite state of the development of their material productive forces. The sum total of these relations of production constitutes the economic structure of society, the real foundation, on which rises a legal and political superstructure and to which correspond definite forms of social consciousness. The mode of production of material life conditions the social, political and intellectual life process in general. It is not the consciousness of men that determines their being, but, on the contrary, their social being that determines their consciousness. At a certain stage of their development, the material productive forces of society come in conflict with the existing relations of production, or—what is but a legal expression for the same thing—with the property relations within which they have been at work hitherto. From forms of development of the productive forces these relations turn into their fetters. Then begins an epoch of social revolution. With the change of the economic foundation the entire immense superstructure is more or less rapidly transformed. In considering such transformations a distinction should always be made between the material transformation of the economic conditions of production, which can be determined with the precision of natural science, and the legal, political, religious, aesthetic or philosophic—in short, ideological forms in which men become conscious of this conflict and fight it out. Just as our opinion of an individual is not based on what he thinks of himself, so can we not judge of such a period of transformation by its own consciousness; on the contrary, this consciousness must be explained rather from the contradictions of material life, from the existing conflict between the social productive forces and the relations of production.

(*Marx/Engels on Literature and Art*, ed. Lee Baxandall and Stefan Morawski, 1974, pp. 85–6.)

1.12 Children's Employment Commission, from the Second Report (1864)

It is said that hitherto the use of steam as the motive power has not met with much favour, but Mr White and Mr Lord state that this power is now used in some cases, although several employers have adopted and abandoned it, owing to the difficulty of checking the speed and the injury caused to the machines by the constant shaking.

At the Army Clothing Depot, Pimlico, where upwards of 700 women are employed, this difficulty appears to have been overcome, and the same may be said of the very large shirt establishment of Messrs Tillie and Henderson, Londonderry, and of Messrs Tait's army clothing manufactory, Limerick, employing 1,000 to 1,200 hands; it may therefore be anticipated that the application of steam power will extend and become general. The introduction of the machine, joined to the extraordinary and increasing demand in foreign, and especially in the colonial markets, for wearing apparel of English manufacture, is accomplishing quite a revolution in these trades; in fact it is evident that the whole employment is at this time in a state of transition, and is undergoing the same change as that effected in the lace trade, weaving, etc., mechanical power superseding hand labour.

Advantages of the Sewing Machine

The history of the sewing machine affords, probably, one of the best illustrations of the benefits conferred upon all classes engaged in industrial pursuits, and especially on the operatives, by the substitution of machinery for hand labour.

It appears from the statement of Mr Tillie, that the machine now performs the work formerly done in London known as the most miserable, and even notorious, of all occupations, under the name of 'slop work', in which grown up women, by working very long hours, could only earn, as in some of the poorest paid branches they still do, from 4s to 6s a week. On comparing the details given further on, it will appear, speaking generally, that the wages of machinists, averaging 14s to 16s a week, are at least one-third higher than those of handworkers in the same department. The economy of production effected by the machine, with the general development of trade in late years, has also led to a great increase in the number of hands. The result of these two conditions combined has, in the aggregate, greatly added to the national wealth. Thus, in the Londonderry district, where the machine shirt business was only introduced 14 years ago by the firm of Messrs Tillie and Henderson, it is estimated by the first-named gentleman 'that the whole sum paid for labour in this branch of manufacture now amounts to nearly a quarter of a million yearly, circulating in cash for the general benefit of all'. Mr Tillie may therefore well say, 'the benefit conferred on this part of Ireland by the introduction of this branch of manufacture is enormous'.

But, in addition to the pecuniary gain, another great boon has been conferred on the operative class by the reduction of the protracted hours of work formerly exacted by the system of hand labour. It will subsequently appear that in the shirt and clothing factories, and especially in Ireland, where the greatest change has taken place, the hours for the most part do not exceed, in the case of young persons and adults, those of the Factory Acts, in fact they are often considerably below these, being at ordinary times only nine or 10 hours. . . .

The introduction of the machine has necessitated the employment, on the whole, of older children and girls, the usual age for commencing being about 14, one consequence of which is that in these factories the great majority of the employed being above 13 are either adults or 'young persons', as defined by the Factory Act, and therefore entitled to work full time, thus facilitating the introduction of legislative measures.

(*Documents in English Economic History: England since 1760*,
ed. B. W. Clapp, 1976, pp. 156–8.)

R. Dudley Baxter, from *National Income* (1868)   I.13

There is in the Atlantic an island—the Peak of Teneriffe—which rises from the sea in a pyramidal form to the height of 12,000 feet, conspicuous from every point of the horizon, and casting its shadow from the morning or evening sun for fifty miles over the ocean. An inhabitant is scarcely aware of its real proportions: for if he lives at its foot, he sees chiefly the lower eminences which rise immediately above him; and if he climbs the heights he is apt to lose sight of the broad base which spreads below. He must leave the land and sail out into the offing, before he can form any accurate picture of the real outline, and grasp as a whole the shape and majesty of his mountain isle. I have often thought that such an island is a good emblem of a wealthy state, with its long low base of labouring population, with its uplands of the middle classes, and with the towering peaks and summits of those with princely incomes. The difficulty is, to ascertain the relative dimensions of these mountain zones. If we take our stand on the lower plateau we are absorbed in its extent and richness, and cannot see or appreciate the ridges which rise tier upon tier above us; and if we devote ourselves to exploring and measuring the higher ranges we are prone to overlook and despise the plains far below us. We must sail out into the offing, till we can see the island as one grand whole, and realize its true proportions.

There can scarcely be an inquiry more interesting to those who take a pride in their country than the investigation of the statistics of our National Income. What are the means and aggregate wages of our labouring population; what the numbers and aggregate profits of the middle classes; what the revenues of our great proprietors and capitalists; and what the pecuniary strength of the nation to bear the burdens annually falling upon us? What capital in land and goods and money is stored up for our subsistence, and for carrying out our enterprises? What is the relative magnitude of our National Debt? What progress has been made since the beginning of the century in the increase of our income and the accumulation of savings? And what are the risks to which our wealth is exposed, and the precautions that ought to be taken for our own protection and for the safety of posterity?

The materials for such an inquiry are abundantly ample; but their enormous mass renders it difficult to present them clearly and in small compass. The long catalogue of occupations of the people, and the infinite variety of wages even in the same occupations, can only be appreciated by those who have endeavoured to reduce them to order. Minute accuracy is unattainable, and we are obliged to work by general averages. The great object is to render those averages trustworthy and simple, and that they should not be undigested masses of figures, of mere lists of unconnected totals, but coherent and lucid. Nor ought important facts to rest upon mere assertion; the authorities for the facts, and the reasons for the calculations, ought in every case to be given, so that the reader may refer and verify for himself . . .

The Income-Classes

The first step towards a reliable estimate of the Income of a nation is to ascertain the number of individuals who possess or earn it. This can be done for the United Kingdom from the Census Tables of 1861, which give in very great detail the occupations of the people, and the number of persons engaged in each. From them it is possible to ascertain, with tolerable accuracy, the number of persons who may be presumed to have independent incomes or wages. They are as follows:–

POPULATION OF ENGLAND AND WALES, 1861

I. *Persons with Incomes or Wages* (Men, boys, women, and girls)		9,289,000
II. *Persons without Incomes or Wages*		10,626,000
	Total accounted for	19,915,000

Besides 151,000 respecting whom nothing was ascertained.

If we could obtain the average income of each occupation we should be able to deduce the aggregate income of the nation. This method is practicable for the occupation pursued by the Manual Labour Class, whose wages are generally at average rates, known to their employers. But it fails with those above the Manual Labour Class, whose earnings are much more variable, and whose incomes are in great part derived from capital. It becomes necessary, therefore, to make a further classification of the persons with independent incomes into the *Upper and Middle Classes* on the one hand, and the *Manual Labour Class* on the other. I purposely adopt the latter term, as less ambiguous than *Working Classes* . . .

The Upper and Middle Classes And The Manual Labour Class

Before plunging into the question of Incomes, I should like to digress for a short time to a point of great interest, viz. to endeavour to determine the total numbers, including families, of the Upper and Middle Classes and the Manual Labour Class of England and Wales. The calculation has often been made on conjectural grounds, and with the most diverse results, usually varying according to the personal predilections of the calculator. The first Table given in the Appendix affords the means of ascertaining their numbers with something like certainty. It gives the total number of males above twenty years of age who in the Census Tables of 1861 have occupations belonging to the Upper and Middle Classes; and shows their number to be 1,194,000. But the males above twenty years of age bear a known proportion to the total population, being as nearly as possible twenty-six per cent, or in round numbers one-fourth. So that we may with accuracy calculate the total numbers of the Upper and Middle Classes at a little less than four times the number of their adult males. Then by subtraction from the total population we can find the total number of the Manual Labour Classes. Performing these operations, and adding six per cent. for the increase since 1861, we find that in England and Wales, out of a total population in 1867 of 21,000,000, the Upper and Middle Classes were 4,870,000 and the Manual Labour Class 16,130,000.

It is a confirmation of these figures that the number of £10 houses in boroughs and counties of England and Wales in the Electoral Returns of 1866 (allowing 50,000 for the difference between rating and rental in the counties) was 1,250,000, of which about 140,000 were occupied by the Manual Labour Class. The remainder, or 1,110,000 houses, correspond nearly with the 4,870,000 persons of the Upper and Middle Classes, and with their servants.

The complete table is as follows:–

ENGLAND AND WALES, 1867

UPPER AND MIDDLE AND MANUAL LABOUR CLASSES

	Persons	
Upper and Middle Classes—		
With Independent Incomes	2,053,000	
Dependent	2,817,000	
		4,870,000
Manual Labour Class—		
Earning Wages	7,785,000	
Dependent	8,345,000	
		16,130,000
Total Population of England and Wales, 1867		21,000,000

Hence the Upper and Middle Classes are 5,000,000 in round numbers, and have nearly three persons dependent for every two with independent income.

The Manual Labour are 16,000,000 in round numbers, and are almost equally divided between earners and non-earners.

In Scotland the same data and principles of calculation, with 3 per cent. increase of population, give—

SCOTLAND, 1867

	Persons
Upper and Middle Classes	692,000
Manual Labour Class	2,460,000
Total Population, 1867	3,152,000

The proportions between the independent incomes or earners and the dependent persons in each class, are the same as in England.

In Ireland the same calculation, but with 4 per cent. decrease of population, gives—

IRELAND, 1867

	Persons
Upper and Middle Classes	1,056,000
Manual Labour Class	4,501,000
Total Population, 1867	5,557,000

For the United Kingdom the several Classes are as follows:—

UNITED KINGDOM, 1867

Upper and Middle Classes—	Persons	
With Independent Incomes	2,759,000	
Dependent	3,859,000	
		6,618,000
Manual Labour Class—		
Earning Wages	10,961,000	
Dependent	12,130,000	
		23,091,000
Total Estimated Population		29,709,000

The per centages are—Upper and Middle Classes, 23 per cent.; Manual Labour Class, 77 per cent.

Putting the result into round numbers, out of a total population of 30,000,000, the Upper and Middle Classes are 7,000,000 and the Manual Labour Class 23,000,000.

Recurring to the simile in which I compared the State to an island; rather more than three-fourths of its surface is formed by the Manual Labour Class, and rather less than one-fourth by the Upper and Middle Classes.

(National Income, 1868, pp. 1–3, 7–8, 13–17.)

Letter from S. C. Nicholson and W. H. Wood to Secretaries of Trades' I.14
Councils, Federations of Trades, and Trade Societies (16 Apr. 1868)

Manchester, April 16th, 1868

Sir:

You are requested to lay the following before your Society. The vital *interests* involved, it is conceived, will justify the officials in convening a special meeting for the consideration thereof.

The Manchester and Salford Trades' Council having recently taken into their serious consideration the present aspect of Trades Unions, and the profound ignorance which prevails in the public mind with reference to their operations and principles, together with the probability of an attempt being made by the Legislature, during the present Session of Parliament, to introduce a measure which might prove detrimental to the interests of such Societies *unless some prompt and decisive action be taken by the working classes themselves*, beg most respectfully to intimate that it has been decided to hold in Manchester, as the main centre of industry in the provinces, a Congress of the representatives of Trades' Councils, Federations of Trades, and Trade Societies in general.

The Congress will assume the character of the Annual Meetings of the Social Science Association in the transactions of which Society the artisan class is almost excluded; and papers previously carefully prepared by such Societies as elect to do so, will be laid before the Congress on the various subjects which at the present time affect the Trade Societies, each paper to be followed by discussion on the points advanced, with a view of the merits and demerits of each question being thoroughly ventilated through the medium of the public press. It is further decided that the subjects treated upon shall include the following:

1 Trade Unions an absolute necessity.
2 Trade Unions and Political Economy.
3 The effect of Trade Unions on foreign competition.
4 Regulation of the hours of labour.
5 Limitation of apprentices.
6 Technical Education.
7 Courts of Arbitration and Conciliation.
8 Co-operation.
9 The present inequality of the law in regard to conspiracy, intimidation, picketing, coercion, etc.
10 Factory Acts Extension Bill, 1867: the necessity of compulsory inspection and its application to all places where women and children are employed.
11 The present Royal Commission on Trades' Unions—how far worthy of the confidence of the Trade Union interests.
12 Legalization of Trade Societies.
13 The necessity of an Annual Congress of Trade Representatives from the various centres of industry.

All Trades' Councils, Federations of Trades, and Trade Societies generally, are respectfully solicited to intimate their adhesion to this project on or before the 12th of May next, together with a notification of the subject of the paper that each body will undertake to prepare, and the number of delegates by whom they will be respectively represented; after which date all information as to the place of meeting, etc., will be supplied.

It is not imperative that all Societies should prepare papers, it being anticipated that the subjects will be taken up by those most capable of expounding the principles sought to be maintained. Several have already adhered to the project, and have signified their intention of taking up the subjects, Nos. 1, 4, 6, and 7.

The Congress will be held on Whit-Tuesday, the 2nd of June next, its duration not to exceed five days; and all expenses in connection therewith, which will be very small, and as economical as possible, will be equalized amongst those Societies sending delegates, and will not extend beyond their sittings.

Communications to be addressed to Mr W. H. Wood, Typographical Institute, 29 Water Street, Manchester.

By order of the Manchester & Salford Trades' Council.

S. C. Nicholson, *President*

W. H. Wood, *Secretary*

(*Documents in English Economic History: England since 1760*, ed B. W. Clapp, 1976, pp. 373–4.)

From Majority Report of the Royal Commission on Trade Unions (1867–9)

I.15

Objects of Trades Unions and Method of Attainment

26. The objects of trades unions are in general of a twofold character:—

I. *First.* Those of an ordinary friendly or benefit society—*viz.*, to afford relief to the members of the union when incapacitated from work by accident or sickness; to allow a sum for the funeral expenses of the members and their wives; and sometimes to provide superannuation allowances for members incapacitated by old age.

II. *Secondly.* Those of trade society proper—*viz.*, to watch over and promote the interests of the working classes in the several trades, and especially to protect them against the undue advantage which the command of a large capital is supposed by them to give to the employers of labour.

27. The objects last referred to are, in the great majority of the existing trades unions, the main objects of the members in associating together. It is, however, found desirable by the promoters of trades unions to combine with these objects the functions of a friendly or benefit society. Additional members and additional funds are thus obtained; and the hold which the society has over its members is strengthened by the consideration that any

member who should subject himself to expulsion for disobedience to the orders of the union, issued in what it deems the interests of trade, would thereby forfeit the superannuation and other benefits to which he would be entitled, it may be, from a long course of subscription continued with the very object of securing to himself those benefits.

28. With respect to the trade purposes of the unions, one of the most constant objects is to obtain for the members the best rate of wages which they can command, and to reduce the number of hours in which the wages are earned. A further object is to bring about a more equal division of work among the members of the trade, and its distribution among a greater number of workmen, than would prevail under the influence of unrestrained competition; and this object is sought by attempting to establish a uniform minimum rate of wages.

29. The agency through which the trades unions endeavour to effect these purposes is of two kinds—direct and indirect. The direct agency is by means of what is termed a 'strike'—a simultaneous cessation from work on the part of the workmen. The strike is the ultimate sanction, as between the workmen and the employer, of all the demands insisted upon by the union. It is usually preceded by an intimation that if the concession required be not granted the men will quit work in a body. If this intimation fails to produce the desired effect, the case is ordinarily brought before the governing body of the union; and if the proposed proceeding is approved, the strike is organized and the men are called off work.

30. The policy and conduct of strikes would seem to constitute an important part of the duties of the council of a union. In the case of the *Amalgamated Society of Carpenters and Joiners*, Mr Applegarth, the secretary, informed us (qu. 54) that the number of strikes involving a large number of men are about 12 in a year. Speaking of the success which had attended the establishment of a branch union at Bradford in raising wages and shortening hours, he says (qu. 145): 'Our men were continually agitating in a very businesslike manner with their employers, and the result has been, as here stated, that they have got their hours reduced and the wages increased.' Their general policy is to take advantage of a brisk trade to insist on a rise of wages, and when trade is slack they resist a fall (Applegarth, qu. 95; Allan, qu. 857–861). It appears, however, in evidence that in many cases leaders of unions fail to consider whether the circumstances of the trade are such as to call for or admit of a rise of wages. It is with them rather a question of the relative strength of the two parties.

31. It does not appear to be borne out by the evidence that the disposition to strike on the part of workmen is in itself the creation of unionism, or that the frequency of strikes increases in proportion to the strength of the union. It is, indeed, affirmed by the leaders of unions that the effect of the established societies is to diminish the frequency, and certainly the disorder, of strikes, and to guarantee a regularity of wages and hours rather

than to engage in constant endeavours to improve them. But supposing such results to follow, as stated, from the establishment and action of a powerful trades union in any trade or district, it is not unreasonable to assume that the diminished frequency of strikes may arise not from any want of disposition to strike on the part of the members of the union, but from the fact that its organization is so powerful as, in most cases, to obtain the concession demanded without recourse to a strike . . .

32. The indirect agency above referred to is of a more complex nature; but it will be found to resolve itself into—

1. An attempt to limit the number of workmen to be employed in any branch of industry, and so to create a monopoly of labour with its attendant power to command a higher rate of wages.

2. To repress competition among the workmen themselves.

33. It is said by some advocates of trades unions that men, if left to independent action, will, in the struggle for employment, by competition with each other lower the rate of wages at which they are willing to work; and will, also, be tempted by the love of gain to injure themselves by working long hours and overtaxing their strength, thereby compelling others to follow their example. It is deemed more for their interest, therefore, that they should by arrangement together refuse to accept less than a certain rate of wages or to work more than a limited number of hours, and should also resort to other expedients for distributing the work equally amongst them, and making it go as far as possible in furnishing them a moderate amount of employment.

34. The monopoly of labour is attempted to be effected by means of rules, or by a practice tacitly adopted among the members of the unions, limiting the number of apprentices to be allowed in a trade, and excluding from work as far as practicable workmen not belonging to the union. The limitation of the number of apprentices is not insisted on by all the unions, but it is a matter to which some of them attach the greatest importance. The question, and the question of the employment of boys to do work which it is urged by the unionists ought to be done by men, have led to many disputes . . .

35. The right to limit the supply of labour in a given trade, and so to raise the rate of wages, is distinctly claimed by some of the unionists. Mr Wilkinson, the secretary of the *National Flint Glassmakers' Friendly Society*, says (qu. 18,717): 'The limitation of apprentices is simply because we consider that as working men who have been brought up in the trade and devoted a number of years to learn it . . . we have a right in a certain measure to limit the supply in accordance with what the demand may be. . . .'

36. On the same ground, objection is sometimes made to the employment of women in certain kinds of work. A union of warpers in Manchester refused to allow the wife and sisters of one of their members to warp. 'It

was against their rules,' they said, 'to allow women to warp, for if women were introduced into their market the wages of the men would be reduced.' . . .

Effects of Trades Unions on the Character of Working Men, and on their Relations with their Employers

45. That trades unions have had certain injurious effects on the character of the working men, as well as on the relations between them and their employers, seems not to admit of doubt. Thus much the evidence which we have collected appears to us to establish. But in respect to the special character and extent of those effects, there is, as might be expected, great discrepancy between the witnesses. The employers complain that trades unions have fostered a spirit of antagonism between themselves and their workmen which formerly did not exist. There is no longer, they say, the cordial and friendly feeling which used to be common between the two classes. The workmen, looking rather to the approval of their unions than to that of their employers, are less anxious than of yore to stand well with the latter; and the employers on their part no longer feel under the same obligation to look after the interests of their workmen and to assist them in periods of difficulty. Misunderstandings which often would be readily settled if there were free and friendly intercourse between them, are exasperated and prolonged. Such are the allegations of the employers. Nor can it be said that they are materially shaken, or even strongly denied, on the part of the unionists. These, in general, seem rather to regard those sentiments of which the employers regret the decline, as founded on mistaken notions of inferiority on the one hand and patronage on the other.

46. But many statements will be found in the evidence implying a deterioration in the character of the workmen in more material respects than these. It is said that the better class among them are losing, under the influence of the trades unions, the character of self-reliance and independence by which they used to be distinguished. The desire of the workman to excel, to do the best in his power to give satisfaction to his employer, to improve himself, and if possible to rise in the world, is damped by the thraldom in which he is held to the rules of his union, and by the systematic disapproval on the part of his fellow unionists of all efforts to go beyond that average level of exertion which it is the aim of the unions to maintain.

47. To this it is replied on the part of the unions, that their real tendency, considered in a wider and more equitable view, is to raise, not depress, the character of the workman, by making him feel that he is not an insulated agent, subject to oppression, or at all events to accidents over which he can exercise no control, but a member of a strong united body, capable at once of defending his rights and of ensuring him a resource in case of temporary need. It is maintained also that the practice of having a

code of working rules agreed to between employers and workmen, such as
the better unions seek to establish, embracing a book of wages, of laws,
and of trade rules, is attended with the best results; that it tends to diminish
and usually to extinguish the occurrence of strikes, and to establish a spirit
of co-operation between masters and workmen . . .

(*English Historical Documents, 1833–74*, ed. G. M. Young and
W. D. Hancock, 1956, vol. 12, pp. 1000–5.)

Hannah Cullwick's Diary (1 Jan. 1871) I.16

This is the beginning of another year, & I am still general servant like, to
Mrs Henderson at 20 Gloucester Crescent. This month on the 16th I shall
o' bin in her service 2 years & a ½, & if I live till the 26th o' May when I
shall be 38 year old, I shall o' bin in service 30 years . . . Now there's such a
little boy kept here I've a deal more to do of jobs that's hard, like digging
coals & carrying 'em up & the boxes, & high windows & the fanlight over
the door to clean & anything as wants strength or height I am sent for or
call'd up to do it. All the cabs that's wanted I get, & if the young ladies
want fetching or taking anywhere I've to walk with them & carry their
cloaks or parcels. I clean all the copper scuttles & dig the coals clean the
tins & help to clean the silver & do the washing up if I'm wanted, & carry
things up as far as the door for dinner. I clean 4 grates & do the fires &
clean the irons, sweep & clean 3 rooms & my attic, the hall & front steps
& the flags & area railings & all that in the street. I clean the water closet
& privy out & the backyard & the area, the back stairs & the passage, the
larder, pantry & boy's room & the kitchen & scullery, all the cupboards
downstairs & them in the storeroom. And at the house cleaning I do the
walls down from the top to the bottom o' the house & clean all the high
paint, & dust the pictures. I get all the meals down stairs & lay the cloth &
wait on the boy & the housemaid as much as they want & if it's my work,
like changing their plates & washing their knife & fork & that . . .

(*The Diaries of Hannah Cullwick*, ed. Liz Stanley, 1984, pp. 152–3.)

From Report of Alexander Redgrave, Factory Inspector, to the Rt. I.17 Hon. H. A. Bruce, Home Secretary (1871)

I continue to receive from the sub-inspectors excellent accounts of the
observance of the various regulations which we have to enforce. The harmonious co-operation of employers of all classes, and the increasing feeling
that the interests of employers and employed are bound together, have
greatly contributed to this end.

Nothing can shew in stronger light the great change that has taken place in the acceptance and observance of the Factory Regulations, than the recommendations in the reports of the factory inspectors 25 years since, contrasted with those which I have frequently felt it my duty to submit.

My former colleagues, hampered by opposition and obstructed on every side, filled their reports with urgent recommendations for increased power, for more stringent regulations, and more certain penalties.

It has been my good fortune to be able to demonstrate, as I trust I have done with sufficient justification, that useless and annoying regulations may be removed, and that a yet readier and more cheerful observance of the law will follow the removal of rules which now serve no useful purpose . . .

(*British Parliamentary Papers, Factories*, 1870–1, vol. 14, p. 401.)

1.18 Emma Paterson, from 'The Organisation of Women's Industry' (Apr. 1879)

There are many reasons for the great disinclination which girls have for domestic service, but it would take too long to go fully into these. In all but large, rich households, where there is much idleness and waste, domestic service is incessant hard work at all hours of the day and sometimes of the night also. It is at the best but a kind of slavery, and when a girl has a home it is only a human feeling, and one that we should respect, if she prefers to undertake work in trades, because she can return at night and on Sundays to the home circle. At a meeting last year of factory women at Bristol who were earning only 5s. or 6s. per week, I urged upon them the advisability of going out to service rather than submit to such low wages, but without an exception the advice was rejected by all . . . One feasible suggestion of an improvement is a system of superior charwomen, under which servants could go home at night. They would then know when their work for the day was over, and their industry could be organised and thus placed more on a footing with other trades. Heads of households might then have to wait upon themselves a little more than they now do but much of the service now regarded as necessary is really only to gratify pride and to keep up appearances. At any rate, girls of the working class and their parents are just as much entitled to freedom of choice as any other persons are and we must try not to 'bump' people, especially women, into what we think are their places.

(*Women's Union Journal*, Apr. 1879; reprinted in *Women in Public 1850–1900*, ed. P. Hollis, 1979, p. 64.)

T. H. S. Escott, from *England: Her People, Polity and Pursuits* (1879)   I.19

[1.] In the constitution of English society at the present day, the three rival elements—the aristocratic, the democratic, and the plutocratic—are closely blended. The aristocratic principle is still paramount, forms the foundation of our social structure, and has been strengthened and extended in its operation by the plutocratic, while the democratic instinct of the race has all the opportunities of assertion and gratification which it can find in a career conditionally open to talents.

[2.] The antagonism between the aristocracy of wealth and birth has long been disappearing. The son of the newly-enriched father is identified in education, social training, habits, prejudices, feelings, with the scions of the houses of Norman descent. At all times there has been a tendency on the part of birth to ally itself with wealth, and it would be found upon examination, that for the greater part of their princely rentals many a noble English stock is indebted to purely commercial sources. Judicious matrimonial alliances have largely assisted in identifying the two principles of wealth and birth. This has continued down to the present day, and the consequence is that though English society may be divided into the higher classes, the middle classes, the lower middle, and that vast multitude, which for the sake of convenience may be described as the proletariate, the feud between the aristocracy of lineage and of revenue is almost at an end. There are typical country gentlemen in the House of Commons and in society, but the country interest is no longer the sworn enemy of the urban interest. Our territorial nobles, our squires, our rural landlords great and small, have become commercial potentates; our merchant-princes have become country gentlemen. The possession of land is the guarantee of respectability, and the love of respectability and land is inveterate in our race.

[3.] The great merchant or banker of to-day is an English gentleman of a finished type. He is possibly a peer, and an active partner in a great City firm; if he is not a peer, the chances are that he is a member of the House of Commons. He is a man of extensive culture, an authority upon paintings, or china, or black-letter books; upon some branch of natural science; upon the politics of Europe; upon the affairs of the world. Does he then neglect his business? By no means. He has, indeed, trustworthy servants and deputies; but he consults personally with his partners, gentlemen in culture and taste scarcely inferior, it may be, to himself; he goes into the City as punctually as his junior clerks; and when he returns from the City he drops for a few minutes into the most exclusive of Westend clubs. His grandfather would have lived with his family above the counting-house, and regarded a trip to Hyde Park as a summer day's journey. As for the descendant, his town-house is in Belgravia or Mayfair, he occupies it for little more than six months out of the twelve, and during the rest of the year lives at his palace in the country, takes a keen interest in the breeding of stock, the cultivation of soil, and the general improvement of property. There is, in fact, but one standard of 'social position' in England, and it is that which is formed by a blending of the plutocratic and aristocratic elements. If it is realised imperfectly in one generation, it will be approximated to more closely in the next, and thus it will go on till the ideal is reached.

[4.] There is a rush just now equally on the part of patrician and plebeian parents to get their sons into business, and noblemen with illustrious titles and boasting the most ancient descent eagerly embrace any good opening in the City which may present itself for their sons. It is perhaps the younger son of an earl or a duke who sees you when you call on your broker to transact business; it may be the heir to a peerage himself who is head partner in the firm which supplies the middle-class household with tea, puts a ring-fence round the park of the Yorkshire squire, or erects a trim conservatory in one of the villa-gardens of suburban Surrey. It may also be remarked that an institution which is the great object of menace and attack on the part of the radical reformers of the age has greatly assisted to knit together the various parts, sections, and interests of the social system, and at the same time that it has dispersed the aristocratic leaven has proved to be a distinctly popularising agency. Primogeniture, the bulwark of an hereditary nobility, is one of the guarantees of the alliance between the upper and the middle classes which has contributed to give us the social stability that other nations have lacked. Imagine primogeniture abolished, and the French system, as a possible alternative to primogeniture, adopted, an equal division of property between the various members of the family. The distinction between elder and younger sons would disappear. Most of the sons of our great landlords would have a competence, and as a probable consequence they would combine together to form an anti-popular and exclusive caste, would intermarry to a much greater extent than at present, would cease to go forth, since the necessity would cease, into the world to make their fortunes, and would erect a hard and fast line of demarcation between classes . . .

[5.] The era of the enlargement of English society dates from the Reform Bill of 1832, and if it has brought with it some contradictions, anomalies, and inconveniences, it has also been instrumental in the accomplishment of great and undoubted good. It has substituted, in a very large degree, the prestige of achievement for the prestige of position. The mere men of fashion, the fops, dandies, and exquisites, the glory of whose life was indolence, and who looked upon anything in the way of occupation as a disgrace, have gone out of date never to return. . . . Before the eventful year 1832, there existed a society in England very like the old exclusive society of Vienna. The chief and indeed almost only road to it lay through politics, and politics were for the most part a rigidly aristocratic profession. Occasionally men of the people made their way out of the crowd, and became personages in and out of the House of Commons; but most of the places under Government were in the hands of the great families, as also were the close boroughs, and the tendency was to fill each from among the young men of birth and fashion. The Reform Bill admitted an entirely new element into political life, and threw open the whole of the political area. A host of applicants for parliamentary position at once came forward, and as a consequence the social citadel was carried by persons who had nothing to do with the purely aristocratic section which had hitherto been paramount. The patrician occupants of the captured stronghold, if they were somewhat taken aback by the blow which had been dealt them, accepted the situation and decided upon their future tactics with equal wisdom and promptitude. If the new-comers were to be successfully competed with, they saw that they must compete with them on the new ground, and must assert their power as the scions of no *fainéant* aristocracy. The impulse given to the whole mass of the patriciate was immense, and the sum of the new-born or newly-displayed energies as surprising as it was satisfactory. The man of pleasure ceased to be the type to which it was expected, as a matter of course, that all those born in the purple should conform.

[6.] The activity thus communicated directed itself into an infinite number of channels, and it has continued operative ever since. Our aristo-crats of to-day are at least fired by a robust ambition. Many of them take up statesmanship as the business of their lives, and work at its routine duties as if it were necessary to the support of existence. Those whose tastes do not incline them in the direction of the senate, write books, paint pic-tures, or carve statues. Perhaps, even probably, they are of a theatrical turn, and subsidise a theatre, or even manage a company. They go into business, or they dedicate their existence to agricultural enterprise. . . .

[7.] The degrees of esteem allotted to the different English professions are exactly what might be expected in a society organised upon such a basis and conscious of such aims. Roughly it may be said professions in England are valued according to their stability, their remunerativeness, their influence, and their recognition by the State. These conditions may par-tially explain the difference which English society draws between the call-ings of the merchant and the stock-broker. Stock-brokers make immense fortunes; but there attaches to them a suspicion of precariousness infinitely in excess of that which, in some degree or other, necessarily attaches to all fortunes accumulated in commerce or trade. The merchant represents an interest which is almost deserving of a place among the estates of the realm, and with the development of which the prosperity and prestige of England are bound up. His house of business is practically a public institution, and the speculative element—the fluctuation of prices and the uncertainty of markets—enters as little as possible into it. Merchants have from time immemorial been the friends and supporters of monarchs—have taken their place in the popular chamber of the legislature, have been elevated to distinguished stations among the titular aristocracy of the land. We have had not only our merchant-princes, but our merchant-peers and merchant-statesmen. The calling has been recognised in our social hierarchy for centuries, and if not exactly a liberal, is an eminently respectable and dignified profession. Nor is the merchant, as a rule, so much absorbed in the affairs of his own business as to be unable to devote as much time as is necessary to the pursuits of society and the affairs of the country. His operations run in a comparatively equal and tranquil channel, and to hint that he lives in an atmosphere of feverish excitement is equivalent to insinuating a doubt of his solvency. It is different with the stock-broker, whose social position is so sudden that it cannot yet be looked upon as assured—whose wealth, though great, has the garish hue of luck, and the glories associated with which may dissolve themselves at any moment into thin air, like Aladdin's palace, and who himself is popularly supposed to be more or less on the tenterhooks of expectation and anxiety from morning to night. The merchant drives to his place of business in a family brougham or barouche; the stock-broker drives to the station, where he takes the morning express to the City, in a smart dog-cart, with a high-stepping horse between the shafts, and a very knowing-looking groom at his side.

[8.] . . . We live in an age whose boast it is that it can appreciate merit or capacity of any kind. Artists and actors, poets and painters, are the much-courted guests of the wealthiest and the noblest in the land—to be met with at their dinner-tables, in their reception-rooms, and in their counting-houses. To all appearance, the fusion between the aristocracy of birth, wealth, and intellect is complete, and the representatives of each appear to meet on a footing of the most perfect and absolute equality. Still the notion prevails that the admission, let us say, of the painter into society is an act of condescension on society's part, none the less real because the condescension is ostentatiously concealed. Nor does the fact that artists occasionally not only amass large fortunes, but contract illustrious matrimonial alliances, militate against the view. It is only possible where an entire class is concerned to speak generally, and to this, as to every other rule, there are exceptions. Why should the rule—always assuming that it is a rule—exist, and what are the explanations of it? As regards painters, there is this to be borne in mind: their calling is a noble one; but in view of the genius of English society, it labours under certain disadvantages. A vague and unreasoning prejudice still exists against the profession of the artist. The keen-scented, eminently decorous British public perceives a certain aroma of social and moral laxity in the atmosphere of the studio, a kind of blended perfume of periodical impecuniosity and much tobacco-smoke. This laxity, moreover, is to a great extent a tradition of art, which artists themselves do not a little to perpetuate. They are, or they affect to be, for the most part a simple-minded, demonstrative, impulsive, eccentric, vagabond race, even as Thackeray has drawn them in his novels. As a matter of fact, many, perhaps most of them, are the reverse of this—shrewd, hard-headed men of business, with as clear a conception as the most acute trader of the value of twenty shillings. But social verdicts are based for the most part on general impressions; and the popular view of the painter—speaking now, as always, of the guild, not of the individual member of it—is that the calling which he elects to follow lacks definitiveness of status, and that it is not calculated to promote those serious, methodical habits which form an integral part of the foundation of English society.

[9.] If this sentiment were to be exhaustively analysed, it would be found that there entered into it considerations which apply to other professions. Attorneys or solicitors, general practitioners, and even illustrious physicians in the daily intercourse of society labour under nearly the same disadvantages as artists. It is therefore natural and logical to ask what is the social differentia of this group of professional men? It is to be found, unless we greatly mistake, in the fact that they are each of them in the habit of receiving money payments direct from those with whom they consort nominally on a footing of social equality. All professional men make their livelihood out of the public in some shape or other. The only thing is that some of them receive the money of the public through an agent, or middleman, and that others do not. A barrister has no immediate pecuniary dealings with his client. An author has no immediate pecuniary dealings with those who read his books or articles. A beneficed clergyman is independent of his congregation for his income. Artists, attorneys, surgeons, dentists, physicians, are paid by fee, or they send in their account and receive—or at least look for—a cheque in settlement. But this is exactly what a tailor, a wine merchant, a butcher, a grocer, or any other retail dealer does. Thus we arrive at the conclusion that whatever the social disadvantage at which artists, attorneys, and doctors may find themselves, it arises from precisely the same cause as that which exists in the case of persons who derive their income from nothing that can be called a liberal or a learned trade . . .

(*England: Her People, Polity and Pursuits*, 1885 edn.,
pp. 22–5, 35–7, 39–41, 42–5.)

From William Ewart Gladstone's speech at Liverpool (28 June 1886)   I.20

[Y]ou are opposed throughout the country by a compact army, and that army is the case of the classes against the masses. I am thankful to say that there are among the classes many happy exceptions. I am thankful to say that there are men wearing coronets on their heads who are as good, as sound, as genuine Liberals as any working man who hears me at this moment. Still, as a general rule, it cannot be pretended that we are supported by the dukes, or by the squires, or by the established clergy, or by the officers of the Army, or by any other body of very respectable persons. And what I observe is this, whenever a profession is highly privileged, whenever a profession is publicly endowed, it is in these cases you will find that almost the whole of the class and the profession are against us. But if I go to more open professions, if I take the Bar . . . if I take the medical profession . . . in these open professions I am thankful to say that we make a very good and respectable muster indeed. . . . Still . . . I am sorry to say, there is class against the mass, classes against the nation.

(*The Times*, 29 June 1886; reprinted in *The Nineteenth-Century Constitution*, ed H. J. Hanham, 1969, p. 205.)

II

Religion: Conformity and Controversy

Edward Miall, from *The British Churches in Relation to the British*   II.1
People (1849)

[1.] I am bound to say, that in watching the operations of our religious institutions, whenever I have endeavoured to put myself in the position of the humbler classes, and have asked myself, 'What is there here to interest such?' I have been at a loss for a reply. I do not arraign architectural magnificence—we cannot, indeed, boast much of it outside of the Establishment—for in continental countries I am not aware that it discourages the humblest worshipper. But here, in Great Britain, we carry our class distinctions into the house of God, whether the edifice be a splendid monument of art, or whether it be nothing superior to a barn. The poor man is made to feel that he is a poor man, the rich is reminded that he is rich, in the great majority of our churches and chapels. The square pew, carpeted, perhaps, and curtained, the graduated scale of other pews, the free-sittings, if there are any, keep up the separation between class and class; and even where the meanly-clad are not conscious of intrusion, as is sometimes painfully the case, the arrangements are generally such as to preclude in their bosoms any momentary feeling of essential equality. We have no negro pews, for we have no prejudice against colour—but we have distinct places for the pennyless, for we have a morbid horror of poverty. Into a temple of worship thus mapped out for varying grades of worshippers, in which the lowly and the unfortunate are forbidden to lose sight of their worldly circumstances, some such, spite of all discouragements, find their way. In the singing it may be, they can join, and mingle their voices and their sympathies with those around them—unless, indeed, the more respectable tenants of the pews, deeming it ill-bred to let themselves be heard, leave the psalmody to the Sunday-school children, and the vulgar. Possibly, their emotions may be elicited by prayer—seldom, we should think, by the discourse. It may be excellent, persuasive, pungent—but, in multitudes of cases, it will also be cast in a mould which none but the educated can appreciate. Let it not be said that this is owing exclusively to their ignorance. 'The common people heard' our Lord 'gladly'—the early reformers won their way to the

inmost hearts of the lowliest of men—and even those who in our day are
judged to be too uncultured to profit by the ministry of God's word from
the pulpit, are sufficiently intelligent to derive interest from a public political meeting, to appreciate the points of a speech from the hustings, and to
feel the force of an argument when put to them in private. No! it is not
altogether ignorance which prevents them from following the generality of
preachers. It is an entire absence of colloquialism from the discourse—an
absence imposed upon the speaker by that sense of propriety which the
aristocratic sentiment engenders. The etiquette of preaching prescribes an
exclusively didactic style—and an address, the aim of which is to save
souls, is supposed to approximate towards perfection, in proportion as it is
free from conversational blemishes and inaccuracies, satisfies a fastidious
and classical taste, and flows on in one unbroken stream from its commencement to its close. The consequence is, that while some few are pleased,
and, perhaps, profited, the mass remain utterly untouched. Oh! for some
revolution to break down for ever, and scatter to the four winds of heaven,
our pulpit formulas and proprieties, and leave men at liberty to discourse
on the sublime verities of the Christian faith, with the same freedom,
variety, and naturalness, with which they would treat other subjects in
other places! . . .

Social and Political Hindrances to the Success of the Churches

[2.] There lies at the bottom of society in this country, and especially in the
metropolis and the more populous towns, a thick sediment of physical destitution, which it is morally impossible for the light of Christianity to
penetrate and purify. . . . Individual and isolated instances may be discovered of the triumph of the divine message in the soul of man, even
where it has had to encounter the disadvantage of the most squalid
poverty. But the few exceptions only serve to prove the rule. It may be
safely laid down that there are positions of physical depression and degradation which disqualify human nature for the appreciation of the gospel.
Men exiled by want from the sympathy, and even notice, of the great mass
of their fellows—driven to subsist precariously and scantily on garbage—
clothed in rags, loathsome both to sight and smell—preyed upon by ver-
min—herding for shelter in dark, damp cellars, or dilapidated and filthy
garrets, or, still worse, packed nightly, in nakedness, body to body, along
the noisome dormitories of cheap lodging-houses—to whom the next
wretched meal is always an uncertainty—in whom a sense of cleanliness
can scarcely ever, by any chance, have been realized—whose mode of life
precludes order, comfort, prudence, reflection—who live half their time in
an atmosphere of poison—who cannot, if they would, escape close and
familiar contact with obscenity and vice—devoid of all moral motive,
because divorced from hope, and denuded of self-respect—men in this
frightful abyss are, as a class, as much below the immediate reach of the

gospel, as the better tended cattle that are driven to the shambles. And to the shame of philanthropy in our land be it spoken, these festering heaps of misery have gone on until just lately, increasing in bulk, unnoticed by society, until they comprehend hundreds of thousands of individuals. Their numbers alone might well alarm us—but there is something more appalling than their numbers. Out of this slimy bed of physical destitution rises perpetually a pestiferous moral exhalation dangerous to all other classes of society—most dangerous to those immediately contiguous to it. Swarms of thieves, trained from infancy to their business of plunder, and of prostitutes turned nightly into our thoroughfares to ply their deadly seduction, carry with them the taint of demoralization into all other sections of the social body. That physical wretchedness which we have self-ishly allowed to accumulate, passing by it, like the Levite, on the other side of the road, avenges itself upon our supineness and neglect, by per-meating the entire mass of uplying humanity with a moral typhus, peril-ous to every family in the land, and carrying into not a few the germ of death.

[3.] What can Christianity do with this terrific mass of rottenness? Rag-ged schools and ragged kirks are admirable institutions in their way—but alone they will never Christianize this region of the shadow of death. Most efficient they are as pioneers of benevolence into the heart of this matted jungle of poverty, ignorance, vice, and crime—but they are pioneers only. They may heroically carry religious truth into the haunts of desperation—but religious truth cannot well abide there. The spiritual man must be, in some measure, at least, contemplative, and contemplation asks privacy—but with the class to which we refer there is scarcely a possibility of retire-ment. In order to develop religious emotions there must be some mainten-ance of self-respect—but self-respect cannot linger amidst the dirt, brutality, and hopelessness, the vicious and polluting sights and sounds of scenes like these. The culture of piety requires a frequent reference of the mind and heart to God, in his works and word—but here almost all the facts met with are embodiments, not of the divine, but the human, and radiate, not purity, but corruption. Where is the city missionary who has not felt this? What single instance of the power of revealed truth has he met with in these outcast parts, that has not suggested to him the necessity, in order to the completion of its triumph, of rescuing the subject of it, if poss-ible, from the appalling depths, and insurmountable disadvantages of his social position? . . .

[4.] I come now to political religionism—or, in other words, that state of sentiment in reference to Christianity, its object, spirit, and means, created and fostered by State interference with its institutions and oper-ations. . . . The truth is, I cannot recognize civil establishments of Christi-anity as organizations for the extension of Christ's kingdom, in any sense. They are not Churches—they are merely political arrangements for the real, or ostensible, attainment of spiritual objects. They are machinery invented, constructed, put in motion, and presided over by 'the powers that be,' professedly for imparting religious instruction, and dispensing gospel ordinances, to all the subjects of the empire—but they want all the characteristics of the machinery appointed by God. They comprehend all the inhabitants of the land without distinction of character. They may be devoid of a single member whose heart is in living sympathy with God, as mirrored in the person and life of his Son, without losing one essential feature of their constitution. They are not an association, but an aggregation merely—for the bond of their union is only nominal.

[5.] We have already cordially admitted that there are many ministers in the Church Establishment in England whose religious character ranks deservedly high. But of three-fourths of them it may be remarked, without the smallest breach of charity, that they are practically ignorant of the great spiritual principles of the gospel, the purifying power of which they have never felt, nor even professed to feel. The office they sustain allies them with the aristocracy, and a benefice ensures to them, in most cases, a certain, and, in not a few, an ample income. The Establishment south of the Tweed has its prizes to attract, and its honours to distribute amongst the sons of our nobility and gentry. Moved by impulses of the most worldly kind, these flock to our universities to prepare themselves for 'holy orders'. The training they undergo is in perfect keeping with the main object they have in view. Theology is the last thing to which their attention is directed—spiritual religion, in any sense worthy of the name, almost the only influence with which they never come in contact. Oxford and Cambridge are notorious as centres of abandoned profligacy. Immorality walks their streets unabashed, and fills the surrounding villages with victims, whose self-respect is destroyed, and whose reputation is for ever blasted. In these places human depravity, heaped up in masses, reeks out its most offensive exhalations. From these schools of corruption go forth, year by year, the legally authorized expositors of Christianity, carrying with them, for the most part, habits imbued to the core with worldliness, and understandings and hearts alike ignorant of 'the things which pertain to life and godliness.' What is the general consequence? The flocks over whom they preside learn nothing from their lips of 'the unsearchable riches of Christ,' see nothing in their lives illustrative of 'the beauties of holiness.' They go through their dull routine of formality, where necessary, in person—where practicable, by proxy, and for the rest, they are—gentlemen. Can it be wondered at that amongst such men, filling such a position, the worst absurdities of priestism should find high and extensive favour? Could they be otherwise than predisposed to take the *virus*, when all their previous practices and habits had been of a character to virtually reduce religion to outward rites, priestly manipulations, and senseless dogmas? Yet these men, like a tissue of net-work, overspread the land from end to end, and, in the dread name of Him whose authority they so little revere, assume to themselves an exclusive right to be regarded as 'the ministers of Jesus Christ'.

[6.] Such a state of things, even if it went no further, places in the way of the British Churches a fearful impediment to the successful prosecution of their spiritual enterprise. It is the substitution, on a national scale, of a name for a reality—a formal pretence for a living power. But the evil does not rest here. This legalized ecclesiasticism claiming exclusive right to dispense God's gospel to the people of these realms, and casting contempt upon all unauthorized efforts puts itself into jealous and active antagonism to the Christian zeal which sends forth into our neglected towns, and amongst our stolid peasantry, labourers of various denominations, for the purpose of rescuing immortal souls from a cruel and fatal bondage. Every one familiarly acquainted with our rural districts can bear witness to facts in proof of this position. Go into almost any village in the empire, and set yourself down there to win souls to Christ, and your bitterest foe, your most energetic and untiring opponent, will prove to be the clergyman—the State-appointed minister of Jesus Christ. The very first symptoms of spiritual life which show themselves among his parishioners—social meetings for prayer, anxious inquiries for the way of salvation, eager attention to the proclamations of the gospel—will attract his vigilant notice, and provoke his severest censure. The thing is so common, and has been so from time immemorial, as to cease to excite surprise. Would you stir up in men's minds serious concern respecting their highest interests, the parish 'priest' will be sure to cross your path at every step. Gather around you the children of the poor to instil into their young and susceptible hearts the truths of the gospel, and instantly, their parents are threatened with a forfeiture of all claims upon parochial charity. Circulate from house to house plain, pungent, religious tracts, and in your second or third visit you will learn that the vicar has forbidden their reception. Assemble a few men and women 'perishing for lack of knowledge,' that you may preach to them the message of reconciliation, and ten to one you will be informed, in the course of a few weeks, that the occupant of the house in which you laboured has been served with a notice to quit. It matters nothing that your efforts are free from all tinge of sectarianism—they are regarded as intrusive, irregular, and mischievous. How many villages are there in this country in which, through clerical influence, it is impossible to hire a room, within the narrow walls of which to proclaim to rustic ignorance the tidings of eternal life! How many more in which, from the same cause, misrepresentation, intimidation, and oppressive power, are brought to bear upon miserable and helpless dependents, to scare them beyond the reach of the gladsome sound of mercy! How many millions of souls, hemmed in on all sides by this worldly system of religion, cry aloud from the depths of

their ruin to earnest Christians for help, whom, nevertheless, State chur-
chism renders it impossible to reach! . . .

(*The Evangelical and Oxford Movements*, ed. E. Jay, 1983, pp. 98–105.)

II.2 Letter from Lord John Russell to the Bishop of Durham (4 Nov. 1850)

Downing Street, 4 November, 1850.

My dear Lord,

I agree with you in considering 'the late aggression of the Pope upon our
Protestantism' as 'insolent and insidious', and I therefore feel as indignant
as you can do upon the subject.

I not only promoted to the utmost of my power the claims of the Roman
Catholics to all civil rights, but I thought it right and even desirable that the
ecclesiastical system of the Roman Catholics should be the means of giving
instruction to the numerous Irish immigrants in London and elsewhere,
who without such help would have been left in heathen ignorance.

This might have been done, however, without any such innovation as
that which we have now seen.

It is impossible to confound the recent measures of the Pope with the
division of Scotland into dioceses by the Episcopal Church, or the arrangement of districts in England by the Wesleyan Conference.

There is an assumption of power in all the documents which have come
from Rome; a pretension of supremacy over the realm of England, and a
claim to sole and undivided sway, which is inconsistent with the Queen's
supremacy, with the rights of our bishops and clergy, and with the spiritual
independence of the nation, as asserted even in Roman Catholic times.

I confess, however, that my alarm is not equal to my indignation.

Even if it shall appear that the ministers and servants of the Pope in this
country have not transgressed the law, I feel persuaded that we are strong
enough to repel any outward attacks. The liberty of Protestantism has been
enjoyed too long in England to allow of any successful attempt to impose a
foreign yoke upon our minds and consciences. No foreign prince or poten-
tate will be at liberty to fasten his fetters upon a nation which has so long
and so nobly vindicated its right to freedom of opinion, civil, political, and
religious.

Upon this subject, then, I will only say that the present state of the law
shall be carefully examined, and the propriety of adopting any proceedings
with reference to the recent assumption of power, deliberately considered.

There is a danger, however, which alarms me much more than any
aggression of a foreign sovereign.

Clergymen of our own Church, who have subscribed the Thirty-Nine
Articles and acknowledged in explicit terms the Queen's supremacy, have

been most forward in leading their flocks 'step by step to the very verge of the precipice'. The honour paid to saints, the claim of infallibility for the Church, the superstitious use of the sign of the cross, the muttering of the liturgy so as to disguise the language in which it is written, the recommendation of auricular confession, and the administration of penance and absolution, all these things are pointed out by clergymen of the Church of England as worthy of adoption, and are now openly reprehended by the Bishop of London in his charge to the clergy of his diocese.

What then is the danger to be apprehended from a foreign prince of no great power compared to the danger within the gates from the unworthy sons of the Church of England herself?

I have little hope that the propounders and framers of these innovations will desist from their insidious course. But I rely with confidence on the people of England; and I will not bate a jot of heart or hope, so long as the glorious principles and the immortal martyrs of the Reformation shall be held in reverence by the great mass of a nation which looks with contempt on the mummeries of superstition, and with scorn at the laborious endeavours which are now making to confine the intellect and enslave the soul.—

I remain, with great respect, etc.

J. RUSSELL

If you think it will be of any use, you have my full permission to publish this letter.

(*The Times*, 7 Nov. 1850; reprinted in E. R. Norman, *Anti-Catholicism in Victorian England*, 1968, pp. 159–61.)

Horace Mann, from the 'Report on the Religious Census' (1851)　II.3

Spiritual Provision and Destitution

There are two methods of pursuing a statistical inquiry with respect to the religion of a people. You may either ask each individual directly, what particular form of religion he professes; or, you may collect such information as to the religious *acts* of individuals as will equally, though indirectly, lead to the same result. The former method was adopted, some few years ago, in Ireland, and is generally followed in the continental states when such investigations as the present are pursued. At the recent Census, it was thought advisable to take the latter course; partly because it had a less inquisitorial aspect,—but especially because it was considered that the outward *conduct* of persons furnishes a better guide to their religious state than can be gained by merely vague professions. In proportion, it was thought, as people truly are connected with particular sects or churches, will be their activity in raising buildings in which to worship and their diligence in afterwards frequenting them; but where there is an absence of such practical regard for a religious creed, but little weight can be attached to any purely formal acquiescence. This inquiry, therefore was confined to obvious *facts* relating to two subjects.—

1. The amount of ACCOMMODATION which the people have provided for religious worship; and, 2. The number of persons as ATTENDANTS, by whom this provision is made use of. . . .

The most important fact which this investigation as to attendance brings before us is, unquestionably, the alarming number of the non-attendants. Even in the least unfavorable aspect of the figures just presented, and assuming (as no doubt is right) that the 5,288,294 absent every Sunday are not always the same individuals, it must be apparent that a sadly formidable portion of the English people are habitual neglecters of the public ordinances of religion. Nor is it difficult to indicate to what particular class of the community this portion in the main belongs. The middle classes have augmented rather than diminished that devotional sentiment and strictness of attention to religious services by which, for several centuries, they have so eminently been distinguished. With the upper classes, too, the subject of religion has obtained of late a marked degree of notice, and a regular church-attendance is now ranked amongst the recognized proprieties of life. It is to satisfy the wants of these two classes that the number of religious structures has of late years so increased. But while the *labouring* myriads of our country have been multiplying with our multiplied material prosperity, it cannot, it is feared, be stated that a corresponding increase has occurred in the attendance of this class in our religious edifices. More especially in cities and large towns it is observable how absolutely insignificant a portion of the congregations is composed of artizans. They fill, perhaps, in youth, our National, British, and Sunday Schools, and there receive the elements of a religious education; but, no sooner do they mingle in the active world of labour than, subjected to the constant action of opposing influences, they soon become as utter strangers to religious ordinances as the people of a heathen country. From whatever cause, in them or in the manner of their treatment by religious bodies, it is sadly certain that this vast, intelligent, and growingly important section of our countrymen is thoroughly estranged from our religious institutions in their present aspect. Probably, indeed, the prevalence of *infidelity* has been exaggerated, if the word be taken in its popular meaning, as implying some degree of intellectual effort and decision; but, no doubt, a great extent of negative, inert indifference prevails, the practical effects of which are much the same. There is a sect, originated recently, adherents to a system called 'Secularism'; the principal tenet being that, as the fact of a future life is (in their view) at all events susceptible of *some* degree of doubt, while the fact and the necessities of a present life are matters of direct sensation, it is therefore prudent to attend exclusively to the concerns of that existence which is certain and immediate—not wasting energies required for present duties by a preparation for remote, and merely possible, contingencies. This is the creed which probably with most exactness indicates the faith which, virtually though not professedly, is entertained by the masses of our working population: by the skilled and unskilled labourer alike—by hosts of minor shopkeepers and Sunday traders—and by miserable denizens of courts and crowded alleys. They are *unconscious Secularists*—engrossed by the demands, the trials, or the pleasures of the passing hour, and ignorant or careless of a future. These are never or but seldom seen in our religious congregations; and the melancholy fact is thus impressed upon our notice that the classes which are most in need of the restraints and consolations of religion are the classes which are most without them. . . .

1. One chief cause of the dislike which the labouring population entertain for religious services is thought to be the maintenance of those distinctions by which they are separated as a class from the class above them. Working men, it is contended, cannot enter our religious structures without having pressed upon their notice some memento of inferiority. The existence of pews and the position of the free seats are, it is said, alone sufficient to deter them from our churches: and religion has thus come to be regarded as a purely middle-class propriety or luxury. It is therefore, by some, proposed to abandon altogether the pew system, and to raise by voluntary contributions the amount now paid as seat rents. The objection and proposal come from churchmen and dissenters too; . . . To other minds, the prevalence of social distinctions, while equally accepted as a potent cause of the absence of the working classes from religious worship, is suggestive of a different remedy. It is urged that the influence of that broad line of demarcation which on week days separates the workman from his master cannot be effaced on Sundays by the mere removal of a physical barrier. The labouring myriads, it is argued, forming to themselves a world apart, have no desire to mingle, even though ostensibly on equal terms, with persons of a higher grade. Their tastes and habits are so wholly uncongenial with the views and customs of the higher orders that they feel an insuperable aversion to an intermixture which would bring them under an intolerable constraint. The same disposition, it is said, which hinders them from mixing in the scenes of recreation which the other classes favour, and induces their selection preferably of such amusements as can be exclusively confined to their own order, will for ever operate to hinder their attendance at religious services unless such services can be devised as shall become exclusively *their* own. An argument in favour of such measures is supposed to be discovered in the fact that the greatest success among these classes is obtained where, as amongst the Methodists, this course is (more perhaps from circumstances than design) pursued. If such a plan were carried out by the Church of England, and by the wealthier Dissenting bodies,

it is thought that some considerable advantage would result. It has consequently been proposed to meet so far the prejudices of the working population; and to strive to get them gradually to establish places of worship for
themselves. Experiments have been already put in operation with the persons lowest in the social scale; and RAGGED CHURCHES are in several
places making a successful start. In several places, too, among Dissenters,
special services in halls and lecture rooms are being held, intended wholly
for the working class; and the success of these proceedings seems to prove
that multitudes will readily frequent such places, where of course there is a
total absence of all class distinctions, who would never enter the exclusive-
looking chapel.

2. A second cause of the alienation of the poor from religious institutions is supposed to be an insufficient sympathy exhibited by professed
Christians for the alleviation of their social burdens—poverty, disease, and
ignorance. It is argued that the various philanthropic schemes which are
from time to time originated, though certainly the offspring of benevolent
minds, are not associated with the Christian church in such a manner as to
gain for it the gratitude of those who thus are benefited. This cause, however, of whatever force it may have been as yet, is certainly in process now
of mitigation; for the clergy everywhere are foremost in all schemes for
raising the condition of the poor, and the ministers and members of the
other churches are not backward in the same good labour.

3. A third cause of the ill-success of Christianity among the labouring
classes is supposed to be a misconception on their part of the motives by
which Christian ministers are actuated in their efforts to extend the
influence of the Gospel. From the fact that clergymen and other ministers
receive in exchange for their services pecuniary support, the hasty inference
is often drawn that it is wholly by considerations of a secular and selfish
kind that their activity and zeal are prompted. Or, even if no sordid
motives are imputed, an impression is not seldom felt that the exhortations
and the pleadings of the ministry are matters merely of professional routine—the requisite fulfilment of official duty. It is obvious that these misapprehensions would be dissipated by a more familiar knowledge; but the evil
of the case is, that the influence of such misapprehensions is sufficient to
prevent that closer intimacy between pastors and their flocks from which
alone such better knowledge can arise. The ministers are distrusted—the
poor keep stubbornly aloof: how shall access to them be obtained? The
employment of LAY-AGENCY has been proposed as the best of many
methods by which minds, indifferent or hostile to the regular clergy, can be
reached. It is thought by some that that unfortunate suspicion, by the poor,
of some concealed and secretly inimical design, by which the regular ministers are often baffled in their missionary enterprises, might be much allayed
if those who introduced the message of Christianity were less removed in
station and pursuits from those whom it is sought to influence.

42

4. Another and a potent reason why so many are forgetful of religious obligations is attributable to their *poverty*: or rather, probably, to certain conditions of life which seem to be inseparable from less than moderate incomes. The scenes and associates from which the poor, however well disposed, can never, apparently, escape; the vice and filth which riot in their crowded dwellings, and from which they cannot fly to any less degraded homes; what awfully effective teaching, it is said, do these supply in opposition to the few infrequent lessons which the Christian minister or missionary, after much exertion, may impart! How feeble, it is urged, the chance, according to the course of human probabilities, with which the intermittent voice of Christianity must strive against the fearful neverceasing eloquence of such surrounding evil!—Better dwellings, therefore, for the labouring classes are suggested as a most essential aid and introduction to the labours of the Christian agent. And, indeed, of secondary influences, few can be esteemed of greater power than this. Perhaps no slight degree of that religious character by which the English middle classes are distinguished is the consequence of their peculiar isolation in distinct and separate houses—thus acquiring almost of necessity, from frequent opportunities of solitude, those habits of reflection which cannot be exercised to the entire exclusion of religious sentiments, but, certainly, however this may be, no doubt can be admitted that a great obstruction to the progress of religion with the working class would be removed if that condition which forbids *all* solitude and *all* reflection were alleviated.

Probably, however, the grand requirement of the case is, after all, a multiplication of the various *agents* by whose zeal religious truth is disseminated. Not chiefly an additional provision of religious *edifices*. The supply of these perhaps, will not much longer, if the present wonderful exertions of the Church of England (aided in but little less degree by other Churches) be sustained, prove very insufficient for the wants of the community. But what is eminently needed is, an agency to bring into the buildings thus provided those who are indifferent or hostile to religious services. The present rate of church-and-chapel-increase brings before our view the prospect, at no distant period, of a state of things in which there will be small deficiency of structures where to worship, but a lamentable lack of worshippers. There is indeed already, even in our present circumstances, too conspicuous a difference between accommodation and attendants. Many districts might be indicated where, although the provision in religious buildings would suffice for barely half of those who might attend, yet scarcely more than half of even this inadequate provision is appropriated. Teeming populations often now surround half empty churches, which would probably remain half empty even if the sittings were all free. The question then is mainly this: By what means are the multitudes thus absent to be brought into the buildings open for their use? Whatever impeding influence may be exerted by the prevalence of class distinctions, the constraints of poverty, or misconceptions of the character and motives of the ministers of religion, it is evident that absence from religious worship is attributable *mainly* to a genuine repugnance to religion itself. And, while this lasts, it is obvious that the stream of Christian liberality, now flowing in the channel of church-building, must produce comparatively small results. New churches and new chapels will arise, and services and sermons will be held and preached within them: but the masses of the population, careless or opposed, will not frequent them. It is not, perhaps, sufficiently remembered that the process by which men in general are to be brought to practical acceptance of Christianity is necessarily *aggressive*. There is no attractiveness, at first, to them in the proceedings which take place within a church or chapel: all is either unintelligible or disagreeable. We can never then, expect that, in response to the mute invitation which is offered by the open door of a religious edifice, the multitudes, all unprepared by previous appeal, will throng to join in what to them would be a mystic worship, and give ear to truths which, though unspeakably beneficent, are also, to such persons, on their first announcement, utterly distasteful. Something more, then, it is argued, must be done. The people who refuse to hear the gospel in the church must have it brought to them in ther own haunts. If ministers, by standing every Sunday in the desk or pulpit, fail to attract the multitudes around, they must by some means make their invitations heard beyond the church or chapel walls. The myriads of our labouring population, really as ignorant of Christianity as were the heathen Saxons at Augustine's landing, are as much in need of missionary enterprise to bring them into practical acquaintance with its doctrines; and until the dingy territories of this alienated nation are invaded by *aggressive* Christian agency, we cannot reasonably look for that more general attendance on religious ordinances which, with many other blessings, would, it is anticipated, certainly succeed an active war of such benevolent hostilities.

Nor, it is urged in further advocacy of these missionary efforts, are the people insusceptible of those impressions which it is the aim of Christian preachers to produce. Although by natural inclination adverse to the entertainment of religious sentiments, and fortified in this repugnance by the habits and associations of their daily life, there still remain within them that vague sense of some tremendous want and those aspirings after some indefinite advancement which afford to zealous preachers a firm hold upon the conscience even of the rudest multitude. Their native and acquired disinclination for religious truth is chiefly of a negative, inert description—strong enough to hinder their spontaneous seeking of the passive object of their dis-esteem—too feeble to present effectual resistance to the inroads of aggressive Christianity invading their own doors. . . .

It is, however, in the facts and figures which succeed that any value which belongs to this inquiry will be found; and these—much labour having been bestowed upon them—are, I think, sufficiently complete to justify whatever inferences may, by those accustomed to statistical investigations, fairly be deduced. If this should be the case, the public will assuredly be grateful, Sir, to you for undertaking, and to Government for sanctioning, as part of the decennial Census, an inquiry which must certainly reveal important facts relating to that most important of all subjects—the religious state of the community. Inquiry upon such a subject will not, surely, be considered as beneath the notice or beyond the province of a Government, if only it be recollected that, apart from those exalted and immeasurable interests with which religion is connected in the destinies of all—on which it is the office rather of the Christian preacher to dilate—no inconsiderable portion of the secular prosperity and peace of individuals and states depends on the extent to which a pure religion is professed and practically followed. If we could imagine the effects upon a people's temporal condition of two different modes of treatment—education separate from religion, and religion separate from education—doubtless we should gain a most impressive lesson of the inappreciable value of religion even to a nation's physical advancement. For, whatever the dissuasive influence, from crime and grosser vice, of those refined ideas which in general accompany augmented knowledge, yet undoubtedly it may occur that, under the opposing influence of social misery, increased intelligence may only furnish to the vicious and the criminal increased facilities for evil. But the wider and more penetrating influence exerted by religious principle—controlling conscience rather than refining taste—is seldom felt without conferring, in addition to its higher blessings, those fixed views and habits which can scarcely fail to render individuals prosperous and states secure. Applying to the regulations of their daily conduct towards themselves and towards society the same high sanctions which control them in their loftier relations, Christian men become, almost inevitably, temperate, industrious, and provident, as part of their religious duty; and Christian citizens acquire respect for human laws from having learnt to reverence those which are divine. The history of men and states shows nothing more conspicuously than this—that in proportion as a pure and practical religion is acknowledged and pursued are individuals materially prosperous and nations orderly and free. It is thus that religion 'has the promise of the life that now is, as well as of that which is to come.'

(*Census of England and Wales, 1851: Religious Worship*, pp. cxix, clviii–clxii, clxvii–clxviii.)

Letter from Charles Darwin to Asa Gray (22 May 1860)   II.4

With respect to the theological view of the question. This is always painful to me. I am bewildered. I had no intention to write atheistically. But I own that I cannot see as plainly as others do, and as I should wish to do, evidence of design and beneficence on all sides of us. There seems to me too much misery in the world. I cannot persuade myself that a beneficent and omnipotent God would have designedly created the Ichneumonidæ[1] with the express intention of their feeding within the living bodies of Caterpillars, or that a cat should play with mice. Not believing this, I see no necessity in the belief that the eye was expressly designed. On the other hand, I cannot anyhow be contented to view this wonderful universe, and especially the nature of man, and to conclude that everything is the result of brute force. I am inclined to look at everything as resulting from designed laws, with the details, whether good or bad, left to the working out of what we may call chance. Not that this notion *at all* satisfies me. I feel most deeply that the whole subject is too profound for the human intellect. A dog might as well speculate on the mind of Newton. Let each man hope and believe what he can. Certainly I agree with you that my views are not at all necessarily atheistical. The lightning kills a man, whether a good one or bad one, owing to the excessively complex action of natural laws. A child (who may turn out an idiot) is born by the action of even more complex laws, and I can see no reason why a man, or other animal, may not have been aboriginally produced by other laws, and that all these laws may have been expressly designed by an omniscient Creator, who foresaw every future event and consequence. But the more I think the more bewildered I become; as indeed I have probably shown by this letter.

Most deeply do I feel your generous kindness and interest.

Yours sincerely and cordially,
CHARLES DARWIN.

(*The Life and Letters of Charles Darwin*, ed. F. Darwin, 2nd edn., 1887, vol. 2, pp. 311–12.)

NOTE
1. Ichneumonidae are wasps that deposit their eggs inside the bodies of live caterpillars. When the egg hatches, the ichneumon larva feeds on the body of the host caterpillar, eventually killing it.

II.5 **Frederic Harrison, from 'Neo-Christianity' (Oct. 1860)**

[1.] This 'Review' at any rate ought not to be silent whilst so much courage and candour call for recognition and support. Nor can we lose the opportunity of insisting on this conspicuous triumph of the principle of free discussion. On the other hand, we should be wanting to our readers if we failed to point out the light which it throws on the position of official belief. When axioms of science and results of criticism, principles and theories for which we have long contended, are preached in the citadels of orthodoxy, we may welcome and proclaim the fact, whilst insisting that they be frankly adopted and pushed to their legitimate conclusions.

[2.] No fair mind can close this volume without feeling it to be at bottom in direct antagonism to the whole system of popular belief. They profess, indeed, to come forward as defenders of the creeds against attacks from without; but their hardest blows fall not on the assaulting, but on the resisting forces. They throw themselves into the breach; but their principal care is to clear it from its oldest and stoutest defenders. In object, in spirit, and in method, in details no less than in general design—this book is incompatible with the religious belief of the mass of the Christian public, and the broad principles on which the Protestantism of Englishmen rests. The most elaborate reasoning to prove that they are in harmony can never be anything but futile and ends in becoming insincere. All attempts to show that these opinions are in accordance with Scripture, the Articles, the Liturgy, or the Church have little practical value, and do no small practical harm. Such reasoning may ease the conscience of troubled inquirers; but is powerless to persuade the mass that *that* is after all the true meaning of that which they have been taught and have believed. Just as their instinct repudiated the ingenious attempts of the Tractarian writers to build a semi-Romish system on the dogmas of our Church; just so it will revolt from any attempt, however sincere, to graft the results and the principles of rationalism on the popular Christianity of the day. Is the crumbling edifice of orthodoxy to be supported by sweeping away the whole of its substructure; and Christian divines taught cheerfully to surrender all that the most exacting criticism assails? The mass of ordinary believers may well ask to be protected from such friends, as their worst and most dangerous enemies. Is it reasonable to suppose, that at this time of day the Christian world will consent to reconsider the whole of its positions; to develop its cardinal doctrines into new forms, and to remodel the whole structure of belief upon an improved theory? Will the complicated and time-worn mechanism bear so radical a repair? Can its pieces be reset and placed in new relations, and the rusted medieval time-piece be restored into the shape of a modern watch? Has it been all a mistaken rendering that men have been believing so long? Is theology then due to a mere confusion of terms? Can religion be set right by sounder canons of interpretation, and the mystery of the unknown cleared up by a more accurate scholarship? Of one thing we may be quite sure, that the public can never be persuaded to make trial of the process. They, at any rate, will never be brought to believe that the Bible is full of errors, or rather untruths; that it does not contain authentic or even contemporary records of facts, and is a medley of late compilers; and yet withal remains the Book of Life, the great source of revealed truth, the standard of holiness, purity, and wisdom. Yet all this our Essayists call upon them to admit, in the very name of Revelation and for the honour and glory of the Bible itself. Let our authors beware of such excessive candour, and rest assured that when the public once begin to read their Bibles in that spirit, they will soon cease to read them at all, and that the Hebrew Scriptures will take their place upon the bookshelf of the learned, beside the Arabian and the Sanscrit poets.

[3.] Nor again is it a more hopeful scheme to preach to the congregations in Church and Chapel, that the central notions of their creed, no less than the volume on which they are based, have been utterly misinterpreted and distorted; yet withal that the creeds must regain their influence under new forms, as the Scriptures, through their new expounders. The men and women around us are told that the whole scheme of salvation has to be entirely rearranged and altered: Divine rewards and punishments; the Fall; original Sin; the vicarious Penalty; and Salvation by faith are all, in the natural sense of the terms, repudiated as immoral delusions. Miracles, inspiration, and prophecy, in their plain and natural sense, are denounced as figments or exploded blunders. The Mosaic history dissolves into a mass of ill-digested legends, the Mosaic ritual into an Oriental System of priestcraft, and the Mosaic origin of the earth and man sinks amidst the rubbish of rabbinical cosmogonies. And yet all this is done in the name of orthodoxy, and for the glory of Christian truth. Nay, unwearied with destroying this great edifice of old belief, our writers enter upon the gigantic and incredible enterprise of rebuilding the whole again from its foundations, upon the same groundplan but with stronger walls; and after forcing the simple believer to unlearn his well-conned creed, they sit down to teach it to him anew with altered words and remodelled phrases. An expurgated Bible resumes its place. Miracles, inspiration, and prophecy reappear under the old names with new meanings: the harmonious whole arises anew in loftier and softer outlines with the cardinal features—with a revised Atonement, a transcendental Fall, a practical Salvation, and an idealized Damnation.

[4.] What consolation can it be to the simple believer to be told that this inversion and his whole creed is all within the letter of the Articles, and the Liturgy, and the Scripture? All the bases of his creed are undermined; the whole external authority on which it rests is swept away; the mysterious book of truth fades into an old collection of poetry and legend; and the scheme of Redemption in which he has been taught to live and die turns out to be a demoralizing invention of men. And yet all this is done to him to strengthen his Christianity, to confirm him as a member of the Church, to give a moral power to his faith, to teach him the true spirit of the Gospel. It is done unto him not by the open foes with whom he has long waged unequal battle to the simple watchwords of 'No human reason,' 'The region of faith,' and so forth; but it is done unto him by doctors, professors, and divines, by those who breed up churchmen and clergymen—by men who teach those who teach him and his children. We can well imagine the bitterness of heart with which he must repudiate this system of cure.

His mental constitution cannot bear so terrific a remedy. They may demonstrate the scientific necessity of the operation they propose; but what if he feel certain of dying under their knives? Old and infirm as he is, they would restore him in a Medean caldron. 'Mine own familiar friend in whom I trusted hath lifted up his heel against me'.

[5.] Thus, in a word, from one end of this book to the other the same process is continued; facts are idealized; dogmas are transformed; creeds are discredited as human and provisional; the authority of the Church and of the Bible to establish any doctrine is discarded; the moral teaching of the Gospel remains; the moral sense of each must decide upon its meaning and its application. Now in all seriousness we would ask, what is the practical issue of all this? Having made all these deductions from the popular belief, what remains as the residuum? How far is the solvent process to be carried? Are all formulae whatever discarded, or what materials remain to form now? In their ordinary, if not plain sense, there has been discarded the Word of God—the Creation—the Fall—the Redemption—Justification, Regeneration, and Salvation—Miracles, Inspiration, Prophecy—Heaven and Hell—Eternal Punishment and a Day of Judgment—Creeds, Liturgies, and Articles—the truth of Jewish history and of Gospel narrative—a sense of doubt thrown over even the Incarnation, the Resurrection, and Ascension—the Divinity of the second Person, and the Personality of the third. It may be that this is a true view of Christianity, but we insist in the name of common sense that it is a new view. Surely it is waste of time to argue that it is agreeable to Scripture, and not contrary to the Canons.

[6.] From the general extracts which we have made, we think it will be seen that this book does radically destroy not a part, but the whole of the popular belief; and that it is designed with very considerable accord and unity of purpose.

[7.] The extent to which scientific criticism has undermined the whole framework of doctrine, is sufficiently manifested by the appearance of this book. The manner in which this decay is met is its characteristic feature. It surrenders, in fact, not merely the various points of the doctrine, but the necessity of retaining any system of doctrine at all. This spirit, indicated throughout the volume, culminates in the concluding essay of Mr. Jowett. It is as difficult to say how many of his young hearers this essay will lead away, as it is to say whither it will lead them. The tone of earnestness, tenderness, and courage that breathes through it will prove very fascinating to their open hearts. It possesses, indeed, most of the qualities requisite for a religious revival. Its sympathy for the spirit of Scripture never runs into servility to the words. It is candid to the present, and throws a halo over the selected portion of the past. It brings down all the influence of grand and hallowed phrases upon minds enfeebled by a long training upon sentences and words. It offers imposing theories of mankind made musical with poetry and text to the young brains who are just constructing their first or second 'Philosophy of Being.' It offers them a bright, not too systematic view of human goodness, and it frees them from the thraldom of intellectual convictions.

[8.] That such a view should have success in such an atmosphere is natural enough. We deny, however, that it can have a chance of success with the men and women around us, or that it bears the remotest resemblance to religion or faiths which sustain societies and nations. It acknowledges in sad and eloquent words the prevailing antagonism between our intellectual convictions and our religious professions. It hopes to mitigate the evil by thrusting the intellectual behind the moral element of the belief. The doctrine it leaves as possibly erroneous and comparatively unimportant; it sums up the Gospels in the practice of the Christian life.

(*Westminster Review*, Oct. 1860.)

II.6 Samuel Wilberforce, from a response to *Essays and Reviews* (Jan. 1861)

[1.] This then we would entreat all who see anything attractive in these views distinctly to contemplate—that, whether right or wrong, they are essentially and completely at variance with the doctrinal teaching of the Church of England, and cannot even under the shelter of any names be advisedly maintained by honest men who hold her ministry.

[2.] But beyond this, another inference of the deepest moment follows we think directly from a clear comprehension of these views. Those who hold them are in a position in which it is impossible to remain. The theory of Mr. Jowett and his fellows is as false to philosophy as to the Church of England. More may be true, or less, but to attempt to halt where they would stop is a simple absurdity.

[3.] They deny, for instance, the possibility of miracles, and so they ideologically suggest that, when it is asserted that our Lord miraculously fed the multitudes in the wilderness, or opened the eyes of the blind, no more is meant than that in the wilderness of this world He fed the souls of thousands with edifying moral discourses, or unsealed the eyes of their spirit to the better contemplation of heavenly and earthly things. Now in passing just let us remark that in this, as in many other things, the latest pretensions to illumination in our own time are but a revival of notions which were broached and were condemned centuries ago; for the same principle of explaining away the miraculous narrative was applied by the Cathari of the middle ages . . .

[4.] But, again, it is not merely that once in the land of shadows all apparitions must of necessity be equipollent, but this treatment of miracles implies a charge of falsehood, of conscious fraud, not only against the writers of the Gospel, but against our blessed Lord himself.

[5.] . . . There is no escape from the conclusion; if they were deceived, he was a deceiver. For he himself again and again appeals to these works as the proof of his own mission, and so the condemnation of those who rejected him. So he says, in direct answer to the question 'Art thou he that should come, or do we look for another?' 'Tell John again the things that ye do hear and see; the blind receive their sight and the lame walk, the lepers are cleansed and the deaf hear, the dead are raised up' (Matt. xi. 4, 5); or, as he says again, 'Though ye believe not me, believe the works' (John x. 38); and again, 'I have greater witness than that of John: for the works which the Father hath given me to finish, the same works that I do bear witness of me' (John v. 36); and again, 'If I had not done among them the works which none other man did, they had not had sin' (John xv. 24).

[6.] There is no escape from this: if He wrought the works, the whole rationalistic scheme crumbles into dust; if He wrought not the works, claiming as He claimed to work them as the very proofs of his mission, He was, in truth, the deceiver that the chief priests declared him to be. Dr Williams makes a miserable effort to escape from this dilemma. 'By appealing,' he says, 'to *Good* WORKS' (sic), 'however wonderful, for his witness, Christ has taught us to have faith mainly in goodness'; as if the appeal of Christ was mainly to the inherent goodness, and not to the manifested power of the works—a fallacy so utterly transparent that it is needless in exposing it to do more than enunciate its terms.

[7.] And they are claimed as brethren by infidels of every shade. The only fault found with them is, that they do not follow out to the legitimate end their openly-proclaimed principles. How can they put aside this universal estimate of their position, held alike by believers and by infidels? . . .

[8.] It is not indeed a 'neo-Christianity,' but it is a new religion, which our Essayists would introduce; and they would act more rationally, more philosophically, and, we believe, less injuriously to religion, if they did as their brother unbelievers invite them to do, renounce the hopeless attempt at preserving Christianity without Christ, without the Holy Ghost, without a Bible, and without a Church . . . In Germany the same attempt has been made; and what has been its issue? The attempt to rationalise Christianity; to remove the supernatural from that which is either a system of supernaturalism or a falsehood; to bring down to the utterance of the voice of man's heart, and of his internal consciousness, that which challenges attention, because it claims to be a revelation from God of that which it had not entered and could not enter the heart of man to conceive;—all this has failed, as it ever must fail. It has issued as its direct result in a wide-spread pantheistic atheism; it has sent souls, wearied out with perpetual speculations, torn by distracting doubts, and feeling that they must have something certain upon which to rest the burden of their being, into the deep delusions of the Roman system; and the few who have escaped even as by fire have come back as worn and weeping penitents to the simple belief of primitive truth, the bright blessedness of which they had been seduced to forsake for the darkness and intricacy of these now abandoned speculations.

[9.] And this is no accidental consequence of such a course. There can be no religious system which is not founded upon definite teaching as to God, and as to His relation to us. The very name of a theology testifies to man's universal sense of this truth, even where it is held unconsciously and instinctively, and not reasoned out into a proposition. Even a false faith, if it is to be effectual at all, must rest upon a theology. To attempt to retain the Bible, as in this system is attempted, as a rule of life; as giving moral precepts; as expressing high and ennobling sentiments; and yet to deprive its voice of the authority of inspiration, and to silence it as to the great doctrines of Christianity,—is to endeavour to maintain unshaken a vast and curiously constructed edifice, when you have deliberately removed all the foundations upon which it is built. The articles of the Christian creed are in truth as much the basis of Christian morals as of Christian faith. The creation of man in the image of God; the supernatural gift of His indwelling presence; the marring of that image, and the losing of that precious gift through man's rebellion; the eternal counsels which planned, and in the fulness of time wrought out, his redemption; the Incarnation; the Cross; the Atonement; the Personal presence with the Church, of God the Holy Ghost, and His utterances through prophet and evangelist, in promise and prediction, of the redemption of the race and its restoration; with the new and blessed light which all these cast on man, on his life, on his death, and on his resurrection;—in these are all the strength of the creed for moral instruction, all the sublimity of its spiritual teaching. Remove the theology, and you take away the morality. You may feed man's intellectual pride, and gratify the morbid appetite of his fancy with the husks of an empty rationalism, but you will leave him the slave of appetite and the bond-slave of passion: you promise him liberty, and you make him anew and hopelessly subject to vanity.

[10.] To suppose that it can be otherwise is not only to contradict the experience afforded to us by every religious system which ever has exercised any real control over man, but it is also by its very suggestion to rob man of his highest faculties. For not hereafter only, when the ransomed shall be perfected, in the full vision of God's countenance, and amidst the uncreated light, is the soul of man capable of communion with his Maker; but here upon earth, in spite of all his remaining infirmities, this may be his portion, and for this his spirit longs. The want of this is the secret of that fevered restlessness which makes, where it exists, the most fully furnished outer life so empty, and the highest intellectualism so poor. It is man's truest greatness that he can acquaint himself with God and be at peace. But for this communing with God to be real, there must be a definite revelation of Him after whom the soul seeks. The mists which hang around 'the Infinite and 'the Absolute' must roll away, and manifest to the believer the revealed countenance of God in Christ; the weary wrestling of the long night of empty speculation must be over, and the angel of the everlasting covenant must reveal his name to the child of dust, whom He Himself hath upheld to struggle with Him until the day break. To tell the sorely tempted soul, to whisper into the already deafening ear, when the pains of dissolution are upon every nerve, shaking the strong man in his citadel of life, that he may perchance 'find a refuge in the bosom of the Universal Parent in the ages to come,' is only to mock the thirsty lips with the illusive water of the driest desert mirage. No, there is indeed no rest for man's spirit in anything but distinct and definite revelation as to himself and as to his God.

[11.] Here, then, is one answer to the first great class of arguments by which our 'new Christians' seek to establish their system. Their promise to reconcile Christianity with the requirements of a remorseless rationalism involves in its primary conditions an essential falsehood.

[12.] Yet this is one of their very chiefest arguments in favour of their system. It is probably the one which is the most attractive, and therefore the most dangerous, because it is that which appeals to the highest qualities of those whom they are seeking to induce to accept them as teachers.

[13.] This essential falsehood is not the only fallacy with which this argument is chargeable. There is a perpetual and most delusive exaggeration of the amount of the difficulties which they profess to remove. It is not true that the highest intellects revolt hopelessly against the old simple Christianity, and that it must either forfeit their adherence or submit to the reconstruction of the rationalist. The greatest, the most comprehensive, and the acutest intellects have received, and daily do receive, even as little children, without abatement and without doubt, the whole Christian revelation. The difficulty is created for the solution. The patient is instructed by the tender sympathy of the would-be physician in the unsuspected existence within him of a lamentable sickness, in order that he may the more readily accept the treatment offered to him. More or less this fallacy runs through every Essay. The supposed opposition between the revelations of instructed science and the written Word of God is full of this fraud. It may be quite true that Christian philosophers have been too eager to invent theories to reconcile what Nature was understood to utter with what Revelation was supposed to declare; and that, as Nature's voice was better understood, the different theories of reconciliation were one after another found to fail. But how could this affect the actual fact? For a long time the astronomical theory of Copernicus was supposed to give the true law of the motions of the heavenly bodies. Problems were solved by it, and mysteries explained. But the further discoveries of science proved the incompleteness of the theory, and it passed wholly away. But did the failure of the reconciling theory affect the motions of the heavenly bodies? Not a whit more are the certain harmonies which exist between God's voice in nature and God's voice in revelation disturbed by the discovery that the particular theory which professed to exhibit their agreement has proved, on further inquiry, inadequate to the solution of the mighty problem which it promised to reduce. How wide a chasm is there between such a failure in a proposed solution and the representation of our essayists that science therefore convicts the author of the Book of Genesis of fraudulently putting forth his own speculations as the result of a revelation from on high!

(*Quarterly Review*, Jan. 1861.)

II.7 **Arthur Stanley, from a response to *Essays and Reviews* (Apr. 1861)**

[1.] But, although the Westminster manifesto fell, as was to be expected, powerless on the ears of those to whom it was addressed, it found ready listeners elsewhere. Partly in genuine alarm, partly in greedy delight at finding such an unlooked-for confirmation of their own uneasy suspicions and dislikes, the partisans of the two chief theological schools in the country caught up and eagerly echoed the note of the infidel journal. They extolled the eloquence and ability of the article; they made its conclusions their own; they discerned, through its inquisitorial gaze, tendencies which up to that moment had escaped even their own keen scent for the track of heresy. Gradually the heterogeneous series began to assume that mystified form which it has worn ever since in the public eye. The Essayists were discovered to be seven in number. They were the 'seven stars in a new constellation,'—or 'the seven extinguishers of the seven lamps of the Apocalypse,'—or 'the seven champions not of Christendom,'—or by the title which unhappily its blasphemous levity and its wicked uncharitableness has not excluded from journals professing to write in the name of religion, 'the Septem contra Christum.' Every part of the volume was now seen to have a close interdependence. In spite of the solemn disclaimer of joint responsibility and concert with which the volume was prefaced, every writer was assumed to have been acquainted with the production of every other. The first essay was supposed to contain in its successive pages the keynotes of the successive dissertations which followed, closing in the last, the climax and conclusion of the whole.

[2.] We pass on to the consideration of the general questions involved in the whole phenomenon, both of the volume and of the alarm that it has excited. Long after it and they have passed away, these questions will continue. It is of the highest interest to ascertain what they are, and how they affect the prospect of religion in this country. They relate mainly to two subjects,—the proper mode of studying and interpreting the Bible, and, closely allied with it, the relative value of the internal and external evidences of Religion. To which may perhaps be added a third, of less general interest, the relation of dogmatical theology to the Bible and to history.

[3.] On all these points but specially on the first, it has been a prodigious mistake to suppose that this volume contains anything new. By friends and foes alike this illusion has been propagated,—'a new Reformation,' 'a neo-Christianity,' 'a new Religion, of Christianity without Christ, without the Holy Ghost, without a Bible, and without a Church'. We will venture to say that, with the possible exception of Professor Powell's Essay, and a few words of Dr. Williams and Mr. Wilson, there is no statement of doctrine or fact in this volume which has not been repeatedly set forth by divines whose deep and sincere faith in the Christian religion cannot be denied without the very worst uncharitableness, and some of whom are actually regarded as luminaries of the Church. Even if the volume could be regarded as an epoch in the Church of England, it cannot possibly be regarded as an epoch in Christendom. If the Westminster or the Quarterly Reviewer had looked ever so cursorily through the works of Herder, Schleiermacher, Lücke, Neander; De Wette, Ewald, or even Tholuck, Olshausen, and Hengstenberg, they would see that the greater part of the passages which have given so much cause for exultation or for offence in this volume, have their counterpart in those distinguished theologians whom we have just cited, and therefore, if they were destined to overthrow Christianity, ought to have done so long ago. But neither is it an epoch in England. The style, the manner, the composition of this book may be offensive or peculiar. But facts and creeds are not revolutionised by manner and style. The principles, even the words, of the Essayists have been known for the last fifty years, through writings popular amongst all English students of the higher branches of theology. If there be a conspiracy, it is one far more formidable than that of the seven Essayists. For it is a conspiracy in which half the rising generation, one quarter of the Bench of Bishops, the most leading spirits of our clergy, have been, and are, and will be engaged, whatever be the results of the present controversy. Coleridge led the way. A whole generation arose under his Germanising influence.

[4.] In justice to the Bishops of St. David's and Hereford, no less than to the Essayists, we must consider the grounds for that right of speech which has been vehemently disputed both by the assailants and the defenders of the book. The 'Westminster' and 'National,' hardly less than the 'Quarterly' and the 'Record,' demand the withdrawal of the Essayists, and, we may add, by implication, of the other eminent persons just named, and of all who agree with them, from their position as English clergymen. The truth or falsehood of the views maintained is treated as a matter almost of indifference. The lay contributor, however offensive his statements, is dismissed 'as comparatively blameless.' But the Christian minister, it is said, has 'parted with his natural liberty.' It is almost openly avowed (and we are sorry to see this tendency as much amongst free-thinking laymen as

amongst fanatical clergymen) that Truth was made for the laity and Falsehood for the clergy—that Truth is tolerable everywhere except in the
mouths of the ministers of the God of Truth—that Falsehood, driven from
every other quarter of the educated world, may find an honoured refuge
behind the consecrated bulwarks of the Sanctuary.

[5.] Against this godless theory of a national Church we solemnly protest. It is a theory tainted with a far deeper unbelief than any that has ever
been charged against the Essayists and Reviewer . . .

[6.] If the Bishops had been successful in their design of terrifying or
driving out of the Church those whom they themselves confess to be
amongst its chief ornaments, not only would the individual loss have been
irreparable, but the heavy blow and discouragement to all Biblical study,—
the breach between religion and science, between devotion and truth,—the
repulsion, (already sufficiently alarming,) of the higher intelligences and
more generous spirits of the rising generation from the sacred profession,—
would have gone far to have reduced the National Church to the level of an
illiterate sect or a mere satellite of the Church of Rome. This danger has
been averted, not merely by the failure of the assailants, but by the silent
resistance of the assailed. Had they wavered under the storm which burst
upon them, the cause of Religion and of religious freedom might have suffered a portentous eclipse. In that calm attitude we trust that they will hold
their ground, 'in the quietness and confidence' which for the present is their
best strength.

[7.] They have by this unexpected turn of events been thrust into an
eminence, not of their own seeking, but from which their voices will be
heard far and near by those who will listen to few besides. Amongst all the
correctives which zealous enemies and anxious friends may wish to supply
to anything erroneous or dangerous in their present teaching, none will be
so effective as the sight of their own self-devotion, the sound of their own
call to duty, to faith, to charity. Judging by the usual course of events, it is
probable that before twenty years are passed, they will be seated in the high
places of the Church, now occupied by those who twenty years ago were
suffering under the obloquy which at present rests on them.

(*Edinburgh Review*, Apr. 1861.)

II.8 Charles Darwin, from *Variation of Animals and Plants under Domestication* (1868)

In accordance with the views maintained by me in this work and elsewhere,
not only the various domestic races, but the most distinct genera and orders
within the same great class—for instance, mammals, birds, reptiles, and
fishes—are all the descendants of one common progenitor, and we must

admit that the whole vast amount of difference between these forms has primarily arisen from simple variability. To consider the subject under this point of view is enough to strike one dumb with amazement. But our amazement ought to be lessened, when we reflect that beings almost infinite in number, during an almost infinite lapse of time, have often had their whole organization rendered in some degree plastic, and that each slight modification of structure which was in any way beneficial under excessively complex conditions of life has been preserved, whilst each which was in any way injurious has been rigorously destroyed. And the long-continued accumulation of beneficial variations will infallibly have led to structures as diversified, as beautifully adapted for various purposes and as excellently co-ordinated, as we see in the animals and plants around us. Hence I have spoken of selection as the paramount power, whether applied by man to the formation of domestic breeds, or by nature to the production of species. I may recur to the metaphor given in a former chapter: if an architect were to rear a noble and commodious edifice, without the use of cut stone, by selecting from the fragments at the base of a precipice wedge-formed stones for his arches, elongated stones for his lintels, and flat stones for his roof, we should admire his skill and regard him as the paramount power. Now, the fragments of stone, though indispensable to the architect, bear to the edifice built by him the same relation which the fluctuating variations of organic beings bear to the varied and admirable structures ultimately acquired by their modified descendants.

Some authors have declared that natural selection explains nothing, unless the precise cause of each slight individual difference be made clear. If it were explained to a savage utterly ignorant of the art of building, how the edifice had been raised stone upon stone, and why wedge-formed fragments were used for the arches, flat stones for the roof, &c.; and if the use of each part and of the whole building were pointed out, it would be unreasonable if he declared that nothing had been made clear to him, because the precise cause of the shape of each fragment could not be told. But this is a nearly parallel case with the objection that selection explains nothing, because we know not the cause of each individual difference in the structure of each being.

The shape of the fragments of stone at the base of our precipice may be called accidental, but this is not strictly correct; for the shape of each depends on a long sequence of events, all obeying natural laws; on the nature of the rock, on the lines of deposition or cleavage, on the form of the mountain, which depends on its upheaval and subsequent denudation, and lastly on the storm or earthquake which throws down the fragments. But in regard to the use to which the fragments may be put, their shape may be strictly said to be accidental. And here we are led to face a great difficulty, in alluding to which I am aware that I am travelling beyond my proper province. An omniscient Creator must have foreseen every consequence which results from the laws imposed by Him. But can it be reasonably maintained that the Creator intentionally ordered, if we use the words in any ordinary sense, that certain fragments of rock should assume certain shapes so that the builder might erect his edifice? If the various laws which have determined the shape of each fragment were not predetermined for the builder's sake, can it be maintained with any greater probability that He specially ordained for the sake of the breeder each of the innumerable variations in our domestic animals and plants;—many of these variations being of no service to man, and not beneficial, far more often injurious to the creatures themselves? Did He ordain that the crop and tail-feathers of the pigeon should vary in order that the fancier might make his grotesque pouter and fantail breeds? Did He cause the frame and mental qualities of the dog to vary in order that a breed might be formed of indomitable ferocity, with jaws fitted to pin down the bull for man's brutal sport? But if we give up the principle in one case,—if we do not admit that the variations of the primeval dog were intentionally guided in order that the greyhound, for instance, that perfect image of symmetry and vigour, might be formed,—no shadow of reason can be assigned for the belief that variations, alike in nature and the result of the same general laws, which have been the groundwork through natural selection of the formation of the most perfectly adapted animals in the world, man included, were intentionally and specially guided. However much we may wish it, we can hardly follow Professor Asa Gray in his belief 'that variation has been led along certain beneficial lines,' like a stream 'along definite and useful lines of irrigation.' If we assume that each particular variation was from the beginning of all time preordained, then that plasticity of organization, which leads to many injurious deviations of structure, as well as the redundant power of reproduction which inevitably leads to a struggle for existence, and, as a consequence, to the natural selection or survival of the fittest, must appear to us superfluous laws of nature. On the other hand, an omnipotent and omniscient Creator ordains everything and foresees everything. Thus we are brought face to face with a difficulty as insoluble as is that of free will and predestination.

(*Variation of Animals and Plants under Domestication*, 1868,
popular edn. 1905, vol. 2, pp. 523–6.)

II.9 Charles Darwin, from *Autobiography* (*c.* 1880)

During these two years[1] I was led to think much about religion. Whilst on board the Beagle I was quite orthodox, and I remember being heartily laughed at by several of the officers (though themselves orthodox) for quoting the Bible as an unanswerable authority on some point of morality. I suppose it was the novelty of the argument that amused them. But I had gradually come by this time (i.e. 1836 to 1839) to see that the Old Testament, from its manifestly false history of the world, with the Tower of Babel, the rain-bow as a sign, &c., &c., and from its attributing to God the feelings of a revengeful tyrant, was no more to be trusted than the sacred books of the Hindoos, or the beliefs of any barbarian. The question then continually rose before my mind and would not be banished,—is it credible that if God were now to make a revelation to the Hindoos, would he permit it to be connected with the belief in Vishnu, Siva, &c., as Christianity is connected with the Old Testament. This appeared to me utterly incredible. By further reflecting that the clearest evidence would be requisite to make any sane man believe in the miracles by which Christianity is supported,— that the more we know of the fixed laws of nature the more incredible do miracles become,—that the men at that time were ignorant and credulous to a degree almost incomprehensible by us—that the Gospels cannot be proved to have been written simultaneously with the events,—that they differ in many important details, far too important as it seemed to me to be admitted as the usual inaccuracies of eye-witnesses;—by such reflections as these which I give not as having the least novelty or value, but as they influenced me, I gradually came to disbelieve in Christianity as a divine revelation.

The fact that many false religions have spread over large portions of the earth like wild-fire had some weight with me. Beautiful as is the morality of the New Testament, it can hardly be denied that its perfection depends in part on the interpretation which we now put on metaphors and allegories. But I was very unwilling to give up my belief.—I feel sure of this for I can well remember often and often inventing day-dreams of old letters between distinguished Romans and manuscripts being discovered at Pompeii or elsewhere which confirmed in the most striking manner all that was written in the Gospels. But I found it more and more difficult, with free scope given to my imagination, to invent evidence which would suffice to convince me. Thus disbelief crept over me at a very slow rate, but was at last complete. The rate was so slow that I felt no distress, and have never since doubted even for a single second that my conclusion was correct. I can indeed hardly see how anyone ought to wish Christianity to be true; for if so, the plain language of the text seems to show that the men who do not believe, and this would include my Father, Brother and almost all my best friends, will be everlastingly punished.

And this is a damnable doctrine.

Although I did not think much about the existence of a personal God until a considerably later period of my life, I will here give the vague conclusions to which I have been driven. The old argument from design in nature, as given by Paley[2], which formerly seemed to me so conclusive, fails, now that the law of natural selection has been discovered. We can no longer argue that, for instance, the beautiful hinge of a bivalve shell must have been made by an intelligent being, like the hinge of a door by man. There seems to be no more design in the variability of organic beings and in the action of natural selection, than in the course which the wind blows. Everything in nature is the result of fixed laws. . . .

Another source of conviction in the existence of God, connected with the reason and not with the feelings, impresses me as having much more weight. This follows from the extreme difficulty or rather impossibility of conceiving this immense and wonderful universe, including man with his capacity of looking far backward and far into futurity, as the result of blind chance or necessity. When thus reflecting I feel compelled to look to a First Cause having an intelligent mind in some degree analogous to that of man; and I deserve to be called a Theist.

This conclusion was strong in my mind about the time, as far as I can remember, when I wrote the Origin of Species; and it is since that time that it has very gradually with many fluctuations become weaker. But then arises the doubt—can the mind of man, which has, as I fully believe, been developed from a mind as low as that possessed by the lowest animal, be trusted when it draws such grand conclusions? May not these be the result of the connection between cause and effect which strikes us as a necessary one, but probably depends merely on inherited experience? Nor must we overlook the probability of the constant inculcation of a belief in God on the minds of children producing so strong and perhaps an inherited effect on their brains, not as yet fully developed, that it would be as difficult for them to throw off their belief in God, as for a monkey to throw off its instinctive fear and hatred of a snake. I cannot pretend to throw the least light on such abstruse problems. The mystery of the beginning of all things is insoluble by us; and I for one must be content to remain an Agnostic.

(*Charles Darwin, Thomas Henry Huxley: Autobiographies*, ed. G. de Beer, 1974, pp. 49–54)

NOTES
1. from Oct. 1836 to Jan. 1839.
2. W. Paley, author of *Natural Theology* (1802). Paley argued that the only satisfactory explanation of the obvious marks of design in plants and animals is that they were created by a good and wise God. Paley's book was standard reading at Cambridge when Darwin was an undergraduate there.

II.10 From lecture by W. K. Clifford on 'Body and Mind', delivered to the Sunday Lecture Society (1 Nov. 1874)

[1.] The subject of this Lecture is one in regard to which a great change has recently taken place in the public mind. Some time ago it was the custom to look with suspicion upon all questions of a metaphysical nature as being questions that could not be discussed with any good result, and which, leading inquirers round and round in the same circle, never came to an end. But quite of late years there is an indication that a large number of people are waking up to the fact that Science has something to say upon these subjects; and the English people have always been very ready to hear what Science can say—understanding by Science what we shall now understand by it, that is, organised common sense.

[2.] . . . The first of these questions is that of the possible existence of consciousness apart from a nervous system, of mind without body. Let us first of all consider the effect upon this question of the doctrines which are admitted by all competent scientific men. All the consciousness that we know of is associated with a brain in a certain definite manner, namely, it is built up out of elements in the same way as part of the action of the brain is built up out of elements; an element of one corresponds to an element in the other; and the mode of connection, the shape of the building, is the same in the two cases. The mere fact that all the consciousness we know of is associated with certain complex forms of matter need only make us exceedingly cautious not to imagine any consciousness apart from matter without very good reason indeed; just as the fact of all swans having turned out white up to a certain time made us quite rightly careful about accepting stories that involved black swans. But the fact that mind and brain are associated in a definite way, and in that particular way that I have mentioned, affords a very strong presumption that we have here something which can be *explained*; that it is possible to find a reason for this exact correspondence. If such a reason can be found, the case is entirely altered; instead of a provisional probability which may rightly make us cautious we should have the highest assurance that Science can give, a practical certainty on which we are bound to act, that there is no mind without a brain. Whatever, therefore, is the probability that an explanation exists of the connection of mind with brain in action, such is also the probability that each of them involves the other. . . .

[3.] The other question which may be asked is this: Can we regard the universe, or that part of it which immediately surrounds us, as a vast brain, and therefore the reality which underlies it as a conscious mind? This question has been considered by the great naturalist Du Bois Reymond, and has received from him that negative answer which I think we also must give. For we found that the particular organisation of the brain which enables its action to run parallel with consciousness amounts to this—that disturbances run along definite channels, and that two disturbances which occur together establish links between the channels along which they run, so that they naturally occur together again. It will, I think, be clear to every one that these are not characteristics of the great interplanetary spaces. Is it not possible, however, that the stars we can see are just atoms in some vast organism, bearing some such relation to it as the atoms which make up our brains bear to us? I am sure I do not know. But it seems clear that the knowledge of such an organism could not extend to events taking place on the earth, and that its volition could not be concerned in them. And if some vast brain existed far away in space, being invisible because not self-luminous, then, according to the laws of matter at present known to us, it could affect the Solar system only by its weight.

[4.] On the whole, therefore, we seem entitled to conclude that during such time as we can have evidence of, no intelligence or volition has been concerned in events happening within the range of the Solar system, except that of animals living on the planets. The weight of such probabilities is, of course, estimated differently by different people, and the questions are only just beginning to receive the right sort of attention. But it does seem to me that we may expect in time to have negative evidence on this point of the same kind and of the same cogency as that which forbids us to assume the existence between the Earth and Venus of a planet as large as either of them.

[5.] Now, about these conclusions which I have described as probable ones, there are two things that may be said. In the first place, it may be said that they make the world a blank, because they take away the objects of very important and widespread emotions of hope and reverence and love, which are human faculties and require to be exercised, and that they destroy the motives for good conduct. To this it may be answered that we have no right to call the world a blank while it is full of men and women, even though our one friend may be lost to us. And in the regular everyday facts of this common life of men, and in the promise which it holds out for the future, there is room enough and to spare for all the high and noble emotions of which our nature is capable. Moreover, healthy emotions are felt about facts and not about phantoms; and the question is not 'What conclusion will be most pleasing or elevating to my feelings?' but 'What is the truth?' For it is not all human faculties that have to be exercised, but only the good ones. It is not right to exercise the faculty of feeling terror or of resisting evidence. And if there are any faculties which prevent us from accepting the truth and guiding our conduct by it, these faculties ought not to be exercised. As for the assertion that these conclusions destroy the motive for good conduct, it seems to me that it is not only utterly untrue, but, because of its great influence upon human action, one of the most dangerous doctrines that can be set forth. The two questions which we have last discussed are exceedingly difficult and complex questions; the ideas and the knowledge which we used in their discussion are the product of long centuries of laborious investigation and thought; and perhaps, although we all make our little guesses, there is not one man in a million who has any right to a definite opinion about them. But it is not necessary to answer these questions in order to tell an honest man from a rogue. The distinction of right and wrong grows up in the broad light of day out of natural causes wherever men live together; and the only right motive to right action is to be found in the social instincts which have been bred into mankind by hundreds of generations of social life. In the target of every true Englishman's allegiance the bull's-eye belongs to his countrymen, who are visible and palpable and who stand around him; not to any far-off shadowy centre beyond the hills, *ultra montes*, either at Rome or in heaven. Duty to one's countrymen and fellow-citizens, which is the social instinct guided by reason, is in all healthy communities the one thing sacred and supreme. If the course of things is guided by some unseen intelligent person, then this instinct is his highest and clearest voice, and because of it we may call him good. But if the course of things is not so guided, that voice loses nothing of its sacredness, nothing of its clearness, nothing of its obligation.

[6.] In the second place it may be said that Science ought not to deal with these questions at all; that while scientific men are concerned with physical facts, they are *dans leur droit*,[1] but that in treating of such subjects as these they are going out of their domain, and must do harm.

[7.] What is the domain of Science? It is all possible human knowledge which can rightly be used to guide human conduct. . . .

(Fortnightly Review, Dec. 1874.)

NOTE
  1. 'Within their own province'.

Alfred Tennyson, from 'In Memoriam' (1850)   II.11

21

I sing to him that rests below,
    And, since the grasses round me wave,
    I take the grasses of the grave,
And make them pipes whereon to blow.

The traveller hears me now and then,   5
    And sometimes harshly will he speak:
    'This fellow would make weakness weak,
And melt the waxen hearts of men.'

Another answers, 'Let him be,
    He loves to make parade of pain,   10
    That with his piping he may gain
The praise that comes to constancy.'

A third is wroth: 'Is this an hour
    For private sorrow's barren song,
    When more and more the people throng   15
The chairs and thrones of civil power?

'A time to sicken and to swoon,
   When Science reaches forth her arms
   To feel from world to world, and charms
Her secret from the latest moon?'   20

Behold, ye speak an idle thing:
   Ye never knew the sacred dust:
   I do but sing because I must,
And pipe but as the linnets sing:

And one is glad; her note is gay,   25
   For now her little ones have ranged;
   And one is sad; her note is changed,
Because her brood is stol'n away.

28

The time draws near the birth of Christ:
   The moon is hid; the night is still;
   The Christmas bells from hill to hill
Answer each other in the mist.

Four voices of four hamlets round,   5
   From far and near, on mead and moor,
   Swell out and fail, as if a door
Were shut between me and the sound:

Each voice four changes on the wind,
   That now dilate, and now decrease,   10
   Peace and goodwill, goodwill and peace,
Peace and goodwill, to all mankind.

This year I slept and woke with pain,
   I almost wish'd no more to wake,
   And that my hold on life would break   15
Before I heard those bells again:

But they my troubled spirit rule,
   For they controll'd me when a boy;
   They bring me sorrow touch'd with joy,
The merry merry bells of Yule.   20

30

With trembling fingers did we weave
   The holly round the Christmas hearth;
   A rainy cloud possess'd the earth,
And sadly fell our Christmas-eve.

At our old pastimes in the hall   5
   We gambol'd, making vain pretence
   Of gladness, with an awful sense
Of one mute Shadow watching all.

We paused: the winds were in the beech:
   We heard them sweep the winter land;   10
   And in a circle hand-in-hand
Sat silent, looking each at each.

Then echo-like our voices rang;
   We sung, tho' every eye was dim,
   A merry song we sang with him   15
Last year: impetuously we sang:

We ceased: a gentler feeling crept
   Upon us: surely rest is meet:
   'They rest,' we said, 'their sleep is sweet,'
And silence follow'd, and we wept.   20

Our voices took a higher range;
   Once more we sang: 'They do not die
   Nor lose their mortal sympathy,
Nor change to us, although they change;

'Rapt from the fickle and the frail   25
   With gather'd power, yet the same,
   Pierces the keen seraphic flame
From orb to orb, from veil to veil.'

Rise, happy morn, rise, holy morn,
   Draw forth the cheerful day from night;   30
   O Father, touch the east, and light
The light that shone when Hope was born.

31

When Lazarus left his charnel-cave,
   And home to Mary's house return'd,
   Was this demanded—if he yearn'd
To hear her weeping by his grave?

'Where wert thou, brother, those four days?'   5
   There lives no record of reply,
   Which telling what it is to die
Had surely added praise to praise.

From every house the neighbours met,
   The streets were fill'd with joyful sound,   10
   A solemn gladness even crown'd
The purple brows of Olivet.

Behold a man raised up by Christ!
   The rest remaineth unreveal'd:
   He told it not; or something seal'd   15
The lips of that Evangelist.

35

Yet if some voice that man could trust
   Should murmur from the narrow house,
   'The cheeks drop in; the body bows;
Man dies: nor is there hope in dust:'

Might I not say? 'Yet even here,   5
   But for one hour, O Love, I strive
   To keep so sweet a thing alive:'
But I should turn mine ears and hear

The moanings of the homeless sea,
   The sound of streams that swift or slow   10
   Draw down Aeonian hills, and sow
The dust of continents to be;

And Love would answer with a sigh,
   'The sound of that forgetful shore
   Will change my sweetness more and more,   15
Half-dead to know that I shall die.'

O me, what profits it to put
   An idle case? If Death were seen
   At first as Death, Love had not been,
Or been in narrowest working shut,   20

Mere fellowship of sluggish moods,
   Or in his coarsest Satyr-shape
   Had bruised the herb and crush'd the grape,
And bask'd and batten'd in the woods.

50

Be near me when my light is low,
   When the blood creeps, and the nerves prick
   And tingle; and the heart is sick,
And all the wheels of Being slow.

Be near me when the sensuous frame   5
     Is rack'd with pangs that conquer trust;
     And Time, a maniac scattering dust,
And Life, a Fury slinging flame.

Be near me when my faith is dry,
     And men the flies of latter spring,   10
     That lay their eggs, and sting and sing
And weave their petty cells and die.

Be near me when I fade away,
     To point the term of human strife,
     And on the low dark verge of life   15
The twilight of eternal day.

53

How many a father have I seen,
     A sober man, among his boys,
     Whose youth was full of foolish noise,
Who wears his manhood hale and green:

And dare we to this fancy give,   5
     That had the wild oat not been sown,
     The soil, left barren, scarce had grown
The grain by which a man may live?

Or, if we held the doctrine sound
     For life outliving heats of youth,   10
     Yet who would preach it as a truth
To those that eddy round and round?

Hold thou the good: define it well:
     For fear divine Philosophy
     Should push beyond her mark, and be   15
Procuress to the Lords of Hell.

54

Oh yet we trust that somehow good
     Will be the final goal of ill,
     To pangs of nature, sins of will,
Defects of doubt, and taints of blood;

That nothing walks with aimless feet;   5
     That not one life shall be destroy'd,
     Or cast as rubbish to the void,
When God hath made the pile complete;

That not a worm is cloven in vain;
    That not a moth with vain desire   10
    Is shrivell'd in a fruitless fire,
Or but subserves another's gain.

Behold, we know not anything;
    I can but trust that good shall fall
    At last—far off—at last, to all,   15
And every winter change to spring.

So runs my dream; but what am I?
    An infant crying in the night:
    An infant crying for the light:
And with no language but a cry.   20

55

The wish, that of the living whole
    No life may fail beyond the grave,
    Derives it not from what we have
The likest God within the soul?

Are God and Nature then at strife,   5
    That Nature lends such evil dreams?
    So careful of the type she seems,
So careless of the single life;

That I, considering everywhere
    Her secret meaning in her deeds,   10
    And finding that of fifty seeds
She often brings but one to bear,

I falter where I firmly trod,
    And falling with my weight of cares
    Upon the great world's altar-stairs   15
That slope thro' darkness up to God,

I stretch lame hands of faith, and grope,
    And gather dust and chaff, and call
    To what I feel is Lord of all.
And faintly trust the larger hope.   20

56

'So careful of the type?' but no.
    From scarped cliff and quarried stone
    She cries, 'A thousand types are gone:
I care for nothing, all shall go.

'Thou makest thine appeal to me: 5
   I bring to life, I bring to death:
   The spirit does but mean the breath:
I know no more.' And he, shall he,

Man, her last work, who seem'd so fair,
   Such splendid purpose in his eyes,   10
   Who roll'd the psalm to wintry skies,
Who build him fanes of fruitless prayer,

Who trusted God was love indeed
   And love Creation's final law—
   Tho' Nature, red in tooth and claw   15
With ravine, shriek'd against his creed—

Who loved, who suffer'd countless ills,
   Who battled for the True, the Just,
   Be blown about the desert dust,
Or seal'd within the iron hills?   20

No more? A monster then, a dream,
   A discord. Dragons of the prime,
   That tare each other in their slime,
Were mellow music match'd with him.

O life as futile, then, as frail!   25
   O for thy voice to soothe and bless!
   What hope of answer, or redress?
Behind the veil, behind the veil.

                         95
By night we linger'd on the lawn,
   For underfoot the herb was dry;
   And genial warmth; and o'er the sky
The silvery haze of summer drawn;

And calm that let the tapers burn   5
   Unwavering: not a cricket chirr'd:
   The brook alone far-off was heard,
And on the board the fluttering urn:

And bats went round in fragrant skies,
   And wheel'd or lit the filmy shapes   10
   That haunt the dusk, with ermine capes
And woolly breasts and beaded eyes;

While now we sang old songs that peal'd
    From knoll to knoll, where, couch'd at ease,
    The white kine glimmer'd, and the trees   15
Laid their dark arms about the field.

But when those others, one by one,
    Withdrew themselves from me and night,
    And in the house light after light
Went out, and I was all alone,   20

A hunger seized my heart; I read
    Of that glad year which once had been,
    In those fall'n leaves which kept their green,
The noble letters of the dead:

And strangely on the silence broke   25
    The silent-speaking words, and strange
    Was love's dumb cry defying change
To test his worth; and strangely spoke

The faith, the vigour, bold to dwell
    On doubts that drive the coward back,   30
    And keen thro' wordy snares to track
Suggestion to her inmost cell.

So word by word, and line by line,
    The dead man touch'd me from the past,
    And all at once it seem'd at last   35
The living soul was flash'd on mine,

And mine in this was wound, and whirl'd
    About empyreal heights of thought,
    And came on that which is, and caught
The deep pulsations of the world,   40

Aeonian music measuring out
    The steps of Time—the shocks of Chance—
    The blows of Death. At length my trance
Was cancell'd, stricken thro' with doubt.

Vague words! but ah, how hard to frame   45
    In matter-moulded forms of speech,
    Or ev'n for intellect to reach
Thro' memory that which I became:

Till now the doubtful dusk reveal'd
 The knolls once more where, couch'd at ease,
 The white kine glimmer'd, and the trees   50
Laid their dark arms about the field:

And suck'd from out the distant gloom
 A breeze began to tremble o'er
 The large leaves of the sycamore,   55
And fluctuate all the still perfume,

And gathering freshlier overhead,
 Rock'd the full-foliaged elms, and swung
 The heavy-folded rose, and flung
The lilies to and fro, and said   60

'The dawn, the dawn,' and died away;
 And East and West, without a breath,
 Mixt their dim lights, like life and death,
To broaden into boundless day.

98

You leave us: you will see the Rhine,
 And those fair hills I sail'd below,
 When I was there with him; and go
By summer belts of wheat and vine

To where he breathed his latest breath,   5
 That City. All her splendour seems
 No livelier than the wisp that gleams
On Lethe in the eyes of Death.

Let her great Danube rolling fair
 Enwind her isles, unmark'd of me: 10
 I have not seen, I will not see
Vienna; rather dream that there,

A treble darkness, Evil haunts
 The birth, the bridal; friend from friend
 Is oftener parted, fathers bend   15
Above more graves, a thousand wants

Gnarr at the heels of men, and prey
 By each cold hearth, and sadness flings
 Her shadow on the blaze of kings:
And yet myself have heard him say,   20

That not in any mother town
   With statelier progress to and fro
   The double tides of chariots flow
By park and suburb under brown

Of lustier leaves; nor more content,   25
   He told me, lives in any crowd,
   When all is gay with lamps, and loud
With sport and song, in booth and tent,

Imperial halls, or open plain;
   And wheels the circled dance, and breaks   30
   The rocket molten into flakes
Of crimson or in emerald rain.

106

Ring out, wild bells, to the wild sky,
   The flying cloud, the frosty light:
   The year is dying in the night;
Ring out, wild bells, and let him die.

Ring out the old, ring in the new,   5
   Ring, happy bells, across the snow:
   The year is going, let him go;
Ring out the false, ring in the true.

Ring out the grief that saps the mind,
   For those that here we see no more;   10
   Ring out the feud of rich and poor,
Ring in redress to all mankind.

Ring out a slowly dying cause,
   And ancient forms of party strife;
   Ring in the nobler modes of life,   15
With sweeter manners, purer laws.

Ring out the want, the care, the sin,
   The faithless coldness of the times;
   Ring out, ring out my mournful rhymes,
But ring the fuller minstrel in.   20

Ring out false pride in place and blood,
   The civic slander and the spite;
   Ring in the love of truth and right,
Ring in the common love of good.

Ring out old shapes of foul disease;   25
   Ring out the narrowing lust of gold;
   Ring out the thousand wars of old,
Ring in the thousand years of peace.

Ring in the valiant man and free,
   The larger heart, the kindlier hand;   30
   Ring out the darkness of the land,
Ring in the Christ that is to be.

118

Contemplate all this work of Time,
   The giant labouring in his youth:
   Nor dream of human love and truth,
As dying Nature's earth and lime;

But trust that those we call the dead   5
   Are breathers of an ampler day
   For ever nobler ends. They say,
The solid earth whereon we tread

In tracts of fluent heat began,
   And grew to seeming-random forms,   10
   The seeming prey of cyclic storms,
Till at the last arose the man;

Who throve and branch'd from clime to clime,
   The herald of a higher race,
   And of himself in higher place,   15
If so he type this work of time

Within himself, from more to more;
   Or, crown'd with attributes of woe
   Like glories, move his course, and show
That life is not as idle ore,   20

But iron dug from central gloom,
   And heated hot with burning fears,
   And dipt in baths of hissing tears,
And batter'd with the shocks of doom

To shape and use. Arise and fly   25
   The reeling Faun, the sensual feast;
   Move upward, working out the beast,
And let the ape and tiger die.

120

I trust I have not wasted breath:
   I think we are not wholly brain,
   Magnetic mockeries; not in vain,
Like Paul with beasts, I fought with Death;

Not only cunning casts in clay: 5
   Let Science prove we are, and then
   What matters Science unto men,
At least to me? I would not stay.

Let him, the wiser man who springs
   Hereafter, up from childhood shape   10
   His action like the greater ape,
But I was *born* to other things.

123

There rolls the deep where grew the tree.
   O earth, what changes hast thou seen!
   There where the long street roars, hath been
The stillness of the central sea.

The hills are shadows, and they flow   5
   From form to form, and nothing stands;
   They melt like mist, the solid lands,
Like clouds they shape themselves and go.

But in my spirit will I dwell,
   And dream my dream, and hold it true;   10
   For tho' my lips may breathe adieu,
I cannot think the thing farewell.

124

That which we dare invoke to bless;
   Our dearest faith; our ghastliest doubt;
   He, They, One, All; within, without;
The Power in darkness whom we guess;

I found Him not in world or sun,   5
   Or eagle's wing, or insect's eye;
   Nor thro' the questions men may try,
The petty cobwebs we have spun:

If e'er when faith had fall'n asleep,
  I heard a voice 'believe no more'   10
  And heard an ever-breaking shore
That tumbled in the Godless deep;

A warmth within the breast would melt
  The freezing reason's colder part,
  And like a man in wrath the heart   15
Stood up and answer'd 'I have felt.'

No, like a child in doubt and fear:
  But that blind clamour made me wise;
  Then was I as a child that cries,
But, crying, knows his father near;   20

And what I am beheld again
  What is, and no man understands;
  And out of darkness came the hands
That reach thro' nature, moulding men.

Epilogue

O true and tried, so well and long,
  Demand not thou a marriage lay;
  In that it is thy marriage day
Is music more than any song.

Nor have I felt so much of bliss   5
  Since first he told me that he loved
  A daughter of our house; nor proved
Since that dark day a day like this;

Tho' I since then have number'd o'er
  Some thrice three years: they went and came,   10
  Remade the blood and changed the frame,
And yet is love not less, but more;

No longer caring to embalm
  In dying songs a dead regret,
  But like a statue solid-set,   15
And moulded in colossal calm.

Regret is dead, but love is more
  Than in the summers that are flown,
  For I myself with these have grown
To something greater than before;   20

Which makes appear the songs I made
   As echoes out of weaker times,
   As half but idle brawling rhymes,
The sport of random sun and shade.

But where is she, the bridal flower,   25
   That must be made a wife ere noon?
   She enters, glowing like the moon
Of Eden on its bridal bower:

On me she bends her blissful eyes
   And then on thee; they meet thy look   30
   And brighten like the star that shook
Betwixt the palms of paradise.

O when her life was yet in bud,
   He too foretold the perfect rose.
   For thee she grew, for thee she grows   35
For ever, and as fair as good.

And thou art worthy; full of power;
   As gentle; liberal-minded, great,
   Consistent; wearing all that weight
Of learning lightly like a flower.   40

But now set out: the noon is near,
   And I must give away the bride;
   She fears not, or with thee beside
And me behind her, will not fear.

For I that danced her on my knee,   45
   That watch'd her on her nurse's arm,
   That shielded all her life from harm
At last must part with her to thee;

Now waiting to be made a wife,
   Her feet, my darling, on the dead;   50
   Their pensive tablets round her head,
And the most living words of life

Breathed in her ear. The ring is on,
   The 'wilt thou' answer'd, and again
   The 'wilt thou' ask'd, till out of twain   55
Her sweet 'I will' has made you one.

Now sign your names, which shall be read,
 Mute symbols of a joyful morn,
 By village eyes as yet unborn;
The names are sign'd, and overhead   60

Begins the clash and clang that tells
 The joy to every wandering breeze;
 The blind wall rocks, and on the trees
The dead leaf trembles to the bells.

O happy hour, and happier hours   65
 Await them. Many a merry face
 Salutes them—maidens of the place,
That pelt us in the porch with flowers.

O happy hour, behold the bride
 With him to whom her hand I gave.   70
 They leave the porch, they pass the grave
That has to-day its sunny side.

To-day the grave is bright for me.
 For them the light of life increased,
 Who stay to share the morning feast,   75
Who rest to-night beside the sea.

Let all my genial spirits advance
 To meet and greet a whiter sun;
 My drooping memory will not shun
The foaming grape of eastern France.   80

It circles round, and fancy plays,
 And hearts are warm'd and faces bloom,
 As drinking health to bride and groom
We wish them store of happy days.

Nor count me all to blame if I   85
 Conjecture of a stiller guest,
 Perchance, perchance, among the rest,
And, tho' in silence, wishing joy.

But they must go, the time draws on,
 And those white-favour'd horses wait;   90
 They rise, but linger; it is late;
Farewell, we kiss, and they are gone.

A shade falls on us like the dark
   From little cloudlets on the grass,
   But sweeps away as out we pass   95
To range the woods, to roam the park,

Discussing how their courtship grew,
   And talk of others that are wed,
   And how she look'd, and what he said,
And back we come at fall of dew.   100

Again the feast, the speech, the glee,
   The shade of passing thought, the wealth
   Of words and wit, the double health,
The crowning cup, the three-times-three,

And last the dance;—till I retire: 105
   Dumb is that tower which spake so loud,
   And high in heaven the streaming cloud,
And on the downs a rising fire:

And rise, O moon, from yonder down,
   Till over down and over dale   110
   All night the shining vapour sail
And pass the silent-lighted town,

The white-faced halls, the glancing rills,
   And catch at every mountain head,
   And o'er the friths that branch and spread   115
Their sleeping silver thro' the hills;

And touch with shade the bridal doors,
   With tender gloom the roof, the wall;
   And breaking let the splendour fall
To spangle all the happy shores   120

By which they rest, and ocean sounds,
   And, star and system rolling past,
   A soul shall draw from out the vast
And strike his being into bounds,

And, moved thro' life of lower phase,   125
   Result in man, be born and think,
   And act and love, a closer link
Betwixt us and the crowning race

Of those that, eye to eye, shall look
   On knowledge; under whose command   130
   Is Earth and Earth's, and in their hand
Is Nature like an open book;

No longer half-akin to brute,
   For all we thought and loved and did,
   And hoped, and suffer'd, is but seed   135
Of what in them is flower and fruit;

Whereof the man, that with me trod
   This planet, was a noble type
   Appearing ere the times were ripe,
That friend of mine who lives in God,   140

That God, which ever lives and loves,
   One God, one law, one element,
   And one far-off divine event,
To which the whole creation moves.

(*Works*, 1884.)

12

Robert Browning, 'How it Strikes a Contemporary' (1852)   II.12

I only knew one poet in my life:
And this, or something like it, was his way.

   You saw go up and down Valladolid,
A man of mark, to know next time you saw.
His very serviceable suit of black   5
Was courtly once and conscientious still,
And many might have worn it, though none did:
The cloak, that somewhat shone and showed the threads,
Had purpose, and the ruff, significance.
He walked and tapped the pavement with his cane,   10
Scenting the world, looking it full in face,
An old dog, bald and blindish, at his heels.
They turned up, now, the alley by the church,
That leads nowhither; now, they breathed themselves
On the main promenade just at the wrong time: 15
You'd come upon his scrutinizing hat,
Making a peaked shade blacker than itself
Against the single window spared some house

Intact yet with its mouldered Moorish work,—
Or else surprise the ferrel of his stick   20
Trying the mortar's temper 'tween the chinks
Of some new shop a-building, French and fine.
He stood and watched the cobbler at his trade,
The man who slices lemons into drink,
The coffee-roaster's brazier, and the boys   25
That volunteer to help him turn its winch.
He glanced o'er books on stalls with half an eye,
And fly-leaf ballads on the vendor's string,
And broad-edge bold-print posters by the wall.
He took such cognizance of men and things,   30
If any beat a horse, you felt he saw;
If any cursed a woman, he took note;
Yet stared at nobody,—you stared at him,
And found, less to your pleasure than surprise,
He seemed to know you and expect as much.   35
So, next time that a neighbour's tongue was loosed,
It marked the shameful and notorious fact,
We had among us, not so much a spy,
As a recording chief-inquisitor,
The town's true master if the town but knew!   40
We merely kept a governor for form,
While this man walked about and took account
Of all thought, said and acted, then went home,
And wrote it fully to our Lord the King
Who has an itch to know things, he knows why,   45
And reads them in his bedroom of a night.
Oh, you might smile! there wanted not a touch,
A tang of . . . well, it was not wholly ease
As back into your mind the man's look came.
Stricken in years a little,—such a brow   50
His eyes had to live under!—clear as flint
On either side the formidable nose
Curved, cut and coloured like an eagle's claw.
Had he to do with A.'s surprising fate?
When altogether old B. disappeared   55
And young C. got his mistress,—was't our friend,
His letter to the King, that did it all?
What paid the bloodless man for so much pains?
Our Lord the King has favourites manifold,
And shifts his ministry some once a month;   60
Our city gets new governors at whiles,—
But never word or sign, that I could hear,

Notified to this man about the streets
The King's approval of those letters conned
The last thing duly at the dead of night.   65
Did the man love his office? Frowned our Lord,
Exhorting when none heard—'Beseech me not!
Too far above my people,—beneath me!
I set the watch,—how should the people know?
Forget them, keep me all the more in mind!'   70
Was some such understanding 'twixt the two?

    I found no truth in one report at least—
That if you tracked him to his home, down lanes
Beyond the Jewry; and as clean to pace,
You found he ate his supper in a room   75
Blazing with lights, four Titians on the wall,
And twenty naked girls to change his plate!
Poor man, he lived another kind of life
In that new stuccoed third house by the bridge,
Fresh-painted, rather smart than otherwise!   80
The whole street might o'erlook him as he sat,
Leg crossing leg, one foot on the dog's back,
Playing a decent cribbage with his maid
(Jacynth, you're sure her name was) o'er the cheese
And fruit, three red halves of starved winter-pears,   85
Or treat of radishes in April. Nine,
Ten, struck the church clock, straight to bed went he.

    My father, like the man of sense he was,
Would point him out to me a dozen times;
''St—'St,' he'd whisper, 'the Corregidor!'   90
I had been used to think that personage
Was one with lacquered breeches, lustrous belt,
And feathers like a forest in his hat,
Who blew a trumpet and proclaimed the news,
Announced the bull-fights, gave each church its turn,   95
And memorized the miracle in vogue!
He had a great observance from us boys;
We were in error; that was not the man.

    I'd like now, yet had haply been afraid,
To have just looked, when this man came to die,   100
And seen who lined the clean gay garret-sides
And stood about the neat low truckle-bed,
With the heavenly manner of relieving guard.

Here had been, mark, the general-in-chief,
Through a whole campaign of the world's life and death,   105
Doing the King's work all the dim day long,
In his old coat and up to knees in mud,
Smoked like a herring, dining on a crust,—
And, now the day was won, relieved at once!
Nor further show or need for that old coat,   110
You are sure, for one thing! Bless us, all the while
How sprucely we are dressed out, you and I!
A second, and the angels alter that.
Well, I could never write a verse,—could you?
Let's to the Prado and make the most of time.   115

(*Men and Women*, 1885; 1972 edn., ed. P. Turner.)

II.13 **Christina Rossetti, Poems**

A Birthday (1862)

My heart is like a singing bird
    Whose nest is in a watered shoot;

My heart is like an apple tree
    Whose boughs are bent with thickset fruit;
My heart is like a rainbow shell   5
    That paddles in a halcyon sea;
My heart is gladder than all these
    Because my love is come to me.

Raise me a dais of silk and down;
    Hang it with vair and purple dyes;   10
Carve it in doves and pomegranates,
    And peacocks with a hundred eyes;
Work it in gold and silver grapes,
    In leaves and silver fleurs-de-lys;
Because the birthday of my life   15
    Is come, my love is come to me.

A Better Resurrection (1862)

I have no wit, no words, no tears;
    My heart within me like a stone
Is numbed too much for hopes or fears;

Look right, look left, I dwell alone;
  I lift mine eyes, but dimmed with grief   5
    No everlasting hills I see;
  My life is in the falling leaf:
    O Jesus, quicken me.

My life is like a faded leaf,
    My harvest dwindled to a husk;   10
Truly my life is void and brief
    And tedious in the barren dusk;
My life is like a frozen thing,
    No bud nor greenness can I see:
Yet rise it shall—the sap of Spring;   15
    O Jesus, rise in me.

My life is like a broken bowl,
    A broken bowl that cannot hold
One drop of water for my soul
    Or cordial in the searching cold;   20
Cast in the fire the perished thing,
    Melt and remould it, till it be
A royal cup for Him my King:
    O Jesus, drink of me.

(Goblin Market and Other Poems, 1862.)

If Only (1866)

If I might only love my God and die!
  But now He bids me love Him and live on,
  Now when the bloom of all my life is gone,
The pleasant half of life has quite gone by.
My tree of hope is lopped that spread so high;   5
  And I forget how Summer glowed and shone,
  While Autumn grips me with its fingers wan,
And frets me with its fitful windy sigh.
When Autumn passes then must Winter numb,
  And Winter may not pass a weary while,   10
    But when it passes Spring shall flower again:
And in that Spring who weepeth now shall smile,
  Yea, they shall wax who now are on the wane,
Yea, they shall sing for love when Christ shall come.

(The Prince's Progress and Other Poems, 1866.)

II.14 Algernon C. Swinburne, 'A Forsaken Garden' (1876–8)

In a coign of the cliff between lowland and highland,
    At the sea-down's edge between windward and lee,
Walled round with rocks as an inland island,
    The ghost of a garden fronts the sea.
A girdle of brushwood and thorn encloses
    The steep square slope of the blossomless bed
Where the weeds that grew green from the graves of its roses
    Now lie dead.

The fields fall southward, abrupt and broken,
    To the low last edge of the long lone land.   10
If a step should sound or a word be spoken,
    Would a ghost not rise at the strange guest's hand?
So long have the grey bare walks lain guestless,
    Through branches and briars if a man make way,
He shall find no life but the sea-wind's, restless   15
    Night and day.

The dense hard passage is blind and stifled
    That crawls by a track none turn to climb
To the strait waste place that the years have rifled
    Of all but the thorns that are touched not of time.   20
The thorns he spares when the rose is taken;
    The rocks are left when he wastes the plain.
The wind that wanders, the weeds wind-shaken,
    These remain.

Not a flower to be pressed of the foot that falls not;   25
    As the heart of a dead man the seed-plots are dry;
From the thicket of thorns whence the nightingale calls not,
    Could she call, there were never a rose to reply.
Over the meadows that blossom and wither
    Rings but the note of a sea-bird's song;   30
Only the sun and the rain come hither
    All year long.

The sun burns sere and the rain dishevels
    One gaunt bleak blossom of scentless breath.
Only the wind here hovers and revels   35
    In a round where life seems barren as death.
Here there was laughing of old, there was weeping,
    Haply, of lovers none ever will know,

Whose eyes went seaward a hundred sleeping
    Years ago.   40

Heart handfast in heart as they stood, 'Look thither,'
    Did he whisper? 'look forth from the flowers to the sea;
For the foam-flowers endure when the rose-blossoms wither,
    And men that love lightly may die—but we?'
And the same wind sang and the same waves whitened,   45
    And or ever the garden's last petals were shed,
In the lips that had whispered, the eyes that had lightened,
    Love was dead.

Or they loved their life through, and then went whither?
    And were one to the end—but what end who knows?   50
Love deep as the sea as a rose must wither,
    As the rose-red seaweed that mocks the rose.
Shall the dead take thought for the dead to love them?
    What love was ever as deep as a grave?
They are loveless now as the grass above them   55
    Or the wave.

All are at one now, roses and lovers,
    Not known of the cliffs and the fields and the sea.
Not a breath of the time that has been hovers
    In the air now soft with a summer to be.   60
Not a breath shall there sweeten the seasons hereafter
    Of the flowers or the lovers that laugh now or weep,
When as they that are free now of weeping and laughter
    We shall sleep.

Here death may deal not again for ever;   65
    Here change may come not till all change end.
From the graves they have made they shall rise up never,
    Who have left nought living to ravage and rend.
Earth, stones, and thorns of the wild ground growing,
    While the sun and the rain live, these shall be;   70
Till a last wind's breath upon all these blowing
    Roll the sea.

Till the slow sea rise and the sheer cliff crumble,
    Till terrace and meadow the deep gulfs drink,
Till the strength of the waves of the high tides humble   75
    The fields that lessen, the rocks that shrink,

85

Here now in his triumph where all things falter,
   Stretched out on the spoils that his own hand spread,
As a god self-slain on his own strange altar,
    Death lies dead.   80

                (*Collected Poetical Works*, 1924, vol. 1.)

II.15 Gerard Manley Hopkins, Poems

God's Grandeur (1877)

The world is charged with the grandeur of God.
   It will flame out, like shining from shook foil;
   It gathers to a greatness, like the ooze of oil
Crushed. Why do men then now not reck his rod?
Generations have trod, have trod, have trod;   5
   And all is seared with trade; bleared, smeared with toil;
   And wears man's smudge and shares man's smell: the soil
Is bare now, nor can foot feel, being shod.

And for all this, nature is never spent;
   There lives the dearest freshness deep down things;   10
And though the last lights off the black West went
   Oh, morning, at the brown brink eastward, springs—
Because the Holy Ghost over the bent
   World broods with warm breast and with ah! bright wings.

The Starlight Night (1877)

Look at the stars! look, look up at the skies!
   O look at all the fire-folk sitting in the air!
   The bright boroughs, the circle-citadels there!
Down in dim woods the diamond delves! the elves'-eyes!
The grey lawns cold where gold, where quickgold lies!   5
   Wind-beat whitebeam! airy abeles set on a flare!
   Flake-doves sent floating forth at a farmyard scare!—
Ah well! it is all a purchase, all is a prize.

Buy then! bid then!—What?—Prayer, patience, alms, vows.
Look, look: a May-mess, like on orchard boughs!   10
   Look! March-bloom, like on mealed-with-yellow sallows!
These are indeed the barn; withindoors house
The shocks. This piece-bright paling shuts the spouse
   Christ home, Christ and his mother and all his hallows.

Hurrahing in Harvest (1877)

Summer ends now; now, barbarous in beauty, the stooks rise
Around; up above, what wind-walks! what lovely behaviour
Of silk-sack clouds! has wilder, wilful-wavier
Meal-drift moulded ever and melted across skies?

I walk, I lift up, I lift up heart, eyes,   5
Down all that glory in the heavens to glean our Saviour;
And, éyes, heárt, what looks, what lips yet gave you a
Rapturous love's greeting of realer, of rounder replies?

And the azurous hung hills are his world-wielding shoulder
Majestic—as a stallion stalwart, very-violet-sweet!—   10
These things, these things were here and but the beholder
Wanting; which two when they once meet,
The heart rears wings bold and bolder
And hurls for him, O half hurls earth for him off under his feet.

Pied Beauty (1877)

Glory be to God for dappled things—
    For skies of couple-colour as a brinded cow;
        For rose-moles all in stipple upon trout that swim;
Fresh-firecoal chestnut-falls, finches' wings;
    Landscape plotted and pieced—fold, fallow, and plough;   5
        And áll trádes, their gear and tackle and trim.

All things counter, original, spare, strange;
    Whatever is fickle, freckled (who knows how?)
        With swift, slow; sweet, sour; adazzle, dim;
He fathers-forth whose beauty is past change: 10
                        Praise him.

Binsey Poplars (1879)

FELLED 1879

My aspens dear, whose airy cages quelled,
    Quelled or quenched in leaves the leaping sun,
All felled, felled, are all felled;
    Of a fresh and following folded rank
            Not spared, not one   5
        That dandled a sandalled
        Shadow that swam or sank
On meadow and river and wind-wandering weed-winding bank.

     O if we but knew what we do
        When we delve or hew—   10
     Hack and rack the growing green!
       Since country is so tender
    To touch, her being só slender,
    That, like this sleek and seeing ball
    But a prick will make no eye at all,   15
    Where we, even where we mean
        To mend her we end her,
      When we hew or delve:
After-comers cannot guess the beauty been.
    Ten or twelve, only ten or twelve   20
      Strokes of havoc únselve.
       The sweet especial scene,
    Rural scene, a rural scene,
    Sweet especial rural scene.

Duns Scotus's Oxford (1879)

Towery city and branchy between towers;
Cuckoo-echoing, bell-swarmèd, lark-charmèd, rook-racked,
    river-rounded;
The dapple-eared lily below thee; that country and town did
Once encounter in, here coped and poisèd powers;

Thou hast a base and brickish skirt there, sours   5
That neighbour-nature thy grey beauty is grounded
Best in; graceless growth, thou hast confounded
Rural rural keeping—folk, flocks, and flowers.

Yet ah! this air I gather and I release
He lived on; these weeds and waters, these walls are what   10
He haunted who of all men most sways my spirits to peace;

Of realty the rarest-veinèd unraveller; a not
Rivalled insight, be rival Italy or Greece;
Who fired France for Mary without spot.

Carrion Comfort (1885)

Not, I'll not, carrion comfort, Despair, not feast on thee;
Not untwist—slack they may be—these last strands of man
In me ór, most weary, cry *I can no more*. I can;
Can something, hope, wish day come, not choose not to be.

But ah, but O thou terrible, why wouldst thou rude on me   5
Thy wring-world right foot rock? lay a lionlimb against me? scan
With darksome devouring eyes my bruisèd bones? and fan,
O in turns of tempest, me heaped there; me frantic to avoid thee and flee?

Why? That my chaff might fly; my grain lie, sheer and clear.
Nay in all that toil, that coil, since (seems) I kissed the rod,   10
Hand rather, my heart lo! lapped strength, stole joy, would laugh, chéer.
Cheer whom though? The hero whose heaven-handling flung me, fóot tród
Me? or me that fought him? O which one? is it each one? That night,
     that year
Of now done darkness I wretch lay wrestling with (my God!) my God.

No Worst . . . (1885)

No worst, there is none. Pitched past pitch of grief,
More pangs will, schooled at forepangs, wilder wring.
Comforter, where, where is your comforting?
Mary, mother of us, where is your relief?
My cries heave, herds-long; huddle in a main, a chief-   5
woe, world-sorrow; on an age-old anvil wince and sing—
Then lull, then leave off. Fury had shrieked 'No ling-
ering! Let me be fell: force I must be brief'.
O the mind, mind has mountains; cliffs of fall
Frightful, sheer, no-man-fathomed. Hold them cheap   10
May who ne'er hung there. Nor does long our small
Durance deal with that steep or deep. Here! creep,
Wretch, under a comfort serves in a whirlwind: all
Life death does end and each day dies with sleep.

Thou Art Indeed Just . . . (1889)

*Justus quidem tu es, Domine, si disputem tecum; verumtamen
justa loquar ad te: Quare via impiorum prosperatur? &c.*

Thou art indeed just, Lord, if I contend
With thee; but, sir, so what I plead is just.
Why do sinners' ways prosper? and why must
Disappointment all I endeavour end?

Wert thou my enemy, O thou my friend,   5
How wouldst thou worse, I wonder, than thou dost
Defeat, thwart me? Oh, the sots and thralls of lust
Do in spare hours more thrive than I that spend,

Sir, life upon thy cause. See, banks and brakes
Now, leavèd how thick! lacèd they are again   10
With fretty chervil, look, and fresh wind shakes

Them; birds build—but not I build; no, but strain,
Time's eunuch, and not breed one work that wakes.
Mine, O thou lord of life, send my roots rain.

(*The Poems of Gerard Manley Hopkins*, ed. R. Bridges, 1918; 4th edn. 1967,
ed. W. H. Gardner.)

III

Moral Values and the Social Order

John Stuart Mill, from 'On the Logic of the Moral Sciences' (1843)

Chapter I. Introductory Remarks

[1.] Concerning the physical nature of man as an organised being,—though there is still much uncertainty and much controversy, which can only be terminated by the general acknowledgment and employment of stricter rules of induction than are commonly recognised,—there is, however, a considerable body of truths which all who have attended to the subject consider to be fully established; nor is there now any radical imperfection in the method observed in this department of science by its most distinguished modern teachers. But the laws of Mind, and, in even a greater degree, those of Society, are so far from having attained a similar state of even partial recognition, that it is still a controversy whether they are capable of becoming subjects of science in the strict sense of the term; . . .

[2.] At the threshold of this inquiry we are met by an objection, which, if not removed, would be fatal to the attempt to treat human conduct as a subject of science. Are the actions of human beings, like all other natural events, subject to invariable laws? Does that constancy of causation, which is the foundation of every scientific theory of successive phenomena, really obtain among them? This is often denied; and, for the sake of systematic completeness, if not from any very urgent practical necessity, the question should receive a deliberate answer in this place. We shall devote to the subject a chapter apart.

Chapter II. Of Liberty and Necessity

[3.] The question whether the law of causality applies in the same strict sense to human actions as to other phenomena, is the celebrated controversy concerning the freedom of the will, which, from at least as far back as the time of Pelagius, has divided both the philosophical and the religious world. The affirmative opinion is commonly called the doctrine of Necessity, as asserting human volitions and actions to be necessary and inevitable. The negative maintains that the will is not determined, like other phenomena, by antecedents, but determines itself; that our volitions are not, properly speaking, the effects of causes, or at least have no causes which they uniformly and implicitly obey.

[4.] I have already made it sufficiently apparent that the former of these opinions is that which I consider the true one; but the misleading terms in which it is often expressed, and the indistinct manner in which it is usually apprehended, have both obstructed its reception and perverted its influence when received. The metaphysical theory of free-will, as held by philosophers, (for the practical feeling of it, common in a greater or less degree to all mankind, is in no way inconsistent with the contrary theory,) was invented because the supposed alternative of admitting human actions to be *necessary* was deemed inconsistent with every one's instinctive consciousness, as well as humiliating to the pride, and even degrading to the moral nature, of man. Nor do I deny that the doctrine, as sometimes held, is open to these imputations; for the misapprehension in which I shall be able to show that they originate unfortunately is not confined to the opponents of the doctrine, but is participated in by many, perhaps we might say by most, of its supporters.

[5.] Correctly conceived, the doctrine called Philosophical Necessity is simply this: that, given the motives which are present to an individual's mind, and given likewise the character and disposition of the individual, the manner in which he will act might be unerringly inferred; that if we knew the person thoroughly, and knew all the inducements which are acting upon him, we could foretell his conduct with as much certainty as we can predict any physical event. This proposition I take to be a mere interpretation of universal experience, a statement in words of what every one is internally convinced of. No one who believed that he knew thoroughly the circumstances of any case, and the characters of the different persons concerned, would hesitate to foretell how all of them would act. Whatever degree of doubt he may in fact feel arises from the uncertainty whether he really knows the circumstances, or the character of some one or other of the persons, with the degree of accuracy required; but by no means from thinking that if he did know these things, there could be any uncertainty what the conduct would be. Nor does this full assurance conflict in the smallest degree with what is called our feeling of freedom. We do not feel ourselves the less free because those to whom we are intimately known are well assured how we shall will to act in a particular case. We often, on the contrary, regard the doubt what our conduct will be as a mark of ignorance of our character, and sometimes even resent it as an imputation. The religious metaphysicians who have asserted the freedom of the will have always maintained it to be consistent with divine foreknowledge of our actions; and if with divine, then with any other foreknowledge. We may be free, and yet another may have reason to be perfectly certain what use we shall make of our freedom. It is not, therefore, the doctrine that our volitions and actions are invariable consequents of our antecedent states of mind, that is either contradicted by our consciousness or felt to be degrading.

[6.] But the doctrine of causation, when considered as obtaining between our volitions and their antecedents, is almost universally conceived as involving more than this. Many do not believe, and very few practically feel, that there is nothing in causation but invariable, certain, and unconditional sequence. There are few to whom mere constancy of succession appears a sufficiently stringent bond of union for so peculiar a relation as that of cause and effect. Even if the reason repudiates, the imagination retains, the feeling of some more intimate connection, of some peculiar tie or mysterious constraint exercised by the antecedent over the consequent. Now this it is which, considered as applying to the human will, conflicts with our consciousness and revolts our feelings. We are certain that, in the case of our volitions, there is not this mysterious constraint. We know that we are not compelled, as by a magical spell, to obey any particular motive. We feel that if we wished to prove that we have the power of resisting the motive, we could do so, (that wish being, it needs scarcely be observed, a *new antecedent*;) and it would be humiliating to our pride, and (what is of more importance) paralysing to our desire of excellence, if we thought otherwise. But neither is any such mysterious compulsion now supposed, by the best philosophical authorities, to be exercised by any other cause over its effect. Those who think that causes draw their effects after them by a mystical tie are right in believing that the relation between volitions and their antecedents is of another nature. But they should go farther, and admit that this is also true of all other effects and their antecedents. If such a tie is considered to be involved in the word necessity, the doctrine is not true of human actions; but neither is it then true of inanimate objects. It would be more correct to say that matter is not bound by necessity, than that mind is so.

[7.] That the free-will metaphysicians, being mostly of the school which rejects Hume's and Brown's analysis of Cause and Effect, should miss their way for want of the light which that analysis affords, cannot surprise us. The wonder is, that the Necessitarians, who usually admit that philosophical theory, should in practice equally lose sight of it. The very same misconception of the doctrine called Philosophical Necessity which prevents the opposite party from recognising its truth, I believe to exist more or less obscurely in the minds of most Necessitarians, however they may in words disavow it. I am much mistaken if they habitually feel that the necessity which they recognise in actions is but uniformity of order, and capability of being predicted. They have a feeling as if there were at bottom a stronger tie between the volitions and their causes: as if, when they asserted that the will is governed by the balance of motives, they meant something more cogent than if they had only said, that whoever knew the motives, and our habitual susceptibilities to them, could predict how we should will to act. They commit, in opposition to their own scientific system, the very same mistake which their adversaries commit in obedience to theirs; and in consequence do really in some instances suffer those depressing consequences which their opponents erroneously impute to the doctrine itself.

[8.] I am inclined to think that this error is almost wholly an effect of the associations with a word, and that it would be prevented by forbearing to employ, for the expression of the simple fact of causation, so extremely inappropriate a term as Necessity. That word, in its other acceptations, involves much more than mere uniformity of sequence: it implies irresistibleness. Applied to the will, it only means that the given cause will be followed by the effect, subject to all possibilities of counteraction by other causes; but in common use it stands for the operation of those causes exclusively, which are supposed too powerful to be counteracted at all. When we say that all human actions take place of necessity, we only mean that they will certainly happen if nothing prevents:—when we say that dying of want, to those who cannot get food, is a necessity, we mean that it will certainly happen, whatever may be done to prevent it. The application of the same term to the agencies on which human actions depend as is used to express those agencies of nature which are really uncontrollable, cannot fail, when habitual, to create a feeling of uncontrollableness in the former also. This, however, is a mere illusion. There are physical sequences which we call necessary, as death for want of food or air; there are others which, though as much cases of causation as the former, are not said to be necessary, as death from poison, which an antidote, or the use of the stomach-pump will sometimes avert. It is apt to be forgotten by people's feelings, even if remembered by their understandings, that human actions are in this last predicament: they are never (except in some cases of mania) ruled by any one motive with such absolute sway that there is no room for the influence of any other. The causes, therefore, on which action depends are never uncontrollable, and any given effect is only necessary provided that the causes tending to produce it are not controlled. That whatever happens could not have happened otherwise unless something had taken place which was capable of preventing it, no one surely needs hesitate to admit. But to call this by the name necessity is to use the term in a sense so different from its primitive and familiar meaning, from that which it bears in the common occasions of life, as to amount almost to a play upon words. The associations derived from the ordinary sense of the term will adhere to it in spite of all we can do; and though the doctrine of Necessity, as stated by most who hold it, is very remote from fatalism, it is probable that most Necessitarians are Fatalists, more or less, in their feelings.

[9.] A Fatalist believes, or half believes, (for nobody is a consistent Fatalist,) not only that whatever is about to happen will be the infallible result of the causes which produce it, (which is the true Necessitarian doctrine,) but, moreover, that there is no use in struggling against it; that it will happen however we may strive to prevent it. Now, a Necessitarian, believing that our actions follow from our characters, and that our characters follow from our organisation, our education, and our circumstances, is apt to be, with more or less of consciousness on his part, a Fatalist as to his own actions, and to believe that his nature is such, or that his education and circumstances have so moulded his character, that nothing can now prevent him from feeling and acting in a particular way, or at least that no effort of his own can hinder it. In the words of the sect[1] which in our own day has most perseveringly inculcated and most perversely misunderstood this great doctrine, his character is formed *for* him and not *by* him; therefore his wishing that it had been formed differently is of no use; he has no power to alter it. But this is a grand error. He has, to a certain extent, a power to alter his character. Its being, in the ultimate resort, formed for him is not inconsistent with its being, in part, formed *by* him as one of the intermediate agents. His character is formed by his circumstances, (including among these his particular organisation,) but his own desire to mould it in a particular way is one of those circumstances, and by no means one of the least influential. We cannot, indeed, directly will to be different from what we are; but neither did those who are supposed to have formed our characters directly will that we should be what we are. Their will had no direct power except over their own actions. They made us what they did make us by willing, not the ends, but the requisite means; and we, when our habits are not too inveterate, can, by similarly willing the requisite means, make ourselves different. If they could place us under the influence of certain circumstances, we in like manner can place ourselves under the influence of other circumstances. We are exactly as capable of making our own character, *if we will*, as others are of making it for us.

[10.] Yes, (answers the Owenite,) but these words, 'if we will,' surrender the whole point, since the will to alter our own character is given us, not by any efforts of ours, but by circumstances which we cannot help; it comes either from external causes or not at all. Most true: if the Owenite stops here, he is in a position from which nothing can expel him. Our character is formed by us as well as for us; but the wish which induces us to attempt to form it is formed for us; and how? Not, in general, by our organisation, nor wholly by our education, but by our experience—experience of the painful consequences of the character we previously had, or by some strong feeling of admiration or aspiration accidentally aroused. But to think that we have no power of altering our character, and to think that we shall not use our power unless we desire to use it, are very different things, and have a very different effect on the mind. A person who does not wish to alter his character cannot be the person who is supposed to feel discouraged or paralysed by thinking himself unable to do it. The depressing effect of the Fatalist doctrine can only be felt where there *is* a wish to do what that doctrine represents as impossible. It is of no consequence what we think forms our character, when we have no desire of our own about forming it, but it is of great consequence that we should not be prevented from forming such a desire by thinking the attainment impracticable, and that if we have the desire we should know that the work is not so irrevocably done as to be incapable of being altered. . . .

[11.] With the corrections and explanations now given, the doctrine of the causation of our volitions by motives, and of motives by the desirable objects offered to us, combined with our particular susceptibilities of desire, may be considered, I hope, as sufficiently established for the purposes of this treatise.

Chapter IV. Of the Laws of Mind

[12.] Here, as throughout our inquiry, we shall . . . understand by the laws of mind those of mental phenomena—of the various feelings or states of consciousness of sentient beings. These, according to the classification we have uniformly followed, consist of Thoughts, Emotions, Volitions, and Sensations . . .

[13.] All states of mind are immediately caused either by other states of mind or by states of body. When a state of mind is produced by a state of mind, I call the law concerned in the case a law of Mind. When a state of mind is produced directly by a state of body, the law is a law of Body, and belongs to physical science.

[14.] With regard to those states of mind which are called sensations, all are agreed that these have for their immediate antecedents states of body. Every sensation has for its proximate cause some affection of the portion of our frame called the nervous system, whether this affection originate in the action of some external object, or in some pathological condition of the nervous organisation itself. The laws of this portion of our nature—the varieties of our sensations and the physical conditions on which they proximately depend—manifestly belong to the province of Physiology.

[15.] Whether the remainder of our mental states are similarly dependent on physical conditions, is one of the *vexatae questiones* in the science of human nature. It is still disputed whether our thoughts, emotions, and volitions are generated through the intervention of material mechanism; whether we have organs of thought and of emotion in the same sense in which we have organs of sensation. Many eminent physiologists hold the affirmative. These contend that a thought (for example) is as much the result of nervous agency as a sensation; that some particular state of our nervous system, in particular of that central portion of it called the brain, invariably precedes, and is presupposed by, every state of our consciousness. According to this theory, one state of mind is never really produced by another; all are produced by states of body. When one thought seems to call up another by association, it is not really a thought which recalls a thought; the association did not exist between the two thoughts, but between the two states of the brain or nerves which preceded the thoughts: one of those states recalls the other, each being attended, in its passage, by the particular state of consciousness which is consequent on it. On this theory the uniformities of succession among states of mind would be mere derivative uniformities, resulting from the laws of succession of the bodily states which cause them. There would be no original mental laws, no Laws of Mind in the sense in which I use the term, at all; and mental science would be a mere branch, though the highest and most recondite branch, of the science of Physiology. M. Comte, accordingly, claims the scientific cognisance of moral and intellectual phenomena exclusively for physiologists; and not only denies to Psychology, or Mental Philosophy properly so called, the character of a science, but places it, in the chimerical nature of its objects and pretensions, almost on a par with astrology.

[16.] But, after all has been said which can be said, it remains incontestable that there exist uniformities of succession among states of mind, and that these can be ascertained by observation and experiment. Further, that every mental state has a nervous state for its immediate antecedent and proximate cause, though extremely probable, cannot hitherto be said to be proved, in the conclusive manner in which this can be proved of sensations; and even were it certain, yet every one must admit that we are wholly ignorant of the characteristics of these nervous states; we know not, and at present have no means of knowing, in what respect one of them differs from another; and our only mode of studying their successions or co-existences must be by observing the successions and co-existences of the mental states of which they are supposed to be the generators or causes. The successions, therefore, which obtain among mental phenomena do not admit of being deduced from the physiological laws of our nervous organisation; and all real knowledge of them must continue, for a long time at least, if not always, to be sought in the direct study, by observation and experiment, of the mental successions themselves. Since, therefore, the order of our mental phenomena must be studied in those phenomena, and not inferred from the laws of any phenomena more general, there is a distinct and separate Science of Mind.

[17.] The relations, indeed, of that science to the science of physiology must never be overlooked or undervalued. It must by no means be forgotten that the laws of mind may be derivative laws resulting from laws of animal life, and that their truth therefore may ultimately depend on physical conditions; and the influence of physiological states or physiological changes in altering or counteracting the mental successions is one of the most important departments of psychological study. But, on the other hand, to reject the resource of psychological analysis, and construct the theory of the mind solely on such data as physiology at present affords, seems to me as great an error in principle, and an even more serious one in practice. Imperfect as is the science of mind, I do not scruple to affirm that it is in a considerably more advanced state than the portion of physiology which corresponds to it; and to discard the former for the latter appears to me an infringement of the true canons of inductive philosophy, which must produce, and which does produce, erroneous conclusions in some very important departments of the science of human nature.

[18.] The subject, then, of Psychology is the uniformities of succession, the laws, whether ultimate or derivative, according to which one mental state succeeds another—is caused by, or at least is caused to follow, another. Of these laws, some are general, others more special. The following are examples of the most general laws.

[19.] First, whenever any state of consciousness has once been excited in us, no matter by what cause, an inferior degree of the same state of consciousness, a state of consciousness resembling the former, but inferior in intensity, is capable of being reproduced in us, without the presence of any such cause as excited it at first. Thus, if we have once seen or touched an object, we can afterwards think of the object though it be absent from our sight or from our touch. If we have been joyful or grieved at some event, we can think of or remember our past joy or grief, though no new event of a happy or painful nature has taken place. When a poet has put together a mental picture of an imaginary object, a Castle of Indolence, a Una,[2] or a Hamlet, he can afterwards think of the ideal object he has created without any fresh act of intellectual combination. This law is expressed by saying, in the language of Hume, that every mental *impression* has its *idea*.

[20.] Secondly, these ideas, or secondary mental states, are excited by our impressions, or by other ideas, according to certain laws which are called Laws of Association. Of these laws the first is, that similar ideas tend to excite one another. The second is, that when two impressions have been frequently experienced (or even thought of), either simultaneously or in immediate succession, then whenever one of these impressions, or the idea of it recurs, it tends to excite the idea of the other. The third law is, that greater intensity in either or both of the impressions is equivalent, in rendering them excitable by one another, to a greater frequency of conjunction. These are the laws of ideas, on which I shall not enlarge in this place, but refer the reader to works professedly psychological, in particular to Mr. James Mill's *Analysis of the Phenomena of the Human Mind*, where the principal laws of association, along with many of their applications, are copiously exemplified, and with a masterly hand.

[21.] These simple or elementary Laws of Mind have been ascertained by the ordinary methods of experimental inquiry; nor could they have been ascertained in any other manner. But a certain number of elementary laws having thus been obtained, it is fair subject of scientific inquiry how far those laws can be made to go in explaining the actual phenomena. It is obvious that complex laws of thought and feeling not only may, but must be generated from these simple laws.

(*A System of Logic*, 8th edn., 1872, Book VI.)

1. A reference to the Owenites.
2. Una is the heroine of Edmund Spenser's *Faerie Queene* (Book I). 'Castle of Indolence' is a reference to James Thomson's poem of that name.

Arthur Hugh Clough, 'Each for Himself is Still the Rule' (1852)   III.2

Each for himself is still the rule,
We learn it when we go to school—
  The devil take the hindmost, o!

And when the schoolboys grow to men,
In life they learn it o'er again—   5
  The devil take the hindmost, o!

For in the church, and at the bar,
On 'Change, at court, where'er they are,
  The devil takes the hindmost, o!

Husband for husband, wife for wife,   10
Are careful that in married life
  The devil take the hindmost, o!

From youth to age, whate'er the game,
The unvarying practice is the same—
  The devil take the hindmost, o!   15

And after death, we do not know,
But scarce can doubt, where'er we go,
  The devil takes the hindmost, o!

Tol rol de rol, tol rol de ro,
The devil take the hindmost, o!   20

(*The Poems of Arthur Hugh Clough*, ed. A. L. P. Norrington, 1968.)

Elizabeth Barrett Browning, 'Lord Walter's Wife' (1862)   III.3

I

'But why do you go,' said the lady,
    while both sate under the yew,
And her eyes were alive in their depth,
    as the kraken beneath the sea-
    blue.

II

'Because I fear you,' he answered;—
  'because you are far too fair,
And able to strangle my soul in a mesh
  of your gold-coloured hair.'

III

'Oh, that,' she said, 'is no reason.
  Such knots are quickly undone,
And too much beauty, I reckon, is
  nothing but too much sun.'

IV

'Yet farewell so,' he answered;—'the
  sunstroke's fatal at times.
I value your husband, Lord Walter,
  whose gallop rings still from the
  limes.'

V

'Oh, that,' she said, 'is no reason.
  You smell a rose through a fence:
If two should smell it, what matter?
  who grumbles, and where's the
  pretence!'

VI

'But I,' he replied,' have promised
  another, when love was free,
To love her alone, alone, who alone
  and afar loves me.'

VII

'Why, that,' she said, 'is no reason.
  Love's always free, I am told.
Will you vow to be safe from the head-
  ache on Tuesday, and think it
  will hold!'

VIII

'But you,' he replied, 'have a
   daughter, a young little child,
   who was laid
In your lap to be pure; so I leave you:
   the angels would make me afraid.'

IX

'Oh, that,' she said, 'is no reason.
   The angels keep out of the way;
And Dora, the child, observes nothing,
   although you should please me
   and stay.'

X

At which he rose up in his anger,—
   'Why, now, you no longer are
   fair!
Why, now, you no longer are fatal, but
   ugly and hateful, I swear.'

XI

At which she laughed out in her scorn,—
   'These men! Oh, these men over-
   nice,
Who are shocked if a colour not virtuous,
   is frankly put on by a vice.'

XII

Her eyes blazed upon him— 'And *you!*
   You bring us your vices so near
That we smell them! You think in our
   presence a thought 'twould de-
   fame us to hear!

XIII

'What reason had you and what right,
   —I appeal to your soul from my
   life,—
To find me too fair as a woman? why,
   sir, I am pure, and a wife.

15

20

25

XIV

'Is the day-star too fair up above you?
    It burns you not. Dare you imply
I brushed you more close than the star
    does, when Walter had set me as
    high?

XV

'If a man finds a woman too fair, he
    means simply adapted too much
To uses unlawful and fatal. The praise!
    —shall I thank you for such?   30

XVI

'Too fair?—not unless you misuse us
    and surely if, once in a while,
You attain to it, straightway you call us
    no longer too fair, but too vile.

XVII

'A moment,—I pray your attention!—I
    have a poor word in my head
I must utter, though womanly custom
    would set it down better unsaid.

XVIII

'You grew, sir, pale to impertinence,
    once when I showed you a ring.   35
You kissed my fan when I dropped it.
    No matter!—I've broken the
    thing.

XIX

'You did me the honour, perhaps, to be
    moved at my side now and then
In the senses—a vice, I have heard,
    which is common to beasts and
    some men.

XX

'Love's a virtue for heroes!—as white
    as the snow on high hills,
And immortal as every great soul is that
    struggles, endures, and fulfils.   40

XXI

'I love my Walter profoundly,—you,
    Maude, though you faltered a
    week,
For the sake of . . . what was it? an eye-
    brow? or, less still, a mole on a
    cheek?

XXII

'And since when all's said, you're too
    noble to stoop to the frivolous cant
About crimes irresistible virtues that
    swindle, betray and supplant,

XXIII

'I determined to prove to yourself that,
    whate'er you might dream or avow   45
By illusion, you wanted precisely no
    more of me than you have now.

XXIV

'There. Look me full in the face!—In
    the face. Understand, if you can,
That the eyes of such women as I am,
    are clean as the palm of a man.

XXV

'Drop his hand, you insult him. Avoid
    us for fear we should cost you
    a scar—
You take us for harlots, I tell you, and
    not for the women we are.   50

XXVI

'You wronged me: but then I con-
    sidered . . . there's Walter! And
    so at the end,
I vowed that he should not be mulcted
    by me, in the hand of a friend.

XXVII

Have I hurt you indeed? We are quits
then. Nay, friend of my Walter,
be mine!
Come Dora, my darling, my angel, and
help me to ask him to dine.'

(*Last Poems*, 1862.)

II.4 Letter from John Ruskin to *The Times* (25 May 1854)

Sir:

Your kind insertion of my notes on Mr. Hunt's principal picture encourages me to hope that you may yet allow me room in your columns for a few
words respecting his second work in the Royal Academy, the 'Awakening
Conscience.' Not that his picture is obscure, or its story feebly told. I am at
a loss to know how its meaning could be rendered more distinctly, but
assuredly it is not understood. People gaze at it in a blank wonder, and
leave it hopelessly; so that, though it is almost an insult to the painter to
explain his thoughts in this instance, I cannot persuade myself to leave it
thus misunderstood. The poor girl has been sitting singing with her
seducer; some chance words of the song, 'Oft in the stilly night,' have
struck upon the numbed places of her heart; she has started up in agony;
he, not seeing her face, goes on singing, striking the keys carelessly with his
gloved hand.

I suppose that no one possessing the slightest knowledge of expression
could remain untouched by the countenance of the lost girl, rent from its
beauty into sudden horror; the lips half open, indistinct in their purple
quivering; the teeth set hard; the eyes filled with the fearful light of futurity,
and with tears of ancient days. But I can easily understand that to many
persons the careful rendering of the inferior details in this picture cannot
but be at first offensive, as calling their attention away from the principle
[*sic*] subject. It is true that detail of this kind has long been so carelessly rendered, that the perfect finishing of it becomes a matter of curiosity, and
therefore an interruption to serious thought. But, without entering into the
question of the general propriety of such treatment, I would only observe
that, at least in this instance, it is based on a truer principle of the pathetic
than any of the common artistical expedients of the schools. Nothing is
more notable than the way in which even the most trivial objects force
themselves upon the attention of a mind which has been fevered by violent
and distressful excitement. They thrust themselves forward with a ghastly
and unendurable distinctness, as if they would compel the sufferer to
count, or measure, or learn them by heart. Even to the mere spectator a

1. W. Holman Hunt: *The Awakening Conscience* 1854

strange interest exalts the accessories of a scene in which he bears witness to human sorrow. There is not a single object in all that room—common, modern, vulgar (in the vulgar sense, as it may be), but it becomes tragical, if rightly read. That furniture so carefully painted, even to the last vein of the rosewood—is there nothing to be learnt from that terrible lustre of it, from its fatal newness; nothing there that has the old thoughts of home upon it, or that is ever to become a part of home? Those embossed books, vain and useless,—they are also new, marked with no happy wearing of beloved leaves; the torn and dying bird upon the floor, the gilded tapestry, with the fowls of the air feeding on the ripened corn; the picture above the fireplace, with its single drooping figure—the woman taken in adultery; nay, the very hem of the poor girl's dress, at which the painter has labored so closely, thread by thread, has story in it, if we think how soon its pure whiteness may be soiled with dust and rain, her outcast feet failing in the street; and the fair garden flowers, seen in that reflected sunshine of the mirror—these also have their language—

> Hope not to find delight in us, they say,
> For we are spotless, Jessy—we are pure.

I surely need not go on. Examine the whole range of the walls of the Academy,—nay, examine those of all our public and private galleries,—and while pictures will be met with by the thousand which literally tempt to evil, by the thousand which are directed to the meanest trivialities of incident or emotion, by the thousand to the delicate fancies of inactive religion, there will not be found one powerful as this to meet full in the front the moral evil of the age in which it is painted; to waken into mercy the cruel thoughtlessness of youth, and subdue the severities of judgment into the sanctity of compassion.

I have the honor to be, Sir,
Your obedient servant,
THE AUTHOR OF 'MODERN PAINTERS.'

III.5 Samuel Smiles, from *Self-Help* (1859)

[1.] 'Heaven helps those who help themselves' is a well-tried maxim, embodying in a small compass the results of vast human experience. The spirit of self-help is the root of all genuine growth in the individual; and, exhibited in the lives of many, it constitutes the true source of national vigour and strength. Help from without is often enfeebling in its effects, but help from within invariably invigorates. Whatever is done *for* men or classes, to a certain extent takes away the stimulus and necessity of doing for themselves; and where men are subjected to over-guidance and over-government, the inevitable tendency is to render them comparatively help-less.

[2.] Even the best institutions can give a man no active aid. Perhaps the utmost they can do is, to leave him *free* to develop himself and improve his individual condition. But in all times men have been prone to believe that their happiness and well-being were to be secured by means of institutions rather than by their own conduct. Hence the value of legislation as an agent in human advancement has always been greatly over-estimated. To constitute the millionth part of a Legislature, by voting for one or two men once in three or five years, however conscientiously this duty may be performed, can exercise but little active influence upon any man's life and character. Moreover, it is every day becoming more clearly understood, that the function of Government is negative and restrictive, rather than positive and active; being resolvable principally into protection—protection of life, liberty, and property. Hence the chief 'reforms' of the last fifty years have consisted mainly in abolitions and disenactments. But there is no power of law that can make the idle man industrious, the thriftless provident, or the drunken sober; though every individual can be each and all of these if he will, by the exercise of his own free powers of action and self-denial. Indeed all experience serves to prove that the worth and strength of a State depend far less upon the form of its institutions than upon the character of its men. For the nation is only the aggregate of individual conditions, and civilization itself is but a question of personal improvement.

[3.] National progress is the sum of individual industry, energy, and uprightness, as national decay is of individual idleness, selfishness, and vice. What we are accustomed to decry as great social evils, will, for the most part, be found to be only the outgrowth of our own perverted life; and though we may endeavour to cut them down and extirpate them by means of Law, they will only spring up again with fresh luxuriance in some other form, unless the conditions of human life and character are radically improved. If this view be correct, then it follows that the highest patriotism and philanthropy consist, not so much in altering laws and modifying institutions, as in helping and stimulating men to elevate and improve themselves by their own free and independent action.

[4.] The Government of a nation itself is usually found to be but the reflux of the individuals composing it. The Government that is ahead of the people will be inevitably dragged down to their level, as the Government that is behind them will in the long run be dragged up. In the order of nature, the collective character of a nation will as surely find its befitting results in its law and government, as water finds its own level. The noble people will be nobly ruled, and the ignorant and corrupt ignobly. Indeed, liberty is quite as much a moral as a political growth—the result of free individual action, energy, and independence.

[5.] It may be of comparatively little consequence how a man is governed from without, whilst everything depends upon how he governs himself from within. The greatest slave is not he who is ruled by a despot, great though that evil be, but he who is in the thrall of his own moral ignorance, selfishness, and vice. There have been, and perhaps there still are, so-called patriots abroad, who hold it to be the greatest stroke for liberty to kill a tyrant, forgetting that the tyrant usually represents only too faithfully the millions of people over whom he reigns. But nations who are enslaved at heart cannot be freed by any mere changes of masters or of institutions; and so long as the fatal delusion prevails, that liberty solely depends upon and consists in government, so long will such changes, no matter at what cost they be effected, have as little practical and lasting result as the shifting of the figures in a phantasmagoria. The solid foundations of liberty must rest upon individual character; which is also the only sure guarantee for social security and national progress. In this consists the real strength of English liberty. Englishmen feel that they are free, not merely because they live under those free institutions which they have so laboriously built up, but because each member of society has to a greater or less extent got the root of the matter within himself; and they continue to hold fast and enjoy their liberty, not by freedom of speech merely, but by their steadfast life and energetic action as free individual men.

[6.] Such as England is, she has been made by the thinking and working of many generations; the action of even the least significant person having contributed towards the production of the general result. Laborious and patient men of all ranks—cultivators of the soil and explorers of the mine—inventors and discoverers—tradesmen, mechanics, and labourers—poets, thinkers, and politicians—all have worked together, one generation carrying forward the labours of another, building up the character of the country, and establishing its prosperity on solid foundations. This succession of noble workers—the artisans of civilization—has created order out of chaos, in industry, science, and art: and as our forefathers laboured for us, and we have succeeded to the inheritance which they have bequeathed to us, so is it our duty to hand it down, not only unimpaired, but improved, to our successors.

[7.] This spirit of self-help, as exhibited in the energetic action of individuals, has in all times been a marked feature in the English character, and furnishes the true measure of our power as a nation. Rising above the heads of the mass, there have always been a series of individuals distinguished beyond others, who have commanded the public homage. But our progress has been owing also to multitudes of smaller and unknown men. Though only the generals' names may be remembered in the history of any great campaign, it has been mainly through the individual valour and heroism of the privates that victories have been won. And life, too, is 'a soldiers' battle,' men in the ranks having in all times been amongst the greatest of workers. Many are the lives of men unwritten, which have nevertheless as powerfully influenced civilization and progress as the more fortunate Great whose names are recorded in biography. Even the humblest person, who sets before his fellows an example of industry, sobriety, and upright honesty of purpose in life, has a present as well as a future influence upon the well-being of his country; for his life and character pass unconsciously into the lives of others, and propagate good example for all time to come.

[8.] Biographies of great, but especially of good men, are, nevertheless, most instructive and useful, as helps, guides and incentives to others. Some of the best are almost equivalent to gospels—teaching high living, high thinking, and energetic action for their own and the world's good. British biography is studded over, as 'with patines of bright gold,' with illustrious examples of the power of self-help, of patient purpose, resolute working, and steadfast integrity, issuing in the formation of truly noble and manly character; exhibiting in language not to be misunderstood, what it is in the power of each to accomplish for himself; and illustrating the efficacy of self-respect and self-reliance in enabling men of even the humblest rank to work out for themselves an honourable competency and a solid reputation.

[9.] Foreign observers have noted, as one of the most marked characteristics of the Englishman, his strong individuality and distinctive personal energy,—refusing to merge himself in institutions, but retaining throughout his perfect freedom of thought, and speech, and action. 'Que j'aime la hardiesse Anglaise! que j'aime les gens qui disent ce qu'ils pensent!' was the expressive exclamation of Voltaire. It is this strong individualism which makes and keeps the Englishman really free, and brings out fully the action of the social body. The energies of the strong form so many living centres of action, round which other individual energies group and cluster themselves; thus the life of all is quickened, and, on great occasions, a powerful energetic action of the nation is secured.

[10.] It is this energy of individual life and example acting throughout society, which constitutes the best practical education of Englishmen. Schools, academies, and colleges, give but the merest beginnings of culture in comparison with it. Far higher and more practical is the life-education daily given in our homes, in the streets, behind counters, in workshops, at the loom and the plough, in counting-houses and manufactories, and in all the busy haunts of men. This is the education that fits Englishmen for doing the work and acting the part of free men. This is that final instruction as members of society, which Schiller designated 'the education of the human race,' consisting in action, conduct, self-culture, self-control,—all that tends to discipline a man truly, and fit him for the proper performance of the duties and business of life,—a kind of education not to be learnt from books, or acquired by any amount of mere literary training. With his usual weight of words, Bacon observes, that 'Studies teach not their own use; but that is a wisdom without them, and above them, won by observation;' a remark that holds true of actual life, as well as of the cultivation of the intellect itself. For all observation serves to illustrate and enforce the lesson, that a man perfects himself by work much more than by reading,—that it is life rather than literature, action rather than study, and character rather than biography, which tend perpetually to renovate mankind. . . .

[11.] It is this individual freedom and energy of action, so cordially recognised by . . . observant foreigners, that really constitutes the prolific source of our national growth. For it is not to one rank or class alone that this spirit of free action is confined, but it pervades all ranks and classes; perhaps its most vigorous outgrowths being observable in the commonest orders of the people. . . .

[12.] The instances of men in this country who, by dint of persevering application and energy, have raised themselves from the humblest ranks of industry to eminent positions of usefulness and influence in society, are indeed so numerous that they have long ceased to be regarded as exceptional. Looking at some of the more remarkable instances, it might almost be said that early encounter with difficulty and adverse circumstances was the necessary and indispensable condition of success. The House of Commons has always contained a considerable number of such self-raised men—fitting representatives of the industrial character of the British people; and it is to the credit of our Legislature that such men have received due honour there. When the late Joseph Brotherton, member for Salford, in the course of the discussion on the Ten Hours Bill, detailed with true pathos the hardships and fatigues to which he had been subjected when working as a factory boy in a cotton mill, and described the resolution which he had then formed, that if ever it was in his power he would endeavour to ameliorate the condition of that class, Sir James Graham rose immediately after him, and declared, amidst the cheers of the House, that he did not before know that Mr. Brotherton's origin had been so humble, but that it rendered him more proud than he had ever before been of the House of Commons, to think that a person risen from that condition should be able to sit side by side, on equal terms, with the hereditary gentry of the land. . . .

[13.] But the same characteristic feature of energetic industry happily has its counterpart amongst the other ranks of the community. The middle and well-to-do classes are constantly throwing out vigorous offshoots in all directions—in science, commerce, and art—thus adding effectively to the working power of the country. Probably the very greatest name in English philosophy is that of Sir Isaac Newton, who was the son of a yeoman, the owner and farmer of a little property at Woolsthorpe, in Lincolnshire, worth only about thirty pounds a year. The distinguished astronomer Adams, the discoverer of Neptune, was born in the same condition of life; his father being a small farmer on one of the bleakest spots on Dartmoor, a region in which, however sterile the soil may be, it is clear that nature is capable of growing the manliest of men. . . .

[**14.**] Riches are so great a temptation to ease and self-indulgence, to which men are by nature prone, that the glory is all the greater of those who, born to ample fortunes, nevertheless take an active part in the work of their generation—who 'scorn delights and live laborious days.' It is to the honour of the wealthier ranks in this country that they are not idlers; for they do their fair share of the work of the state, and usually take more than their fair share of its dangers. . . .

[**15.**] But it is principally in the departments of politics and literature that we find the most energetic labourers amongst our higher classes. Success in these lines of action, as in all others, can only be achieved through industry, practice, and study; and the great Minister, or parliamentary leader, must necessarily be amongst the very hardest of workers. Such are Palmerston and Derby, Russell and Disraeli, Gladstone and Bulwer. These men have had the benefit of no Ten Hours Bill, but have often, during the busy season of Parliament, worked 'double shift,' almost day and night. One of the most illustrious of such workers in modern times was unquestionably the late Sir Robert Peel. He possessed in an extraordinary degree the power of continuous intellectual labour, nor did he spare himself. His career, indeed, presented a remarkable example of how much a man of comparatively moderate powers can accomplish by means of assiduous application and indefatigable industry. During the forty years that he held a seat in Parliament, his labours were prodigious. He was a most conscientious man, and whatever he undertook to do, he did thoroughly. . . .

[**16.**] Illustrious as are the instances of strong individuality which we have thus rapidly cited, the number might be largely increased even from the list of living men. One of our most distinguished writers has, it is true, lamented the decay of that strength of individual character which has been the glory of the English nation; yet, if we mistake not, no age in our history so little justifies such a lament as the present. Never did sudden calamity more severely test the individual pluck, endurance, and energy of a people, than did the recent outbreak of the rebellion in India; but it only served to bring out the unflinching self-reliance and dormant heroism of the English race. In that terrible trial all proved almost equally great—women, civilians, and soldiers—from the general down through all grades to the private and bugleman. The men were not picked—they belonged to the same every-day people whom we daily meet at home—in the streets, in workshops, in the fields, at clubs; yet when sudden disaster fell upon them, each and all displayed a wealth of personal resources and energy, and became as it were individually heroic. Indeed in no age of England have the finest qualities of men been so brilliantly displayed; and there are perhaps no names in our history which outshine those of the modern heroes of India. Montalembert avows that they 'do honour to the human race.' Citing the great names of Havelock, Nicholson, Peel, Wilson, and Neill—to which might be added that of Outram, 'the Bayard of India'—he goes on to say, 'it is not only such names, great beyond comparison, it is the bearing in every respect of this handful of Englishmen, surprised in the midst of peace and prosperity by the most frightful and most unforeseen of catastrophes. Not one of them shrank or trembled—all, military and civilians, young and old, generals and soldiers, resisted, fought, and perished with a coolness and intrepidity which never faltered. It is in this circumstance that shines out the immense value of public education, which invites the Englishman from his youth to make use of his strength and his liberty, to associate, resist, fear nothing, be astonished at nothing, and to save himself, by his own sole exertions, from every sore strait in life.'

[17.] Equally brilliant instances of individual force of character are also to be found in more peaceful and scientific walks. Is there not Livingstone, with a heroism greater than that of Xavier, penetrating the wilds of South Africa on his mission of Christian civilization; Layard, labouring for years to disinter the remains of the buried city of Babylon; Rawlinson, the decipherer of their cuneiform inscriptions; Brooke, establishing a nucleus of European enterprise and colonization amongst the piratical tribes of the Indian Ocean; Franklin, Maclure, Collinson, M'Clintock, and others, cleaving their way through storms, and ice, and darkness, to solve the problem of the north-west passage;—enterprises which, for individual daring, self-denial, energy, and heroism, are unsurpassed by those of any age or country.

(*Self-Help*, 1859, Ch. 1.)

III.6 **Ford Madox Brown, on *Work* (1865)**

[1.] This picture, on account of which, in a great measure the present exhibition has been organised, was begun in 1852 at Hampstead. The background, which represents the main street of that suburb not far from the heath, was painted on the spot.

[2.] At that time extensive excavations, connected with the supply of water, were going on in the neighbourhood, and seeing and studying daily as I did the British excavator, or *navvy*, as he designates himself, in the full swing of his activity (with his manly and picturesque costume, and with the rich glow of colour, which exercise under a hot sun will impart), it appeared to me that he was at least as worthy of the powers of an English painter, as the fisherman of the Adriatic, the peasant of the Campagna, or the Neopolitan lazzarone. Gradually this idea developed itself into that of 'Work' as it now exists, with the British excavator for a central group, as the outward and visible type of *Work*. Here are presented the young navvy in the pride of manly health and beauty; the strong fully developed navvy who does his work and loves his beer; the selfish old bachelor navvy, stout

2. Ford Madox Brown: *Work* 1863

of limb, and perhaps a trifle tough in those regions where compassion is said to reside; the navvy of strong animal nature, who, but that he was, when young, taught to work at useful work, might even now be working at the useless crank. Then Paddy with his larry and his pipe in his mouth.

[3.] The young navvy who occupies the place of hero in this group, and in the picture, stands on what is termed a landing-stage, a platform placed half-way down the trench; two men from beneath shovel the earth up to him, and he shovels it on to the pile outside.

[4.] Next in value of significance to these, is the ragged wretch who has never been *taught* to *work*; with his restless gleaming eyes, he doubts and despairs of every one. But for a certain effeminate gentleness of dis-position and a love of nature, he might have been a burglar! He lives in Flower and Dean Street, where the policemen walk two and two, and the worst cut-throats surround him, but he is harmless; and before the dawn you may see him miles out in the country, collecting his wild weeds and singular plants to awaken interest, and perhaps find a purchaser in some sprouting botanist. When exhausted he will return to his den, his creel of flowers then rests in an open court-yard, the thoroughfare for the crowded inmates of this haunt of vice, and played in by mischievous boys, yet the basket rarely gets interfered with, unless through the unconscious lurch of some drunkard. The bread-winning implements are sacred with the very poor.

[5.] In the very opposite scale from the man who can't work, at the further corner of the picture, are two men who appear as having nothing to do. These are the brainworkers, who, seeming to be idle, work, and are the cause of well-ordained work and happiness in others. Sages, such as in ancient Greece, published their opinions in the market square. Perhaps one of these may already, before he or others know it, have moulded a nation to his pattern, converted a hitherto combative race to obstinate passivity; with a word may have centupled the tide of emigration, with another, have quenched the political passions of both factions—may have reversed men's notions upon criminals, upon slavery, upon many things, and still be walk-ing about little known to some. The other, in friendly communion with the philosopher, smiling perhaps at some of his wild sallies and cynical thrusts (for Socrates at times strangely disturbs the seriousness of his auditory by the mercilessness of his jokes—against vice and foolishness), is intended for a kindred and yet very dissimilar spirit. A clergyman, such as the Church of England offers examples of—a priest without guile—a gentleman without pride, much in communion with the working classes, 'honouring all men', 'never weary in well-doing.' Scholar, author, philosopher, and teacher, too, in his way, but not above practical efforts, if even for a small result in good. Deeply penetrated as he is with the axiom that each unit of humanity feels as much as all the rest combined, and impulsive and hopeful in nature, so that the remedy suggests itself to him concurrently with the evil.

[6.] Next to these, on the shaded bank, are different characters out of work, haymakers in quest of employment; a stoic from the Emerald Island, with hay stuffed in his hat to keep the draught out, and need for his stoicism just at present, being short of baccy—a young shoeless Irishman, with his wife, feeding their first-born with cold pap—an old sailor turned haymaker, and two young peasants in search of harvest work, reduced in strength, perhaps by fever—possibly by famine.

[7.] Behind the Pariah, who never has learned to work, appears a group, of a very different class, who, from an opposite cause, have perhaps not been sufficiently used to work either. These are the *rich*, who have no need to work—not at least for bread—*the 'bread of life'* being neither here nor there. The pastry-cook's tray the symbol of superfluity, accompanies these. It is peculiarly English: I never saw it abroad that I remember, though something of the kind must be used. For some years after returning to England I could never quite get over a certain socialistic twinge on seeing it pass, unreasonable as the feeling may have been. Past the pastry-cook's tray come two married ladies. The elder and more serious of the two devotes her energies to tract distributing, and has just flung one entitled, 'The Hodman's Haven, or drink for thirsty souls', to the somewhat unpromising specimen of navvy humanity descending the ladder: he scorns it, but with good nature. This well-intentioned lady has, perhaps, never reflected that excavators may have notions to the effect that ladies might be benefited by receiving tracts containing navvies' ideas! nor yet that excavators are skilled workmen, shrewd thinkers chiefly, and, in general, men of great experience in life, as life presents itself to them.

[8.] In front of her is the lady whose only business in life as yet is to dress and look beautiful for our benefit. She probably possesses everything that can give enjoyment to life; how then can she but enjoy the passing moment, and like a flower feed on the light of the sun? Would anyone wish it otherwise?—Certainly, not I, dear lady. Only in your own interest, seeing that certain blessings cannot be insured for ever—as for instance, health may fail, beauty fade, pleasures through repetition pall—I will not hint at the greater calamities to which flesh is heir—seeing all this, were you less engaged watching that exceedingly beautiful tiny greyhound in a red jacket that *will* run through that lime, I would beg to call your attention to my group of small, exceedingly ragged, dirty children in the foreground of my picture, where you are about to pass. I would, if permitted, observe that, though at first they may appear just such a group of ragged dirty brats as anywhere get in the way and make a noise, yet, being considered attentively, they like insects, molluscs, miniature plants, &c., develop qualities to form a most interesting study, and occupy the mind at times when all else might fall to attract. That they are motherless, the baby's black ribbons and their extreme dilapidation indicate, making them all the more worthy of consideration, a mother, however destitute, would scarcely leave the eldest one in such a plight. As to the father, I have no doubt he drinks, and will be sentenced in the police-court for neglecting them. The eldest girl, not more than ten, poor child! is very worn looking and thin, her frock, evidently the compassionate gift of some grown-up person, she has neither the art nor the means to adapt to her own diminutive proportions—she is fearfully untidy therefore, and her way of wrenching her brother's hair looks vixenish and against her. But then a germ or rudiment of good housewifery seems to pierce through her disordered envelope, for the younger ones are taken care of, and nestle to her as to a mother—the sunburnt baby, which looks wonderfully solemn and intellectual as all babies do, as I have no doubt your own little cherub looks at this moment asleep in its charming basinet, is fat and well-to-do, it has even been put into poor mourning for mother. The other little one, though it sucks a piece of carrot in lieu of a sugar-plum, and is shoeless, seems healthy and happy, watching the workmen. The care of the two little ones is an anxious charge for the elder girl, and she has become a premature scold through having to manage that *boy*—that boy, though a merry, good-natured-looking good Bohemian, is evidently the plague of her life, as boys always are. Even now he *will* not leave that workman's barrow alone, and gets his hair well-pulled, as is natural. The dog which accompanies them is evidently of the same outcast sort as themselves. The having to do battle for his existence in a hard world has soured his temper, and he frequently fights, as by his torn ear you may know; but the poor children may do as they like with him, rugged democrat as he is, he is gentle to them, only he hates minions of aristocracy in red jackets. The old bachelor navvy's small valuable bull-pup, also instinctively distrusts outlandish-looking dogs in jackets.

[9.] The couple on horseback in the middle distance, consists of a gentleman, still young, and his daughter. (The rich and the poor both marry early, only those of moderate incomes procrastinate.) This gentleman is evidently very rich, probably a Colonel in the army, with a seat in Parliament, and fifteen thousand a-year, and a pack of hounds. He is not an over-dressed man of the tailor's dummy sort—he does not put his fortune on his back, he is too rich for that; moreover, he looks to me an honest true-hearted gentleman (he was painted from one I know), and could he only be got to hear what the two sages in the corner have to say, I have no doubt he would be easily won over. But the road is blocked, and the daughter says we must go back, papa, round the other way.

[10.] The man with the beer-tray, calling beer ho! so lustily, is a specimen of town pluck and energy contrasted with country thews and sinews. He is humpbacked, dwarfish, and in all matters of taste, vulgar as Birmingham can make him look in the 19th century. As a child he was probably starved, stunted with gin, and suffered to get run over. But energy has brought him through to be a prosperous beer man, and 'very much respected,' and in his way he also is a sort of hero; that black eye was got probably doing the police of his master's establishment, and in an encounter with some huge ruffian whom he has conquered in fight, and hurled out through the swing-doors of the palace of gin prone on the pavement. On the wall are posters and bills; one of the 'Boy's Home, 41, Euston Road,' which the lady who is giving tracts will no doubt subscribe to presently and place the urchin playing with the barrow in; one of 'the Working Men's College, Great Ormond Street,' or if you object to these, then a police bill offering £50 reward in a matter of highway robbery. Back in the distance we see the Assembly-room of the 'Flamstead Institute of Arts', where Professor Snoöx is about to repeat his interesting lecture on the habits of the domestic cat. Indignant pusses up on the roofs are denying his theory in toto.

[11.] The less important characters in the background require little comment. Bobus, our old friend, 'the sausage-maker of Houndsditch', from *Past and Present*, having secured a colossal fortune (he boasts of it *now*), by anticipating the French Hippophage Society in the introduction of horse flesh as a *cheap* article of human food, is at present going in for the county of Middlesex, and, true to his old tactics, has hired all the idlers in the neighbourhood to carry his boards. These being one too many for the bearers, an old woman has volunteered to carry the one in excess.

[12.] The episode of the policeman who has caught an orange-girl in the heinous offence of resting her basket on a post, and who himself administers justice in the shape of a push, that sends her fruit all over the road, is one of common occurrence, or used to be—perhaps the police now 'never do such things.'

[13.] I am sorry to say that most of my friends, on examining this part of my picture, have laughed over it as a good joke. Only two men saw the circumstance in a different light, one of them was the young Irishman, who feeds his infant with pap. Pointing to it with his thumb, his mouth quivering at the reminiscence, he said, 'that, Sir, *I* know to be true.' The other was a clergyman, his testimony would perhaps have more weight. I dedicate this portion of the work to the Commissioners of Police.

[14.] Through this picture I have gained some experience of the navvy class, and I have usually found, that if you can break through the upper crust of *mauvaise honte*, which surrounds them in common with most Englishmen, and which, in the case of the navvies, I believe to be the cause of much of their bad language, you will find them serious intelligent men, and with much to interest in their conversation, which, moreover, contains about the same amount of morality and sentiment that is commonly found among men in the active and hazardous walks of life; for that their career is one of hazard and danger, none should doubt. Many stories might be told of navvies' daring and endurance, were this the place for them. One incident peculiarly connected with this picture is the melancholy fact, that one of the very men who sat for it lost his life by a scaffold accident, before

I had yet quite done with him. I remember the poor fellow telling me, among other things, how he never but once felt nervous with his work, and this was, having to trundle barrows of earth over a plank-line crossing a rapid river at a height of *eighty feet* above the water. But it was not the height he complained of, it was the *gliding motion of the water underneath*.

[15.] I have only to observe in conclusion, that the effect of hot July sunlight attempted in this picture, has been introduced, because it seems peculiarly fitted to display work in all its severity, and not from any predilection for this kind of light over any other. Subjects, according to their nature, require different effects of light.

> (On *Work*, 1865; quoted in Julian Treuherz, *Pre-Raphaelite Paintings for the Manchester City Art Gallery*, 1980, pp. 53–9.)

III.7 John Ruskin, from *Sesame and Lilies* (1865)

[1.] We are foolish, and without excuse foolish, in speaking of the 'superiority' of one sex to the other, as if they could be compared in similar things. Each has what the other has not: each completes the other, and is completed by the other: they are in nothing alike, and the happiness and perfection of both depends on each asking and receiving from the other what the other only can give.

[2.] Now their separate characters are briefly these. The man's power is active, progressive, defensive. He is eminently the doer, the creator, the discoverer, the defender. His intellect is for speculation and invention; his energy for adventure, for war, and for conquest wherever war is just, wherever conquest necessary. But the woman's power is for rule, not for battle,—and her intellect is not for invention or creation, but for sweet ordering, arrangement, and decision. She sees the qualities of things, their claims, and their places. Her great function is Praise: she enters into no contest, but infallibly adjudges the crown of contest. By her office, and place, she is protected from all danger and temptation. The man, in his rough work in open world, must encounter all peril and trial:—to him, therefore, the failure, the offence, the inevitable error: often he must be wounded, or subdued, often misled, and *always* hardened. But he guards the woman from all this; within his house, as ruled by her, unless she herself has sought it, need enter no danger, no temptation, no cause of error or offence. This is the true nature of home—it is the place of Peace; the shelter, not only from all injury, but from all terror, doubt, and division. In so far as the anxieties of the outer life penetrate into it, and the inconsistently-minded, unknown, unloved, or hostile society of the outer world is allowed by either husband or wife to cross the threshold, it ceases to be home; it is then only a part of that outer world which you have roofed over, and lighted fire in . . .

[3.] And wherever a true wife comes, this home is always round her. The stars only may be over her head; the glowworm in the night-cold grass may be the only fire at her foot: but home is yet wherever she is; and for a noble woman it stretches far round her, better than ceiled with cedar, or painted with vermilion, shedding its quiet light far, for those who else were homeless.

[4.] This, then, I believe to be,—will you not admit it to be,—the woman's true place and power? But do not you see that, to fulfil this, she must—as far as one can use such terms of a human creature—be incapable of error? So far as she rules, all must be right, or nothing is. She must be enduringly, incorruptibly good; instinctively, infallibly wise— wise, not for self-development, but for self-renunciation: wise, not that she may set herself above her husband, but that she may never fail from his side . . .

[5.] Generally, we are under an impression that a man's duties are public, and a woman's private. But this is not altogether so. A man has a personal work or duty, relating to his own home, and a public work or duty, which is the expansion of the other, relating to the state. So a woman has a personal work or duty, relating to her own home, and a public work or duty, which is also the expansion of that.

[6.] Now, the man's work for his own home is, as has been said, to secure its maintenance, progress, and defence; the woman's to secure its order, comfort, and loveliness.

[7.] Expand both these functions. The man's duty, as a member of a commonwealth, is to assist in the maintenance, in the advance, in the defence of the state. The woman's duty, as a member of the commonwealth, is to assist in the ordering, in the comforting, and in the beautiful adornment of the state.

[8.] What the man is at his own gate, defending it, if need be, against insult and spoil, that also, not in a less, but in a more devoted measure, he is to be at the gate of his country, leaving his home, if need be, even to the spoiler, to do his more incumbent work there.

[9.] And, in like manner, what the woman is to be within her gates, as the centre of order, the balm of distress, and the mirror of beauty: that she is also to be without her gates, where order is more difficult, distress more imminent, loveliness more rare.

[10.] And as within the human heart there is always set an instinct for all its real duties . . . as there is the intense instinct of love, which rightly disciplined, maintains all the sanctities of life . . . so there is in the human heart an inextinguishable instinct, the love of power, which, rightly directed, maintains all the majesty of law and life, and misdirected, wrecks them.

[11.] Deep rooted in the innermost life of the heart of man, and of the heart of woman, God set it there, and God keeps it there. Vainly, as falsely, you blame or rebuke the desire of power!—For Heaven's sake, and for Man's sake, desire it all you can. But *what* power? That is all the question. Power to destroy? . . . Not so. Power to heal, to redeem, to guide, and to guard. Power of the sceptre and shield . . . Will you not covet such power as this, and seek such throne as this, and be no more housewives, but queens?

[12.] . . . Your fancy is pleased with the thought of being noble ladies, with a train of vassals. Be it so; you cannot be too noble, and your train cannot be too great; but see to it that your train is of vassals whom you serve and feed, not merely of slaves who serve and feed *you*; and that the multitude which obeys you is of those whom you have comforted, not oppressed,—whom you have redeemed, not led into captivity.

[13.] And this, which is true of the lower or household dominion, is equally true of the queenly dominion,—that highest dignity is open to you, if you will also accept that highest duty. Rex et Regina—Roi et Reine— 'Right-doers'; they differ but from the Lady and Lord, in that their power is supreme over the mind as over the person—that they not only feed and clothe, but direct and teach. And whether consciously or not, you must be, in many a heart, enthroned: there is no putting by that crown; queens you must always be; queens to your lovers; queens to your husbands and your sons; queens of higher mystery to the world beyond, which bows itself, and will for ever bow, before the myrtle crown, and the stainless sceptre of womanhood. But, alas! you are too often idle and careless queens, grasping at majesty in the least things, while you abdicate it in the greatest; and leaving misrule and violence to work their will among men, . . . There is not a war in the world, no, nor an injustice, but you women are answerable for it; not in that you have provoked, but in that you have not hindered. Men, by their nature, are prone to fight; they will fight for any cause, or for none. It is for you to choose their cause for them, and to forbid them when there is no cause. There is no suffering, no injustice, no misery in the earth, but the guilt of it lies with you. Men can bear the sight of it, but you should not be able to bear it. Men may tread it down without sympathy in their own struggle; but men are feeble in sympathy, and contracted in hope; it is you only who can feel the depths of pain, and conceive the way of its healing. Instead of trying to do this, you turn away from it; you shut yourselves within your park walls and garden gates; and you are content to know that there is beyond them a whole world in wilderness—a world of secrets which you dare not penetrate, and of suffering which you dare not conceive.

[14.] I tell you that this is to me quite the most amazing among the phenomena of humanity. I am surprised at no depths to which, when once warped from its honour, that humanity can be degraded. I do not wonder at the miser's death, with his hands, as they relax, dropping gold. I do not wonder at the sensualist's life, with the shroud wrapped about his feet. I do not wonder at the single-handed murder of a single victim, done by the assassin in the darkness of the railway, or reed-shadow of the marsh. I do not even wonder at the myriad-handed murder of multitudes, done boastfully in the daylight, by the frenzy of nations, and the immeasurable, unimaginable guilt, heaped up from hell to heaven, of their priests, and kings. But this is wonderful to me— . . . to see the tender and delicate woman among you, with her child at her breast, and a power, if she would wield it, over it, and over its father, purer than the air of heaven, and stronger than the seas of earth . . . to see her abdicate this majesty to play at precedence with her next-door neighbour. . . .

[15.] But it is little to say of a woman, that she only does not destroy where she passes. She should revive; the harebells should bloom, not stoop, as she passes . . . You have heard it said . . . that flowers only flourish rightly in the garden of some one who loves them. I know you would like that to be true; you would think it a pleasant magic if you could flush your flowers into brighter bloom by a kind look upon them: nay, more, if your look had the power, not only to cheer, but to guard—if you could bid the black blight turn away, and the knotted caterpiller spare—if you could bid the dew fall upon them in the drought, and say to the south wind, in the frost—'Come, thou south, and breathe upon my garden, that the spices of it may flow out.' This you would think a great thing? And do you think it not a greater thing, that all this . . . you *can* do, for fairer flowers than these—flowers that could bless you for having blessed them, and will love you for having loved them;—flowers that have thoughts like yours, and lives like yours; which, once saved, you save for ever? Is this only a little power? Far among the moorlands and the rocks,—far in the darkness of the terrible streets,—these feeble florets are lying, with all their fresh leaves torn, and their stems broken—will you never go down to them, nor set them in order in their little fragrant beds, nor fence them in their shuddering from the fierce wind?

[16.] Did you ever hear, . . . of a . . . Madeleine, who went down to her garden in the dawn, and found One waiting at the gate, whom she supposed to be the gardener? Have you not sought Him often; sought Him in vain, all through the night; sought Him in vain at the gate of that old garden where the fiery sword is set? He is never there; but at the gate of *this* garden He is waiting always—waiting to take your hand—ready to go down to see the fruits of the valley, to see whether the vine has flourished, and the pomegranate budded. There you shall see with Him the little tendrils of the vines that His hand is guiding—there you shall see the pomegranate springing where His hand cast the sanguine seed;—more: you shall see the troops of the angel keepers that, with their wings, wave away the hungry birds from the pathsides where He has sown, and call to each other between the vineyard rows, 'Take us the foxes, the little foxes, that spoil the vines, for our vines have tender grapes.' Oh—you queens—you queens! among the hills and happy greenwood of this land of yours, shall the foxes have holes and the birds of the air have nests; and in your cities shall the stones cry out against you, that they are the only pillows where the Son of Man can lay His head?

(*Sesame and Lilies*, 1865; 1909 edn., pp. 72–4, 87–95.)

III.8 **From sermon preached by Henry Liddon (9 June 1876)**

[1.] A first effect of poverty . . . is the confiscation of a poor man's best time and thought, from sheer necessity, to the task of providing food and clothing for himself and his family. Many men who are far from being poor have to work for a livelihood But a man can work hard, if he can at will command a holiday. A man can work hard, if his work is also felt to be a source of refinement, of instruction, of discipline, of recreation; if it enlightens his mind, if it purifies his affections. As a rule, a poor man's work is not of that description: it is, from all points of view save that of the wages it yields, unremunerative, because it is more or less mechanical. It cannot be interrupted unless from sheer necessity; the poor man cannot afford to lose a day's wages, and therefore, though feeling depressed or ill, he cannot forego a day's work. As he works he is not thinking of his place in the moral universe, although he is at least as capable of true nobility as is any other human being; he is thinking of the next meal, of the next pay-day, of the next rent-day. The next rent-day is probably his most distant horizon. Rarely can he aspire to win an independence, and so to purchase exemption from the necessity which is laid upon him of supporting existence by incessant toil. Who does not see how this liability must clog and depress the human spirit; how it chokes up the avenues through which even natural light and heat penetrate within the understanding and the heart? Some room must be made for religion amidst the thoughts and occupations of life before it can inspire or control them; and in the case of the poor man, who has to work hard for his daily bread, and to whom all mental effort is very serious, the difficulty of even getting a hearing for the good tidings which Christ our Lord has brought to earth from heaven is often great indeed.

   [2.] Another effect of poverty is that it often blights those domestic scenes of happiness which prepare the way of religion in the soul. In the natural course of things, kindliness, courtesy, refinement, are the products of home life; the home is the centre and the manufactory of these natural graces. It is to his family that a man escapes when his day's toil is over. At home he forgets the passions and the rivalries, be they great or small, of his

public life, whatever its sphere or scale of importance; at home the finer
side of human nature has a chance of growing, as being sure of its nutri-
ment and its welcome. At home a man knows, if nowhere else, what it is to
be interpreted generously, to be trusted, to be loved; here he finds a field for
the play of those affections in the exercise of which earthly happiness
mainly consists. But for this two things are needed; competency and order.
And how often are these wanting in the households of the poor! Many of
us must have visited cabins in which a numerous family inhabits a single
room; in which the young, the aged, the sick, the hale, the parents and children, herd together by day and by night; in which the mother, who should
be a presiding genius of kindliness and of cleanliness, is the representative
of ill-humour and of dirt; in which all that protects ordinary intercourse
against coarseness, and ordinary tempers against irritation, and average
health against disease, and modest efforts to improve against brutal interference, is too often absent; in which all is so crowded that there is no room
for delicacy, for reserve, for the charities, for the properties of common
life. . . .

[3.] Worse off, it has been truly said, may be the poor man, whom civilization has made what he is, than was his savage ancestor; for worse his lot
who lives in the back lane of a great city, where pure air, and light, and
room, and cleanliness are denied him, than that of the man of another time,
who roamed in the forest beneath the sky of heaven, and who could at least
command, amid whatever disadvantages, the requisites for healthy animal
existence, and for the unstinted play of pure affections. Yes! A comfortless
home is often even more fatal to character than to health. It chills the affections; it sours the temper; it ends by doing more. Nothing is more common
than to hear severe language applied to the poor man's habit of spending
his evenings at the public house. But who of us, when by chance walking at
night through the neglected quarters of a great town, has observed how, at
more or less frequent intervals, the monotony of dreariness and squalor is
broken by the brilliant lights and the ostentatious hospitalities of these
establishments, can wonder that the poor man is attracted by the contrast
which they present to all that characterizes his home, and that, yielding to
their fatal welcome, he essays to drown in an hour of brute half-conscious-
ness the memory of the griefs that too sorely embitter his domestic life? It is
the road to ruin, without a doubt. But it is not for those of us who have
never felt even the shadow of the troubles which are eating out his heart to
cast a stone at him.

[4.] The worst result of poverty is that it often destroys self-respect. Self-
respect is a different thing, as it is needless to add, from the most venial
form of self-complacency. The forfeiture of self-respect does not necessarily
take place when a poor man becomes a pensioner on the bounty of others.
A man who receives from his fellow-man that assistance which, if their circumstances were reversed, he would gladly bestow, undergoes no moral

damage in consequence; he is merely a party to a transaction which effects on a small scale an equitable redistribution of property. If, indeed, he prefers dependence to exertion: if, forgetful of the intrinsic nobleness of work, he attempts to purchase leisure by the servilities of beggary, then, beyond doubt, his manhood is impaired, and he is in a fair way to be and to do much that is fatal to the respect which a good man should entertain for the sanctities of his life. But of itself, dependence does not degrade. Children are not the worse for depending on their parents; servants are not injured by the kindness of their employers; tenants are not humiliated by the considerate liberality of the landlord; nor do we any of us suffer because we are all indebted for all that we are and have to the Eternal Bounty, and he knows us too well, and has too good a care of us, to have ordered anything really inconsistent with our true well-being. No, his dependence does not threaten the poor man's self-respect; but, especially in large centres of life, he is peculiarly exposed to the ravages of a passion which, if yielded to, degrades and brands the soul with a fatal certainty. Certainly, envy is no monopoly of the poor; it makes itself felt in all sections of society. . . . From their narrow and squalid homes they go abroad to gaze on the mansions of the great and wealthy; at their scanty meals they discuss the splendid banquets which can command every luxury but appetite; as they pursue their daily toil, they see around them men of their own race and age to whom life is made so easy as to become little less than a protracted weariness. . . .

[5.] Poverty of course is and means a great deal more than has thus been stated. But at least let us bear in mind that it involves, very commonly, the exhaustion of life by mechanical work, the degradation of character in the home and in the usual expedients to escape from it, and the loss of self-respect, and of all that that loss implies, through the continued, unappeased, ever-increasing envy of the lot of others. Not that poverty has not produced its heroes, who have vanquished its disadvantages with stern determination. We have here to consider, not the splendid exceptions, but the average result. And that result may, within limits, be counteracted by wise philanthropy and by wise laws. When a sufficient number of regular holidays are secured by law, as in bygone ages the Church did secure them by her festivals for the working poor; when the hours of daily labour are kept within reasonable limits; when homes have been provided for the people on any considerable scale in which the first conditions of healthy living shall be insisted on; when it shall have been made fairly possible for every poor man so to better his condition by work as to escape from poverty into comfort; and when education shall have done all that may be done towards furthering this result, legislation and philanthropy will have achieved what may be fairly required of them. Useful knowledge, practical kindness, and beneficent laws—these are not the Gospel; but, like philosophy, they are, or may be, its handmaids. They may make its task smooth and grateful; they may associate themselves with its victories, or they may prepare its way.

[6.] But for more important results a higher force is needed; nothing less than the Christian faith itself. The faith of Christ reverses the disadvantages of poverty with decisive force. It acts upon poverty not from without, but from within; it begins not with legislation, but with hearts and minds; not with circumstances, but with convictions. When this faith is received, it forthwith transfigures the idea of labour: labour is no longer deemed a curse, but a discipline; work of all kinds is sensibly ennobled by being done with and for Jesus Christ; and by this association it acquires the character of a kind of worship. When this faith is received, it sweetens, consecrates, elevates the affections of the husband, of the father, of the child; it sets the physical difficulties of a pauper household at defiance by referring them to the Holy Home of Nazareth; or it lifts the whole conception of human relationships into an atmosphere where the risks to which they are ordinarily exposed have ceased to exist. When this faith is embraced it changes the estimate of different conditions in life; the first become last, and the last first.

(*Sermons and Society*, ed. Paul A. Welsby, 1970, pp. 281–6.)

George Eliot, from *Daniel Deronda* (1876)   III.9

Imagine a rambling, patchy house, the best part built of grey stone, and red-tiled, a round tower jutting at one of the corners, the mellow darkness of its conical roof surmounted by a weather-cock making an agreeable object either amidst the gleams and greenth of summer or the low-hanging clouds and snowy branches of winter: the grounds shady with spreading trees: a great cedar flourishing on one side, backward some Scotch firs on a broken bank where the roots hung naked, and beyond, a rookery: on the other side a pool overhung with bushes, where the water-fowl fluttered and screamed: all around, a vast meadow which might be called a park, bordered by an old plantation and guarded by stone lodges which looked like little prisons. Outside the gate the country, once entirely rural and lovely, now black with coal-mines, was chiefly peopled by men and brethren with candles stuck in their hats, and with a diabolic complexion which laid them peculiarly open to suspicion in the eyes of the children at Gadsmere—Mrs Glasher's four beautiful children, who had dwelt there for about three years. Now, in November, when the flower-beds were empty, the trees leafless, and the pool blackly shivering, one might have said that the place was sombrely in keeping with the black roads and black mounds which seemed to put the district in mourning;—except when the children were playing on the gravel with the dogs for their companions. But Mrs Glasher under her present circumstances liked Gadsmere as well as she would have liked any other abode. The complete seclusion of the place, which the unattractiveness of the country secured, was exactly to her taste. When she drove her two ponies with a waggonet full of children, there were no gentry in carriages to be met, only men of business in gigs; at church there were no eyes she cared to avoid, for the curate's wife and the curate himself were either ignorant of anything to her disadvantage, or ignored it: to them she was simply a widow lady, the tenant of Gadsmere; and the name of Grandcourt was of little interest in that district compared with the names of Fletcher and Gawcome, the lessees of the collieries.

It was full ten years since the elopement of an Irish officer's beautiful wife with young Grandcourt, and a consequent duel where the bullets wounded the air only, had made some little noise. Most of those who remembered the affair now wondered what had become of that Mrs Glasher whose beauty and brilliancy had made her rather conspicuous to them in foreign places, where she was known to be living with young Grandcourt.

That he should have disentangled himself from that connection seemed only natural and desirable. As to her it was thought that a woman who was understood to have forsaken her child along with her husband had probably sunk lower. Grandcourt had of course got weary of her. He was much given to the pursuit of women: but a man in his position would by this time desire to make a suitable marriage with the fair young daughter of a noble house. No one talked of Mrs Glasher now, any more than they talked of the victim in a trial for manslaughter ten years before: she was a lost vessel after whom nobody would send out an expedition of search; but Grandcourt was seen in harbour with his colours flying, registered as seaworthy as ever.

(*Daniel Deronda*, 1876, Ch. xxx.)

III.10 John Stuart Mill, from *Principles of Political Economy* (1848)

(a) Property

[1.] Private property, as an institution, did not owe its origin to any of those considerations of utility, which plead for the maintenance of it when established. Enough is known of rude ages, both from history and from analogous states of society in our own time, to show that tribunals (which always precede laws) were originally established, not to determine rights, but to repress violence and terminate quarrels. With this object chiefly in view, they naturally enough gave legal effect to first occupancy, by treating as the aggressor the person who first commenced violence, by turning, or attempting to turn, another out of possession. The preservation of the peace, which was the original object of civil government, was thus attained; while by confirming, to those who already possessed it, even what was not the fruit of personal exertion, a guarantee was incidentally given to them and others that they would be protected in what was so.

[2.] In considering the institution of property as a question in social philosophy, we must leave out of consideration its actual origin in any of the existing nations of Europe. We may suppose a community unhampered by any previous possession; a body of colonists, occupying for the first time an uninhabited country; bringing nothing with them but what belonged to them in common, and having a clear field for the adoption of the institutions and polity which they judged most expedient; required, therefore, to choose whether they would conduct the work of production on the principle of individual property, or on some system of common ownership and collective agency.

[3.] If private property were adopted, we must presume that it would be accompanied by none of the initial inequalities and injustices which obstruct the beneficial operation of the principle in old societies. Every full-grown man or woman, we must suppose, would be secured in the unfettered use and disposal of his or her bodily and mental faculties; and the instruments of production, the land and tools, would be divided fairly among them, so that all might start, in respect to outward appliances, on equal terms. It is possible also to conceive that in this original apportionment, compensation might be made for the injuries of nature, and the balance redressed by assigning to the less robust members of the community advantages in the distribution, sufficient to put them on a par with the rest. But the division, once made, would not again be interfered with; individuals would be left to their own exertions and to the ordinary chances, for making an advantageous use of what was assigned to them. If individual property, on the contrary, were excluded, the plan which must be adopted would be to hold the land and all instruments of production as the joint property of the community, and to carry on the operations of industry on the common account. The direction of the labour of the community would devolve upon a magistrate or magistrates, whom we may suppose elected by the suffrages of the community, and whom we must assume to be voluntarily obeyed by them. The division of the produce would in like manner be a public act. The principle might either be that of complete equality, or of apportionment to the necessities or deserts of individuals, in whatever manner might be comfortable to the ideas of justice or policy prevailing in the community.

[4.] Examples of such associations, on a small scale, are the monastic orders, the Moravians and others: and from the hopes which they hold out of relief from the miseries and iniquities of a state of much inequality of wealth, schemes for a larger application of the same idea have reappeared and become popular at all periods of active speculation on the first principles of society. In an age like the present, when a general reconsideration of all first principles is felt to be inevitable, and when more than at any former period of history the suffering portions of the community have a voice in the discussion, it was impossible but that ideas of this nature should spread far and wide. The late revolutions in Europe have thrown up a great amount of speculation of this character, and an unusual share of attention has consequently been drawn to the various forms which these ideas have assumed: nor is this attention likely to diminish, but on the contrary, to increase more and more.

[5.] The assailants of the principle of individual property may be divided into two classes: those whose scheme implies absolute equality in the distribution of the physical means of life and enjoyment, and those who admit inequality, but grounded on some principle, or supposed principle, of justice or general expediency, and not, like so many of the existing social inequalities, dependent on accident alone. At the head of the first class, as the earliest of those belonging to the present generation, must be placed Mr Owen and his followers. . . . The characteristic name for this economical system is Communism, a word of continental origin, only of late introduced into this country. The word Socialism, which originated among the English Communists, and was assumed by them as a name to designate their own doctrine, is now, on the Continent, employed in a larger sense; not necessarily implying Communism, or the entire abolition of private property, but applied to any system which requires that the land and the instruments of production should be the property, not of individuals, but of communities or associations, or of the government. Among such systems, the two of highest intellectual pretension are those which, from the names of their real or reputed authors, have been called St Simonism and Fourierism; the former, defunct as a system, but which during the few years of its public promulgation, sowed the seeds of nearly all the Socialist tendencies which have since spread so widely in France: the second, still flourishing in the number, talent, and zeal of its adherents.

[6.] Whatever may be the merits or defects of these various schemes, they cannot be truly said to be impracticable. No reasonable person can doubt that a village community, composed of a few thousand inhabitants cultivating in joint ownership the same extent of land which at present feeds that number of people, and producing by combined labour and the most improved processes the manufactured articles which they required, could raise an amount of productions sufficient to maintian them in comfort; and would find the means of obtaining, and if need be, exacting, the quantity of labour necessary for this purpose, from every member of the association who was capable of work.

[7.] The objection ordinarily made to a system of community of property and equal distribution of the produce, that each person would be incessantly occupied in evading his fair share of the work, points, undoubt edly, to a real difficulty. But those who urge this objection, forget how great an extent the same difficulty exists under the system on which nine-tenths of the business of society is now conducted. The objection supposes, that honest and efficient labour is only to be had from those who are them-selves individually to reap the benefit of their own exertions. But how small a part of all the labour performed in England, from the lowest paid to the highest, is done by persons working for their own benefit? From the Irish reaper or hodman to the chief justice or the minister of state, nearly all the work of society is remunerated by day wages or fixed salaries. A factory operative has less personal interest in his work than a member of a Com-munist association, since he is not, like him, working for a partnership of which he is himself a member. It will no doubt be said, that though the labourers themselves have not, in most cases, a personal interest in their work, they are watched and superintended, and their labour directed, and the mental part of the labour performed, by persons who have. Even this, however, is far from being universally the fact. In all public, and many of the largest and most successful private undertakings, not only the labours of detail, but the control and superintendence are entrusted to salaried offi-cers. And though the 'master's eye', when the master is vigilant and intelli-gent, is of proverbial value, it must be remembered that in a Socialist farm or manufactory, each labourer would be under the eye not of one master, but of the whole community. In the extreme case of obstinate perseverance in not performing the due share of work, the community would have the same resources which society now has for compelling conformity to the necessary conditions of the association. Dismissal, the only remedy at pres-ent, is no remedy when any other labourer who may be engaged does no better than his predecessor: the power of dismissal only enables an employer to obtain from his workmen the customary amount of labour, but that customary labour may be of any degree of inefficiency. Even the labourer who loses his employment by idleness or negligence, has nothing worse to suffer, in the most unfavourable case, than the discipline of a workhouse, and if the desire to avoid this be a sufficient motive in the one system, it would be sufficient in the other. I am not undervaluing the strength of the incitement given to labour when the whole or a large share of the benefit of extra exertion belongs to the labourer. But under the pres-ent system of industry this incitement, in the great majority of cases, does not exist. If Communistic labour might be less vigorous than that of a peasant proprietor, or a workman labouring on his own account, it would probably be more energetic than that of a labourer for hire, who has no personal interest in the matter at all. The neglect by the uneducated classes of labourers for hire, of the duties which they engage to perform, is in the present state of society most flagrant. Now it is an admitted condition of the Communist scheme that all shall be educated: and this being supposed, the duties of the members of the association would doubtless be as diligently performed as those of the generality of salaried officers in the middle or higher classes; who are not supposed to be necessarily unfaithful to their trust, because so long as they are not dismissed, their pay is the same in however lax a manner their duty is fulfilled. Undoubtedly, as a general rule, remuneration by fixed salaries does not in any class of functionaries produce the maximum of zeal; and this is as much as can be reasonably alleged against Communistic labour.

[8.] That even this inferiority would necessarily exist, is by no means so certain as is assumed by those who are little used to carry their minds beyond the state of things with which they are familiar. Mankind are capable of a far greater amount of public spirit than the present age is accustomed to suppose possible. History bears witness to the success with which large bodies of human beings may be trained to feel the public interest their own. And no soil could be more favourable to the growth of such a feeling, than a Communist association, since all the ambition, and the bodily and mental activity, which are now exerted in the pursuit of separate and self-regarding interests, would require another sphere of employment, and would naturally find it in the pursuit of the general benefit of the community. . . .

[9.] Another of the objections to Communism is similar to that, so often urged against poor-laws: that if every member of the community were assured of subsistence for himself and any number of children, on the sole condition of willingness to work, prudential restraint on the multiplication of mankind would be at an end, and population would start forward at a rate which would reduce the community through successive stages of increasing discomfort to actual starvation. There would certainly be much ground for this apprehension if Communism provided no motives to restraint, equivalent to those which it would take away. But Communism is precisely the state of things in which opinion might be expected to declare itself with greatest intensity against this kind of selfish intemperance. Any augmentation of numbers which diminished the comfort or increased the toil of the mass, would then cause (which now it does not) immediate and unmistakable inconvenience to every individual in the association; inconvenience which could not then be imputed to the avarice of employers, or the unjust privileges of the rich. In such altered circumstances opinion could not fail to reprobate, and if reprobation did not suffice, to repress by penalties of some description, this or any other culpable self-indulgence at the expense of the community. The Communistic scheme, instead of being peculiarly open to the objection drawn from danger of over-population, has the recommendation of tending in an especial degree to the prevention of that evil.

[10.] A more real difficulty is that of fairly apportioning the labour of the community among its members. There are many kinds of work, and by what standard are they to be measured one against another? Who is to judge how much cotton spinning, or distributing goods from the stores, or bricklaying, or chimney sweeping, is equivalent to so much ploughing? The difficulty of making the adjustment between different qualities of labour is so strongly felt by Communist writers, that they have usually thought it necessary to provide that all should work by turns at every description of useful labour: an arrangement which by putting an end to the division of employments, would sacrifice so much of the advantage of co-operative production as greatly to diminish the productiveness of labour. Besides, even in the same kind of work, nominal equality of labour would be so great a real inequality, that the feeling of justice would revolt against its being enforced. All persons are not equally fit for all labour; and the same quantity of labour is an unequal burthen on the weak and the strong, the hardy and the delicate, the quick and the slow, the dull and the intelligent.

[11.] But these difficulties, though real, are not necessarily insuperable. The apportionment of work to the strength and capacities of individuals, the mitigation of a general rule to provide for cases in which it would operate harshly, are not problems to which human intelligence, guided by a sense of justice, would be inadequate. And the worst and most unjust arrangement which could be made of these points, under a system aiming at equality, would be so far short of the inequality and injustice with which labour (not to speak of remuneration) is now apportioned, as to be scarcely worth counting in the comparison. We must remember too that Communism, as a system of society, exists only in idea; that its difficulties, at present, are much better understood than its resources; and that the intellect of mankind is only beginning to contrive the means of organising it in detail, so as to overcome the one and derive the greatest advantage from the other.

[12.] If, therefore, the choice were to be made between Communism with all its chances, and the present state of society with all its sufferings and injustices; if the institution of private property necessarily carried with it as a consequence, that the produce of labour should be apportioned as we now see it, almost in an inverse ratio to the labour—the largest portions to those who have never worked at all, the next largest to those whose work is almost nominal, and so in a descending scale, the remuneration dwindling as the work grows harder and more disagreeable, until the most fatiguing and exhausting bodily labour cannot count with certainty on being able to earn even the necessaries of life; if this, or Communism, were the alternative, all the difficulties, great or small, of Communism would be but as dust in the balance. But to make the comparison applicable, we must compare Communism at its best, with the régime of individual property, not as it is, but as it might be made. The principle of private property has never yet had a fair trial in any country; and less so, perhaps, in this country than in some others. The social arrangements of modern Europe commenced from a distribution of property which was the result, not of just partition, or acquisition by industry, but of conquest and violence: and notwithstanding what industry has been doing for many centuries to modify the work of force, the system still retains many and large traces of its origin. The laws of property have never yet conformed to the principles on which the justification of private property rests. They have made property of things which never ought to be property, and absolute property where only a qualified property ought to exist. They have not held the balance fairly between human beings, but have heaped impediments upon some, to give advantage to others; they have purposely fostered inequalities and prevented all from starting fair in the race. That all should indeed start on perfectly equal terms, is inconsistent with any law of private property: but if as much pains as has been taken to aggravate the inequality of chances arising from the natural working of the principle, had been taken to temper that inequality by every means not subversive of the principle itself; if the tendency of legislation had been to favour the diffusion, instead of the concentration of wealth—to encourage the subdivision of the large masses, instead of striving to keep them together; the principle of individual property would have been found to have no necessary connexion with the physical and social evils which almost all Socialist writers assume to be inseparable from it.

[13.] Private property, in every defence made of it, is supposed to mean, the guarantee to individuals, of the fruits of their own labour and abstinence. The guarantee to them of the fruits of the labour and abstinence of others, translated to them without any merit or exertion of their own, is not of the essence of the institution, but a mere incidental consequence, which when it reaches a certain height, does not promote, but conflicts with the ends which render private property legitimate. To judge of the final destination of the institution of property, we must suppose everything rectified, which causes the institution to work in a manner opposed to that equitable principle, of proportion between remuneration and exertion, on which in every vindication of it that will bear the light, it is assumed to be grounded. We must also suppose two conditions realised, without which neither Communism nor any other laws or institutions could make the condition of the mass of mankind other than degraded and miserable. One of these conditions is, universal education; the other, a due limitation of the numbers of the community. With these, there could be no poverty even under the present social institutions: and these being supposed, the question of Socialism is not, as generally stated by Socialists, a question of flying to the sole refuge against the evils which now bear down humanity; but a mere question of comparative advantages, which futurity must determine. We are too ignorant either of what individual agency in its best form, or Socialism in its best form, can accomplish, to be qualified to decide which of the two will be the ultimate form of human society.

[14.] If a conjecture may be hazarded, the decision will probably depend mainly on one consideration, viz. which of the two systems is consistent with the greatest amount of human liberty and spontaneity. After the means of subsistence are assured, the next in strength of the personal wants of human beings is liberty; and (unlike the physical wants, which as civilisation advances become more moderate and more amenable to control) it increases instead of diminishing in intensity, as the intelligence and the moral faculties are more developed. The perfection both of social arrangements and of practical morality would be, to secure to all persons complete independence and freedom of action, subject to no restriction but that of not doing injury to others: and the education which taught, or the social institutions which required them to exchange the control of their own actions for any amount of comfort or affluence, or to renounce liberty for the sake of equality, would deprive them of one of the most elevated characteristics of human nature. It remains to be discovered how far the preservation of this characteristic would be found compatible with the communistic organisation of society. No doubt, this, like all the other objections to the Socialist schemes, is vastly exaggerated. The members of the association need not be required to live together more than they do now, nor need they be controlled in the disposal of their individual share of the produce, and of the probably large amount of leisure which, if they limited their production to things really worth producing, they would possess. Individuals need not be chained to an occupation, or to a particular locality. The restraints of Communism would be freedom in comparison with the present condition of the majority of the human race. The generality of labourers in this and most other countries, have as little choice of occupation or freedom of locomotion, are practically as dependent on fixed rules and on the will of others, as they could be on any system short of actual slavery; to say nothing of the entire domestic subjection of one half the species, . . . But it is not by comparison with the present bad state of society that the claims of Communism can be estimated; nor is it sufficient that it should promise greater personal and mental freedom than is now enjoyed by those who have not enough of either to deserve the name. The question is whether there would be any asylum left for individuality of character; whether public opinion would not be a tyrannical yoke; whether the absolute dependence of each on all, and surveillance of each by all, would not grind all down into a tame uniformity of thoughts, feelings, and actions. This is already one of the glaring evils of the existing state of society, notwithstanding a much greater diversity of education and pursuits, and a much less absolute dependence of the individual on the mass, than would exist in the Communistic régime. No society in which eccentricity is a matter of reproach, can be in a wholesome state. It is yet to be ascertained whether the Communistic scheme would be consistent with that multiform development of human nature, those manifold unlikenesses, that diversity of tastes and talents, and variety of intellectual points of view, which not only form a great part of the interest of human life, but by bringing intellects into a stimulating collision, and by presenting to each innumerable notions that he would not have conceived of himself, are the mainspring of mental and moral progression.

(*Principles of Political Economy*, 1848, 1865 edn.)

(b) The Probable Future of the Labouring Classes

[1.] When I speak, either in this place or elsewhere, of 'the labouring classes', or of labourers as a 'class', I use those phrases in compliance with custom, and as descriptive of an existing, but by no means a necessary or permanent state of social relations. I do not recognise as either just or salutary, a state of society in which there is any 'class' which is not labouring; any human beings exempt from bearing their share of the necessary labours of human life, except those unable to labour, or who have fairly earned rest by previous toil. So long, however, as the great social evil exists of a non-labouring class, labourers also constitute a class, and may be spoken of, though only provisionally, in that character.

[2.] Considered in its moral and social aspect, the state of the labouring people has latterly been a subject of much more speculation and discussion than formerly; and the opinion, that it is not now what it ought to be, has become very general. The suggestions which have been promulgated, and the controversies which have been excited, on detached points rather than on the foundations of the subject, have put in evidence the existence of two conflicting theories, respecting the social position desirable for manual labourers. The one may be called the theory of dependence and protection, the other that of self-dependence.

[3.] According to the former theory, the lot of the poor, in all things which affect them collectively, should be regulated *for* them, not *by* them. They should not be required or encouraged to think for themselves, or give to their own reflection or forecast an influential voice in the determination of their destiny. It is supposed to be the duty of the higher classes to think for them, and to take the responsibility of their lot, as the commander and officers of an army take that of the soldiers composing it. This function, it is contended, the higher classes should prepare themselves to perform conscientiously, and their whole demeanour should impress the poor with a reliance on it, in order that, while yielding passive and active obedience to the rules prescribed for them, they may resign themselves in all other respects to a trustful *insouciance*, and repose under the shadow of their protectors. The relation between rich and poor, according to this theory (a theory also applied to the relation between men and women), should be only partly authoritative: it should be amiable, moral, and sentimental: affectionate tutelage on the one side, respectful and grateful deference on the other. The rich should be *in loco parentis* to the poor, guiding and restraining them like children. Of spontaneous action on their part there should be no need. They should be called on for nothing but to do their day's work, and to be moral and religious. Their morality and religion should be provided for them by their superiors, who should do all that is necessary to ensure their being, in return for labour and attachment, properly fed, clothed, housed, spiritually edified, and innocently amused.

[4.] This is the ideal of the future, in the minds of those whose dissatisfaction with the Present assumes the form of affection and regret towards the Past. Like other ideals, it exercises an unconscious influence on the opinions and sentiments of numbers who never consciously guide themselves by any ideal. It has also this in common with other ideals, that it has never been historically realised. It makes its appeal to our imaginative sympathies in the character of a restoration of the good times of our forefathers. But no times can be pointed out in which the higher classes of this or any other country performed a part even distantly resembling the one assigned to them in this theory. It is an idealisation, grounded on the conduct and character of here and there an individual. All privileged and powerful classes, as such, have used their power in the interest of their own selfishness, and have indulged their self-importance in despising, and not in lovingly caring for, those who were, in their estimation, degraded, by being under the necessity of working for their benefit. I do not affirm that what has always been must always be, or that human improvement has no tendency to correct the intensely selfish feelings engendered by power; but though the evil may be lessened, it cannot be eradicated, until the power itself is withdrawn. This, at least, seems to me undeniable, that long before the superior classes could be sufficiently improved to govern in the tutelary manner supposed, the inferior classes would be too much improved to be so governed. . . .

[5.] Of the working men, at least in the more advanced countries of Europe, it may be pronounced certain, that the patriarchal or paternal system of government is one to which they will not again be subject. That question was decided, when they were taught to read, and allowed access to newspapers and political tracts; when dissenting preachers were suffered to go among them, and appeal to their faculties and feelings in opposition to the creeds professed and countenanced by their superiors; when they were brought together in numbers, to work socially under the same roof; when railways enabled them to shift from place to place, and change their patrons and employers as easily as their coats; when they were encouraged to seek a share in the government, by means of the electoral franchise. The working classes have taken their interests into their own hands, and are perpetually showing that they think the interests of their employers not identical with their own, but opposite to them. Some among the higher classes flatter themselves that these tendencies may be counteracted by moral and religious education; but they have let the time go by for giving an education which can serve their purpose. The principles of the Reformation have reached as low down in society as reading and writing, and the poor will not much longer accept morals and religion of other people's prescribing. I speak more particularly of this country, especially the town population, and the districts of the most scientific agriculture or the highest wages, Scotland and the north of England. Among the more inert and less modernised agricultural population of the southern counties, it might be possible for the gentry to retain, for some time longer, something of the ancient deference and submission of the poor, by bribing them with high wages and constant employment; by ensuring them support, and never requiring them to do anything which they do not like. But these are two conditions which never have been combined, and never can be, for long together. . . .

[6.] It is on a far other basis that the well-being and well-doing of the labouring people must henceforth rest. The poor have come out of leading-strings, and cannot any longer be governed or treated like children. To their own qualities must now be commended the care of their destiny. Modern nations will have to learn the lesson, that the well-being of a people must exist by means of the justice and self-government . . . of the individual citizens. The theory of dependence attempts to dispense with the necessity of these qualities in the dependent classes. But now, when even in position they are becoming less and less dependent, their minds less and less acquiescent in the degree of dependence which remains, the virtues of independence are those which they stand in need of. Whatever advice, exhortation, or guidance is held out to the labouring classes, must henceforth be tendered to them as equals, and accepted by them with their eyes open. The prospect of the future depends on the degree in which they can be made rational beings.

[7.] There is no reason to believe that prospect other than hopeful. The progress indeed has hitherto been, and still is, slow. But there is a spontaneous education going on in the minds of the multitude, which may be greatly accelerated and improved by artificial aids. The instruction obtained from newspapers and political tracts may not be the most solid kind of instruction, but it is an immense improvement upon none at all. What it does for a people, has been admirably exemplified during the cotton crisis, in the case of the Lancashire spinners and weavers; who have acted with the consistent good sense and forbearance so justly applauded, simply because, being readers of newspapers, they understood the causes of the calamity which had befallen them, and knew that it was in no way imputable either to their employers or to the Government. It is not certain that their conduct would have been as rational and exemplary, if the distress had preceded the salutary measure of fiscal emancipation which gave existence to the penny press. The institutions for lectures and discussion, the collective deliberations on questions of common interest, the trades unions, the political agitation, all serve to awaken public spirit, to diffuse variety of ideas among the mass, and to excite thought and reflection in the more intelligent. Although the too early attainment of political franchise by the least educated class might retard, instead of promoting, their improvement, there can be little doubt that it has been greatly stimulated by the attempt to acquire them. In the meantime, the working classes are now part of the public; in all discussions on matters of general interest they, or a portion of them, are now partakers; all who use the press as an instrument may, if it so happens, have them for an audience; the avenues of instruction through which the middle classes acquire such ideas as they have, are accessible to, at least, the operatives in the towns. With these resources, it cannot be doubted that they will increase in intelligence, even by their own unaided efforts; while there is reason to hope that great improvements both in the quality and quantity of school education will be effected by the exertions either of Government or of individuals, and that the progress of the mass of the people in mental cultivation, and in the virtues which are dependent on it, will take place more rapidly, and with fewer intermittences and aberrations, than if left to itself.

[8.] From this increase of intelligence, several effects may be confidently anticipated. First: that they will become even less willing than at present to be led and governed, and directed into the way they should go, by the mere authority and *prestige* of superiors. If they have not now, still less will they have hereafter, any deferential awe, or religious principle of obedience, holding them in mental subjection to a class above them. The theory of dependence and protection will be more and more intolerable to them, and they will require that their conduct and condition shall be essentially self-governed. . . .

(c) Co-operatives

[1.] It is hardly possible to take any but a hopeful view of the prospects of mankind, when in the two leading countries of the world, the obscure depths of society contain simple working men whose integrity, good sense, self-command, and honourable confidence in one another, have enabled them to carry these noble experiments to the triumphant issue which the facts recorded in the preceding pages attest.

[2.] From the progressive advance of the co-operative movement, a great increase may be looked for even in the aggregate productiveness of industry. The sources of the increase are two-fold. In the first place, the class of mere distributors, who are not producers but auxiliaries of production, and whose inordinate numbers, far more than the gains of capitalists, are the cause why so great a portion of the wealth produced does not reach the producers—will be reduced to more modest dimensions. Distributors differ from producers in this, that when producers increase, even though in any given department of industry they may be too numerous, they actually produce more: but the multiplication of distributors does not make more distribution to be done, more wealth to be distributed; it does but divide the same work among a greater number of persons, seldom even cheapening the process. By limiting the distributors to the number really required for making the commodities accessible to the consumers—which is the direct effect of the co-operative system—a vast number of hands will be set free for production, and the capital which feeds and the gains which remunerate them will be applied to feed and remunerate producers. This great economy of the world's resources would be realised, even if co-operation stopped at associations for purchase and consumption, without extending to production.

[3.] The other mode in which co-operation tends, still more efficaciously, to increase the productiveness of labour, consists in the vast stimulus given to productive energies, by placing the labourers as a mass, in a relation to their work which would make it their principle and their interest—at present it is neither—to do the utmost instead of the least possible in exchange for their remuneration. It is scarcely possible to rate too highly this material benefit, which yet is as nothing compared with the moral revolution in society that would accompany it: the healing of the standing feud between capital and labour; the transformation of human life, from a conflict of classes struggling for opposite interests, to a friendly rivalry in the pursuit of a good common to all; the elevation of the dignity of labour, a new sense of security and independence in the labouring class, and the conversion of each human being's daily occupation into a school of the social sympathies and the practical intelligence.

[4.] Such is the noble ideal which the promoters of Co-operation should have before them. But to attain, in any degree, these objects, it is indispensable that all, and not some only, of those who do the work, should be identified in interest with the prosperity of the undertaking. Associations which, when they have been successful, renounce the essential principle of the system, and become joint-stock companies of a limited number of shareholders, who differ from those of other companies only in being working men; associations which employ hired labourers without any interest in the profits (and I grieve to say that the Manufacturing Society even of Rochdale has thus degenerated), are, no doubt, exercising a lawful right in honestly employing the existing system of society to improve their position as individuals; but it is not from them that anything needs be expected towards replacing that system by a better. Neither will such societies, in the long run, succeed in keeping their ground against individual competition. Individual management by the one person principally interested, has great advantages over every description of collective management: co-operation has but one thing to oppose to those advantages—the common interest of all the workers in the work. When individual capitalists, as they will certainly do, add this to their points of advantage; when, even if only to increase their gains, they take up the practice which these co-operative societies have dropped, and connect the pecuniary interest of every person in their employment with the most efficient and most economical management of the concern; they are likely to gain an easy victory over societies which retain the defects, while they cannot possess the full advantages, of the old system.

[5.] Under the most favourable supposition it will be desirable, and perhaps for a considerable length of time, that individual capitalists associating their workpeople in the profits, should co-exist with even those co-operative societies which are faithful to the co-operative principle. Unity of authority makes many things possible, which could not, or would not, be undertaken, subject to the chance of divided councils, or changes in the management. A private capitalist, exempt from the control of a body, if he is a person of capacity, is considerably more likely than almost any association to run judicious risks, and originate costly improvements. Co-operative societies may be depended upon for adopting improvements after they have been tested by success; but individuals are more likely to commence things previously untried. Even in ordinary business, the competition of capable persons who in the event of failure are to have all the loss, and in case of success the greater part of the gain, will be very useful in keeping the managers of co-operative societies up to the due pitch of activity and vigilance.

[6.] When, however, co-operative societies shall have sufficiently multiplied, it is not probable that any but the least valuable workpeople will any longer consent to work all their lives for wages merely: and both private capitalists and associations will gradually find it necessary to make the entire body of labourers participants in profits. Eventually, and in perhaps a less remote future than may be supposed, we may, through the co-operative principle, see our way to a change in society, which could combine the freedom and independence of the individual, with the moral, intellectual, and economical advantages of aggregate production; and which, without violence or spoliation, or even any sudden disturbance of existing habits and expectations, would realise, at least in the industrial department, the best aspirations of the democratic spirit, by putting an end to the division of society into the industrious and the idle, and effacing all social distinctions but those fairly earned by personal services and exertions. Associations like those which we have described, by the very process of their success, are a course of education in those moral and active qualities by which alone success can be either deserved or attained. As associations multiplied, they would tend more and more to absorb all workpeople, except those who have too little understanding, or too little virtue, to be capable of learning to act on any other system than that of narrow selfishness. As this change proceeded owners of capital would gradually find it to their advantage, instead of maintaining the struggle of the old system with workpeople of only the worst description, to lend their capital to the associations; to do this at a diminishing rate of interest, and at last, perhaps, even to exchange their capital for terminable annuities. In this or some such mode, the existing accumulations of capital might honestly, and by a kind of spontaneous process, become in the end the joint property of all who participate in their productive employment: a transformation which, thus effected (and assuming of course that both sexes participate equally in the rights and in the government of the association),[1] would be the nearest approach to social justice, and the most beneficial ordering of industrial affairs for the universal good, which it is possible at present to foresee.

(d) Socialism

[1.] I agree, then, with the Socialist writers in their conception of the form which industrial operations tend to assume in the advance of improvement; and I entirely share the opinion that the time is ripe for commencing this transformation, and that it should by all just and effectual means be aided and encouraged. But while I agree and sympathise with Socialists in this practical portion of their aims, I utterly dissent from the most conspicuous and vehement part of their teaching, their declamations against competition. With moral conceptions in many respects far ahead of the existing arrangements of society, they have in general very confused and erroneous notions of its actual working; and one of their greatest errors, as I conceive, is to charge upon competition all the economical evils which at present exist. They forget that wherever competition is not, monopoly is; and that monopoly, in all its forms, is the taxation of the industrious for the support of indolence, if not of plunder. They forget, too, that with the exception of competition among labourers, all other competition is for the benefit of the labourers, by cheapening the articles they consume; that competition even in the labour market is a source not of low but of high wages, wherever the

---

[1] In this respect also the Rochdale Society has given an example of reason and justice, worthy of the good sense and good feeling manifested in their general proceedings. 'The Rochdale Store', says Mr Holyoake, 'renders incidental but valuable aid towards realising the civil independence of women. Women may be members of this Store, and vote in its proceedings. Single and married women join. Many married women become members because their husbands will not take the trouble, and others join in it in self-defence, to prevent the husband from spending their money in drink. The husband cannot withdraw the savings at the Store standing in the wife's name, unless she signs the order. Of course, as the law still stands, the husband could by legal process get possession of the money. But a process takes time, and the husband gets sober and thinks better of it before the law can move.'

competition *for* labour exceeds the competition *of* labour, as in America, in the colonies, and in the skilled trades; and never could be a cause of low wages, save by the overstocking of the labour market through the too great numbers of the labourers' families; while, if the supply of labourers is excessive, not even socialism can prevent their remuneration from being low. Besides, if association were universal, there would be no competition between labourer and labourer; and that between association and association would be for the benefit of the consumers, that is, of the associations; of the industrious classes generally.

[2.] I do not pretend that there are no inconveniences in competition, or that the moral objections urged against it by Socialist writers, as a source of jealousy and hostility among those engaged in the same occupation, are altogether groundless. But if competition has its evils, it prevents greater evils. . . . It is the common error of Socialists to overlook the natural indolence of mankind; their tendency to be passive, to be the slaves of habit, to persist indefinitely in a course once chosen. Let them once attain any state of existence which they consider tolerable, and the danger to be apprehended is that they will thenceforth stagnate; will not exert themselves to improve, and by letting their faculties rust, will lose even the energy required to preserve them from deterioration. Competition may not be the best conceivable stimulus, but it is at present a necessary one, and no one can foresee the time when it will not be indispensable to progress. Even confining ourselves to the industrial department, in which, more than in any other, the majority may be supposed to be competent judges of improvements; it would be difficult to induce the general assembly of an association to submit to the trouble and inconvenience of altering their habits by adopting some new and promising invention, unless their knowledge of the existence of rival associations made them apprehend that what they would not consent to do, others would, and that they would be left behind in the race.

[3.] Instead of looking upon competition as the baneful and antisocial principle which it is held to be by the generality of Socialists, I conceive that, even in the present state of society and industry, every restriction of it is an evil, and every extension of it, even if for the time injuriously affecting some class of labourers, is always an ultimate good. To be protected against competition is to be protected in idleness, in mental dullness; to be saved the necessity of being as active and as intelligent as other people; and if it is also to be protected against being underbid for employment by a less highly paid class of labourers, this is only where old custom or local and partial monopoly has placed some particular class of artisans in a privileged position as compared with the rest; and the time has come when the interest of universal improvement is no longer promoted by prolonging the privileges of a few. If the slopsellers and others of their class have lowered the wages of tailors, and some other artisans, by making them an affair of competition instead of custom, so much the better in the end. What is now required is not to bolster up old customs, whereby limited classes of labouring people obtain partial gains which interest them in keeping up the present organisation of society, but to introduce new general practices beneficial to all; and there is reason to rejoice at whatever makes the privileged classes of skilled artisans feel, that they have the same interests, and depend for their remuneration on the same general causes, and must resort for the improvement of their condition to the same remedies, as the less fortunately circumstanced and comparatively helpless multitude.

(*Principles of Political Economy*, 1848, 1865 edn., Books II and IV.)

III.11 William Morris, from *Useful Work Versus Useless Toil* (1885)

The above title may strike some of my readers as strange. It is assumed by most people now-a-days that all work is useful, and by most *well-to-do* people that all work is desirable. Most people, well-to-do or not, believe that, even when a man is doing work which appears to be useless, he is earning his livelihood by it—he is 'employed', as the phrase goes; and most of those who are well-to-do cheer on the happy worker with congratulations and praises, if he is only 'industrious' enough and deprives himself of all pleasure and holidays in the sacred cause of labour. In short it has become an article of the creed of modern morality that all labour is good in itself—a convenient belief to those who live on the labour of others. But as to those on whom they live, I recommend them not to take it on trust, but to look into the matter a little deeper.

Let us grant, first, that the race of man must either labour or perish. Nature gives us absolutely nothing gratis; we must win it by toil of some sort or degree. Let us see, then, if she does not give us some compensation for this compulsion to labour, since certainly in other matters she takes care to make the acts necessary to the continuance of life in the individual and the race not only endurable, but even pleasurable.

Yet, first, we must say in the teeth of the hypocritical praise of all labour, whatsoever it may be, of which I have made mention, that there is some labour which is so far from being a blessing that it is a curse; that it would be better for the community and for the worker if the latter were to fold his hands and refuse to work, and either die or let us pack him off to the workhouse or prison—which you will.

Here, you see, are two kinds of work—one good, the other bad; one not far removed from a blessing, a lightening of life; the other a mere curse, a burden to life.

What is the difference between them, then? This: one has hope in it, the other has not. It is manly to do the one kind of work, and manly also to refuse to do the other.

What is the nature of the hope which, when it is present in work, makes it worth doing?

It is threefold, I think—hope of rest, hope of product, hope of pleasure in the work itself; and hope of these also in some abundance and of good quality; rest enough and good enough to be worth having; product worth having by one who is neither a fool nor an ascetic; pleasure enough for all for us to be conscious of it while we are at work; not a mere habit, the loss of which we shall feel as a fidgetty man feels the loss of the bit of string he fidgets with.

I have put the hope of rest first because it is the simplest and most natural part of our hope. Whatever pleasure there is in some work, there is certainly some pain in all work, the beast-like pain of stirring up our slumbering energies to action, the beast-like dread of change when things are pretty well with us; and the compensation for this animal pain is animal rest. We must feel while we are working that the time will come when we shall not have to work. Also the rest, when it comes, must be long enough to allow us to enjoy it; it must be longer than is merely necessary for us to recover the strength we have expended in working, and it must be animal rest also in this, that it must not be disturbed by anxiety, else we shall not be able to enjoy it. If we have this amount and kind of rest we shall, so far, be no worse off than the beasts.

As to the hope of product, I have said that nature compels us to work for that. It remains for *us* to look to it that we *do* really produce something, and not nothing, or at least nothing that we want or are allowed to use. If we look to this and use our wills we shall, so far, be better than machines.

The hope of pleasure in the work itself: how strange that hope must seem to some of my readers—to most of them! Yet I think that to all living things there is a pleasure in the exercise of their energies, and that even beasts rejoice in being lithe and swift and strong. But a man at work, making something which he feels will exist because he is working at it and wills it, is exercising the energies of his mind and soul as well as of his body. Memory and imagination help him as he works. Not only his own thoughts, but the thoughts of the men of past ages guide his hands; and, as a part of the human race, he creates. If we work thus we shall be men, and our days will be happy and eventful.

Thus worthy work carries with it the hope of pleasure in rest, the hope of the pleasure in our using what it makes, and the hope of pleasure in our daily creative skill.

All other work but this is worthless; it is slaves' work—mere toiling to live, that we may live to toil.

Therefore, since we have, as it were, a pair of scales in which to weigh the work now done in the world, let us use them. Let us estimate the worthiness of the work we do, after so many thousand years of toil, so many promises of hope deferred, such boundless exultation over the progress of civilisation and the gain of liberty.

Now, the first thing as to the work done in civilisation and the easiest to notice is that it is portioned out very unequally amongst the different classes of society. First, there are people—not a few—who do no work, and make no pretence of doing any. Next, there are people, and very many of them, who work fairly hard, though with abundant easements and holidays, claimed and allowed; and lastly, there are people who work so hard that they may be said to do nothing else than work, and are accordingly called 'the working classes', as distinguished from the middle classes and the rich, or aristocracy, whom I have mentioned above.

It is clear that this inequality presses heavily upon the 'working' class, and must visibly tend to destroy their hope of rest at least, and so, in that particular, make them worse off than mere beasts of the field; but that is not the sum and end of our folly of turning useful work into useless toil, but only the beginning of it.

For first, as to the class of rich people doing no work, we all know that they consume a great deal while they produce nothing. Therefore, clearly, they have to be kept at the expense of those who do work, just as paupers have, and are a mere burden on the community. In these days there are many who have learned to see this, though they can see no further into the evils of our present system, and have formed no idea of any scheme for getting rid of this burden; though perhaps they have a vague hope that changes in the system of voting for members of the House of Commons may, as if by magic, tend in that direction. With such hopes or superstitions we need not trouble ourselves. Moreover, this class, once thought most necessary to the State, is scant of numbers, and has now no power of its own, but depends on the support of the class next below it—the middle class. In fact, it is really composed either of the most successful men of that class, or of their immediate descendants.

As to the middle class, including the trading, manufacturing and professional people of our society, they do, as a rule, seem to work quite hard enough, and so at first sight might be thought to help the community, and not burden it. But by far the greater part of them, though they work, do not produce, and even when they do produce, as in the case of those engaged (wastefully indeed) in the distribution of goods, or doctors, or (genuine) artists and literary men, they consume out of all proportion to their due share. The commercial and manufacturing part of them, the most powerful part, spend their lives and energies in fighting amongst themselves for their respective shares of the wealth which they *force* the genuine workers to provide for them; the others are almost wholly the hangers-on of these: they are the parasites of property, sometimes, as in the case of lawyers, undisguisedly so; sometimes, as the doctors and others above-mentioned, professing to be useful but too often of no use save as supporters of the system of folly, fraud and tyranny of which they form a part. And all these we must remember, have, as a rule, one aim in view: not the production of utilities, but the gaining of a position either for themselves or their children in which they will not have to work at all. It is their ambition and the end of their whole lives to gain, if not for themselves yet at least for their children, the proud position of being obvious burdens on the community. For their work itself, in spite of the sham dignity with which they surround it, they care nothing: save a few enthusiasts, men of science, art or letters, who, if they are not the salt of the earth, are at least (and O, the pity of it!) the salt of the miserable system of which they are the slaves, which hinders and thwarts them at every turn and even sometimes corrupts them.

Here then is another class, this time very numerous and all-powerful, which produces very little and consumes enormously, and is therefore supported, as paupers are, by the real producers. The class that remains to be considered produces all that is produced, and supports both itself and the other classes, though it is placed in a position of inferiority to them; real inferiority, mind you, involving a degradation both of mind and body. But it is a necessary consequence of this tyranny and folly that again many of these workers are not producers. A vast number of them once more are merely parasites of property, some of them openly so, as the soldiers by land and sea who are kept on foot for the perpetuating of national rivalries and enmities, and for the purposes of the national struggle for the share of the product of unpaid labour. But besides this obvious burden on the producers and the scarcely less obvious one of domestic servants, there is first the army of clerks, shop-assistants and so forth who are engaged in the service of the private war for wealth, which as above said, is the real occupation of the well-to-do middle class. This is a larger body of workers than might be supposed, for it includes amongst others all those engaged in what I should call competitive salesmanship, or, to use a less dignified word, the puffery of wares, which has now got to such a pitch that there are many things which cost far more to sell than they do to make.

Next there is the mass of people employed in making all those articles of folly and luxury, the demand for which is the outcome of the existence of the rich non-producing classes; things which people leading a manly and uncorrupted life would not ask for or dream of. These things, whoever may gainsay me, I will for ever refuse to call wealth; they are not wealth, but waste. Wealth is what nature gives us and what a reasonable man can make out of the gifts of nature for his reasonable use. The sunlight, the fresh air, the unspoiled face of the earth, food, raiment and housing, necessary and decent; the storing up of knowledge of all kinds, and the power of disseminating it; means of free communication between man and man; works of art, the beauty which man creates when he is most a man, most aspiring and thoughtful—all things which serve the pleasure of people, free, manly and uncorrupted. This is wealth. Nor can I think of anything worth having which does not come under one or other of these heads. But think, I beseech you, of the product of England, the workshop of the world, and will you not be bewildered, as I am, at the thought of the mass of things which no sane man could desire, but which our useless toil makes—and sells?

Now, further, there is even a sadder industry yet forced on many, very many, of our workers—the making of wares which are necessary to them and, their brethren, *because they are an inferior class.* For if many men live without producing, nay, must live lives so empty and foolish that they *force* a great part of the workers to produce wares which no one needs, not even the rich, it follows that most men must be poor; and, living as they do on wages from those whom they support, cannot get for their use the *goods* which men naturally desire, but must put up with miserable makeshifts for them, with coarse food that does not nourish, with rotten raiment which does not shelter, with wretched houses which may well make a town-dweller in civilisation look back with regret to the tent of the nomad tribe, or the cave of the pre-historic savage. Nay, the workers must even lend a hand to the great industrial invention of the age—adulteration, and by its help produce for their own use shams and mockeries of the luxury of the rich; for the wage-earners must always live as the wage-payers bid them, and their very habits of life are *forced* on them by their masters.

But it is waste of time to try to express in words due contempt of the productions of the much-praised cheapness of our epoch. It must be enough to say that this cheapness is necessary to the system of exploiting on which modern manufacture rests. In other words, our society includes a great mass of slaves, who must be fed, clothed, housed and amused as slaves, and that their daily necessity compels them to make the slave-wares whose use is the perpetuation of their slavery.

To sum up, then, concerning the manner of work in civilised states, these states are composed of three classes—a class which does not even pretend to work, a class which pretends to work but which produces nothing, and a class which works, but is compelled by the other two classes to do work which is often unproductive. . . .

(William Morris: News from Nowhere and Selected Writings and Designs,
ed. A. Briggs, 1962, pp. 117–22.)

III.12 **William Morris, from 'How I Became a Socialist' (1894)**

I am asked by the Editor to give some sort of a history of the above conversion, and I feel that it may be of some use to do so, if my readers will look upon me as a type of a certain group of people, but not so easy to do clearly, briefly, and truly. Let me, however, try. But first, I will say what I mean by being a Socialist, since I am told that the word no longer expresses definitely and with certainty what it did ten years ago. Well, what I mean by Socialism is a condition of society in which there should be neither rich nor poor, neither master nor master's man, neither idle nor overworked, neither brain-sick brain workers, nor heart-sick hand workers, in a word, in which all men would be living in equality of condition, and would manage their affairs unwastefully, and with the full consciousness that harm to one would mean harm to all—the realization at last of the meaning of the word COMMONWEALTH.

Now this view of Socialism which I hold today, and hope to die holding, is what I began with; I had no transitional period, unless you may call such a brief period of political radicalism during which I saw my ideal clear enough, but had no hope of any realization of it. That came to an end some months before I joined the (then) Democratic Federation, and the meaning of my joining that body was that I had conceived a hope of the realization of my ideal. If you ask me how much of a hope, or what I thought we Socialists then living and working would accomplish towards it, or when there would be effected any change in the face of society, I must say, I do not know. I can only say that I did not measure my hope nor the joy that it brought me at the time. For the rest, when I took that step I was blankly ignorant of economics; I had never so much as opened Adam Smith, or heard of Ricardo, or of Karl Marx. Oddly enough, I *had* read some of Mill, . . . and the result, so far as I was concerned, was to convince me that Socialism was a necessary change, and that it was possible to bring it about in our own days. . . .

But in this telling how I fell into *practical* Socialism I have begun, as I perceive, in the middle, for in my position of a well-to-do man, not suffering from the disabilities which oppress a working man at every step, I feel that I might never have been drawn into the practical side of the question if an ideal had not forced me to seek towards it. For politics as politics, i.e., not regarded as a necessary if cumbersome and disgustful means to an end, would never have attracted me, nor when I had become conscious of the wrongs of society as it now is, and the oppression of poor people, could I have ever believed in the possibility of a *partial* setting right of those wrongs. In other words, I could never have been such a fool as to believe in the happy and 'respectable' poor.

If, therefore, my ideal forced me to look for practical Socialism, what was it that forced me to conceive of an ideal? Now, here comes in what I said of my being (in this paper) a type of a certain group of mind.

Before the uprising of *modern* Socialism almost all intelligent people either were, or professed themselves to be, quite contented with the civilization of this century. Again, almost all of these really were thus contented, and saw nothing to do but to perfect the said civilization by getting rid of a few ridiculous survivals of the barbarous ages. To be short, this was the *Whig* frame of mind, natural to the modern prosperous middle-class men, who, in fact, as far as mechanical progress is concerned, have nothing to ask for, if only Socialism would leave them alone to enjoy their plentiful style.

But besides these contented ones there were others who were not really contented, but had a vague sentiment of repulsion to the triumph of civilization, but were coerced into silence by the measureless power of Whiggery. Lastly, there were a few who were in open rebellion against the said Whiggery—a few, say two, Carlyle and Ruskin. The latter, before my days of practical Socialism, was my master towards the ideal aforesaid, and, looking backward, I cannot help saying, by the way, how deadly dull the world would have been twenty years ago but for Ruskin! It was through him that I learned to give form to my discontent, which I must say was not by any means vague. Apart from the desire to produce beautiful things, the leading passion of my life has been and is hatred of modern civilization. What shall I say of it now, when the words are put into my mouth, my hope of its destruction—what shall I say of its supplanting by Socialism?

What shall I say concerning its mastery of and its waste of mechanical power, its commonwealth so poor, its enemies of the commonwealth so rich, its stupendous organization—for the misery of life! Its contempt of simple pleasures which everyone could enjoy but for its folly? Its eyeless vulgarity which has destroyed art, the one certain solace of labour? . . . Think of it! Was it all to end in a counting-house on the top of a cinder-heap, with Podsnap's drawing-room in the offing, and a Whig committee dealing out champagne to the rich and margarine to the poor in such convenient proportions as would make all men contented together, though the pleasure of the eyes was gone from the world, and the place of Homer was to be taken by Huxley? . . . So there I was in for a fine pessimistic end of life, if it had not somehow dawned on me that amidst all this filth of civilization the seeds of a great change, what we others call Social-Revolution, were beginning to germinate. The whole face of things was changed to me by that discovery, and all I had to do then in order to become a Socialist was to hook myself on to the practical movement, which, as before said, I have tried to do as well as I could.

To sum up, then, the study of history and the love and practice of art forced me into a hatred of the civilization which, if things were to stop as they are, would turn history into inconsequent nonsense, and make art a collection of the curiosities of the past, which would have no serious relation to the life of the present.

But the consciousness of revolution stirring amidst our hateful modern society prevented me, luckier than many others of artistic perceptions, from crystallizing into a mere railer against 'progress' on the one hand, and on the other from wasting time and energy in any of the numerous schemes by which the quasi-artistic of the middle classes hope to make art grow when it has no longer any root, and thus I became a practical Socialist. . . .

(Justice, 16 June 1894.)

IV

Culture: Production, Consumption, and Status

Letters from John Ruskin to *The Times*.   IV.1

(a) 13 May 1851

Sir,

Your usual liberality will, I trust, give a place in your columns to this expression of my regret that the tone of the critique which appeared in *The Times* of Wednesday last on the works of Mr. Millais and Mr. Hunt now in the Royal Academy, should have been scornful as well as severe.

I regret it, first, because the mere labour bestowed on those works, and their fidelity to a certain order of truth, (labour and fidelity which are altogether indisputable,) ought at once to have placed them above the level of mere contempt; and, secondly, because I believe these young artists to be at a most critical period of their career—at a turning-point, from which they may either sink into nothingness or rise to very real greatness: and I believe also, that whether they choose the upward or the downward path, may in no small degree depend upon the character of the criticism which their works have to sustain. I do not wish in any way to dispute or invalidate the general truth of your critique on the Royal Academy; nor am I surprised at the estimate which the writer formed of the pictures in question when rapidly compared with works of totally different style and aim: nay, when I first saw the chief picture by Millais in the Exhibition of last year, I had nearly come to the same conclusion myself. But I ask your permission, in justice to artists who have at least given much time and toil to their pictures, to institute some more serious inquiry into their merits and faults than your general notice of the Acadamy could possibly have admitted.

Let me state, in the first place, that I have no acquaintance with any of these artists, and very imperfect sympathy with them. No one who has met with any of my writings will suspect me of desiring to encourage them in their Romanist and Tractarian tendencies. . . .

But, before entering into such particulars, let me correct an impression which your article is likely to induce in most minds, and which is altogether false. These Pre-Raphaelites (I cannot compliment them on common sense in choice of a *nom de guerre*) do *not* desire nor pretend in any way to imitate antique paintings as such. They know very little of ancient paintings who suppose the works of these young artists to resemble them. As far as I can judge of their aim—for, as I said, I do not know the men themselves— the Pre-Raphaelites intend to surrender no advantage which the knowledge or inventions of the present time can afford to their art. They intend to return to early days in this one point only—that, as far as in them lies, they will draw either what they see, or what they suppose might have been the actual facts of the scene they desire to represent, irrespective of any conventional rules of picture-making; and they have chosen their unfortunate though not inaccurate name because all artists did this before Raphael's time, and after Raphael's time did *not* this, but sought to paint fair pictures, rather than represent stern facts; of which the consequence has been that, from Raphael's time to this day, historical art has been in acknowledged decadence.

Now, Sir, presupposing that the intention of these men was to return to archaic *art* instead of to archaic *honesty*, your critic borrows Fuseli's expression respecting ancient draperies 'snapped instead of folded,' and asserts that in these pictures there is a '*servile* imitation of *false* perspective'. To which I have just this to answer:

That there is not one single error in perspective in four out of the five pictures in question; and that in Millais' 'Mariana' there is but this one— that the top of the green curtain in the distant window has too low a vanishing-point; and that I will undertake, if need be, to point out and prove a dozen worse errors in perspective in any twelve pictures, containing architecture, taken at random from among the works of the popular painters of the day.

Secondly; that, putting aside the small Mulready, and the works of Thorburn and Sir W. Ross, and perhaps some others of those in the miniature room which I have not examined, there is not a single study of drapery in the whole Academy, be it in large works or small, which for perfect truth, power, and finish could be compared for an instant with the black sleeve of the Julia, or with the velvet on the breast and the chain mail of the Valentine, of Mr. Hunt's picture; or with the white draperies on the table of Mr. Millais' 'Mariana', and of the right-hand figure in the same painter's 'Dove returning to the Ark'.

And further: that as studies both of drapery and of every minor detail, there has been nothing in art so earnest or so complete as these pictures since the days of Albert Dürer. This I assert generally and fearlessly. On the other hand, I am perfectly ready to admit that Mr. Hunt's 'Sylvia' is not a person whom Proteus or anyone else would have been likely to fall in love

3. John Everett Millais: *Mariana* 1851

4. John Everett Millais: *The Dove Returning to the Ark* 1851

5. W. Holman Hunt: *Valentine Rescuing Sylvia* 1851

with at first sight; and that one cannot feel very sincere delight that Mr. Millais' 'Wives of the Sons of Noah' should have escaped the Deluge; with many other faults besides on which I will not enlarge at present, because I have already occupied too much of your valuable space, and I hope to enter into more special criticism in a future letter.

(*The Lamp of Beauty: Writings on Art by John Ruskin*, ed. Joan Evans, 1959, 1980 edn., pp. 47–9.)

(b)   30 May 1851

Sir

Your obliging insertion of my former letter encourages me to trouble you with one or two further notes respecting the pre-Raphaelite pictures. I had intended, in continuation of my first letter, to institute as close an inquiry as I could into the character of the morbid tendencies which prevent these works from favourably arresting the attention of the public; but I believe there are so few pictures in the Academy whose reputation would not be grievously diminished by a deliberate inventory of their errors, that I am disinclined to undertake so ungracious a task with respect to this or that particular work. These points, however, may be noted, partly for the consideration of the painters themselves, partly that forgiveness of them may be asked from the public in consideration of high merits in other respects.

The most painful of these defects is unhappily also the most prominent—the commonness of feature in many of the principal figures. In Mr. Hunt's 'Valentine defending Sylvia', this is, indeed, almost the only fault. Further examination of this picture has even raised the estimate I had previously formed of its marvellous truth in detail and splendour in colour; nor is its general conception less deserving of praise: the action of Valentine, his arm thrown round Sylvia, and his hand clasping hers at the same instant as she falls at his feet, is most faithful and beautiful, nor less so the contending of doubt and distress with awakening hope in the half-shadowed, half-sunlit countenance of Julia. Nay, even the momentary struggle of Proteus with Sylvia just past, is indicated by the trodden grass and broken fungi of the foreground. But all this thoughtful conception, and absolutely inimitable execution, fail in making immediate appeal to the feelings, owing to the unfortunate type chosen for the face of Sylvia. Certainly this cannot be she whose lover was

> As rich in having such a jewel,
> As twenty seas, if all their sands were pearl.

Nor is it, perhaps, less to be regretted that, while in Shakespeare's play there are nominally 'Two Gentlemen', in Mr. Hunt's picture there should only be one—at least, the kneeling figure on the right has by no means the look of a gentleman. But this may be on purpose, for any one who remembers the conduct of Proteus throughout the previous scenes will, I think, be disposed to consider that the error lies more in Shakespeare's nomenclature than in Mr. Hunt's ideal.

No defence can, however, be offered for the choice of features in the left-hand figure of Mr. Millais' 'Dove returning to the Ark'. I cannot understand how a painter so sensible of the utmost refinement of beauty in other objects should deliberately choose for his model a type far inferior to that of average humanity, and unredeemed by any expression save that of dull self-complacency. Yet let the spectator who desires to be just turn away from this head, and contemplate rather the tender and beautiful expression of the stooping figure, and the intense harmony of colour in the exquisitely finished draperies; let him note also the ruffling of the plumage of the wearied dove, one of its feathers falling on the arm of the figure which holds it, and another to the ground, where, by-the-bye, the hay is painted not only elaborately, but with the most perfect ease of touch and mastery of effect, especially to be observed because this freedom of execution is a modern excellence, which it has been inaccurately stated that these painters despise, but which, in reality, is one of the remarkable distinctions between their painting and that of Van Eyck or Memling, which caused me to say in my first letter that 'those knew little of ancient painting who supposed the works of these men to resemble it'.

Next to this false choice of feature, and in connection with it, is to be noted the defect in the colouring of the flesh. The hands, at least in the pictures in Millais, are almost always ill painted, and the flesh tint in general is wrought out of crude purples, and dusky yellows. It appears just possible that much of this evil may arise from the attempt to obtain too much transparency—an attempt which has injured also not a few of the best works of Mulready. I believe it will be generally found that close study of minor details is unfavourable to flesh painting; it was noticed of the drawing by John Lewis, in the old water-colour exhibition of 1850 (a work which, as regards its treatment of detail, may be ranged in the same class with the pre-Raphaelite pictures), that the faces were the worst painted portions of the whole.

The apparent want of shade is, however, perhaps the fault which most hurts the general eye. The fact is, nevertheless, that the fault is far more in the other pictures of the Academy than in the pre-Raphaelite ones. It is the former that are false, not the latter, except so far as every picture must be false which endeavours to represent living sunlight with dead pigments. I think Mr. Hunt has a slight tendency to exaggerate reflected lights; and if Mr. Millais has ever been near a piece of good painted glass, he ought to have known that its tone is more dusky and sober than that of his Mariana's window. But for the most part these pictures are rashly condemned because the only light which we are accustomed to see represented is that which falls on the artist's model in his dim painting-room, not that of sun-shine in the fields.

I do not think I can go much further in fault-finding. I had, indeed, some-thing to urge respecting what I supposed to be the Romanizing tendencies of the painters; but I have received a letter assuring me that I was wrong in attributing to them anything of the kind . . . And so I wish them all heartily good speed, believing in sincerity that if they temper the courage and energy which they have shown in the adoption of their systems with patience and discretion in framing it, and if they do not suffer themselves to be driven by harsh or careless criticism into rejection of the ordinary means of obtaining influence over the minds of others, they may, as they gain experience, lay in our England the foundations of a school of art nobler than the world has seen for three hundred years.

(*The Lamp of Beauty: Writings on Art by John Ruskin*, ed. Joan Evans, 1959, 1980 edn., pp. 50–2.)

IV.2 Reviews of the 1852 Royal Academy Exhibition

(a) The Private View, *The Times* (1 May 1852)

Not far remote from the production . . . of an experienced painter like Mr Maclise must be placed the more crude and grotesque illuminations of Mr Millais and his friends. We see no reason to qualify or retract the censure we thought it our duty to pass last year on their very unfortunate produc-tions, and we regret to find, on the present occasion, the same absence of any real sense of beauty, the same want of enlarged and elevated treatment. We do not confound the works of Mr Millais or Mr Hunt with the 'Medi-cine Man' of Mr Manley or the 'Baa Lambs' of Mr Brown, but there must be something strangely perverse in an imagination which souses Ophelia in a weedy ditch, and robs the drowning struggle of that love-lorn maiden of all pathos and beauty, while it studies every petal of the darnel and ane-mone floating on the eddy, and picks out a robin on the pollard from which Ophelia fell. Nevertheless we readily acknowledge an improvement in some of the productions of this singular school. Mr Millais's *Huguenot* is neither offensive nor absurd, though it is stiff and ungraceful; the details are executed with indisputable nicety, and the principal figure is not devoid of feeling. Mr Hunt's picture of the *Hireling Shepherd*, though in itself more ludicrous and repulsive, was held by not a few of the artists and con-noisseurs assembled yesterday at the Academy to denote powers which might one day reach a safer channel. Shepherds and shepherdesses with such firey complexions, such wiry hair, and such elephantine feet were not born in Arcady; but here again are signs of patient study and of misdirected imitative skill which may rise above the wretched conceit that now seems to enthrall them. To this part of the exhibition we shall, ere long, take occasion to return, for it belongs essentially to the minuteness of style which threatens to become the latest characteristic of modern English art. . . .

The Times, 1 May 1852

(b) The Times (14 May 1852)

We have already remarked that the chief interest of the present exhibition is to be sought in the novelty and progressive merit of the works produced by the younger generation of artists, and the discussions excited by their peculiarities and their theories of art must supply, as far as such a want can be supplied, the absence of those commanding works of genius which we receive with enthusiasm and delight. The tendencies of these junior artists are diametrically opposed to the traditional merits and defects of the English school of painting as it has existed for the last half-century. Instead of breadth, effect, and a vague feeling for the grand and the beautiful, conveyed by a somewhat loose and random style of execution, they aim at excessive precision, minute particularity, a fidelity of detail which they cannot at present combine with general truth of vision, and a study of accessories which is not easily applied to deep interest or poetic feeling. They have applied themselves to remedy an undoubted defect in their predecessors. They are more correct in their drawing, more close in their adherence to natural objects, and less disposed to slur over what they cannot imitate. As studies or efforts at self improvement such practices would be laudable; but in the production of pictures they have not risen above what Fuseli termed 'the elaborate anguish of missal painting'. We are contented to hope that they are still at an early stage of their work, and that the higher graces and meanings of art which they have not attained will one day be added to them. Otherwise they must not complain if the world applies to them the expressions which the same critic applied to those artists of the time preceding Raphael, whom they have rather affectedly taken as their guides . . .

   . . . If any of the higher qualities of art can be traced in these productions, they exist not so much by these peculiarities as in spite of them. We discover genius in Mr Millais, and hope that Mr Hunt may surmount the eccentricities which give his figures minuteness without delicacy, as Gulliver describes the stumps of a human beard to be inexpressibly disgusting to Lilliputian eyes. But, with patience and labour, the same nicety is arrived at in such works as Mr R. Martineau's *Kits Writing Lesson* (in the octagon room) or Mr Collinsons' *St Elizabeth of Hungary* which is the worst of the series. In short, there is in all this a good deal of manner and affectation which may be acquired without a spark of genius or feeling, and the lower the subject to which it is applied the better. Reserve it for vegetables, or for still life, and it may have its value; but to touch the feelings or the imagination we require more harmony and taste. Compare, for example, Mr Millais' Ophelia in her pool, where she makes us think of a dairymaid in a frolic, with Mr O'Neill's affecting and beautiful delineation of the same touching creation, which hangs on the left hand wall beside it. Nothing can be finer, were it only as a study of love-struck madness, than the pallid complexion, the full wet eye, the overwrought brain, the broken heart of Mr O'Neill's picture. There is death in so much love and sorrow, though it be yet afar off; but Mr Millais has attempted to render the very act of drowning as if it were some freak of rude health instead of the climax of distraction. The public very naturally prefer Mr Millais' second picture 'The Lady and the Huguenot'. In this composition, as in the interlude of Pyramus and Thisbe, which it slightly brings to mind, the Wall plays a very important part. Its mosses, its stains, its cracks, and its tendrils of ivy are a surprising example of patient observation and skilful reproduction; yet the tone of the background is excellent and unobtrusive; and the colour of the whole composition so deep and rich as to efface everything near it. The expression of the female figure is admirably wrought with tenderness and terror, and, with the true characteristic of an original conception, it gains upon the eye and fixes itself upon the mind; the lover is stiff, tall, and a thorough Calvinist; the position of his right arm is awkward, and his right leg has disappeared altogether, which gives him the appearance of what ornithologists call a *wader*. But Mr Millais has unquestionably moved the public to interest as well as curiosity; and though we still smile at some of his puerilities, we recognise with pleasure in his works an earnest will and an increasing power of execution; we hope to see him cured of his singularities, and in turn he will gradually educate the public to appreciate his merit and to reward his perseverance.

The Times, 14 May 1852

(c) The *Athenaeum* (22 May 1852)

In this Exhibition, the Pre-Raphaelites, as they are called, attract great attention—and however the minds of beholders may be perplexed, curiosity at least is active. These neologists, or palaeontologists, in Art are not losing ground; their strict observations and minute imitation of Nature seem even to have awakened some of the 'older masters' of the Royal Academy to the necessity of paying more attention than they hitherto have to colour and detail. In fact, Raphaelism in Art seems in some respects to be a part and parcel of the spirit of the present age and akin to tractarianism in faith. It is the reaction and an antagonism to the conventional, the sensual and the unbelieving—and has the falsehood and exaggeration common to reactions in general. Its object is, to give new life to dry bones, and to spiritualize the formal and the material. It is the protest of the nineteenth century against the seventeenth and the eighteenth especially. This psychological reaction commenced some fifty years ago in metaphysical Germany; and what Tieck, Schlegel and Plattner thought, Overbeck and Cornelius painted, with others who thought that Art was purer and truer and holier one hour *before* Raphael was born than one hour *after* he died. Such is the faith of the Pre-Raphaelites. Art, they say, culminated in him,—after a gradual, healthful, beautiful growth. . . .

We shall not repeat our former remarks on the obvious blemishes of these reformers,—nor dwell on their conceits, puerilities, pedantries or finical prettinesses of thought and of treatment, at variance with and beneath true Art. We have pointed out their contempt of aerial and linear perspective and of chiar-oscuro. One trick may be substituted for another,—and in the close but misdirected observance and imitation of everything, and in a neglect of selection, the relative value of form and colour may be lost sight of, until the surfeited eye sickens at an atomic analysis which demands the microscope to examine and the leisure of monastic illuminators to execute it. In some measure this is the reaction against ultra-Turnerism; which left too much to the imagination, and only shadowed forth what might and ought to have been better expressed by outline and detail. But this reaction carried to the extreme involves a sacrifice of the end to the means. Assuredly, neither Giotto nor Cimabue, were they now living, would reject the modern discoveries and appliances of science and cling to the ways and means of the painters of missals and of glass windows. These pioneers of Art toiled to clear the way for progress,—and never would have retrograded by restoring the obsolete, reproducing the faulty, or for a moment ignoring the advantages hardly won in so long a battle. Nor have we much ultimate fear of men like Mr. Millais. Mind and talent will manifest themselves whatever the vehicle, and will pierce through and ultimately reject the eccentric and the fantastic; and already we see, to some extent, the bursting of his self-imposed bonds. The danger to be apprehended is, that the disciples of this modern antique school will out-Herod their teacher, and imitate blemishes rather than excellencies,—restoring the form without revivifying the spirit,—regathering the rubrical symbolic husks without the kernel. They will labour in vain,—for the incredulity, scepticism and science of the nineteenth century are not to be contented with the pictorial pap and panada that satisfied the simple faith and ignorance of mankind's mediaeval infancy.

Mr. Millais—the Raphael of our Pre-Raphaelites, and whose powers of thought, execution and industry are undeniable—contributes three pictures. *Ophelia* has been the subject of much discussion and difference of opinion, condemnation and admiration. The moment chosen is, that of the drowning of the ill-fated maiden, as told in 'Hamlet'. The willow branch on which she has clambered has broken; and she floats awhile on the 'glassy stream'—rendered, however, too much like a still pond,—borne up by her clothes, and chanting snatches, until she is pulled down by her 'garments, heavy with their drink.' On looking closely into the painting, the finish is marvellous. The pollard trunk, the velvetty green rind of the 'envious sliver', the moss and flowers and vegetable details, are positively mirrored as in a glass. The water-lily is the botanical study of a Linneus:— every incident and accident is depicted. Some of the leaves are green and vigorous, others are spotted, corroded and broken:—no form or phase is unobserved or omitted. Ophelia sinks so composedly and gradually, that the idea of one of Dr. Arnott's comfortable water-beds is suggested. Gorgeous as is her fantastic dress and gay the blue and red flowers of her 'weedy trophies,' the flesh tints of her face and hands entirely hold their own. The expression aimed at is, that of an incapability of estimating 'her own distress.' The open mouth is somewhat gaping and gabyish,—the expression is in no way suggestive of her past tale. There is no pathos, no melancholy, no one brightening up, no last lucid interval. If she die swan-like with a song, there is no sound or melody, no poetry in this strain. Rightly to appreciate the general chromatic effect, this picture should be looked at from a little distance, when it becomes quite luminous.

No. 156, a small portrait of *Mrs. Patmore* is a painted daguerreotype. The nose of the full face actually projects, the red ribbon and flowers are finished off with a miniature nicety; yet the solidity and substance of the flesh will stand comparison with the real living faces of the fair gazers who shame so many of the chalky milk-and-water—London milk-and-water— inanities and unrealities suspended around, as if to point out the differences between dear nature and such libels.

Mr. Millais's best work is, No. 478. A Huguenot refuses to permit his Catholic mistress to bind round his arm her handkerchief as a white badge by which he might escape the massacre on St. Bartholomew's Day. The lovers meet under an ivy-mantled mossy red brick wall; and minute delineation cannot be carried further than in this wall. The weather stains and infinite variety of tints convey the impression of reality itself. Nothing is left to the imagination. Equal attention has been lavished on the nasturtium and red flowers in the foreground:—for, to particularize details instead of aiming at general effects is one end which these worshippers of truth hold too sacred to be compromised. If this principle is to be logically carried out, critics have a right to inquire how these nasturtiums bloom and flower so tenderly on the 24th of August, and whether jonquils and dogroses blossom simultaneously. To pass, however, from the almanack to Art.—The lovers are locked in a close embrace,—and, for want of atmospheric perspective, seem somewhat jammed into the wall. Some additional awkwardness arises in the attitude of the lover from only one of his legs being shown,—and that one not of the most elegant shape. A full daylight falls on the wan face which is upturned to his with a touching expression of mingled beseeching, imploring, saddened, and terrified tenderness. Her pure perfect love is for him and for his soul, for this world and for the next. He looks wistfully down on her,—fully conscious of the sacrifice he is about to make in this struggle between love and creed; and while he draws her nearer to his heart with one hand, with the other—truer to his Calvinism—he firmly unlooses the scarf which she fondly tries to fasten. Her pale countenance is heightened by her sable costume, and the pathos is increased by the rich fantastic purple of the once gay lover. The depth of colour and luminous glow will be best felt by the killing effect which this picture produces on some of its unfortunate neighbours. It would be curious to see this power tested by a juxtaposition with *The Destruction of Sodom* by Mr. Martin. This is one of that artist's usual pictorial pyrotechnics. The grand display of fireworks takes place under a crimson stalactitical arch-work of most explosive and Demdaniel character. These Biblical subjects are popular,—as in the case of those by West. Taken from the book with which the many are most familiar, the subject rather than the art attracts. Mr. Martin, whose conception is colossal and grandiose, is monotonous in colouring. His lurid flames rather ascend from below than descend from above. The dark lines of square towers are opposed with no great art to the fiery chasm of the crater centre. The white figures of Lot and his daughters are too cold under circumstances where the refraction must have been most warm. There is some good granulation and texture painting in the rocks to the right,—which, however, are coloured too much like the plumage of woodcocks.—Mr. Hunt follows closely on Mr. Millais with *The Hireling Shepherd*. The neglected sheep 'lie in the corn,' while the stout peasant idles with a buxom lass. Mr. Hunt who has 'an oath in heaven' to tell 'the whole truth and nothing but the truth,' carries anti-eclecticism to the absurd. Like Swift, he revels in the repulsive. These rustics are of the coarsest breed,—ill favoured, ill fed, ill washed. Not to dwell on cutaneous and other minutiae,—they are literal transcripts of stout, sunburnt, out-of-door labourers. Their faces, bursting with a plethora of health, and a trifle too flushed and rubicund, suggest their over-attention to the beer or cyder keg on the boor's back. The youth holds a death's-head moth up to his sweetheart, and presses on while she draws back half scared, half amused. The faces and arms are stippled in with miniature care, and tinted as if both had fed on madder or been busy with raspberries, and would be none the worse for a course of brimstone. Downright literal truth is followed out in every accessory; each sedge, moss, and weed—each sheep—each tree pollard or pruned—each crop, beans or corn—is faithfully imitated. Summer heat pervades the atmosphere,—the grain is ripe,—the swifts skim about,—and the purple clouds cast purple shadows. The woman cools her red-hot feet near some scanty water, which is cold, chalky, and white. The romp and rubicundity of this pair contrast with the pallor and pathos of Mr. Millais's picture.

Mr. Hunt's 'Love in Idleness' may be compared with *Love and Labour* by Mr. Redgrave. This is a charming bit of rural incident,—redolent of sweet upland grass. A row of mowers—somewhat too much in a row—are cresting a hill slope, and keeping a workmanlike time with step and scythe right pleasing to farmer's eye. Their heads, however, are varied. Behind rises a gentle hill on which chequered gleams and shadows play charmingly about. The soft turf, as well as the waving grass, is nicely marked with varied, short, silken tints. The blue sea opens beyond a clump of trees, admirably massed and toned with rich, deep blues that serve as a background for the two principal figures,—a rustic lad and lass, who make love while the labourers make hay, or mow—to speak by the card. The female is pulling a flower to pieces while her swain looks on and woos. His bare legs can scarcely be considered appropriate, or fitted for field work where snakes and thistles do abound,—her attitude is awkward, and her poorly coloured draperies are cast in mean and common-place folds. The accessories in the foreground—the kegs, bottles, baskets, and so forth—are excellently made out and painted. The general effect of the landscape is delicious.

Some of the disciples of Mr. Millais already evince a tendency to exaggerate his mannerisms. Thus, Mr. Collins shows us *May in the Regent's Park* from a window in Sussex Place; and so minute is the scale—the very 'form and pressure' of the flowers, red, white and blue, and of the shrubs—that we could creep about and through them. The botanical predominates altogether over the artistical,—and to a vicious and mistaken extreme. In nature there is air as well as earth,—she masses and generalizes where these facsimile makers split hairs and particularize. They take a branch, a flower, a blade of grass, place it close before them and as closely copy it,—forgetting that these objects, at the distance imagined in the picture, and reduced to its scale, could by no means be seen with such *hortus siccus* minuteness. . . . No. 1091 is taken from the legend of *St. Elizabeth of Hungary*. This maiden of precocious piety was wont, when she found the chapel door shut, to kneel at its outside. The representations of texture are perfect; the strong wall is as true as is the oak graining of the door. The hinges are most mediaeval and Puginesque,—the costume of blue and green shot silk is Byzantine. The hands and face of the maiden adhere nicely to the flat surface,—but the expression is rather pouting than devout, and the countenance is more pinky and school-girlish than saint-like.

Mr. W. H. Millais in No. 1120 carries his minute imitations into the farm yard,—and depicts with much care and patience red brick walls and buildings, brown trees, pigs, poultry, and straw litter. —Mr. W. C. Thomas in No. 448 restores Laura to Avignon as it was in her lifetime. The sage

Sennuccio, orientally attired, touches his white 'wide-awake' to a pale and plain lady, and reproves a mediaevally clad coxcomb who looks upon the pious maiden somewhat irreverently, and as a modern dandy might at a fair Bennettite Belgravian;—a beggar woman and a boy on a pineapple-laden donkey approve of the sage Sennuccio. The pavement reminds us of apple dumplings. The composition is well studied,—although the general tones are flat and tame. Here, as is common in the case of these ultra Pre-Raphaelites, the mediaeval missal recurs to the spectator.—No. 463, by Mr. F. M. Brown, is more ambitious:—*The Saviour washes Peter's Feet.* This artist appears to have studied at Valencia, where mulberries are plentiful as blackberries. He has closely observed the works of Joannes, where the purple tone is so predominant. In this picture it pervades everything— the hair, the naked limbs of the Saviour, and the dress of St. Peter,—who either feels himself unworthy of the honour done him by his divine Master, or by his feet's action makes us feel the water to be too hot. Certainly the copper utensil which contains it seems filled with either blood or raspberries undergoing the jam process. The Apostles in general, seated at a table, take no interest in the lavation,—appearing rather bored:—so much has the artist rejected the conventional attitudes usual on this occasion. St. John must be cited as an exception; he leans over with affection and attention. To these crimson tints, No. 455, a portrait of *Captain W. Cook*, by Mr. A. Craig, and No. 473, a portrait of *Thomas Cooke* Esq., by Mr. Patten, are certainly two solid sable supporters:—but too many 'cooks' sometimes spoil the best compositions.

In the portrait department, Mr. Knight maintains his reputation in six pictures, marked with his decided expression of individuality and power of representing costume and texture. An over-tendency to purple tones in his fleshes may be noticed. The portrait of *Mr. Thomas Vaughan*, 'during half a century a faithful servant of the Royal Academy' is very forcible, and keeps its own while surrounded by real life. Intelligence still beams in the bright eye, while coming senility hangs on the lip. The hands and the various veins are carefully studied. In *The Bishop of Exeter*, we miss the keen searching spirit of the eye, and the peculiar complexion of the countenance. The prelate—pale and temperate in reality—appears to belong to the order of abbots 'purple as their wines.' The blushing genial tints, the fruit of feasts not fasts, seem more appropriate bestowed on *The Lord Mayor, St. John Musgrove.* His worship's costume is admirable, and the gold embroidery is effective without being too much bedizened or made out. The countenance is radiant and full of placidity and good nature. In No. 158 we recognize the same master touch. The likeness must be perfect. The head is placed too high on the canvas, and the stick—we conclude a portrait was no doubt forced on the artist.—*A Student* is the portrait of a bright eyed ingenuous youth; and it is not possible to paint the texture of velvet with greater force or truth than in this picture. . . .

Among the painters of history, Mr. Ward is here the observed of all observers. He lends but one picture, *Charlotte Corday going to Execution*. In this incident—professedly historically treated—the portrait of the heroine is, we understand, not authentic. Clad in a crimson, somewhat sack-like dress, the garb and colour of a murderess, she quits her cell for the scaffold. This Judith, who had freed the world from the miscreant Marat, advances with erect step and serious but collected countenance, fully conscious of her doom, and prepared to meet it. On the whole, as the immediate centre of action and interest, this figure must, we think, be considered a failure. She descends into an outer cell, where Robespierre, Danton and Desmoulins are assembled to gaze on the features and speculate on the expression of one whose 'fanaticism' might have doomed them also to death. Her air of quiet resignation contrasts with that of a red-capped Dame de la Halle,—one of those furies of the Revolution whose children devoured sisters and mothers. The action of this virago is masculine, without any great meaning. Robespierre, dressed as a silken dandy, with his bouquet, presents a mixture of the *petit maître* and the *tigre singe*. He holds in a huge mastiff. More humanity beams in the eye of the brute than in those of any of the bipeds, a good old curé excepted. Near this muscadin of the guillotine is seated Danton,—the personification in mind, body and dress of a coarse, bloated, top-booted ruffian. An open archway discloses the scaffold and the infuriated hordes of mob spectators. This portico is feebly painted and wants air:—otherwise, the subject is, for the most part, handled with great force of design and fierce intensity of colour. The details—the masonry, the tiles, the rusted iron bars, the sentinels and the cat—are conscientiously studied and wrought out. The general character of subject and treatment is very French. There is blood on the hand, and a tricolor terrorism that grieves the eye with glare and executive hardness. There is no gradation, no tenderness, no mercy in the tones. The specialities of the guillotine have been enforced and insisted on. The picture attracts, in addition to its truth and power, by exciting a curiosity akin to the morbid feeling which hurries multitudes to witness a real execution. For our own part, we take no pleasure in beholding a woman led to premature death while furies and ruffians live.

Mr. Maclise sends but one picture.—*Alfred and the Saxon King disguised as a Minstrel in the Tent of Guthrum the Dane*. A yellowish tent, decorated with warlike implements, is hung up to branches of oaks, flowering red and white May, and long-leaved chesnuts. In the foreground are grouped chain-mailed warriors lying down 'at ease.' Some are gambling with dice—winners, losers and indifferent; others are drinking deeply—in all the different stages of inebriety, from the friendly convivial to the dead drunk. Alfred in palmer guise, scowls on them, and strikes his harp, to which the crowned king listens. The monarch reclines, with his court, on a gorgeous couch cribbed, cabined and confined in a punt-like tent too small for so great a company. In fact, the soldiers in the foreground are the real heroes and masters of the melodramatic scene,—otherwise they never could be permitted to misbehave in every way under the very eye of their commander. We feel that the whole performance is a sham. There is no breath of life—no vitality—no reality in these forms—which in colour and hardness might be lay figures dead and dressed, or wooden toys from Nuremberg. We cannot sympathize with these Gog-Magog beings, who have nothing in common with our humanity, and may be the denizens of Mars or of some other planet. Such is the outline of this fricasee of limbs,—this gorgeous kaleidoscope of colour, action and attitude, and all in the superlative degree. Indeed, few things seem too large for Mr. Maclise's conception, none too minute for his detail. He is too rich,—and we strain. Our pictorial athlete has the power of a giant without his forbearance. Full of energy and in the highest condition, his blows are misdirected and his strength wasted. The only power that he wants is, that of selection. His gems are cast profusely about, as it were, unstrung,—and we know not which to pick up first, or where to begin. In vain we look for some key-note—some emphatic principal interest. . . . The facility and exuberance are incontestable—the imitation of still life is wonderful—the nicety of detail and execution—the flowers, mosses, weeds, armour—the heraldic tricking and infinite accessories—might make a Pre-Raphaelite despair. How much talent is here frittered away and labour wasted, to the positive injury of the main interest of the subject? We know few artists to whom the easy summer trips to Madrid would be more beneficial than to Mr. Maclise. At the first glance at Velasquez, there only to be seen, he would learn the art of allowing the imagination of the spectator to come into play. Woe to the author who says all he can say, leaving nothing in the inkstand!—and woe to the painter who leaves nothing on his palette! . . .

(*The Athenaeum*, 22 May 1852, pp. 581–3.)

Letter from Lowell Mason (Sept. 1852)   IV.3

Whatever may be the reason, the *fact* is certain, that in England the *Messiah* is vastly more popular than any other oratorio. The best judges of music, professors and amateurs, the learned and the unlearned, the noble and the ignoble, the great and the little, those who ride in proud carriages, with servants liveried with buff and scarlet, and those who walk through the rain with a cotton umbrella, the old and grave, the young and gay, those who love music, and those who do not know whether they have any love for it or not;—all do homage to this mighty production of Handel. Handel is the Shakespeare of music; there has never been but one Handel, and it is not at all probable that there will ever be another. Handel has written but one *Messiah*, nor could he, had he lived until this time, have written another. He might have improved upon this, but another of equal merit, he could not have produced. This oratorio has been heard for a century, and it is as fresh and new now as ever; indeed the more it is heard the better it is appreciated. This oratorio, too, has done much for charity; it has succored the orphan, comforted the widow, and relieved the distressed. . . . The amount received at the performance of the *Messiah*, this morning, was somewhat more than THIRTEEN THOUSAND AND FIVE HUNDRED DOLLARS.

(*Musical Letters from Abroad*, 1854, Letter XLIII.)

IV.4 John Ruskin, from 'The Nature of Gothic' (1853)

I shall endeavour therefore to give the reader in this chapter an idea, at once broad and definite, of the true nature of *Gothic* architecture, properly so called; . . .

§ II. The principal difficulty in doing this arises from the fact that every building of the Gothic period differs in some important respect from every other; and many include features which, if they occurred in other buildings, would not be considered Gothic at all; so that all we have to reason upon is merely, if I may be allowed so to express it, a greater or less degree of *Gothicness* in each building we examine. And it is this Gothicness,—the character which, according as it is found more or less in a building, makes it more or less Gothic,—of which I want to define the nature; and I feel the same kind of difficulty in doing so which would be encountered by any one who undertook to explain, for instance, the nature of Redness, without any actually red thing to point to, but only orange and purple things. Suppose he had only a piece of heather and a dead oak-leaf to do it with. He might say, the colour which is mixed with the yellow in this oak-leaf, and with the blue in this heather, would be red, if you had it separate; but it would be difficult, nevertheless, to make the abstraction perfectly intelligible: and it is so in a far greater degree to make the abstraction of the Gothic character intelligible, because that character itself is made up of many mingled ideas, and can consist only in their union. That is to say, pointed arches do not constitute Gothic, nor vaulted roofs, nor flying buttresses, nor grotesque sculptures; but all or some of these things, and many other things with them, when they come together so as to have life. . . .

§ VI. I believe, then, that the characteristic or moral elements of Gothic are the following, placed in the order of their importance:

1. Savageness.
2. Changefulness.
3. Naturalism.

J. Ruskin   J. C. Armytage

6. Windows of the Fourth Order, from *Stones of Venice* 1853

4. Grotesqueness.
5. Rigidity.
6. Redundance.

These characters are here expressed as belonging to the building; as belonging to the builder, they would be expressed thus:—1. Savageness, or Rudeness. 2. Love of Change. 3. Love of Nature. 4. Disturbed Imagination. 5. Obstinacy. 6. Generosity. And I repeat, that the withdrawal of any one, or any two, will not at once destroy the Gothic character of a building, but the removal of a majority of them will. I shall proceed to examine them in their order. . . .

§ IX. If, however, the savageness of Gothic architecture, merely as an expression of its origin among Northern nations, may be considered, in some sort, a noble character, it possesses a higher nobility still, when considered as an index, not of climate, but of religious principle. . . . The Greek gave to the lower workman no subject which he could not perfectly execute. The Assyrian gave him subjects which he could only execute imperfectly, but fixed a legal standard for his imperfection. The workman was, in both systems, a slave.

§ X. But in the mediaeval, or especially Christian, system of ornament, this slavery is done away with altogether; Christianity having recognized, in small things as well as great, the individual value of every soul. But it not only recognizes its value; it confesses its imperfection, in only bestowing dignity upon the acknowledgment of unworthiness . . . And it is, perhaps, the principal admirableness of the Gothic schools of architecture, that they thus receive the results of the labour of inferior minds; and out of fragments full of imperfection, and betraying that imperfection in every touch, indulgently raise up a stately and unaccusable whole.

§ XI. But the modern English mind has this much in common with that of the Greek, that it intensely desires, in all things, the utmost completion or perfection compatible with their nature. This is a noble character in the abstract, but becomes ignoble when it causes us to forget the relative dignities of that nature itself, and to prefer the perfectness of the lower nature to the imperfection of the higher; . . . And this is what we have to do with all our labourers; to look for the *thoughtful* part of them, and get that out of them, whatever we lose for it, whatever faults and errors we are obliged to take with it. For the best that is in them cannot manifest itself, but in company with much error. Understand this clearly: You can teach a man to draw a straight line, and to cut one; to strike a curved line, and to carve it; and to copy and carve any number of given lines or forms, with admirable speed and perfect precision; and you find his work perfect of its kind: but if you ask him to think about any of those forms, to consider if he cannot find any better in his own head, he stops; his execution becomes hesitating; he thinks, and ten to one he thinks wrong; ten to one he makes a mistake in the first touch he gives to his work as a thinking being. But you have made a man of him for all that. He was only a machine before, an animated tool.

§ XII. And observe, you are put to stern choice in this matter. You must either make a tool of the creature, or a man of him. You cannot make both. Men were not intended to work with the accuracy of tools, to be precise and perfect in all their actions. If you will have that precision out of them, and make their fingers measure degrees like cog-wheels, and their arms strike curves like compasses, you must unhumanize them. All the energy of their spirits must be given to make cogs and compasses of themselves. All their attention and strength must go to the accomplishment of the mean act. The eye of the soul must be bent upon the finger-point, and the soul's force must fill all the invisible nerves that guide it, ten hours a day, that it may not err from its steely precision, and so soul and sight be worn away, and the whole human being be lost at last—a heap of sawdust, so far as its intellectual work in this world is concerned; saved only by its Heart, which cannot go into the form of cogs and compasses, but expands, after the ten hours are over, into fireside humanity. On the other hand, if you will make a man of the working creature, you cannot make a tool. Let him but begin to imagine, to think, to try to do anything worth doing; and the engine-turned precision is lost at once. Out come all his roughness, all his dulness, all his incapability; shame upon shame, failure upon failure, pause after pause: but out comes the whole majesty of him also; and we know the height of it only, when we see the clouds settling upon him. And, whether the clouds be bright or dark, there will be transfiguration behind and within them.

§ XIII. And now, reader, look round this English room of yours, about which you have been proud so often, because the work of it was so good and strong, and the ornaments of it so finished. Examine again all those accurate mouldings, and perfect polishings, and unerring adjustments of the seasoned wood and tempered steel. Many a time you have exulted over them, and thought how great England was, because her slightest work was done so thoroughly. Alas! if read rightly, these perfectnesses are signs of a slavery in our England a thousand times more bitter and more degrading than that of the scourged African, or helot Greek. . . .

§ XIV. And, on the other hand, go forth again to gaze upon the old cathedral front, where you have smiled so often at the fantastic ignorance of the old sculptors: examine once more those ugly goblins, and formless monsters, and stern statues, anatomiless and rigid; but do not mock at them, for they are signs of the life and liberty of every workman who struck the stone; a freedom of thought, and rank in scale of being, such as no laws, no charters, no charities can secure; but which it must be the first aim of all Europe at this day to regain for her children. . . .

§ XVI. We have much studied and much perfected, of late, the great civilized invention of the division of labour; only we give it a false name. It is not, truly speaking, the labour that is divided; but the men:—Divided into mere segments of men—broken into small fragments and crumbs of life; so that all the little piece of intelligence that is left in a man is not enough to make a pin, or a nail, but exhausts itself in making the point of a pin, or the head of a nail. Now it is a good and desirable thing, truly, to make many pins in a day; but if we could only see with what crystal sand their points were polished,—sand of human soul, much to be magnified before it can be discerned for what it is,—we should think there might be some loss in it also. And the great cry that rises from all our manufacturing cities, louder than their furnace blast, is all in very deed for this,—that we manufacture everything there except men; we blanch cotton, and strengthen steel, and refine sugar, and shape pottery; but to brighten, to strengthen, to refine, or to form a single living spirit, never enters into our estimate of advantages. And all the evil to which that cry is urging our myriads can be met only in one way: not by teaching nor preaching, for to teach them is but to show them their misery, and to preach to them, if we do nothing more than preach, is to mock at it. It can be met only by a right understanding, on the part of all classes, of what kinds of labour are good for men, raising them, and making them happy; by a determined sacrifice of such convenience, or beauty, or cheapness as is to be got only by the degradation of the workman; and by equally determined demand for the products and results of healthy and ennobling labour.

§ XVII. And how, it will be asked, are these products to be recognized, and this demand to be regulated? Easily: by the observance of three broad and simple rules:

1. Never encourage the manufacture of any article not absolutely necessary, in the production of which *Invention* has no share.

2. Never demand an exact finish for its own sake, but only for some practical or noble end.

3. Never encourage imitation or copying of any kind, except for the sake of preserving record of great works. . . .

§ XXII. I should be led far from the matter in hand, if I were to pursue this interesting subject. Enough, I trust, has been said to show the reader that the rudeness or imperfection which at first rendered the term 'Gothic' one of reproach is indeed, when rightly understood, one of the most noble characters of Christian architecture, and not only a noble but an *essential* one. It seems a fantastic paradox, but it is nevertheless a most important truth, that no architecture can be truly noble which is *not* imperfect. . . .

§ XXVI. The second mental element above named was CHANGEFULNESS, or Variety.

I have already enforced the allowing independent operation to the inferior workman, simply as a duty *to him*, and as ennobling the architecture by rendering it more Christian. We have now to consider what reward we obtain for the performance of this duty, namely, the perpetual variety of every feature of the building.

Wherever the workman is utterly enslaved, the parts of the building must of course be absolutely like each other; for the perfection of his execution can only be reached by exercising him in doing one thing, and giving him nothing else to do. The degree in which the workman is degraded may be thus known at a glance, by observing whether the several parts of the building are similar or not; and if, as in Greek work, all the capitals are alike, and all the mouldings unvaried, then the degradation is complete; if, as in Egyptian or Ninevite work, though the manner of executing certain figures is always the same, the order of design is perpetually varied, the degradation is less total; if, as in Gothic work, there is perpetual change both in design and execution, the workman must have been altogether set free.

§ XXVII. How much the beholder gains from the liberty of the labourer may perhaps be questioned in England, where one of the strongest instincts in nearly every mind is that Love of Order which makes us desire that our house windows should pair like our carriage horses, and allows us to yield our faith unhesitatingly to architectural theories which fix a form for everything, and forbid variation from it. I would not impeach love of order: it is one of the most useful elements of the English mind; it helps us in our commerce and in all purely practical matters; and it is in many cases one of the foundation stones of morality. Only do not let us suppose that love of order is love of art. . . .

§ XXVIII. But our higher instincts are not deceived. We take no pleasure in the building provided for us, resembling that which we take in a new book or a new picture. We may be proud of its size, complacent in its correctness, and happy in its convenience. We may take the same pleasure in its symmetry and workmanship as in a well-ordered room, or a skilful piece of manufacture. And this we suppose to be all the pleasure that architecture was ever intended to give us. The idea of reading a building as we would read Milton or Dante, and getting the same kind of delight out of the stones as out of the stanzas, never enters our minds for a moment. . . .

§ XXX. And this we confess in deeds, though not in words. All the pleasure which the people of the nineteenth century take in art, is in pictures, sculpture, minor objects of virtù, or mediaeval architecture, which we enjoy under the term picturesque: no pleasure is taken anywhere in modern buildings, and we find all men of true feeling delighting to escape out of modern cities into natural scenery: hence, as I shall hereafter show, that peculiar love of landscape which is characteristic of the age. It would be well, if, in all other matters, we were as ready to put up with what we dislike, for the sake of compliance with established law, as we are in architecture.

(*Stones of Venice*, 1853, vol. 2, Ch. VI.)

IV.5 **John Ruskin, from 'The Opening of the Crystal Palace considered in Some of its Relations to the Prospects of Art' (1854)**

I read the account in the 'Times' newspaper of the opening of the Crystal Palace at Sydenham, as I ascended the hill between Vevay and Chatel St Denis, and the thoughts which it called up haunted me all day long, as my road wound among the grassy slopes of the Simmenthal. There was a strange contrast between the image of that mighty palace, raised so high above the hills on which it is built as to make them seem little else than a basement for its glittering stateliness, and those low larch huts, half hidden beneath their coverts of forest, and scattered like grey stones along the masses of far away mountain. Here, man contending with the power of Nature for his existence; there, commanding them for his recreation: here a feeble folk nested among the rocks with the wild goat and the coney, and retaining the same quiet thoughts from generation to generation; there, a great multitude triumphing in the splendour of immeasurable habitation, and haughty with hope of endless progress and irresistible power.

It is indeed impossible to limit, in imagination, the beneficent results which may follow from the undertaking thus happily begun. For the first time in the history of the world, a national museum is formed in which a whole nation is interested; formed on a scale which permits the exhibition of monuments of art in unbroken symmetry, and of the productions of nature in unthwarted growth,—formed under the auspices of science which can hardly err, and of wealth which can hardly be exhausted; and placed in the close neighbourhood of a metropolis overflowing with a population weary of labour, yet thirsting for knowledge, where contemplation may be consistent with rest, and instruction with enjoyment. It is impossible, I repeat, to estimate the influence of such an institution on the minds of the working-classes. How many hours once wasted may now be profitably dedicated to pursuits in which interest was first awakened by some accidental display in the Norwood palace; how many constitutions, almost broken, may be restored by the healthy temptation into the country air,—how many intellects, once dormant, may be roused into activity within the crystal walls, and how these noble results may go on multiplying and increasing and bearing fruit seventy times sevenfold, as the nation pursues its career,—are questions as full of hope as incapable of calculation. But with all these grounds for hope there are others for despondency, giving rise to a group of melancholy thoughts, of which I can neither repress the importunity nor forbear the expression.

For three hundred years, the art of architecture has been the subject of the most curious investigation; its principles have been discussed with all earnestness and acuteness; its models in all countries and of all ages have been examined with scrupulous care, and imitated with unsparing expenditure. And of all this refinement of enquiry,—this lofty search after the ideal,—this subtlety of investigation and sumptuousness of practice,—the great result, the admirable and long—expected conclusion is, that in the centre of the nineteenth century, we suppose ourselves to have invented a new style of architecture, when we have magnified a conservatory!

In Mr Laing's speech, at the opening of the palace, he declares that '*an entirely novel order of architecture*, producing, by means of unrivalled mechanical ingenuity, the most marvellous and beautiful effects, sprang into existence to provide a building.' In these words, the speaker is not merely giving utterance to his own feelings. He is expressing the popular view of the facts, nor that a view merely popular, but one which has been encouraged by nearly all the professors of art of our time.

It is to this, then, that our Doric and Palladian pride is at last reduced! We have vaunted the divinity of the Greek ideal—we have plumed ourselves on the purity of our Italian taste—we have cast our whole souls into the proportions of pillars, and the relations of orders—and behold the end! Our taste, thus exalted and disciplined, is dazzled by the lustre of a few rows of panes of glass; and the first principles of architectural sublimity, so far sought, are found all the while to have consisted merely in sparkling and in space.

Let it not be thought that I would depreciate (were it possible to depreciate) the mechanical ingenuity which has been displayed in the erection of the Crystal Palace, or that I underrate the effect which its vastness may continue to produce on the popular imagination. But mechanical ingenuity is *not* the essence either of painting or architecture: and largeness of dimension does not necessarily involve nobleness of design. There is assuredly as much ingenuity required to build a screw frigate, or a tubular bridge as a hall of glass;—all these are works characteristic of the age; and all, in their several ways, deserve our highest admiration; but not admiration of the kind that is rendered to poetry or to art. We may cover the German Ocean with frigates, and bridge the Bristol Channel with iron, and roof the county of Middlesex with crystal, and yet not possess one Milton, or Michael Angelo.

Well, it may be replied, we need our bridges, and have pleasure in our palaces; but we do not want Miltons, nor Michael Angelos.

Truly, it seems so; for, in the year in which the first Crystal Palace was built, there died among us a man whose name, in after ages, will stand with those of the great of all time [i.e. J. M. W. Turner (1775–1851)]. Dying, he bequeathed to the nation the whole mass of his most cherished works: and for these three years, while we have been building this colossal receptacle for casts and copies of the art of other nations, these works of our own greatest painter have been left to decay in a dark room near Cavendish Square, under the custody of an aged servant.

This is quite natural. But it is also memorable.

There is another interesting fact connected with the history of the Crystal Palace as it bears on that of the art of Europe, namely, that in the year 1851, when all that glittering roof was built, in order to exhibit the petty arts of our fashionable luxury—the carved bedsteads of Vienna, and glued toys of Switzerland, and gay jewellery of France—in that very year, I say, the greatest pictures of the Venetian masters were rotting at Venice in the rain, for want of roof to cover them, with holes made by cannon shot through their canvass.

There is another fact, however, more curious than either of these, which will hereafter be connected with the history of the palace now in building; namely, that at the very period when Europe is congratulated on the invention of a new style of architecture, because fourteen acres of ground have been covered with glass, the greatest examples in existence of true and noble Christian architecture were being resolutely destroyed; and destroyed by the effects of the very interest which was slowly beginning to be excited by them.

Under the firm and wise government of the third Napoleon, France has entered on a new epoch of prosperity, one of the signs of which is a zealous care for the preservation of her noble public buildings. Under the influence of this healthy impulse, repairs of the most extensive kind are at this moment proceeding, on the cathedrals of Rheims, Amiens, Rouen, Chartres, and Paris; (probably also in many other instances unknown to me). These repairs were, in many cases, necessary up to a certain point; and they have been executed by architects as skilful and learned as at present exist,—executed with noble disregard of expense, and sincere desire on the part of their superintendents that they should be completed in a manner honourable to the country.

They are nevertheless more fatal to the monuments they are intended to preserve, than fire, war, or revolution. For they are undertaken, in the plurality of instances, under an impression, which the efforts of all true antiquaries have as yet been unable to remove, that it is possible to reproduce the mutilated sculpture of past ages in its original beauty . . .

I have great respect for human nature. But I would rather leave it to others than myself to pronounce how far such a temptation is always likely to be resisted, and how far, when repairs are once permitted to be undertaken, a fabric is likely to be spared from mere interest in its beauty, when its destruction, under the name of restoration, has become permanently remunerative to a large body of workmen. . .

The peculiar character of the evil which is being wrought by this age is its utter irreparableness. Its newly formed schools of art, its extending galleries, and well-ordered museums will assuredly bear some fruit in time, and give once more to the popular mind the power to discern what is great, and the disposition to protect what is precious. But it will be too late. We shall wander through our palaces of crystal, gazing sadly on copies of pictures torn by cannon-shot, and on casts of sculpture dashed to pieces long ago. We shall gradually learn to distinguish originality and sincerity from the decrepitudes of imitation and palsies of repetition; but it will be only in hopelessness to recognise the truth, that architecture and painting can be 'restored' when the dead can be raised.—and not till then.

('The Opening of the Crystal Palace . . . ', 1854, pp. 1–5.)

Charles Dickens, from 'On Strike' (11 Feb. 1854)   IV.6

Travelling down to Preston a week from this date, I chanced to sit opposite to a very acute, very determined, very emphatic personage, with a stout railway rug so drawn over his chest that he looked as if he were sitting up in bed with his great coat, hat, and gloves on, severely contemplating your humble servant from behind a large blue and grey checked counterpane. In calling him emphatic, I do not mean that he was warm; he was coldly and bitingly emphatic as a frosty wind is.

'You are going through to Preston, sir?' says he, as soon as we were clear of the Primrose Hill tunnel.

The receipt of his question was like the receipt of a jerk of the nose; he was so short and sharp.

'Yes.'

'This Preston strike is a nice piece of business!' said the gentleman. 'A pretty piece of business!'

'It is very much to be deplored,' said I, 'on all accounts.'

'They want to be ground. That's what they want, to bring 'em to their senses,' said the gentleman; whom I had already began to call in my own mind Mr. Snapper, and whom I may as well call by that name here as by any other.

I deferentially enquired, who wanted to be ground?

'The hands,' said Mr. Snapper. 'The hands on strike, and the hands who help 'em.'

I remarked that if that was all they wanted, they must be a very unreasonable people, for surely they had had a little grinding, one way and another, already. Mr. Snapper eyed me with sternness, and after opening and shutting his leathern-gloved hands several times outside his counterpane, asked me abruptly, 'Was I a delegate?'

I set Mr. Snapper right on that point, and told him I was no delegate.

'I am glad to hear it,' said Mr. Snapper. 'But a friend to the Strike, I believe?'

'Not at all,' said I.

'A friend to the Lock-out?' pursued Mr. Snapper.

'Not in the least,' said I.

177

Mr. Snapper's rising opinion of me fell again, and he gave me to understand that a man *must* either be a friend to the Masters or a friend to the Hands.

'He may be a friend to both,' said I.

Mr. Snapper didn't see that; there was no medium in the Political Economy of the subject. I retorted on Mr. Snapper, that Political Economy was a great and useful science in its own way and its own place; but that I did not transplant my definition of it from the Common Prayer Book, and make it a great king above all gods. Mr. Snapper tucked himself up as if to keep me off, folded his arms on the top of his counterpane, leaned back, and looked out of window.

'Pray what would you have, sir,' enquired Mr. Snapper, suddenly withdrawing his eyes from the prospect to me, 'in the relations between Capital and Labor, *but* Political Economy?'

I always avoid the stereotyped terms in these discussions as much as I can, for I have observed, in my little way, that they often supply the place of sense and moderation. I therefore took my gentleman up with the words employers and employed, in preference to Capital and Labor.

'I believe,' said I, 'that into the relations between employers and employed, as into all the relations of this life, there must enter something of feeling and sentiment; something of mutual explanation, forbearance, and consideration; something which is not to be found in Mr. McCulloch's dictionary, and is not exactly stateable in figures; otherwise those relations are wrong and rotten at the core and will never bear sound fruit.'

Mr. Snapper laughed at me. As I thought I had just as good reason to laugh at Mr. Snapper, I did so, and we were both contented.

'Ah!' said Mr. Snapper, patting his counterpane with a hard touch. 'You know very little of the improvident and unreasoning habits of the common people, *I* see.'

'Yet I know something of those people, too,' was my reply. 'In fact, Mr. ——,' I had so nearly called him Snapper! 'in fact, sir, I doubt the existence at this present time of many faults that are merely class faults. In the main, I am disposed to think that whatever faults you may find to exist, in your own neighbourhood for instance, among the hands, you will find tolerably equal in amount among the masters also, and even among the classes above the masters. They will be modified by circumstances, and they will be the less excusable among the better-educated, but they will be pretty fairly distributed. I have a strong expectation that we shall live to see the conventional adjectives now apparently inseparable from the phrases working people and lower orders, gradually fall into complete disuse for this reason.'

'Well, but we began with strikes,' Mr. Snapper observed impatiently. 'The masters have never had any share in strikes.'

'Yet I have heard of strikes once upon a time in that same county of Lancashire,' said I, 'which were not disagreeable to some masters when they wanted a pretext for raising prices.'

'Do you mean to say those masters had any hand in getting up those strikes?' asked Mr. Snapper.

'You will perhaps obtain better information among persons engaged in some Manchester branch trades, who have good memories,' said I.

Mr. Snapper had no doubt, after this, that I thought the hands had a right to combine?

'Surely,' said I. 'A perfect right to combine in any lawful manner. The fact of their being able to combine and accustomed to combine may, I can easily conceive, be a protection to them. The blame even of this business is not all on one side. I think the associated Lock-out was a grave error. And when you Preston masters—'

'I am not a Preston master,' interrupted Mr. Snapper.

'When the respectable combined body of Preston masters,' said I, 'in the beginning of this unhappy difference, laid down the principle that no man should be employed henceforth who belonged to any combination—such as their own—they attempted to carry with a high hand a partial and unfair impossibility, and were obliged to abandon it. This was an unwise proceeding, and the first defeat.'

Mr. Snapper had known, all along, that I was no friend to the masters.

'Pardon me,' said I, 'I am unfeignedly a friend to the masters, and have many friends among them.'

'Yet you think these hands in the right?' quoth Mr. Snapper.

'By no means,' said I; 'I fear they are at present engaged in an unreasonable struggle, wherein they began ill and cannot end well.'

Mr. Snapper, evidently regarding me as neither fish, flesh, nor fowl, begged to know after a pause if he might enquire whether I was going to Preston on business?

Indeed I was going there, in my unbusiness-like manner, I confessed, to look at the strike.

'To look at the strike!' echoed Mr. Snapper, fixing his hat on firmly with both hands. 'To look at it! Might I ask you now, with what object you are going to look at it?'

'Certainly,' said I. 'I read, even in liberal pages, the hardest Political Economy—of an extraordinary description too sometimes, and certainly not to be found in the books—as the only touchstone of this strike. I see, this very day, in a to-morrow's liberal paper, some astonishing novelties in the politico-economical way, showing how profits and wages have no connection whatever; coupled with such references to these hands as might be made by a very irascible General to rebels and brigands in arms. Now, if it be the case that some of the highest virtues of the working people still shine through them brighter than ever in their conduct of this mistake of theirs, perhaps the fact may reasonably suggest to me—and to others besides me—that there is some little thing wanting in the relations between them and their employers, which neither political economy nor Drum-head proclamation writing will altogether supply, and which we cannot too soon or too temperately unite in trying to find out.'

Mr. Snapper, after again opening and shutting his gloved hands several times, drew the counterpane higher over his chest, and went to bed in disgust. He got up at Rugby, took himself and counterpane into another carriage, and left me to pursue my journey alone.

When I got to Preston it was four o'clock in the afternoon. The day being Saturday and market-day, a foreigner might have expected, from among so many idle and not over-fed people as the town contained, to find a turbulent, ill-conditioned crowd in the streets. But, except for the cold smokeless factory chimneys, the placards at the street corners, and the groups of working people attentively reading them, nor foreigner nor Englishman could have had the least suspicion that there existed any interruption to the usual labours of the place. The placards thus perused were not remarkable for their logic certainly, and did not make the case particularly clear; but, considering that they emanated from, and were addressed to, people who had been out of employment for three-and-twenty consecutive weeks, at least they had little passion in them, though they had not much reason. Take the worst I could find:

FRIENDS AND FELLOW OPERATIVES,

Accept the grateful thanks of twenty thousand struggling Operatives, for the help you have showered upon Preston since the present contest commenced.

Your kindness and generosity, your patience and long-continued support deserve every praise, and are only equalled by the heroic and determined perseverance of the outraged and insulted factory workers of Preston, who have been struggling for some months, and are, at this inclement season of the year, bravely battling for the rights of themselves and the whole toiling community.

For many years before the strike took place at Preston, the Operatives were the down trodden and insulted serfs of their Employers, who in times of good trade and general prosperity, wrung from their labour a California of gold, which is now being used to crush those who created it, still lower and lower in the scale of civilization. This has been the result of our commercial prosperity!—*more wealth for the rich and more poverty for the Poor!* Because the workpeople of Preston protested against this state of things,—because they combined in a fair and legitimate way for the purpose of getting a reasonable share of the reward of their own labour, the *fair dealing* Employers of Preston, to their eternal shame and disgrace, *locked up* their Mills, and at one fell swoop deprived, as they thought, from twenty to thirty thousand human beings of the means of existence. Cruelty and tyranny always defeat their own object; it was so in this case, and to the honour and credit of the working classes of this country, we have to record, that, those whom the rich and wealthy sought to destroy, the poor and industrious have protected from harm. This love of justice and hatred of wrong, is a noble feature in the character and disposition of the working man, and gives us hope that in the future, this world will become what its great architect intended, not a place of sorrow, toil, oppression and wrong, but the dwelling place and the abode of peace, plenty, happiness and love, where avarice and all the evil passions engendered by the present system of fraud and injustice shall not have a place.

The earth was not made for the misery of its people; intellect was not given to man to make himself and fellow creatures unhappy. No, the fruitfulness of the soil and the wonderful inventions—the result of mind—all proclaim that these things were bestowed upon us for our happiness and well-being, and not for the misery and degredation of the human race.

It may serve the manufacturers and all who run away with the lion's share of labour's produce, to say that the *impartial* God intended that there should be a *partial* distribution of his blessings. But we know that it is against nature to believe, that those who plant and reap all the grain, should not have enough to make a mess of porridge; and we know that those who weave all the cloth should not want a yard to cover their persons, whilst those who never wove an inch have more calico, silks and satins, than would serve the reasonable wants of a dozen working men and their families.

This system of giving everything to the few, and nothing to the many, has lasted long enough, and we call upon the working people of this country to be determined to establish a new and improved system—a system that shall give to all who labour, a fair share of those blessings and comforts which their toil produce; in short, we wish to see that divine precept enforced, which says, 'Those who will not work, shall not eat.'

The task is before you, working men; if you think the good which would result from its accomplishment, is worth struggling for, set to work and cease not, until you have obtained the *good time coming*, not only for the Preston Operatives, but for yourselves as well.

By Order of the Committee.

Murphy's Temperance Hotel, Chapel Walks,
  Preston, January 24th, 1854.

It is a melancholy thing that it should not occur to the Committee to consider what would become of themselves, their friends, and fellow operatives, if those calicoes, silks, and satins, were *not* worn in very large quantities; but I shall not enter into that question. As I had told my friend Snapper, what I wanted to see with my own eyes, was, how these people acted under a mistaken impression, and what qualities they showed, even at that disadvantage, which ought to be the strength and peace—not the weakness and trouble—of the community. I found, even from this literature, however, that all masters were not indiscriminately unpopular. Witness the following verses from the New Song of the Preston Strike:

> There's Henry Hornby, of Blackburn, he is a jolly brick,
> He fits the Preston masters nobly, and is very bad to trick;
> He pays his hands a good price, and I hope he will never sever,
> So we'll sing success to Hornby and Blackburn for ever.

There is another gentleman, I'm sure you'll all lament,
In Blackburn for him they're raising a monument,
You know his name, 'tis of great fame, it was late Eccles of honour,
May Hopwood, and Sparrow, and Hornby live for ever.

So now it is time to finish and end my rhyme,
We warn these Preston Cotton Lords to mind for future time.
With peace and order too I hope we shall be clever,
We sing success to Stockport and Blackburn for ever.
    Now, lads, give your minds to it.

The balance sheet of the receipts and expenditure for the twenty-third week of the strike was extensively posted. The income for that week was two thousand one hundred and forty pounds odd. . . .

That evening, the Delegates from the surrounding districts were coming in, according to custom, with their subscription lists for the week just closed. These delegates meet on Sunday as their only day of leisure; when they have made their reports, they go back to their homes, and their Monday's work. On Sunday morning, I repaired to the Delegates' meeting.

These assemblages take place in a cockpit, which, in the better times of our fallen land, belonged to the late Lord Derby for the purposes of the intellectual recreation implied in its name. I was directed to the cockpit up a narrow lane, tolerably crowded by the lower sort of working people. Personally, I was quite unknown in the town, but every one made way for me to pass, with great civility, and perfect good humour. Arrived at the cockpit door, and expressing my desire to see and hear, I was handed through the crowd, down into the pit, and up again, until I found myself seated on the topmost circular bench, within one of the secretary's tables, and within three of the chairman. Behind the chairman was a great crown on the top of a pole, made of parti-coloured calico, and strongly suggestive of May-day. There was no other symbol or ornament in place.

It was hotter than any mill or factory I have ever been in; but there was a stove down in the sanded pit, and delegates were seated close to it, and one particular delegate often warmed his hands at it, as if he were chilly. The air was so intensely close and hot, that at first I had but a confused perception of the delegates down in the pit, and the dense crowd of eagerly listening men and women (but not very many of the latter) filling all the benches and choking such narrow standing-room as there was. When the atmosphere cleared a little on better acquaintance, I found the question under discussion to be, Whether the Manchester Delegates in attendance from the Labor Parliament, should be heard?

If the Assembly, in respect of quietness and order, were put in comparison with the House of Commons, the Right Honorable the Speaker himself would decide for Preston. The chairman was a Preston weaver, two or three and fifty years of age, perhaps; a man with a capacious head, rather long dark hair growing at the sides and back, a placid attentive face, keen eyes, a particularly composed manner, a quiet voice, and a persuasive action of his right arm. Now look'ee heer my friends. See what t' question is. T' question is, sholl these heer men be heerd. Then 't cooms to this, what ha' these men got t' tell us? Do they bring mooney? If they bring mooney t'ords t' expenses o' this strike, they're welcome. For, Brass, my friends, is what we want, and what we must ha' (hear hear hear!). Do they coom to us wi' any suggestion for the conduct of this strike? If they do, they're welcome. Let 'em give us their advice and we will hearken to 't. But, if these men coom heer, to tell us what t' Labor Parliament is, or what Ernest Jones's opinions is, or t' bring in politics and differences amoong us when what we want is 'armony, brotherly love, and con-cord; then I say t' you, decide for yoursel' carefully, whether these men ote to be heerd in this place. (Hear hear hear! and No no no!) Chairman sits down, earnestly regarding delegates, and holding both arms of his chair. Looks extremely sensible; his plain coarse working man's shirt collar easily turned down over his loose Belcher neckerchief. Delegate who has moved that Manchester delegates be heard, presses motion—Mr. Chairman, will that delegate tell us, as a man, that these men have anything to say concerning this present strike and lock-out, for we have a deal of business to do, and what concerns this present strike and lock-out is our business and nothing else is. (Hear hear hear!)—Delegate in question will not compromise the fact; these men want to defend the Labor Parliament from certain charges made against them.—Very well, Mr. Chairman, Then I move as an amendment that you do not hear these men now, and that you proceed wi' business— and if you don't I'll look after you, I tell you that. (Cheers and laughter)— Coom lads, prove 't then!—Two or three hands for the delegates; all the rest for the business. Motion lost, amendment carried, Manchester deputation not to be heard.

But now, starts up the delegate from Throstletown, in a dreadful state of mind. Mr. Chairman, I hold in my hand a bill; a bill that requires and demands explanation from you, sir; an offensive bill; a bill posted in my town of Throstletown without my knowledge, without the knowledge of my fellow delegates who are here beside me; a bill purporting to be posted by the authority of the massed committee sir, and of which my fellow delegates and myself were kept in ignorance. Why are we to be slighted? Why are we to be insulted? Why are we to be meanly stabbed in the dark? Why is this assassin-like course of conduct to be pursued towards us? Why is Throstletown, which has nobly assisted you, the operatives of Preston, in this great struggle, and which has brought its contributions up to the full sevenpence a loom, to be thus degraded, thus aspersed, thus traduced, thus despised, thus outraged in its feelings by un-English and unmanly conduct? Sir, I hand you up that bill, and I require of you, sir, to give me a satisfactory explanation of that bill. And I have that confidence in your known

183

integrity, sir, as to be sure that you will give it, and that you will tell us who is to blame, and that you will make reparation to Throstletown for this scandalous treatment. Then, in hot blood, up starts Gruffshaw (professional speaker) who is somehow responsible for this bill. O my friends, but explanation is required here! O my friends, but it is fit and right that you should have the dark ways of the real traducers and apostates, and the real un-English stabbers, laid bare before you. My friends when this dark conspiracy first began—But here the persuasive right hand of the chairman falls gently on Gruffshaw's shoulder. Gruffshaw stops in full boil. My friends, these are hard words of my friend Gruffshaw, and this is not the business—No more it is, and once again, sir, I, the delegate who said I would look after you, do move that you proceed to business!—Preston has not the strong relish for personal altercation that Westminster hath. Motion seconded and carried, business passed to, Gruffshaw dumb.

Perhaps the world could not afford a more remarkable contrast than between the deliberate collected manner of these men proceeding with their business, and the clash and hurry of the engines among which their lives are passed. Their astonishing fortitude and perseverance; their high sense of honor among themselves; the extent to which they are impressed with the responsibility that is upon them of setting a careful example, and keeping their order out of any harm and loss of reputation; the noble readiness in them to help one another, of which most medical practitioners and working clergymen can give so many affecting examples; could scarcely ever be plainer to an ordinary observer of human nature than in this cockpit. To hold, for a minute, that the great mass of them were not sincerely actuated by the belief that all these qualities were bound up in what they were doing, and that they were doing right, seemed to me little short of an impossibility. As the different delegates (some in the very dress in which they had left the mill last night) reported the amounts sent from the various places they represented, this strong faith on their parts seemed expressed in every tone and every look that was capable of expressing it. One man was raised to enthusiasm by his pride in bringing so much; another man was ashamed and depressed because he brought so little; this man triumphantly made it known that he could give you, from the store in hand, a hundred pounds in addition next week, if you should want it; and that man pleaded that he hoped his district would do better before long; but I could as soon have doubted the existence of the walls that enclosed us, as the earnestness with which they spoke (many of them referring to the children who were to be born to labor after them) of 'this great, this noble, gallant, godlike struggle.' Some designing and turbulent spirits among them, no doubt there are; but I left the place with a profound conviction that their mistake is generally an honest one, and that it is sustained by the good that is in them, and not by the evil.

Neither by night nor by day was there any interruption to the peace of the streets. Nor was this an accidental state of things, for the police records of the town are eloquent to the same effect. I traversed the streets very much, and was, as a stranger, the subject of a little curiosity among the idlers; but I met with no rudeness or ill-temper. More than once, when I was looking at the printed balance-sheets to which I have referred, and could not quite comprehend the setting forth of the figures, a bystander of the working class interposed with his explanatory forefinger and helped me out. Although the pressure in the cockpit on Sunday was excessive, and the heat of the room obliged me to make my way out as I best could before the close of the proceedings, none of the people whom I put to inconvenience showed the least impatience; all helped me, and all cheerfully acknowledged my word of apology as I passed. It is very probable, notwithstanding, that they may have supposed from my being there at all—I and my companion were the only persons present, not of their own order—that I was there to carry what I heard and saw to the opposite side; indeed one speaker seemed to intimate as much.

On the Monday at noon, I returned to this cockpit, to see the people paid. It was then about half filled, principally with girls and women. They were all seated, waiting, with nothing to occupy their attention; and were just in that state when the unexpected appearance of a stranger differently dressed from themselves, and with his own individual peculiarities of course, might, without offence, have had something droll in it even to more polite assemblies. But I stood there, looking on, as free from remark as if I had come to be paid with the rest. In the place which the secretary had occupied yesterday, stood a dirty little common table, covered with five-penny piles of halfpence. Before the paying began, I wondered who was going to receive these very small sums; but when it did begin, the mystery was soon cleared up. Each of these piles was the change for sixpence, deducting a penny. All who were paid, in filing round the building to prevent confusion, had to pass this table on the way out; and the greater part of the unmarried girls stopped here, to change, each a sixpence, and subscribe her weekly penny in aid of the people on strike who had families. A very large majority of these girls and women were comfortably dressed in all respects, clean, wholesome and pleasant-looking. There was a prevalent neatness and cheerfulness, and an almost ludicrous absence of anything like sullen discontent. . . .

In any aspect in which it can be viewed, this strike and lock-out is a deplorable calamity. In its waste of time, in its waste of a great people's energy, in its waste of wages, in its waste of wealth that seeks to be employed, in its encroachment on the means of many thousands who are laboring from day to day, in the gulf of separation it hourly deepens between those whose interests must be understood to be identical or must be destroyed, it is a great national affliction. But, at this pass, anger is of no use, starving out is of no use—for what will that do, five years hence, but overshadow all the mills in England with the growth of a bitter remembrance?—political economy is a mere skeleton unless it has a little human covering and filling out, a little human bloom upon it, and a little human warmth in it. Gentlemen are found, in great manufacturing towns, ready enough to extol imbecile mediation with dangerous madmen abroad; can none of them be brought to think of authorised mediation and explanation at home? I do not suppose that such a knotted difficulty as this, is to be at all untangled by a morning-party in the Adelphi; but I would entreat both sides now so miserably opposed, to consider whether there are no men in England, above suspicion, to whom they might refer the matters in dispute, with a perfect confidence above all things in the desire of those men to act justly, and in their sincere attachment to their countrymen of every rank and to their country. Masters right, or men right; masters wrong, or men wrong; both right, or both wrong; there is certain ruin to both in the continuance or frequent revival of this breach. And from the ever-widening circle of their decay, what drop in the social ocean shall be free!

(*Household Words*, 11 Feb. 1854.)

IV.7 J. Ewing Ritchie, from *The Night Side of London* (1857)

The Canterbury Hall

'Give me the songs of the people, and you may make its laws,' said old Fletcher, of Saltoun, with a knowledge of human nature which statesmen do not frequently possess. Necessity is a stern taskmaster, and the workman in the factory, and the clerk in the counting-house, and the shopman behind the counter, are generally compelled to stick pretty close to work, and to the eye of the observer present very much the same appearance. They come at certain hours, they go at certain hours, and perform their daily toil with a certain amount of effectiveness and skill. Very little credit is due to them for this—their livelihood depends upon their being diligent and active—and hence I know little of the individual by merely witnessing him toiling for his daily bread. I must follow him home; I must be with him in his hours of relaxation; I must listen to the songs he sings and the jokes he attempts; I must see what is his idea of pleasure, and thus only can I get at the man as he is. Even his church or chapel goings I cannot take as indications of his real nature. He may go because his parents go, because his master goes, because his friends go, because he has been trained to go, because society expects him to go,—for a hundred reasons all equally vain in the eyes of Him who searcheth the heart and trieth the reins of the children of men, but no man is a hypocrite where his pleasures are concerned. I can gather more about him from the way in which he spends his leisure hours than I can from his active employments of the day. They are poor miserable philosophers indeed, and guilty of an enormous blunder, who, in their investigation into the moral and social condition of the people, refuse to notice the amusements of the people in their hours of gaiety and ease. I make, then, no apology for introducing you to Canterbury Hall.

The Upper Marsh, Westminster-road, is what is called a low neighbourhood. It is not far from Astley's Theatre. Right through it runs the South Western Railway, and everywhere about it are planted pawnbrokers' shops, with an indescribable amount of dirty second-hand clothes, and monster gin-palaces, with unlimited plate-glass and gas. Go along there what hour of the day you will, these gin-palaces are full of ragged children, hideous old women, and drunken men. 'The bane and the antidote,' you may say, 'are thus side by side.' True, but you forget that youth in its search for pleasure is blind, and sees not the warning till it is too late; and of the hundreds rushing on to the Canterbury Hall for a quiet glass, none think they will fall so low as the victims of intemperance reeling, cursing, fighting, blaspheming, in their path. But let us pass on. A well-lighted entrance attached to a public-house indicates that we have reached our destination. We proceed up a few stairs, along a passage lined with handsome engravings, to a bar, where we pay sixpence if we take a seat in the body of the hall, and nine-pence if we do the nobby and ascend into the balcony. We make our way leisurely along the floor of the building, which is really a very handsome hall, well lighted, and capable of holding fifteen hundred persons; the balcony extends round the room in the form of a horse shoe. At the opposite end to which we enter is the platform, on which is placed a grand piano and a harmonium, on which the performers play in the intervals when the professional singers have left the stage. The chairman sits just beneath them. It is dull work to him; but there he must sit every night smoking cigars and drinking, from seven till twelve o'clock. I fancy I detect a little touch of rouge just on the top of his cheek; he may well need it, for even on a fine summer night like this the room is crowded, and almost every gentleman present has a pipe or a cigar in his mouth. Let us look round us; evidently the majority present are respectable mechanics, or small tradesmen with their wives and daughters and sweethearts there. Now and then you see a midshipman, or a few fast clerks and warehousemen, who confidentially inform each other that there is 'no end of talent here,' and that Miss —— 'is a doosed fine gal;' and here, as elsewhere, we see a few of the class of unfortunates, whose staring eyes would fain extort an admiration which their persons do not justify. Every one is smoking, and every one has a glass before him; but the class that come here are economical, and chiefly confine themselves to pipes and porter. The presence of the ladies has also a beneficial effect; I see no indication of intoxication, and certainly none of the songs are obscene. . . .

But, compared with many of the places frequented by both sexes, Canterbury Hall is a respectable place. I may think that more rational amusement might be found than by sitting smoking and drinking in a large room on a hot summer's night. I may have my doubts whether all go home sober—the presence of a policeman in the room indicated that at times there was need for his services—but I believe the association of song and drinking and amusements pernicious in the extreme; and, knowing that man needs relaxation—that he must have his hour of amusement as well as of work—I cannot too earnestly press upon the advocates of Temperance reform the desirableness of their out-bidding the public-house in the attempts to cater for the entertainment of the people.

(*The Night Side of London*, 1857, pp. 58–65.)

IV.8 Karl Marx, from *Introduction to the Critique of Political Economy* (1857)

It is well known that certain periods of highest development of art stand in no direct connection with the general development of society, nor with the material basis and the skeleton structure of its organization. Witness the example of the Greeks as compared with modern art or even Shakespeare. As concerns certain forms of art, e.g., the epos, it is even acknowledged that as soon as the production of art as such appears they can never be produced in their epoch-making, classical aspect; and accordingly, that in the domain of art certain of its important forms are possible only at an undeveloped stage of art development. If that is true of the mutual relations of different modes of art within the domain of art itself, it is far less surprising that the same is true of the relations of art as a whole to the general development of society. The difficulty lies only in the general formulation of these contradictions. No sooner are they made specific than they are clarified.

Let us take for instance the relationship of Greek art and then Shakespeare's to the present. It is a well known fact that Greek mythology was not only the arsenal of Greek art but also the very ground from which it had sprung. Is the view of nature and of social relations which shaped Greek imagination and thus Greek [mythology] possible in the age of automatic machinery and railways and locomotives and electric telegraphs? Where does Vulcan come in as against Roberts & Co., Jupiter as against the lightning rod, and Hermes as against the Crédit Mobilier? All mythology masters and dominates and shapes the forces of nature in and through the imagination; hence it disappears as soon as man gains mastery over the forces of nature. What becomes of the Goddess Fame side by side with Printing House Square? Greek art presupposes the existence of Greek mythology, i.e., that nature and even the forms of society itself are worked up in the popular imagination in an unconsciously artistic fashion. That is its material. Not, however, any mythology taken at random, nor any accidental unconsciously artistic elaboration of nature (including with the latter everything objective, hence society too). Egyptian mythology could never be the soil of the womb which would give birth to Greek art. But in any event [there had to be] *a* mythology. There could be no social development which excludes all mythological relation to nature, all mythologizing relation to it, and which accordingly claims from the artist an imagination free of mythology.

Looking at it from another side: is Achilles possible where there are powder and lead? Or is the *Iliad* at all possible in a time of the hand-operated or the later steam press? Are not singing and reciting and the muse necessarily put out of existence by the printer's bar; and do not necessary prerequisites of epic poetry accordingly vanish?

But the difficulty does not lie in understanding that the Greek art and epos are bound up with certain forms of social development. It rather lies in understanding why they still afford us aesthetic enjoyment and in certain respects prevail as the standard and model beyond attainment.

A man cannot become a child again unless he becomes childish. But doesn't he enjoy the naive ways of the child, and mustn't he himself strive to reproduce its truth again at a higher stage? Isn't the character of every epoch revived perfectly true to nature in child nature? Why should the historical childhood of humanity, where it had obtained its most beautiful development, not exert an eternal charm as an age that will never return? There are ill-bred children and precocious children. Many of the ancient peoples belong to these categories. But the Greeks were normal children. The charm their art has for us does not stand in contradiction with the undeveloped stage of the social order from which it had sprung. It is much more the result of the latter, and inseparately connected with the circumstance that the unripe social conditions under which the art arose and under which alone it could appear can never return.

(*Marx/Engels on Literature and Art*, ed. Lee Baxandall and
Stefan Morawski, 1974, pp. 136–8.)

Mrs Isabella Beeton, from *Beeton's Book of Household Management* IV.9 (1859–61)

THE MISTRESS

Strength and honour are her clothing; and she shall rejoice in time to come. She openeth her mouth with wisdom; and in her tongue is the law of kindness. She looketh well to the ways of her household; and eateth not the bread of idleness. Her children arise up, and call her blessed; her husband also, and he praiseth her.

Proverbs, xxi. 25–28.

1. As with the Commander of an army, or the leader of any enterprise, so it is with the mistress of a house. Her spirit will be seen through the whole establishment; and just in proportion as she performs her duties intelligently and thoroughly, so will her domestics follow in her path. Of all those acquirements, which more particularly belong to the feminine character, there are none which take a higher rank, in our estimation, than such as enter into a knowledge of household duties; for on these are perpetually dependent the happiness comfort and well-being of a family. In this opinion we are borne out by the author of 'The Vicar of Wakefield', who says: 'The modest virgin, the prudent wife, and the careful matron, are much more serviceable in life than petticoated philosophers, blustering heroines, or virago queens. She who makes her husband and her children happy, who reclaims the one from vice and trains up the other to virtue, is a much greater character than ladies deserted in romances, whose whole occupation is to murder mankind with shafts from their quiver, or their eyes.' . . .

19. The treatment of servants is of the highest possible moment, as well to the mistress as to the domestics themselves. On the head of the house the latter will naturally fix their attention; and if they perceive that the mistress's conduct is regulated by high and correct principles, they will not fail to respect her. If, also, a benevolent desire is shown to promote their comfort, at the same time that a steady performance of their duty is exacted, then their respect will not be unmingled with affection, and they will be still more solicitous to continue to deserve her favour. . . .

21. The following table of the average yearly wages paid to domestics, with the various members of the household placed in the order in which they are usually ranked, will serve as a guide to regulate the expenditure of an establishment:—

	When not found in livery	When found in livery
The House Steward	From £40 to £80	—
The Valet	,, 25 to 50	From £20 to £30
The Butler	,, 25 to 50	—
The Cook	,, 20 to 40	—
The Gardener	,, 20 to 40	—
The Footman	,, 20 to 40	,, 15 to 25
The Under Butler	,, 15 to 30	,, 15 to 25
The Coachman	—	,, 20 to 35
The Groom	,, 15 to 30	,, 12 to 20
The Under Footman	—	,, 12 to 20
The Page or Footboy	,, 8 to 18	,, 6 to 14
The Stableboy	,, 6 to 12	—

	When no extra allowance is made for Tea, Sugar, and Beer	When an extra allowance is made for Tea, Sugar, and Beer
The Housekeeper	From £20 to £45	From £18 to £40
The Lady's-Maid	,, 12 to 25	,, 10 to 20
The Head Nurse	,, 15 to 30	,, 13 to 26
The Cook	,, 14 to 30	,, 12 to 26
The Upper Housemaid	,, 12 to 20	,, 10 to 17
The Upper Laundry-Maid	,, 12 to 18	,, 10 to 15
The Maid-of-all-work	,, 9 to 14	,, 7½ to 11
The Under Housemaid	,, 8 to 12	,, 6½ to 10
The Still-room Maid	,, 9 to 14	,, 8 to 12
The Nursemaid	,, 8 to 12	,, 5 to 10
The Under Family-Maid	,, 9 to 14	,, 8 to 12
The Kitchen-Maid	,, 9 to 14	,, 8 to 12
The Scullery-Maid	,, 5 to 9	,, 4 to 8

These quotations of wages are those usually given in or near the metropolis; but, of course, there are many circumstances connected with locality, and also having reference to the long service on the one hand, or the inexperience on the other, of domestics, which may render the wages still higher or lower than those named above. All the domestics mentioned in the above table would enter into the establishment of a wealthy nobleman. The number of servants, of course, would become smaller in proportion to the lesser size of the establishment; and we may here enumerate a scale of servants suited to various incomes, commencing with—

About £1,000 a year—A cook, upper housemaid, nursemaid, under housemaid, and a man servant.

About £750 a year—A cook, housemaid, nursemaid and footboy.

About £500 a year—A cook, housemaid, and nursemaid.

About £300 a year—A maid-of-all-work and nursemaid.

About £200 or £150 a year—A maid-of-all-work (and girl occasionally).

(*Beeton's Book of Household Management*, 1859–61, Part 1, Chapter 1.)

Robert Kerr, from 'The Battle of the Styles', a paper read at the Architectural Exhibition (1860)   IV.10

A certain controversy had for some time been going on, both in the architectural profession and in society at large, between the advocates of the Classic styles of design and the promoters of Mediaeval taste. We were at the present day twitted with having no style of our own, borrowing where we could, and after all being even unable to agree how to borrow; there being attached to all this the insinuation of a contemptible decrepitude of taste; but if the argument he had now to submit should appear to be sound, the verdict of the audience would not be in accordance with such an idea. His account of the controversy would extend over about a hundred years; and it became naturally divided into several separate stages or chapters of narrative, namely, Palladianism, eighteenth-century Classicism, eighteenth-century Gothicism, nineteenth-century Classicism, nineteenth-century Gothicism, the new Italian school, Eclecticism, Ecclesiology, Latitudinarianism, and, lastly, a glance at our present position and prospects.

Palladianism—To obtain a proper contrast between Gothic style and that of modern times, we ought to place ourselves at the period of about A.D. 1500, and on the soil of Italy. Looking at society, then, past and present, we should perceive that an old social system was going out, and a new one coming in. The old one was the Gothic system of Mediaeval Europe, with feudalism and ecclesiasticism as essential elements: the new was the modern European system, with commercial enterprise and popular freedom for its bases. The fine arts, always changing with social change, were also in a state of transition; and, amongst the rest, the fine art of architecture. . . .

Eighteenth Century Gothicism— . . . Horace Walpole set a Gothic fashion and built Strawberry Hill, on the Thames, in professed imitation of a 'deserted convent.' James Wyatt was the architect. The principle of the Picturesque also came about this time into recognition in landscape gardening and otherwise; a movement in the same direction. Cathedral restorations were entered upon somewhat largely, under Wyatt, the very work now being swept away by our more correctly-educated Gothic architects, executed in most erroneous style and even in fictitious material. But Antiquarianism soon brought itself to bear upon the new style . . .

Nineteenth Century Classicism—The French revolution and the war divided the Europe of the eighteenth century, lately under discussion, from that of the nineteenth century, now in hand. During the war the Greek taste had slowly advanced . . . After the peace, the then rising men . . . employed the new facilities of travel to admirable purpose. . . . Greek taste was thus in full practice; and not only had Palladian been cast ignominiously aside, but the Roman works themselves were pronounced corrupt . . .

Nineteenth Century Gothicism— . . . The first great public triumph of Gothic style was in the case of the Houses of Parliament, 1835. . . . the arguments in favour of genuine old English building for the palace of the English Legislature were readily accepted on almost all hands. The styles for competition were 'Gothic and Elizabethan.' Barry, in easy triumph, carried off the palm with a Gothic design universally admired. . . . If now by a new class of critics that great work was pronounced imperfect, it was not by any failure in its own promise, but by the introduction of a new spirit of art, namely, that of ecclesiasticism, to be presently treated of. . . .

The New Italian School—In the pseudo-Augustan age of George IV, the tendency of style in ordinary building was towards the increasing modification of Palladian by Graecism of detail. It was so even with Nash, although he could scarcely be called a Graeco-Palladian so much as a Cockney-Palladian . . . It was reserved, however, for Barry to introduce in the Travellers' Clubhouse the genuine palatial Italian of the sixteenth century. The Reform Club followed. . . . The success of Barry's Italian was complete, and ever since, the style had been the favourite all over England, and had produced most numerous and varied works of great excellence.

Eclecticism— . . . The principle of eclecticism was that all authentic styles were on an equal platform of eligibility for adoption, according to circumstances. Copyism and precedent thus enlarged their authority . . . An apportionment of styles soon became recognized,—for churches, Gothic; for mansions and the like, chiefly Tudor; for civil and municipal edifices, generally Italian; for grand monumental buildings, Greek or Roman,—all one happy family, into which no jar was expected to appear for ever. Many practitioners excelled in diverse styles, as Barry in both Italian and Gothic, and after him Scott; and to the present day there were a large body of metropolitan and provincial architects who designed most admirably in all styles alike. This was the triumph of eclecticism. . . .

Ecclesiology—From 1835 to 1840 the sentiment of ecclesiasticism came very decidedly into view, through the means of the well-known movement in the Church, in favour of ritualism, which, of necessity, materially affected church architecture. In 1835, Pugin the younger opened his energetic assault upon Classic practice in his 'Contrasts,' followed in 1841 by his 'True Principles,' in which he laid down rules for sound design, and, subsequently, by the 'Apology,' which treated of the availableness of Mediaeval style for all modern requirements . . . In 1841 was founded the Cambridge Camden Society: the publication of the 'Ecclesiologist' followed: symbolism, in great force, came into request: Pre-Raffaellitism in painting lent its aid: archaeological societies were established in all quarters: the clergy began to take a lively interest in architectural revival: church building and restoration were largely entered upon; and the effect upon the profession was great and rapid. A new school of architects arose, confining themselves entirely to ecclesiastical work, and repudiating the Classical styles altogether. Mr Scott soon took the lead.

Latitudinarianism— . . . The young men and students began to revolt against archaeology and the authority of precedent, and when they formed themselves, in 1847, into a junior society,—the Architectural Association,—the enfranchisement of design was their motto, and there were many amongst the most esteemed designers now who attributed much of their success to the discussions and competitions of that society. Then came

Mr Ruskin. He was claimed by some as an ecclesiologist, but without reason: he was a latitudinarian from first to last. He preferred Gothic for its picturesque and romantic character, but why did he lean so much on Venice? Because, said he, Venice was peculiarly mercantile and non-ecclesiastical. A commonwealth of this kind, existing in the midst of feudalism and ecclesiasticism, would consequently possess in its art the elements of the styles of both conditions, that is, both the old Gothic and the new Classic elements. Mr Ruskin's first work, in 1843, the 'Modern Painters,' took the ground that the ancients, instead of being our superiors, were our inferiors,—latitudinarianism the most daring. In 1849 he applied himself to architecture in his 'Seven Lamps,' and in 1851 he began 'The Stones of Venice.' In 1849 Mr Fergusson published his 'Inquiry into the Principles of Beauty,' in which he also proved himself an extreme latitudinarian. Since that time the principle had been strengthened continually.

But the high priest of all latitudinarians was Mr Ruskin. Not to speak of his elegance of diction and graceful form of thought, which were but the superficial covering of solid matter beneath, the honest pluck and audacity at the root of all was delightful . . .

In conclusion, *the battle of the styles* seemed thus to be approaching near the end of all honourable and creditable conflict, namely, alliance. If Classicism was tending towards the early Italian, the Gothic germ of the later style, and becoming also more and more picturesque, and, therefore, more and more Gothic (the picturesque being the essence of Gothic taste); and if Gothicism was similarly tending towards the examples of Italy, and becoming more and more graceful and refined, and therefore more Classic (grace and proportion being the Classic essence); then it might surely be said that the rival styles, mutually modified, were approaching one common centre. The result might not be any new style,—for it was questionable whether the phraseology of architecture, except in respect of new materials, was not exhausted long ago (like that of music, and perhaps that of painting and sculpture); but there would be a federation and union of purpose; the *quasi* Classic on one side of the way, and the *quasi* Gothic on the other, although clearly distinguishable in criticism, would display accordance and sympathy, and look each other fairly in the face.

(*The Builder*, vol. 18, 1860.)

IV.11 **Evidence given by Mr Daniel Saunders to the Select Committee on Theatrical Licences and Regulation of Music Halls (1866)**

MR. DANIEL SAUNDERS, called in; and Examined.

7377. Mr. *Locke.*] I BELIEVE that you are the manager of Day's Music Hall, at Birmingham?—Yes.

7378. How long have you been manager of that house?—About three years and a half.

7379. How many persons is it capable of accommodating?—2,500.

7380. How are you licensed?—By the magistrates.

7381. What license have you?—A music and dancing license. . . .

7398. How many performers have you engaged there?—Probably 120.

7399. Will you inform the Committee what is the description of your performance?—The best thing I can do, I think, is to give you a programme of an evening's entertainment (*handing in a specimen programme.*)

7400. 'Day's Crystal Palace Concert Hall, Smallbrook-street, Birmingham; Sole Proprietor, Mr. James Day. Thursday, May 10th 1866.' You begin with a concert, I see?—Yes.

7401. 'During which will be exhibited an Act Drop, "The New Street Station" '?—Yes.

7402. Does that come in the middle of the concert?—Yes; in the middle of the concert, while the overture is being played.

7403. 'Grand Garland Divertissement, supported by Miss Fanny Lauri and a New London Corps de Ballet; scenery by Messrs. E. Day and J. Watson;' what was that ballet?—That was a ballet of the usual kind, with appropriate scenery; the scenery in this case was a scene by moonlight.

7404. Did that ballet tell a story?—No; it told no story.

7405. 'Grand Selection from Bellini's favourite opera "Norma," ' and several other pieces?—Yes.

7406. Did those singers sing in character?—No; in evening dress.

7407. Now I see here, 'Comic Entertainment, by Mr. J. G. Forde;' what is that?—He is what is called a patter-comic singer, after the style of Mr. Charles Mathews.

7408. Then there is a gymnastic entertainment by the Brothers Ridley, 'Reading—Mr. Reuben Roe; Waltz (Gungl) Orchestra;' that is merely music given by the orchestra, I suppose?—Just so.

7409. Then you had a pantomimic ballet, called 'The Adventures of Lord Dundreary, supported by the celebrated Lauri family; Comic Song, Serio-comic Song, and Ethiopian Entertainment.' You had this pantomimic ballet, the 'Adventures of Lord Dundreary;' did that come within the provisions of the 6 & 7 Victoria?—According to my interpretation of it, it does.

7410. Have you been at all proceeded against by the theatrical managers of Birmingham?—We have.

7411. When was that?—That was about 18 months ago.

7412. What was the performance that they objected to?—It was the representation of the Ghost Illusion.

7413. Was that representation of the Ghost Illusion in a piece?—Yes; it was introduced into a piece, which was the vehicle for it.

7414. How many actors were there in that piece?—There were two on the stage, and all the rest were underneath.

7415. You had the same kind of contrivance that they had at the Canterbury Hall?—Yes.

7416. With two performers on the stage, and all the others were merely reflections?—Yes; shadows.

7417. You were proceeded against; and the case was ultimately decided in the Court of Common Pleas?—Yes. . . .

(*British Parliamentary Papers, Stage and Theatre*, 2, 1866, p. 259.)

IV.12 Thomas Wright, from *Some Habits and Customs of the Working Classes by a Journeyman Engineer* (1867)

The regular frequenters of the gallery may be divided into the roughs, the hypocrites or snobs, and the orderlies. Of these the roughs are the most numerous division; it consists of those who come to the theatre with unwashed faces and in ragged and dirty attire, who bring bottles of drink with them, who *will* smoke despite of the notice that 'smoking is strictly prohibited,' and that 'officers will be in attendance;' who favour the band with a stamping accompaniment, and take the most noisy part in applauding or giving 'the call' to the performers. The females of this class are generally accompanied by infants, who are sure to cry and make a disturbance at some interesting point in the performance. The snobs comprise those who will tell you that they prefer the gallery to any other part of the house, and that they would still go into it if the price of admission into it was as high as that charged for admission to the pit or boxes; nevertheless, they seem very ill at ease in the place of their choice, and shrink from the glances of the occupants of the pit and boxes. The snob, also, is of those who stand on the back seats, and while talking loudly among themselves, but *at* the other occupants of the gallery, are at great pains to inform you that they have merely come into the gallery for a 'spree,' or 'just to see what kind of place it is,' but who strangely enough are to be found there two or three nights a week, and are amongst the most deeply attentive portion of the audience. The orderlies are those who, while they admit that the gallery is the least comfortable, and it may be the least respectable part of the house, and that they would much rather be in the boxes, go into the gallery because it is the *cheapest* part of the house—because they can go into that part twice for the same amount of money that they would have to pay to go into any other part once.

Considering that the gods are, as a rule, passionately fond of the drama, the majority of them are surprisingly ignorant of all relating to it. Many of them have never heard of Betterton, Garrick, Kemble, or the other great theatrical names of a few generations back. And even since the tercentenary festival, I have sat side by side with a god who, after a thoughtful pause, hesitatingly confessed that he had heard something of a theatrical 'bloke' named Shakespeare, and believed he had written the play of 'Jack Sheppard,' but could not say whether he lived in the time of Alfred the Great or George the Fourth. . . . Another time, while on a visit to Manchester, I went into the Theatre Royal there. In order to secure a good seat, I had gone in half an hour before the time announced for the performance to commence. While waiting for the rise of the curtain, I entered into conversation with the man beside whom I was seated, and from him I learned that the drama with which the entertainments of the evening were to begin had been running for some weeks past, and that he had seen it twice. 'What do you think of that?' asked my new-found acquaintance at the end of the first act. 'It's very good indeed,' I answered. 'Oh, that's nothing!' said he, evidently disappointed by my tone of admiration; '*the murders haven't come yet.*' 'That's cutting, isn't it?' observed my acquaintance as the curtain descended on the last act of the drama. 'Oh, yes,' I said, in a slightly indifferent tone. 'Well, it made me cry, anyhow,' he said, with an emphasis that implied that that was an exceedingly strong and incontrovertible proof of the 'cutting' nature of the drama. 'Yes, it did,' he continued, seeing that I made no reply; 'and so I must go and have a pint of beer; will you come?' 'No thank you.' 'Well, will you mind my seat till I come back?' 'Oh, yes,' I said. There was a song and dance between the pieces, and while the dance was on my acquaintance returned. 'What's next?' he asked when he had resumed his seat. 'A farce,' I answered, looking at the playbill. 'A farce,' he said, repeating my words in a tone of inquiry; 'what's a farce?' 'Something laughable,' I explained. 'Oh, then, I don't like a farce,' he said. 'I like something deep, I do.'

And this predilection for 'something deep' is a general characteristic of the gods, who at all times prefer a melodrama or tragedy to a farce, however 'laughable' or 'screaming' the latter may be. But a burlesque, with its grotesque and beautiful dresses, cleverly arranged dances, and parodies on 'new and popular songs,' often finds favour in their sight; though the few good and the many feeble and farfetched puns which a burlesque generally contains are quite thrown away upon the great majority of them. That the celestials are often noisy, and are sometimes given to discharging nutshells, peas, orange-peel, and other annoying, though harmless missiles, at the heads of the devoted occupants of the 'regions below;' and that their 'chaff' often assumes an unpleasantly personal tone, previous to and during the intervals of the performance, is but too true. . . .

(*Some Habits and Customs* . . . , 1867, pp. 158–62.)

IV.13 **Matthew Arnold, from *Culture and Anarchy* (1869)**

Introduction

[1.] In one of his speeches a short time ago, that fine speaker and famous Liberal, Mr Bright, took occasion to have a fling at the friends and preachers of culture. 'People who talk about what they call *culture!*' said he contemptuously; 'by which they mean a smattering of the two dead languages of Greek and Latin.' And he went on to remark, in a strain with which modern speakers and writers have made us very familiar, how poor a thing this culture is, how little good it can do to the world, and how absurd it is for its possessors to set much store by it. And the other day a younger Liberal than Mr Bright, one of a school whose mission it is to bring into order and system that body of truth with which the earlier Liberals merely fumbled, a member of the University of Oxford, and a very clever writer, Mr Frederic Harrison, developed, in the systematic and stringent manner of his school, the thesis which Mr Bright had pro-pounded in only general terms. 'Perhaps the very silliest cant of the day,' said Mr Frederic Harrison, 'is the cant about culture. Culture is a desir-able quality in a critic of new books, and sits well on a professor of *belles lettres*; but as applied to politics, it means simply a turn for small fault-finding, love of selfish ease, and indecision in action. The man of culture is in politics one of the poorest mortals alive. For simple pedantry and want of good sense no man is his equal. No assumption is too unreal, no end is too unpractical for him. But the active exercise of politics requires com-mon sense, sympathy, trust, resolution and enthusiasm, qualities which your man of culture has carefully rooted up, lest they damage the delicacy of his critical olfactories. Perhaps they are the only class of responsible beings in the community who cannot with safety be entrusted with power.'

[2.] Now for my part I do not wish to see men of culture asking to be entrusted with power; and, indeed, I have freely said, that in my opinion the speech most proper, at present, for a man of culture to make to a body of his fellow-countrymen who gets him into a committee-room, is Socra-tes's: *Know thyself!* and this is not a speech to be made by men wanting to be entrusted with power. For this very indifference to direct political action I have been taken to task by the *Daily Telegraph*, coupled, by a strange per-versity of fate, with just that very one of the Hebrew prophets whose style I admire the least, and called 'an elegant Jeremiah.' It is because I say (to use the words which the *Daily Telegraph* puts in my mouth):—'You mustn't make a fuss because you have no vote,—that is vulgarity; you mustn't hold big meetings to agitate for reform bills and to repeal corn laws,—that is the very height of vulgarity,'—it is for this reason that I am called, sometimes an elegant Jeremiah, sometimes a spurious Jeremiah, a Jeremiah about the reality of whose mission the writer in the *Daily Telegraph* has his doubts. It is evident, therefore, that I have so taken my line as not to be exposed to the whole brunt of Mr Frederic Harrison's censure. Still, I have often spoken in praise of culture, I have striven to make all my works and ways serve the interests of culture. I take culture to be something a great deal more than what Mr Frederic Harrison and others call it: 'a desirable quality in a critic of new books.' Nay, even though to a certain extent I am disposed to agree with Mr Frederic Harrison, that men of culture are just the class of responsible beings in this community of ours who cannot properly, at present, be entrusted with power, I am not sure that I do not think this the fault of our community rather than of the men of culture. In short, although, like Mr Bright and Mr Frederic Harrison, and the editor of the *Daily Telegraph*, and a large body of valued friends of mine, I am a Liberal, yet I am a Liberal tempered by experience, reflexion, and renouncement, and I am, above all, a believer in culture. Therefore I propose now to try and enquire, in the simple unsystematic way which best suits both my taste and my powers, what culture really is, what good it can do, what is our own special need of it; and I shall seek to find some plain grounds on which a faith in culture,—both my own faith in it and the faith of others,—may rest securely.

Chapter 1

Sweetness and Light

[3.] The disparagers of culture make its motive curiosity; sometimes, indeed, they make its motive mere exclusiveness and vanity. The culture which is supposed to plume itself on a smattering of Greek and Latin is a culture which is begotten by nothing so intellectual as curiosity; it is valued either out of sheer vanity and ignorance, or else as an engine of social and class distinction, separating its holder, like a badge or title, from other people who have not got it. No serious man would call this *culture*, or attach any value to it, as culture, at all. To find the real ground for the very differing estimate which serious people will set upon culture, we must find some motive for culture in the terms of which may lie a real ambiguity; and such a motive the word *curiosity* gives us.

[4.] I have before now pointed out that we English do not, like the foreigners, use the word in a good sense as well as in a bad sense. With us the word is always used in a somewhat disapproving sense. A liberal and intelligent eagerness about the things of the mind may be meant by a foreigner when he speaks of curiosity, but with us the word always conveys a certain notion of frivolous and unedifying activity. In the *Quarterly Review*, some little time ago, was an estimate of the celebrated French critic, M. Sainte-Beuve, and a very inadequate estimate it in my judgment was. And its inadequacy consisted chiefly in this: that in our English way it left out of sight the double sense really involved in the word *curiosity*, thinking enough was said to stamp M. Sainte-Beuve with blame if it was said that he was impelled in his operations as a critic by curiosity, and omitting either to perceive that M. Sainte-Beuve himself, and many other people with him, would consider that this was praiseworthy and not blameworthy, or to point out why it ought really to be accounted worthy of blame and not of praise. For as there is a curiosity about intellectual matters which is futile, and merely a disease, so there is certainly a curiosity,—a desire after the things of the mind simply for their own sakes and for the pleasure of seeing them as they are,—which is, in an intelligent being, natural and laudable. Nay, and the very desire to see things as they are, implies a balance and regulation of mind which is not often attained without fruitful effort, and which is the very opposite of the blind and diseased impulse of mind which is what we mean to blame when we blame curiosity. Montesquieu says:—'The first motive which ought to impel us to study is the desire to augment the excellence of our nature, and to render an intelligent being yet more intelligent.' This is the true ground to assign for the genuine scientific passion, however manifested, and for culture, viewed simply as a fruit of this passion; and it is a worthy ground, even though we let the term *curiosity* stand to describe it.

[5.] But there is of culture another view, in which not solely the scientific passion, the sheer desire to see things as they are, natural and proper in an intelligent being, appears as the ground of it. There is a view in which all the love of our neighbour, the impulses towards action, help, and beneficence, the desire for removing human error, clearing human confusion, and diminishing human misery, the noble aspiration to leave the world better and happier than we found it,—motives eminently such as are called social,—come in as part of the grounds of culture, and the main and preeminent part. Culture is then properly described not as having its origin in curiosity, but as having its origin in the love of perfection; it is *a study of perfection*. It moves by the force, not merely or primarily of the scientific passion for pure knowledge, but also of the moral and social passion for doing good. As, in the first view of it, we took for its worthy motto Montesquieu's words: 'To render an intelligent being yet more intelligent!' so, in the second view of it, there is no better motto which it can have than these words of Bishop Wilson: 'To make reason and the will of God prevail!'

[6.] Only, whereas the passion for doing good is apt to be over-hasty in determining what reason and the will of God say, because its turn is for acting rather than thinking and it wants to be beginning to act; and whereas it is apt to take its own conceptions, which proceed from its own state of development and share in all the imperfections and immaturities of this, for a basis of action; what distinguishes culture is, that it is possessed by the scientific passion as well as by the passion of doing good; that it demands worthy notions of reason and the will of God, and does not readily suffer its own crude conceptions to substitute themselves for them. And knowing that no action or institution can be salutary and stable which are not based on reason and the will of God, it is not so bent on acting and instituting, even with the great aim of diminishing human error and misery ever before its thoughts, but that it can remember that acting and instituting are of little use, unless we know how and what we ought to act and to institute.

[7.] This culture is more interesting and more far-reaching than that other, which is founded solely on the scientific passion for knowing. But it needs times of faith and ardour, times when the intellectual horizon is opening and widening all round us, to flourish in. And is not the close and bounded intellectual horizon within which we have long lived and moved now lifting up, and are not new lights finding free passage to shine in upon us? For a long time there was no passage for them to make their way in upon us, and then it was of no use to think of adapting the world's action to them. Where was the hope of making reason and the will of God prevail among people who had a routine which they had christened reason and the will of God, in which they were inextricably bound, and beyond which they had no power of looking? But now the iron force of adhesion to the old routine,—social, political, religious,—has wonderfully yielded; the iron force of exclusion of all which is new has wonderfully yielded. The danger now is, not that people should obstinately refuse to allow anything but their old routine to pass for reason and the will of God, but either that they should allow some novelty or other to pass for these too easily, or else that they should underrate the importance of them altogether, and think it enough to follow action for its own sake, without troubling themselves to make reason and the will of God prevail therein. Now, then, is the moment for culture to be of service, culture which believes in making reason and the will of God prevail, believes in perfection, is the study and pursuit of perfection, and is no longer debarred, by a rigid invincible exclusion of whatever is new, from getting acceptance for its ideas, simply because they are new.

[8.] The moment this view of culture is seized, the moment it is regarded not solely as the endeavour to see things as they are, to draw towards a knowledge of the universal order which seems to be intended and aimed at in the world, and which it is a man's happiness to go along with or his misery to go counter to,—to learn, in short, the will of God,—the moment, I say, culture is considered not merely as the endeavour to *see* and *learn* this, but as the endeavour, also, to make it *prevail*, the moral, social, and beneficent character of culture becomes manifest. The mere endeavour to see and learn the truth for our own personal satisfaction is indeed a commencement for making it prevail, a preparing the way for this, which always serves this, and is wrongly, therefore, stamped with blame absolutely in itself and not only in its caricature and degeneration. But perhaps it has got stamped with blame, and disparaged with the dubious title of curiosity, because in comparison with this wider endeavour of such great and plain utility it looks selfish, petty, and unprofitable.

[9.] And religion, the greatest and most important of the efforts by which the human race has manifested its impulse to perfect itself—religion, that voice of the deepest human experience,—does not only enjoin and sanction the aim which is the great aim of culture, the aim of setting ourselves to ascertain what perfection is and to make it prevail; but also, in determining generally in what human perfection consists, religion comes to a conclusion identical with that which culture,—culture seeking the determination of this question through *all* the voices of human experience which have been heard upon it, of art, science, poetry, philosophy, history, as well as of religion, in order to give a greater fulness and certainty to its solution,—likewise reaches. Religion says: *The kingdom of God is within you*; and culture, in like manner, places human perfection in an *internal* condition, in the growth and the predominance of our humanity proper, as distinguished from our animality. It places it in the ever-increasing efficacy and in the general harmonious expansion of those gifts of thought and feeling, which make the peculiar dignity, wealth, and happiness of human nature. As I have said on a former occasion: 'It is in making endless additions to itself, in the endless expansion of its powers, in endless growth in wisdom and beauty, that the spirit of the human race finds its ideal. To reach this ideal, culture is an indispensable aid, and that is the true value of culture.' Not a having and a resting, but a growing and a becoming, is the character of perfection as culture conceives it; and here, too, it coincides with religion.

[10.] And because men are all members of one great whole, and the sympathy which is in human nature will not allow one member to be indifferent to the rest or to have a perfect welfare independent of the rest, the expansion of our humanity, to suit the idea of perfection which culture forms, must be a *general* expansion. Perfection, as culture conceives it, is not possible while the individual remains isolated. The individual is required, under pain of being stunted and enfeebled in his own development if he disobeys, to carry others along with him in his march towards perfection, to be continually doing all he can to enlarge and increase the volume of the human stream sweeping thitherward. And here, once more, culture lays on us the same obligation as religion, which says, as Bishop Wilson has admirably put it, that 'to promote the kingdom of God is to increase and hasten one's own happiness.'

[11.] But, finally, perfection,—as culture from a thorough disinterested study of human nature and human experience learns to conceive it,—is a harmonious expansion of *all* the powers which make the beauty and worth of human nature, and is not consistent with the over-development of any one power at the expense of the rest. Here culture goes beyond religion, as religion is generally conceived by us.

[12.] If culture, then, is a study of perfection, and of harmonious perfection, general perfection, and perfection which consists in becoming something rather than in having something, in an inward condition of the mind and spirit, not in an outward set of circumstances,—it is clear that culture, instead of being the frivolous and useless thing which Mr Bright, and Mr Frederic Harrison, and many other Liberals are apt to call it, has a very important function to fulfil for mankind. And this function is particularly important in our modern world, of which the whole civilisation is, to a much greater degree than the civilisation of Greece and Rome, mechanical and external, and tends constantly to become more so. But above all in our own country has culture a weighty part to perform, because here that mechanical character, which civilisation tends to take everywhere, is shown in the most eminent degree. Indeed nearly all the characters of perfection, as culture teaches us to fix them, meet in this country with some powerful tendency which thwarts them and sets them at defiance. The idea of perfection as an *inward* condition of the mind and spirit is at variance with the mechanical and material civilisation in esteem with us, and nowhere, as I have said, so much in esteem as with us. The idea of perfection as a *general* expansion of the human family is at variance with our strong individualism, our hatred of all limits to the unrestrained swing of the individual's personality, our maxim of 'every man for himself.' Above all, the idea of perfection as a *harmonious* expansion of human nature is at variance with our want of flexibility, with our inaptitude for seeing more than one side of a thing, with our intense energetic absorption in the particular pursuit we happen to be following. So culture has a rough task to achieve in this country. Its preachers have, and are likely long to have, a hard time of it, and they will much oftener be regarded, for a great while to come, as elegant or spurious Jeremiahs, than as friends and benefactors. That, however, will not prevent their doing in the end good service if they persevere. And meanwhile, the mode of action they have to pursue, and the sort of habits they must fight against, ought to be made quite clear for every one to see, who may be willing to look at the matter attentively and dispassionately.

[13.] Faith in machinery is, I said, our besetting danger; often in machinery most absurdly disproportioned to the end which this machinery, if it is to do any good at all, is to serve; but always in machinery, as if it had a value in and for itself. What is freedom but machinery? what is population but machinery? what is coal but machinery? what are railroads but machinery? what is wealth but machinery? what are, even, religious organisations but machinery? Now almost every voice in England is accustomed to speak of these things as if they were precious ends in themselves, and therefore had some of the characters of perfection indisputably joined to them. . . . Every one must have observed the strange language current during the late discussions as to the possible failure of our supplies of coal. Our coal, thousands of people were saying, is the real basis of our national greatness; if our coal runs short, there is an end of the greatness of England. But what *is greatness?*—culture makes us ask. Greatness is a spiritual condition worthy to excite love, interest, and admiration; and the outward proof of possessing greatness is that we excite love, interest, and admiration. If England were swallowed up by the sea to-morrow, which of the two, a hundred years hence, would most excite the love, interest, and admiration of mankind,—would most, therefore, show the evidences of having possessed greatness,—the England of the last twenty years, or the England of Elizabeth, of a time of splendid spiritual effort, but when our coal, and our industrial operations depending on coal, were very little developed? Well, then, what an unsound habit of mind it must be which makes us talk of things like coal or iron as constituting the greatness of England, and how salutary a friend is culture, bent on seeing things as they are, and thus dissipating delusions of this kind and fixing standards of perfection that are real!

[14.] Wealth, again, that end to which our prodigious works for material advantage are directed,—the commonest of commonplaces tells us how men are always apt to regard wealth as a precious end in itself; and certainly they have never been so apt thus to regard it as they are in England at the present time. Never did people believe anything more firmly, than nine Englishmen out of ten at the present day believe that our greatness and welfare are proved by our being so very rich. Now, the use of culture is that it helps us, by means of its spiritual standard of perfection, to regard wealth as but machinery, and not only to say as a matter of words that we regard wealth as but machinery, but really to perceive and feel that it is so. If it were not for this purging effect wrought upon our minds by culture, the whole world, the future as well as the present, would inevitably belong to the Philistines. The people who believe most that our greatness and welfare are proved by our being very rich, and who most give their lives and thoughts to becoming rich, are just the very people whom we call Philistines. Culture says: 'Consider these people, then, their way of life, their habits, their manners, the very tones of their voice; look at them attentively; observe the literature they read, the things which give them pleasure, the words which come forth out of their mouths, the thoughts which make the furniture of their minds; would any amount of wealth be worth having with the condition that one was to become just like these people by having it?' And thus culture begets a dissatisfaction which is of the highest possible value in stemming the common tide of men's thoughts in a wealthy and industrial community, and which saves the future, as one may hope, from being vulgarised, even if it cannot save the present. . . .

[**15.**] In thus making sweetness and light to be characters of perfection, culture is of like spirit with poetry, follows one law with poetry. Far more than on our freedom, our population, and our industrialism, many amongst us rely upon our religious organisations to save us. I have called religion a yet more important manifestation of human nature than poetry, because it has worked on a broader scale for perfection, and with greater masses of men. But the idea of beauty and of a human nature perfect on all its sides, which is the dominant idea of poetry, is a true and invaluable idea, though it has not yet had the success that the idea of conquering the obvious faults of our animality, and of a human nature perfect on the moral side,—which is the dominant idea of religion,—has been enabled to have; and it is destined, adding to itself the religious idea of a devout energy, to transform and govern the other.

[**16.**] The best art and poetry of the Greeks, in which religion and poetry are one, in which the idea of beauty and of a human nature perfect on all sides adds to itself a religious and devout energy, and works in the strength of that, is on this account of such surpassing interest and instructiveness for us, though it was,—as, having regard to the human race in general, and, indeed, having regard to the Greeks themselves, we must own,—a premature attempt, an attempt which for success needed the moral and religious fibre in humanity to be more braced and developed than it had yet been. But Greece did not err in having the idea of beauty, harmony, and complete human perfection, so present and paramount. It is impossible to have this idea too present and paramount; only, the moral fibre must be braced too. And we, because we have braced the moral fibre, are not on that account in the right way, if at the same time the idea of beauty, harmony, and complete human perfection, is wanting or misapprehended amongst us; and evidently it *is* wanting or misapprehended at present. And when we rely as we do on our religious organisations, which in themselves do not and cannot give us this idea, and think we have done enough if we make them spread and prevail, then, I say, we fall into our common fault of overvaluing machinery. . . .

[**17.**] The impulse of the English race towards moral development and self-conquest has nowhere so powerfully manifested itself as in Puritanism. Nowhere has Puritanism found so adequate an expression as in the religious organisation of the Independents. The modern Independents have a newspaper, the *Nonconformist*, written with great sincerity and ability. The motto, the standard, the profession of faith which this organ of theirs carries aloft, is: 'The Dissidence of Dissent and the Protestation of the Protestant religion.' There is sweetness and light, and an ideal of complete harmonious human perfection! One need not go to culture and poetry to find language to judge it. Religion, with its instinct for perfection, supplies language to judge it, language, too, which is in our mouths every day. 'Finally, be of one mind, united in feeling,' says St Peter. There is an ideal which judges the Puritan ideal: 'The Dissidence of Dissent and the Protestation of the Protestant religion!' And religious organisations like this are what people believe in, rest in, would give their lives for! Such, I say, is the wonderful virtue of even the beginnings of perfection, of having conquered even the plain faults of our animality, that the religious organisation which has helped us to do it can seem to us something precious, salutary, and to be propagated, even when it wears such a brand of imperfection on its forehead as this. And men have got such a habit of giving to the language of religion a special application, of making it a mere jargon, that for the condemnation which religion itself passes on the shortcomings of their religious organisations they have no ear; they are sure to cheat themselves and to explain this condemnation away. They can only be reached by the criticism which culture, like poetry, speaking a language not to be sophisticated, and resolutely testing these organisations by the ideal of a human perfection complete on all sides, applies to them.

[18.] But men of culture and poetry, it will be said, are again and again failing, and failing conspicuously, in the necessary first stage to a harmonious perfection, in the subduing of the great obvious faults of our animality, which it is the glory of these religious organisations to have helped us to subdue. True, they do often so fail. They have often been without the virtues as well as the faults of the Puritan; it has been one of their dangers that they so felt the Puritan's faults that they too much neglected the practice of his virtues. I will not, however, exculpate them at the Puritan's expense. They have often failed in morality, and morality is indispensable. And they have been punished for their failure, as the Puritan has been rewarded for his performance. They have been punished wherein they erred; but their ideal of beauty, of sweetness and light, and a human nature complete on all its sides, remains the true ideal of perfection still; just as the Puritan's ideal of perfection remains narrow and inadequate, although for what he did well he has been richly rewarded . . . I say that the English reliance on our religious organisations and on their ideas of human perfection just as they stand, is like our reliance on freedom, on muscular Christianity, on population, on coal, on wealth,—mere belief in machinery, and unfruitful; and that it is wholesomely counteracted by culture, bent on seeing things as they are, and on drawing the human race onwards to a more complete, a harmonious perfection.

[19.] Culture, however, shows its single-minded love of perfection, its desire simply to make reason and the will of God prevail, its freedom from fanaticism, by its attitude towards all this machinery, even while it insists that it *is* machinery. Fanatics, seeing the mischief men do themselves by their blind belief in some machinery or other,—whether it is wealth and industrialism, or whether it is the cultivation of bodily strength and activity, or whether it is a political organisation,—or whether it is a religious organisation,—oppose with might and main the tendency to this or that political and religious organisation, or to games and athletic exercises, or to wealth and industrialism, and try violently to stop it. But the flexibility which sweetness and light give, and which is one of the rewards of culture pursued in good faith, enables a man to see that a tendency may be necessary, and even, as a preparation for something in the future, salutary, and yet that the generations or individuals who obey this tendency are sacrificed to it, that they fall short of the hope of perfection by following it; and that its mischiefs are to be criticised, lest it should take too firm a hold and last after it has served its purpose.

[20.] ... But what was it, this liberalism, as Dr Newman saw it, and as it really broke the Oxford movement? It was the great middle-class liberalism, which had for the cardinal points of its belief the Reform Bill of 1832, and local self-government, in politics; in the social sphere, free-trade, unrestricted competition, and the making of large industrial fortunes; in the religious sphere, the Dissidence of Dissent and the Protestantism of the Protestant religion. I do not say that other and more intelligent forces than this were not opposed to the Oxford movement: but this was the force which really beat it; this was the force which Dr Newman felt himself fighting with; this was the force which till only the other day seemed to be the paramount force in this country, and to be in possession of the future; this was the force whose achievements fill Mr Lowe with such inexpressible admiration, and whose rule he was so horror-struck to see threatened. And where is this great force of Philistinism now? It is thrust into the second rank, it is become a power of yesterday, it has lost the future. A new power has suddenly appeared, a power which it is impossible yet to judge fully, but which is certainly a wholly different force from middle-class liberalism; different in its cardinal points of belief, different in its tendencies in every sphere. It loves and admires neither the legalisation of middle-class Parliaments, nor the local self-government of middle-class vestries, nor the unrestricted competition of middle-class industrialists, nor the dissidence of middle-class Dissent and the Protestantism of middle-class Protestant religion. I am not now praising this new force, or saying that its own ideals are better; all I say is, that they are wholly different. And who will estimate how much the currents of feeling created by Dr Newman's movements, the keen desire for beauty and sweetness which it nourished, the deep aversion it manifested to the hardness and vulgarity of middle-class liberalism, the strong light it turned on the hideous and grotesque illusions of middle-class Protestantism,—who will estimate how much all these contributed to swell the tide of secret dissatisfaction which has mined the ground under the self-confident liberalism of the last thirty years, and has prepared the way for its sudden collapse and supersession? It is in this manner that the sentiment of Oxford for beauty and sweetness conquers, and in this manner long may it continue to conquer!

[21.] In this manner it works to the same end as culture, and there is plenty of work for it yet to do. I have said that the new and more democratic force which is now superseding our middle-class liberalism cannot yet be rightly judged. It has its main tendencies still to form. We hear promises of its giving us administrative reform, law reform, reform of education, and I know not what; but those promises come rather from its advocates, wishing to make a good plea for it and to justify it for superseding middle-class liberalism, than from clear tendencies which it has itself yet developed. But meanwhile it has plenty of well-maintained friends against whom culture may with advantage continue to uphold steadily its ideal of human perfection; that this is *an inward spiritual activity, having for its characters increased sweetness, increased light, increased life, increased sympathy.* Mr Bright, who has a foot in both worlds, the world of middle-class liberalism and the world of democracy, but who brings most of his ideas from the world of middle-class liberalism in which he was bred, always inclines to inculcate that faith in machinery to which, as we have seen, Englishmen are so prone, and which has been the bane of middle-class liberalism. He complains with a sorrowful indignation of people who 'appear to have no proper estimate of the value of the franchise;' he leads his disciples to believe,—what the Englishman is always too ready to believe,—that the having a vote, like the having a large family, or a large business, or large muscles, has in itself some edifying and perfecting effect upon human nature. Or else he cries out to the democracy,—'the men,' as he calls them, 'upon whose shoulders the greatness of England rests,'—he cries out to them: 'See what you have done! I look over this country and see the cities you have built, the railroads you have made, the manufactures you have produced, the cargoes which freight the ships of the greatest mercantile navy the world has ever seen! I see that you have converted by your labours what was once a wilderness, these islands, into a fruitful garden; I know that you have created this wealth, and are a nation whose name is a word of power throughout all world.' Why, this is just the very style of laudation with which Mr Roebuck or Mr Lowe debauch the minds of the middle classes, and make such Philistines of them. It is the same fashion of teaching a man to value himself not on what he *is*, not on his progress in sweetness and light, but on the number of the railroads he has constructed, or the bigness of the tabernacle he has built. Only the middle classes are told they have done it all with their energy, self-reliance, and capital, and the democracy are told they have done it all with their hands and sinews. But teaching the democracy to put its trust in achievements of this kind is merely training them to be Philistines to take the place of the Philistines whom they are superseding; and they too, like the middle class, will be encouraged to sit down at the banquet of the future without having on a wedding garment, and nothing excellent can then come from them. . . .

[22.] Other well-meaning friends of this new power are for leading it, not in the old ruts of middle-class Philistinism, but in ways which are naturally alluring to the feet of democracy, though in this country they are novel and untried ways. I may call them the ways of Jacobinism. Violent indignation with the past, abstract systems of renovation applied whole-sale, a new doctrine drawn up in black and white for elaborating down to the very smallest details a rational society for the future,—these are the ways of Jacobinism. . . . Culture is always assigning to system-makers and systems a smaller share in the bent of human destiny than their friends like. A current in people's minds sets towards new ideas; people are dissatisfied with their old narrow stock of Philistine ideas, Anglo-Saxon ideas, or any other; and some man, some Bentham or Comte, who has the real merit of having early and strongly felt and helped the new current, but who brings plenty of narrowness and mistakes of his own into his feeling and help of it, is credited with being the author of the whole current, the fit person to be entrusted with its regulation and to guide the human race.

[23.] . . . Jacobinism, in its fierce hatred of the past and of those whom it makes liable for the sins of the past, cannot away with the inexhaustible indulgence proper to culture, the consideration of circumstances, the severe judgment of actions joined to the merciful judgment of persons. 'The man of culture is in politics,' cries Mr Frederic Harrison, 'one of the poorest mortals alive!' Mr Frederic Harrison wants to be doing business, and he complains that the man of culture stops him with a 'turn for small fault-finding, love of selfish ease, and indecision in action.' Of what use is cul-ture, he asks, except for 'a critic of new books or a professor of *belles lettres*?' Why, it is of use because, in presence of the fierce exasperation which breathes, or rather, I may say, hisses, through the whole production in which Mr Frederic Harrison asks that question, it reminds us that the perfection of human nature is sweetness and light. It is of use because, like religion,—that other effort after perfection,—it testifies that, where bitter envying and strife are, there is confusion and every evil work.

[24.] The pursuit of perfection, then, is the pursuit of sweetness and light. He who works for sweetness and light, works to make reason and the will of God prevail. He who works for machinery, he who works for hatred, works only for confusion. Culture looks beyond machinery, culture hates hatred; culture has one great passion, the passion for sweetness and light. It has one even yet greater!—the passion for making them *prevail*. It is not satisfied till we *all* come to a perfect man; it knows that the sweetness and light of the few must be imperfect until the raw and unkindled masses of humanity are touched with sweetness and light. If I have not shrunk from saying that we must work for sweetness and light, so neither have I shrunk from saying that we must have a broad basis, must have sweetness and light for as many as possible. Again and again I have insisted how those are the happy moments of humanity, how those are the marking epochs of a people's life, how those are the flowering times for literature and art and all the creative power of genius, when there is a *national* glow of life and thought, when the whole of society is in the fullest measure permeated by thought, sensible to beauty, intelligent and alive. Only it must be *real* thought and *real* beauty; *real* sweetness and *real* light. Plenty of people will try to give the masses, as they call them, an intellectual food prepared and adapted in the way they think proper for the actual condition of the masses. The ordinary popular literature is an example of this way of working on the masses. Plenty of people will try to indoctrinate the masses with the set of ideas and judgments constituting the creed of their own profession or party. Our religious and political organisations give an example of this way of working on the masses. I condemn neither way; but culture works differently. It does not try to teach down to the level of inferior classes; it does not try to win them for this or that sect of its own, with ready-made judgments and watchwords. It seeks to do away with classes; to make the best that has been thought and known in the world current everywhere; to make all men live in an atmosphere of sweetness and light, where they may use ideas, as it uses them itself, freely,—nourished, and not bound by them.

[25.] This is the *social idea*; and the men of culture are the true apostles of equality. The great men of culture are those who have had a passion for diffusing, for making prevail, for carrying from one end of society to the other, the best knowledge, the best ideas of their time; who have laboured to divest knowledge of all that was harsh, uncouth, difficult, abstract, professional, exclusive; to humanise it, to make it efficient outside the clique of the cultivated and learned, yet still remaining the *best* knowledge and thought of the time, and a true source, therefore, of sweetness and light. Such a man was Abelard in the Middle Ages, in spite of all his imperfections, and thence the boundless emotion and enthusiasm which Abelard excited. . . .

(*Culture and Anarchy*, 1869, 3rd edn., 1882, Introduction and Ch. 1.)

IV.14 George Henry Lewes, from 'Dickens in Relation to Criticism' (Feb. 1872)

[1.] The old feud between authors and critics, a feud old as literature, has not arisen on the ground of chariness in praise, but rather on the ground of deficient sympathy, and the tendency to interpret an author's work according to some standard which is not his. Instead of placing themselves at his point of view, and seeing what he has attempted, how far he has achieved the aim, and whether the aim itself were worthy of achievement, critics have thrust between his work and the public some vague conception of what they required, and measured it by an academic or conventional standard derived from other works. Fond as an author necessarily is of praise, and pained as he must always be by blame, he is far more touched by a sympathetic recognition of his efforts, and far more hurt by a misrepresentation of them. No hyperbole of laudation gives a tithe of the delight which is given by sympathetic insight. Unhappily for the author, this can but sparingly be given by critics, who trust less to their emotions than to their standards of judgment; for the greater the originality of the writer, and the less inclination he has for familiar processes and already-trodden tracks, the greater must be the resistance he will meet with from minds accustomed to move in those tracks, and to consider excellence confined within them. It is in the nature of the critical mind to judge according to precedent; and few minds have flexibility enough to adopt at once a novelty which is destined in its turn to become a precedent.

[2.] There is another source of pain. Besides the very great difficulties of independent judgment, of adjusting the mental focus to new objects under new perspectives, and the various personal considerations which trammel even open minds—considerations of friendship, station, renown, rivalry, etc.—there is the immense difficulty which all men find in giving anything like an adequate expression to their judgments. It is easy for us to say that a book has stirred, or instructed us; but it is by no means easy to specify the grounds of our pleasure, or profit, except in a very general way; and when we attempt to do so we are apt to make ludicrous mistakes. Thus it is that the criticism which begins with a general expression of gratitude to the author, will often deeply pain him by misplaced praise, or blame misdirected.

[3.] Longinus declares that criticism is the last result of abundant experience; he might have added that even the amplest experience is no safeguard against utter failure. For it is true in Art as in the commonest details of life, that our perceptions are mainly determined by our pre-perceptions, our conceptions by our preconceptions. Hence I have long maintained the desirability of preserving as far as possible the individual character of criticism. The artist in his work gives expression to his individual feelings and conceptions, telling us how Life and Nature are mirrored in his mind; we may fairly state how this affects us, whether it accords with our experience, whether it moves or instructs us; but we should be very chary of absolute judgments, and be quite sure of our ground before venturing to assume that the public will feel, or ought to feel, as we feel. Now it is the tendency of criticism to pronounce absolute verdicts, to speak for all; and the exasperation of the artist at finding individual impressions given forth as final judgments is the main cause of the outcry against criticism. The writer who would feel little irritation on hearing that A. and B. were unmoved by his pathos, dead to his humour, unenlightened by his philosophy, may be excused if he writhe under the authoritative announcement that his pathos is maudlin, his humour flat, his philosophy shallow.

He may be convicted of bad grammar, bad drawing, bad logic; and if the critic advances reasons for particular objections, these reasons may be weighed, and perhaps accepted with resignation if not without pain; but no verdict which does not distinctly carry its evidence can be accepted as more than an individual judgment; and in matters of Art there is always great difficulty, sometimes a sheer impossibility, in passing from the individual to the universal. It is impossible to resist feeling. If an author makes me laugh, he is humorous; if he makes me cry, he is pathetic. In vain will any one tell me that such a picture is not laughable, not pathetic; or that I am wrong in being moved.

[4.] While from these and other causes, especially from the tendency to exaggerate what is painful, authors have deeply resented 'the malevolence' of critics—a malevolence which has been mostly incompetence, or inconsiderateness—it is not less true that there has been much heartfelt gratitude given by authors to critics who have sympathised with and encouraged them; and many lasting friendships have been thus cemented. It was thus that the lifelong friendship of Dickens and his biographer began, and was sustained. Nor is it just to object to Mr. Forster's enthusiasm on the ground of his friendship, since he may fairly answer, 'Dickens was my friend because I so greatly admired him.' One thing is certain: his admiration was expressed long before all the world had acknowledged Dickens's genius, and was continued through the long years when the majority of writers had ceased to express much fervour of admiration, preferring rather to dwell on his shortcomings and exaggerations.

[5.] And this brings me to the noticeable fact that there probably never was a writer of so vast a popularity whose genius was so little *appreciated* by the critics. The very splendour of his successes so deepened the shadow of his failures that to many eyes the shadows supplanted the splendour. Fastidious readers were loath to admit that a writer could be justly called great whose defects were so glaring. They admitted, because it was indisputable, that Dickens delighted thousands, that his admirers were found in all classes, and in all countries; that he stirred the sympathy of masses not easily reached through Literature, and always stirred healthy, generous emotions; that he impressed a new direction on popular writing, and modified the Literature of his age, in its spirit no less than in its form; but they nevertheless insisted on his defects as if these outweighed all positive qualities; and spoke of him either with condescending patronage, or with sneering irritation. Surely this is a fact worthy of investigation? Were the critics wrong, and if so, in what consisted their error? How are we to reconcile this immense popularity with this critical contempt? The private readers and the public critics who were eager to take up each successive number of his works as it appeared, whose very talk was seasoned with quotations from and allusions to these works, who, to my knowledge, were wont to lay aside books of which they could only speak in terms of eulogy, in order to bury themselves in the 'new number' when the well-known green cover made its appearance—were nevertheless at this very time niggard in their praise, and lavish in their scorn of the popular humorist. It is not long since I heard a very distinguished man express measureless contempt for Dickens, and a few minutes afterwards, in reply to some representations on the other side, admit that Dickens had 'entered into his life.'

[6.] Dickens has proved his power by a popularity almost unexampled, embracing all classes. Surely it is a task for criticism to exhibit the sources of that power? If everything that has ever been alleged against the works be admitted, there still remains an immense success to be accounted for. It was not by their defects that these works were carried over Europe and America. It was not their defects which made them the delight of grey heads on the bench, and the study of youngsters in the counting-house and school-room. Other writers have been exaggerated, untrue, fantastic, and melodramatic; but they have gained so little notice that no one thinks of pointing out their defects. It is clear, therefore, that Dickens had powers which enabled him to triumph in spite of the weaknesses which clogged them; and it is worth inquiring what those powers were, and their relation to his undeniable defects.

[7.] I am not about to attempt such an inquiry, but simply to indicate two or three general points of view. It will be enough merely to mention in passing the primary cause of his success, his overflowing fun, because even uncompromising opponents admit it. They may be ashamed of their laughter, but they laugh. A revulsion of feeling at the preposterousness or extravagance of the image may follow the burst of laughter, but the laughter is irresistible, whether rational or not, and there is no arguing away such a fact.

[8.] Great as Dickens is in fun, so great that Fielding and Smollett are small in comparison, he would have been only a passing amusement for the world had he not been gifted with an imagination of marvellous vividness, and an emotional, sympathetic nature capable of furnishing that imagination with elements of universal power. Of him it may be said with less exaggeration than of most poets, that he was of 'imagination all compact': if the other higher faculties were singularly deficient in him, this faculty was imperial. He was a seer of visions; and his visions were of objects at once familiar and potent. Psychologists will understand both the extent and the limitation of the remark, when I say that in no other perfectly sane mind (Blake, I believe, was not perfectly sane) have I observed vividness of imagination approaching so closely to hallucination.

[9.] . . . What seems preposterous, impossible to us, seemed to him simple fact of observation. When he imagined a street, a house, a room, a figure, he saw it not in the vague schematic way of ordinary imagination, but in the sharp definition of actual perception, all the salient details obtruding themselves on his attention. He, seeing it thus vividly, made us also see it; and believing in its reality however fantastic, he communicated something of his belief to us. He presented it in such relief that we ceased to think of it as a picture. So definite and insistent was the image, that even while knowing it was false we could not help, for a moment, being affected, as it were, by his hallucination.

[10.] This glorious energy of imagination is that which Dickens had in common with all great writers. It was this which made him a creator, and made his creations universally intelligible, no matter how fantastic and unreal. His types established themselves in the public mind like personal experiences. Their falsity was unnoticed in the blaze of their illumination. Every humbug seemed a Pecksniff, every nurse a Gamp, every jovial improvident a Micawber, every stinted serving-wench a Marchioness. Universal experiences became individualised in these types; an image and a name were given, and the image was so suggestive that it seemed to *express* all that it was found to *recall*, and Dickens was held to have depicted what his readers supplied. Against such power criticism was almost idle. In vain critical reflection showed these figures to be merely masks,—not characters, but personified characteristics, caricatures and distortions of human nature,—the vividness of their presentation triumphed over reflection: their creator managed to communicate to the public his own unhesitating belief. Unreal and impossible as these types were, speaking a language never heard in life, moving like pieces of simple mechanism always in one way (instead of moving with the infinite fluctuations of organisms, incalculable yet intelligible, surprising yet familiar), these unreal figures affected the uncritical reader with the force of reality; and they did so in virtue of their embodiment of some real characteristic vividly presented. The imagination of the author laid hold of some well-marked physical trait, some peculiarity of aspect, speech, or manner which every one recognised at once; and the force with which this was presented made it occupy the mind to the exclusion of all critical doubts: only reflection could detect the incongruity. . . . Just as the wooden horse is brought within the range of the child's emotions, and dramatizing tendencies, when he can handle and draw it, so Dickens's figures are brought within the range of the reader's interests, and receive from these interests a sudden illumination, when they are the puppets of a drama every incident of which appeals to the sympathies. With a fine felicity of instinct he seized upon situations having an irresistible hold over the domestic affections and ordinary sympathies. He spoke in the mother-tongue of the heart, and was always sure of ready listeners. He painted the life he knew, the life every one knew; for if the scenes and manners were unlike those we were familiar with, the feelings and motives, the joys and griefs, the mistakes and efforts of the actors were universal, and therefore universally intelligible; so that even critical spectators who complained that these broadly painted pictures were artistic daubs, could not wholly resist their effective suggestiveness. He set in motion the secret springs of sympathy by touching the domestic affections. He painted nothing ideal, heroic; but all the resources of the bourgeois epic were in his grasp. The world of thought and passion lay beyond his horizon. But the joys and pains of childhood, the petty tyrannies of ignoble natures, the genial pleasantries of happy natures, the life of the poor, the struggles of the street and back parlour, the insolence of office, the sharp social contrasts, east-wind and Christmas jollity, hunger, misery, and hot punch— these he could deal with, so that we laughed and cried, were startled at the revelation of familiar facts hitherto unnoted, and felt our pulses quicken as we were hurried along with him in his fanciful flight.

[11.] ... Dickens once declared to me that every word said by his characters was distinctly *heard* by him; I was at first not a little puzzled to account for the fact that he could hear language so utterly unlike the language of real feeling, and not be aware of its preposterousness; but the surprise vanished when I thought of the phenomena of hallucination. And here it may be needful to remark in passing that it is not because the characters are badly drawn and their language unreal, that they are to be classed among the excesses of imagination; otherwise all the bad novelists and dramatists would be credited with that which they especially want— powerful imagination. His peculiarity is not the incorrectness of the drawing, but the vividness of the imagination which while rendering that incorrectness insensible to him, also renders it potent with multitudes of his fellowmen. For although his weakness comes from excess in one direction, the force which is in excess must not be overlooked; and it is overlooked or undervalued by critics who, with what I have called the bias of opposition, insist only on the weakness.

[12.] This leads me to the second point, the bias of technical estimate. The main purpose of Art is delight. Whatever influences may radiate from that centre,—and however it may elevate or modify,—the one primary condition of influence is stirred emotion. No Art can teach which does not move; no Art can move without teaching. Criticism has to consider Art under two aspects, that of emotional pleasure, and that of technical pleasure. We all—public and critics—are susceptible of the former, are capable of being moved, and are delighted with what stirs the emotions, filling the mind with images having emotional influence; but only the critics are much affected by technical skill, and the pleasure it creates. *What* is done, what is suggested, constitutes the first aspect; *how* it is done the second. We all delight in imitation, and in the skill which represents one object in another medium; but the refinements of skill can only be appreciated by study. ...

[13.] How easily the critic falls into the mistake of overvaluing technical skill, and not allowing for the primary condition, how easily he misjudges works by applying to them technical rules derived from the works of others, need not here be dwelt on. What I wish to indicate is the bias of technical estimate which, acting with that bias of opposition just noted, has caused the critics to overlook in Dickens the great artistic powers which are proved by his immense success; and to dwell only on those great artistic deficiencies which exclude him from the class of exquisite writers. He worked in delf, not in porcelain. But his prodigal imagination created in delf forms which delighted thousands. He only touched common life, but he touched it to 'fine issues'; and since we are all susceptible of being moved by pictures of children in droll and pathetic situations, and by pictures of common suffering and common joy, any writer who can paint such pictures with sufficient skill to awaken these emotions is powerful in proportion to the emotion stirred. That Dickens had this skill is undisputed; and if critical reflection shows that the means he employs are not such as will satisfy the technical estimate, and consequently that the pictures will not move the cultivated mind, nor give it the deep content which perfect Art continues to create, making the work a 'joy for ever,' we must still remember that in the present state of Literature, with hundreds daily exerting their utmost efforts to paint such pictures, it requires prodigious force and rare skill to impress images that will stir the universal heart. Murders are perpetrated without stint, but the murder of Nancy is unforgettable. Children figure in numberless plays and novels, but the deaths of little Nell and little Paul were national griefs. Seduction is one of the commonest of tragedies, but the scene in Peggotty's boat-house burns itself into the memory. Captain Cuttle and Richard Swiveller, the Marchioness and Tilly Slowboy, Pecksniff and Micawber, Tiny Tim and Mrs. Gamp, may be imperfect presentations of human character, but they are types which no one can forget. Dr. Johnson explained the popularity of some writer by saying, 'Sir, *his* nonsense suited *their* nonsense'; let us add, 'and his sense suited their sense,' and it will explain the popularity of Dickens. Readers to whom all the refinements of Art and Literature are as meaningless hieroglyphs, were at once laid hold of by the reproduction of their own feelings, their own experiences, their own prejudices, in the irradiating splendour of his imagination; while readers whose cultivated sensibilities were alive to the most delicate and evanescent touches were, by virtue of their common nature, ready to be moved and delighted at his pictures and suggestions. The cultivated and uncultivated were affected by his admirable *mise en scène*, his fertile invention, his striking selection of incident, his intense vision of physical details. Only the cultivated who are made fastidious by cultivation paused to consider the pervading commonness of the works, and remarked that they are wholly without glimpses of a nobler life; and that the writer presents an almost unique example of a mind of singular force in which, so to speak, sensations never passed into ideas. Dickens sees and feels, but the logic of feeling seems the only logic he can manage. Thought is strangely absent from his works. I do not suppose a single thoughtful remark on life or character could be found throughout the twenty volumes. Not only is there a marked absence of the reflective tendency, but one sees no indication of the past life of humanity having ever occupied him; keenly as he observes the objects before him, he never connects his observations into a general expression, never seems interested in general relations of things. Compared with that of Fielding or Thackeray, his was merely an *animal* intelligence, *i.e.*, restricted to perceptions. On this ground his early education was more fruitful and less injurious than it would have been to a nature constructed on a more reflective and intellectual type. It furnished him with rare and valuable experience, early developed his sympathies with the lowly and struggling, and did not starve any intellectual ambition. He never was and never would have been a student.

[**14.**] My acquaintance with him began soon after the completion of 'Pickwick.' Something I had written on that book pleased him, and caused him to ask me to call on him. (It is pleasant for me to remember that I made Thackeray's acquaintance in a similar way.) He was then living in Doughty Street; and those who remember him at that period will understand the somewhat disturbing effect produced on my enthusiasm for the new author by the sight of his bookshelves, on which were ranged nothing but three-volume novels and books of travel, all obviously the presentation copies from authors and publishers, with none of the treasures of the bookstall, each of which has its history, and all giving the collection its individual physiognomy. A man's library expresses much of his hidden life. I did not expect to find a bookworm, nor even a student, in the marvellous 'Boz'; but nevertheless this collection of books was a shock. He shortly came in, and his sunny presence quickly dispelled all misgivings. He was then, as to the last, a delightful companion, full of sagacity as well as animal spirits; but I came away more impressed with the fulness of life and energy than with any sense of distinction. I believe I only saw him once more before I went to Germany, and two years had elapsed when next we met. While waiting in his library (in Devonshire Terrace) I of course glanced at the books. The well-known paper boards of the three-volume novel no longer vulgarised the place; a goodly array of standard works, well-bound, showed a more respectable and conventional ambition; but there was no physiognomy in the collection. A greater change was visible in Dickens himself. In these two years he had remarkably developed. His conversation turned on graver subjects than theatres and actors, periodicals and London life. His interest in public affairs, especially in social questions, was keener. He still remained completely outside philosophy, science, and the higher literature, and was too unaffected a man to pretend to feel any interest in them. But the vivacity and sagacity which gave a charm to intercourse with him had become weighted with a seriousness which from that time forward became more and more prominent in his conversation and his writings. He had already learned to look upon the world as a scene where it was the duty of each man in his own way to make the lot of the miserable Many a little less miserable; and, having learned that his genius gave him great power, he was bent on using that power effectively. He was sometimes laughed at for the importance he seemed to attach to everything relating to himself, and the solemnity with which he spoke of his aims and affairs; but this belonged to his quality. *Il se prenait au sérieux*, and was admirable because he did so. Whatever faults he may have committed there were none attributable to carelessness. He gave us his best. If the effort were sometimes too strained, and the desire for effect too obtrusive, there was no lazy indulgence, no trading on a great renown, no 'scumbling' in his work. 'Whatever I have tried to do in life,' he said, speaking through Copperfield, 'I have tried with all my heart to do well. Never to put one hand to anything on which I could throw my whole self, and never to affect depreciation of my work, whatever it was, I now find to have been my golden rules.' . . .

[15.] In bringing these detached observations to a close, let me resume their drift by saying that while on the one hand the critics seem to me to have been fully justified in denying him the possession of many technical excellencies, they have been thrown into unwise antagonism which has made them overlook or undervalue the great qualities which distinguished him; and that even on technical grounds their criticism has been so far defective that it failed to recognise the supreme powers which ensured his triumph in spite of all defects. For the reader of cultivated taste there is little in his works beyond the stirring of their emotions—but what a large exception! We do not turn over the pages in search of thought, delicate psychological observation, grace of style, charm of composition; but we enjoy them like children at a play, laughing and crying at the images which pass before us. And this illustration suggests the explanation of how learned and thoughtful men can have been almost as much delighted with the works as ignorant and juvenile readers; how Lord Jeffrey could have been so affected by the presentation of Little Nell, which most critical readers pronounce maudlin and unreal. Persons unfamiliar with theatrical representations, consequently unable to criticise the acting, are stirred by the suggestions of the scenes presented; and hence a great philosopher, poet, or man of science, may be found applauding an actor whom every play-going apprentice despises as stagey and inartistic.

(*Fortnightly Review*, Feb. 1872.)

IV.15 From 'Holidays and How to Keep Them' (6 July 1872)

And remember, too, that recreation is a vital element of the holiday. This word has been abused, and has somehow got to degrade itself with a lower sense than it deserves. In a true holiday we gather new life for work. We generate fresh steam in our boilers. We give ourselves and our small family of wits an airing in the sunshine, that they may get another store of energy . . . a holiday should be—true recreation. Not mere indulgence, not debauch, not the wanton yielding to the sheer spirit of licence; but recreation, renewal, for the wholesomer stronger discharge of our duty when we get home. That is no 'holy' day when the man comes back to his work with bleared eyes, a racking head-ache, and a shaky hand. Such holidays do no real good. It is true that in this age, in some places, work is so pressing that a man is drained of more strength than he ought to part with, and then nature avenges herself, and tempts him to accelerate the process of escape from care by indulgence in that intemperance which is the curse of our land. A delusive attempt. The drunken holiday may indeed put away all thought or remembrance of toil for a few hours, but it is itself a terrible draft upon the life which the holiday-maker professes to renew.

. . . I am loth to commend a visit to the seaside as it is generally paid. To be sure, you have the sea . . . the beach, either sand . . . or shingle . . . You can certainly have this at most watering-places; but the style and shallow fashion of these is, to my mind, monotonously oppressive. There is often a sort of toyshop look about them, and a donkey-driving, band-listening, telescopic weariness of pertinacity which is soon tiresome. Then, too generally, you are like flies in a web, the prey of the lodging-house keepers, who, poor people, of course suck as much as possible out of the visitors whom they catch. If you want to combine sea air and exercise in a short holiday, take a walking tour by the seaside, and use the frequented watering-places only as stations in which to rest for a night or for a meal. . . .

(*Leisure Hour*, 6 July 1872)

Walter Pater, from *The Renaissance* (1873)   IV.1€

To burn always with this hard, gemlike flame, to maintain his ecstasy, is success in life. In a sense it might even be said that our failure is to form habits: for, after all, habit is relative to a stereotyped world, and meantime it is only the roughness of the eye that makes any two persons, things, situations, seem alike. While all melts under our feet, we may well grasp at any exquisite passion, or any contribution to knowledge that seems by a lifted horizon to set the spirit free for a moment, or any stirring of the senses, strange dyes, strange colours, and curious odours, or work of the artist's hands, or the face of one's friend. Not to discriminate every moment some passionate attitude in those about us, and in the very brilliancy of their gifts some tragic dividing of forces on their ways, is, on this short day of frost and sun, to sleep before evening. With the sense of the splendour of our experience and of its awful brevity, gathering all we are into one desperate effort to see and touch, we shall hardly have time to make theories about

7. Lord Leighton of Stretton: *Captive Andromache* 1888

the things we see and touch. What we have to do is to be for ever curiously testing new opinions and courting new impressions, never acquiescing in a facile orthodoxy of Comte, or of Hegel, or of our own. Philosophical theories or ideas, as points of view, instruments of criticism, may help us to gather up what might otherwise pass unregarded by us. 'Philosophy is the microscope of thought.' The theory or idea or system which requires of us the sacrifice of any part of this experience, in consideration of some interest into which we cannot enter, or some abstract theory we have not identified with ourselves, or of what is only conventional, has no real claim upon us.

One of the most beautiful passages of Rousseau is that in the sixth book of the *Confessions* where he describes the awakening in him of the literary sense. An undefinable taint of death had clung always about him, and now in early manhood he believed himself smitten by mortal disease. He asked himself how he might make as much as possible of the interval that remained; and he was not biassed by anything in his previous life when he decided that it must be by intellectual excitement, which he found just then in the clear, fresh writings of Voltaire. Well! we are all *condamnés*, as Victor Hugo says: we are all under sentence of death but with a sort of indefinite reprieve—*les hommes sont tous condamnés à mort avec des sursis indéfinis*: we have an interval, and then our place knows us no more. Some spend this interval in listlessness, some in high passions, the wisest, at least among 'the children of this world,' in art and song. For our one chance lies in expanding that interval, in getting as many pulsations as possible into the given time. Great passions may give us this quickened sense of life, ecstasy and sorrow of love, the various forms of enthusiastic activity, disinterested or otherwise, which come naturally to many of us. Only be sure it is passion—that it does yield you this fruit of a quickened, multiplied consciousness. Of such wisdom, the poetic passion, the desire of beauty, the love of art for its own sake, has most. For art comes to you proposing frankly to give nothing but the highest quality to your moments as they pass, and simply for those moments' sake.

(*The Renaissance* 1873, 1961 edn., Conclusion, pp. 222–4.)

Thomas Wright, from *Our New Masters* (1873)   IV.17

[1.] This, broadly put, is the condition of the mass of the working classes, and to its material hardships is added a sense of injustice suffered, which rankles all the deeper from being blind and impotent. They are certainly born unto trouble. To labour with but scant reward, to endure with but little prospect of relief, is their lot from the cradle to the grave, and, to crown all, they are but too often told that their evil fate will go with them beyond the grave. While they read in The Book that it is the rich who will find it hard to enter the kingdom of heaven, they are assured by those who assume to speak with authority upon such matters that it is they, the poor, who are likely to be excluded from the heavenly paradise, as they have been from the earthly. At an annual meeting of the Scripture Readers' Society held at Sheffield a few years ago, the Archbishop of York stated that 'out of a district with two thousand families, nine hundred and fourteen, or nearly one-half, entered themselves as going to no place of worship whatever.' From which he drew this conclusion: 'that one-half of them had been accustomed to live, and had settled down to live, in a state which professed no hope hereafter, and confessed no God here.' In the case of the Archbishop some allowance is probably due to the sermonesque rounding of a period, but his doctrine as to the meaning of non-attendance at places of worship is substantially the one that is preached to the working classes by Scripture readers and others—and it is a doctrine that does more than any other to keep the poor from places of worship. Uneducated though they may be, ignorant of theology as they mostly are, their common sense still tells them that to make church-going the be-all and end-all, as a test of religion, is to confound religion with the observance of one of its mere mechanical rites; to put a premium upon hypocrisy and cheap self-righteousness. In individual instances they see the strictest religion—in the church-going sense of the term—associated with an utter want of Christianity; and, scoffing at the narrow-mindedness that puts so supreme a meaning upon so (comparatively) secondary a thing, they come to think but very lightly of church-going altogether. That it would in some respects be better for the working classes if they attended places of worship in the same degree that other classes do, may be freely conceded. But to say of them because they do not, they have no hope hereafter, or even that they have no real religion or true Christianity, is, upon the part of those indulging in such utterances, saying in periphrastic language that they know nothing whatever of the working classes. . . . Though there is much in their life that at times is almost enough to drive them to doubt the existence of a principle of eternal justice, they do firmly believe in it; believe that though it is often set aside here, it will be asserted hereafter. Such a belief is to them a hope. They *do* 'profess hope hereafter'—the hope of a brighter, better, juster, more all-equal hereafter, by which they cannot but be gainers, as those who have not had their good things in this life will get them there. And it is well for society that the masses have this hope and belief. If they had not, if they *were* hopeless as regards the hereafter, were really persuaded that—

Vain as the has-been is the great to-be,

then would they not endure the present as patiently as they have done, and do. If they thought that all that they could know of good or evil was to be found in this world alone, can it be doubted that they would attempt to seize a larger share of the good things than now falls to their portion? and though they might be frustrated in such an endeavour, they would destroy others, even if they were themselves destroyed in the effort. Of those who speak of the working classes in relation to religion, as the Archbishop of York did on the occasion to which we have referred, it may be safely and charitably said, 'They know not what they say;' they cannot have realised the terrible significance of the idea of those who have so little to hope for here having no hope hereafter. If ever such a state of things does come to pass, a time will have arrived when there will be no highly-paid and narrow-thoughted prelates to moralise about it. In the essentials of Christianity—the feelings of brotherly and neighbourly love and kindness, and the virtue of patience—the working classes are not lacking. Their non-attendance at places of worship has not the grave meaning that even many of the more charitably inclined in other classes attach to it, and the reasons for it are simple and not far to seek. To many of the poor and uneducated, as well as to many of the rich and educated, the actualities of public worship are repellent rather than attractive. To minds that do not regard public worship as an essential of religion, but only an optional accessory, formalised services, however fine in their conception, become ineffective and meaningless by constant and mechanical repetition. Then sermons are, as a rule—for there are many noble exceptions—dull, and exhibit a sameness and mechanicality that cannot but remind *attentive and intelligent* hearers that the manufacture of sermons is as distinctively and commercially a trade as is the manufacture of three-volume novels. They are often delivered either with an evident lack of all earnestness, or with an earnestness that it is as palpable is directed solely to clerical mannerisms and oratorical effects; and in tone they are more sectarian than broadly or charitably Christian.

[2.] These things constitute the ground upon which many of the more thoughtful of the working classes justify themselves for not attending places of worship. Another reason often assigned is, that Sunday being the only day the working classes have entirely to themselves, they require it for rest, fresh air, and certain phases of social intercourse that the limited leisure of other days does not admit of their carrying out. But the reason most frequently given to Scripture readers, district visitors, ministers, and others who put working men to the question concerning their non-attendance at places of worship is, that they—the working men—have not clothes good enough to go in. 'What a paltry, contemptible reason!' perhaps some reader exclaims. Indeed, what a no-reason, what an *excuse*; and with the ministers and Scripture readers they would doubtless make the obvious reply—'God does not look at clothes.' But there is an equally obvious—to working men—answer to that: 'Congregations and the guardians of the temples do.' Nowhere do the 'pomps and vanities of this wicked world' assert themselves more strongly than in 'the house of God.' Any moderately close observer who has given attention to the point must know that such is the case. Broadcloth and silk shrink from fustian and print in the church, as much or more than they do in the theatre. It is generally those who attend worship well dressed who are inclined to regard a working man's plea of want of good clothes as an evasive one, but they might easily see for themselves that the reason is a substantial one. Let them enter a strange place of worship dressed, as tens of thousands of working men would have to be, in a washed and worn suit of 'working' moleskin, or cord, and note the result. Let them see whether any half-filled pew will be opened for them as it would be for a well-dressed stranger; let them observe the different expression of the glance cast upon them and a well-dressed stranger, and notice how they will be avoided as the congregation streams out at the close of the service. Let them do this, and they will be convinced that want of good clothes alone may be *the* reason for working men not attending places of worship. It would be no reason for a high-souled Christian omitting to fulfil what he conceived to be a duty. But, as we have pointed out, the working classes generally do not regard attendance at a place of worship as an essential; and it is not every man who *is* sufficiently high-souled to brave even a petty social martyrdom.

[3.] To some it may appear that we have dwelt at an unnecessary length upon this point of the existence of a religious feeling among the working classes; but though, at a first glance, the question may seem distantly incidental, it has, in the connection in which we have been considering it, a really important bearing upon our subject. The statistics quoted by the Archbishop of York, though gathered from a single district of a single town, are, as regards the matter upon which they bear, largely representative of the condition of things among the working classes generally. The Archbishop's deduction from the figures is also largely representative, and showing, as it does, that the working classes are very much misknown upon a point that cannot but have a material influence upon both their present and prospective ideas and actions, it was necessary to combat it, to show that in this case narrowness of view meant also falsity of view. If the working classes had no comforting belief here, no hope hereafter, the constitution of society would be very different from what it is, and the attempt to estimate the prospects of those classes would involve an altogether different set of circumstances and probabilities from those that now offer themselves for consideration. . . .

[4.] To come now to the favourable, the hopeful view of these prospects. The things needful to the improvement of the condition of the working classes are a general and higher education; a friendly, open, non-aggressive federation of the labouring classes throughout the civilized world; and Christianity. These are, in our opinion, the three grand essentials, comprehending within themselves the many minor ones necessary to the desired end. To speak of Christianity as one of the wants in a matter that is generally held to be wholly political is, we know, to lay ourselves open to a charge of Utopianism, idealism, and so forth; and as the charge of being unpracticable is the most damaging that can be brought against a writer dealing with such a question as our present one, we hasten to explain. In all civilized communities there always has been, and it may be taken for granted that there always will be, a stronger and weaker race of men, the stronger, though fewer in numbers, rising above and ruling their weaker brethren. The form and name of the relations between ruler and rulers may alter, but the relation has always existed, and with the same relative result—the earth and the fulness thereof falling to the lot of the strong, the hardest toil and bitterest suffering to that of the weak. And so substantially it will continue to be, if we have not Christianity to make the strong men merciful, to bring them to love their neighbours as themselves, and to cease to act upon such principles as that self is the first law of nature, and the weak must go to the wall. It may, of course, be said that we have Christianity, that we are a Christian country. But this is only nominally the case. Though we have undoubtedly many individual Christians among us, we are *not* a Christian nation—have not a general, living, fruitful Christianity. The Christianity which we speak of as being one of the things needful for the permanent and general improvement of the condition of the working classes is not that of mere creeds, rites, and Sunday church-going; not the formal Christianity which is adopted as an element of respectability, but the Christianity of Christ, of the Sermon on the Mount, a Christianity under which brotherly love would abound, and the spirit of which would be visible in the life of the week-day, work-day world, which would lead the rich to consider the poor, employers to be kind to and thoughtful for the employed, and the latter class to be just and honest to employers, not the mere eye-servants and time-servers that so many of them now are. This is the sort of Christianity that we want, and it is strictly practical to say that if we do not get it, whatever else may or can be done for the benefit of the working classes, will be less efficient without such Christianity than it would be in conjunction with it.

[5.] The hopefulness of the outlook in regard to the condition of the working classes lies, in our opinion, in the fact that progress is already being made in two of the three things that we have spoken of as needful, while there are not wanting some slight signs and tokens favourable to the idea of progression in the third—Christianity. The anxiety, the warmth, and even the intolerance of feeling that are being displayed in connection with the Christianity of creed-ism, Ritualism, vestment controversies, and the like, may, we think, be taken as indicating a tendency, a direction of mind, that may ultimately result in a more extended development of that truer, nobler Christianity of which, as we have said, there are many individual instances among us—a Christianity that would cause an unjust balance to be an abomination to the conscience of man as well as to the

Lord, and the now prevailing worship of mammon to be recognised as the ignoble idolatry it is.

(*Our New Masters*, 1873, pp. 86–93, 103–6.)

IV.18 **George Bernard Shaw**

(a) **A Concert (28 Feb. 1877)**

The second Crystal Palace concert of this year took place on Saturday afternoon, the 17th. The program included Cherubini's earnest and refined overture to Medea, Haydn's Oxford symphony, and an overture to Alfieri's tragedy of Saul, the latter being heard for the first—and possibly the last—time in England. It is a fair specimen of a modern concert overture, being provided with a program which instructs us as to the intention of the various passages. Thus, the trombone solos, which, we should mention, were played without any of the noisy vulgarity which our experience elsewhere has led us to associate with that instrument, are illustrative of the wrath of Saul; the harp indicates the soothing minstrelsy of David; and when a trumpet and side drum leave the orchestra and perform vigorously in the lobby, we know that the Philistines are approaching, and that the end of the overture is at hand. Excepting such brief suggestions as Beethoven prefixed to the movements of a very few of his works, or the fanciful titles which Schumann gave to his pianoforte pieces, detailed programs seem to be a complete mistake. They may impart a certain interest to a composition for those who are incapable of appreciating abstract music, but they do so at the expense of the dignity of an art whose true province is foreign to the illustration of commonplace and material detail. In the present case, however, the program is emotional rather than incidental, and Signor Bazzini's overture, if not strikingly original, is sufficiently entertaining to justify its introduction by Mr Manns.

Mlle Marie Krebs played Beethoven's fourth concerto in her characteristic style, crisply and steadily. Throughout the concert the orchestra acquitted themselves most satisfactorily. The performances to which we are accustomed in London seem to move in a narrow circle from weak incompetence or coarse violence to the perfection of lifeless finish, according to the incapacity, the misdirected energy, or the cold autocracy which distinguished the conductors. At Sydenham, thanks to Mr Manns, we can hear an orchestra capable of interpreting with refinement and expression the greatest instrumental compositions, more especially those of Beethoven.

(*Hornet*, 28 Feb. 1877.)

(b) The Handel Festival (4 July 1877)

Another Handel Festival has passed away, bearing testimony in its progress to the undiminished popularity of our most imposing musical institution. The occasion, considering its magnitude, affords but little matter for comment. The stale wonderment which the great chorus never fails to elicit has already been exhausted; and Sir Michael Costa has probably enjoyed the triennial laugh in his sleeve over the journalistic exaggerations of the difficulties he has had to contend with. As a matter of fact, the time for regarding an *ensemble* of 4,000 performers as a prodigy has gone by; and the sooner we begin to consider the feasibility of adding another thousand or so to the number, and varying the *repertoire* a little, the longer our national interest in the Festival is likely to last. We do not mean to imply that the highest interests of music would be served by increasing a choir already so large as to entail conditions of performance incompatible with strict justice to the master. But a justification of such a course might be found in the increase of sensational attraction; for the aims of the Festival-givers necessarily are, firstly, commercial; secondly, phenomenal; and, lastly, artistic.

The performance of The Messiah on the first day was excellent in the choral numbers, and generally respectable in the *arias*. It would be invidious to select any particular chorus for mention. All were executed with perfect precision; and the text was enunciated with surprising distinctness. It is unfortunate that spirited renderings are considered incompatible with the safe conduct of large masses. However, all that could be done to relieve the somewhat mechanical rigidity of the great choruses by careful observance of *forte* and *piano* was done to the utmost, and the effect was, on the whole, stirring and impressive. The orchestra, though at times rather brassy, was satisfactory, the phrasing being conscientiously followed with the result of a fairly artistic reading. The solos were the weak points of the performance, except in a very few instances. Mlle Albani sang her first recitatives out of tune, and in the subsequent *arias* made no effect, Rejoice greatly being conspicuously weak. Madame Patey acquitted herself most meritoriously in the numbers allotted to her, which produced an impression due to her care and earnestness. Madame Edith Wynne, in I know that my Redeemer liveth, struck the first really sympathetic chord in her listeners, and suggested regrets that her share in the performance was not greater. Mr Cummings sang the tenor music in the first part feebly as [is] his wont, but with more finish than usual. Owing to the high pitch of the organ, Mr Sims Reeves was not available for the Passion music; but Mr Vernon Rigby reproduced his mannerisms with more success than usually falls to the lot of imitators. Mr Santley did not seem in as happy a mood as usual. Nevertheless, he sang Why do the nations and The trumpet shall sound as perfectly as could have been desired. Herr Henschel took the rest of the baritone music; and it is sufficient to say of him that his bad pronunciation was his misfortune, and his bad phrasing his fault. . . . We cannot omit this opportunity of warning conductors against the common error of endeavoring to make all performances of The Messiah as like the Festival one as possible. The transept of the Crystal Palace is larger even than the Albert Hall; and the crashing brass and retarded rhythms which are appropriate enough to the vast Handel orchestra become misplaced and intolerably offensive in any smaller space.

(*Hornet*, 4 July 1877.)

IV.19 Anthony Trollope, from *An Autobiography* (1883)

When this was done, and the new furniture had got into its place, and my little book-room was settled sufficiently for work, I began a novel, to the writing of which I was instigated by what I conceived to be the commercial profligacy of the age. Whether the world does or does not become more wicked as years go on, is a question which probably has disturbed the minds of thinkers since the world began to think. That men have become less cruèl, less violent, less selfish, less brutal, there can be no doubt;—but have they become less honest? If so, can a world, retrograding from day to day in honesty, be considered to be in a state of progress? We know the opinion on this subject of our philosopher Mr. Carlyle. If he be right, we are all going straight away to darkness and the dogs. But then we do not put very much faith in Mr. Carlyle,—nor in Mr. Ruskin and his other followers. The loudness and extravagance of their lamentations, the wailing and gnashing of teeth which comes from them, over a world which is supposed to have gone altogether shoddy-wards, are so contrary to the convictions of men who cannot but see how comfort has been increased, how health has been improved, and education extended,—that the general effect of their teaching is the opposite of what they have intended. It is regarded simply as Carlylism to say that the English-speaking world is growing worse from day to day. And it is Carlylism to opine that the general grand result of increased intelligence is a tendency to deterioration. . . .

(*An Autobiography*, 1883, 1980 edn., Ch.xx, pp. 353–4.)

IV.20 The Inauguration of the Royal College of Music (1 June 1883)

The College was inaugurated on the 7th ult. by his Royal Highness the Prince of Wales. At present it occupies the building formerly used by the National Training School for Music at Kensington, and facing the west side of the Albert Hall. The building is not adapted to large assemblies, and the ceremony, we are told in the report in the *Times*, from which we are about to quote further, had necessarily somewhat of a private character: 'The Prince of Wales, the President and, it may be added, the founder of the institution, accompanied by the Princess of Wales and the Princes Victor and George, the Duke and Duchess of Edinburgh, and Princess Christian, arrived about noon at the College, where their Royal Highnesses were received by the trustees. . . . the Director, Mr. George Grove, D.C.L., and the honorary secretary, Mr. Charles Morley. . . . Among others present were the Prime Minister and Miss Gladstone, the Archbishop of Canterbury and his chaplain, the Rev. Randall Davidson, Earl Cadogan, the Bishop of Bath and Wells. . . .'

At the conclusion of the ceremony the Royal party visited in turn all the class-rooms in the building, where the students and pupils were already in their places, with the professors of the various departments of instruction. So that the mechanism of the new conservatorium was set to work at once, and has already been busy for at least three weeks in a mission of a more than usually comprehensive nature; designed ultimately to collect and promote the latent musical talent not only of London and the home counties, and of the United Kingdom, but of India and the colonies and even of the United States and all English-speaking countries and nations. With these more than national and even more than Imperial objects the College commences with a subscribed fund amounting to £110,000; by the aid of which, and as a bold but wise beginning, fifty scholarships have been established. Of these, thirty-five confer a free education in music, and fifteen provide not only a free education, but also a maintenance for the scholars. Half the scholarships are held by boys and half by girls. 'London, with its vast population,' said the Prince of Wales in his inaugural speech, 'sends only twelve out of the fifty. The remaining thirty-eight come as follows: twenty-eight from fourteen different counties in England, two from Scotland, six from Ireland, one from Wales and one from Jersey.' The scholars were selected from 1,588 candidates examined by local boards. Subsequently 480 were sent up for a final examination conducted by the various professors at the College in Kensington. The result was the unanimous election of seventeen scholars for the pianoforte, thirteen for singing, eight for the violin, six for composition, two for the violoncello, one for the organ, one for the clarinet, one for the flute and one for the harp. In addition to the fifty scholars, forty-two persons have entered their names as paying students in the College. . . .

In the eloquent speech delivered by his Royal Highness the Prince of Wales a far higher view was taken of the mission of the College than might have been suggested even by national musical requirements, much less local rivalries. With that genuine kindliness, always the soundest basis of good taste and happy allusions, his Royal Highness expressed the deep personal gratification he felt at the manner in which the country had replied to his appeal for aid in establishing the College. The sincerity of the Prince's words may open the hearts and purses of many whose minds are not usually sensitive to the claims of mere music. We have not the slightest doubt that before long the whole sum needed to worthily accomplish the intentions of the founders of the College will be subscribed by the nation. Meanwhile, there is no object in pandering to our national failing—hypocrisy—and slurring over the fact that the £110,000 subscribed, equal to a twelve-thousandth part of the national income, or to about one-third of a farthing per head of the population, is by no means munificent or encouraging. The subscription is the result of fourteen months' whipping of the country, since the bishops, ministers, clergy of all denominations, the nobles and municipal dignitaries of the kingdom assembled in the banqueting room of St. James's Palace, and swore fealty to the designs of the Prince of Wales and his Royal brothers in regard to the establishment of a College of Music. Boxes for voluntary contributions in the streets and lanes would have produced more. There are, of course, abundant reasons for this apparent niggardliness. Some of these reasons are political, some religious, and others are only moral and even musical. But the main reason is that whilst the heart of the country is true to the project and to the Prince, the national intellectual bias is opposed to what it is pleased to consider non-essentials. We are all honourable men and lovers of music; but, to the ordinary educated Englishman, music is an abstraction until united with some essential, such as sectarian opinion, or utilised for charitable purposes, or made incarnate in a brass band ministering to the works of the flesh and of fashion. . . . The Prince of Wales has told us that amongst the successful competitors for scholarships in the new College were a mill-girl, the daughter of a bricklayer, the son of a blacksmith, and the son of a farm labourer. Each of these is, perhaps, drawn from some particular fold and will be watched by anxious shepherds who will only be partially reassured by being told, in the words of the Prince of Wales, that among the higher objects of the Royal College of Music are the discovery of latent musical ability, and the extension to those who, with natural gifts, have been blessed with little of this world's goods, of the opportunity of obtaining instruction, and joining together in the study of an art which softens asperities, inspires kindly feeling between various classes and proves that all mankind are kin—an art that, as he says, is in the best sense the most popular because, at the least expense, it provides for the happiness or pleasure of the greatest number: 'The time has come,' said the Prince, 'when class can no longer stand aloof from class, and that man does his duty best who works most earnestly in bridging over the gulf between different classes which it is the tendency of increased wealth and increased civilisation to widen. I claim for music the merit that it has a voice which speaks in different tones, perhaps, but with equal force to the cultivated and the ignorant, to the peer and the peasant. I claim for music a variety of expression which belongs to no other art, and therefore adapts it more than any other art to produce that union of feeling which I much desire to promote.'

These words are genuine, and are not the words of common liberalism or of common benevolence. They are redolent of the political philosophy of the day. In their very nonconformity we lose sight of the presence of the Archbishop of Canterbury. With the remembrance of such frankness and universal liberality on the part of the President of the Royal College of Music, it cannot possibly happen that the purse-strings of the nation will be tightened by narrow prejudices, local jealousies, provincial vanities, obsolete economic doctrine, intellectual fastidiousness or any of the smaller causes which might induce the general public to discuss the *cui bono* of the new institution. It is at present a question for the general public. As for the musical world, it will have ample time to mature its judgment and suggest changes after the College is in working order.

(*Musical Times*, 1 June 1883.)

William Morris, from 'The Worker's Share of Art' (Apr. 1885)   IV.21

I can imagine some of our comrades smiling bitterly at the above title, and wondering what a Socialist journal can have to do with art; so I begin by saying that I understand only too thoroughly how 'unpractical' the subject is while the present system of capital and wages lasts. Indeed that is my text.

What, however, is art? whence does it spring? Art is man's embodied expression of interest in the life of man; it springs from man's pleasure in his life; pleasure we must call it, taking all human life together, however much it may be broken by the grief and trouble of individuals; and as it is the expression of pleasure in life generally, in the memory of the deeds of the past, and the hope of those of the future, so it is especially the expression of man's pleasure in the deeds of the present; in his work.

Yes, that may well seem strange to us at present! Men today may see the pleasure of unproductive energy—energy put forth in games and sports; but in productive energy—in the task which must be finished before we can eat, the task which will begin again tomorrow, and many a tomorrow without change or end till *we* are ended—pleasure in that?

Yet I repeat that the chief source of art is man's pleasure in his daily necessary work, which expresses itself and is embodied in that work itself; nothing else can make the common surroundings of life beautiful, and whenever they are beautiful it is a sign that men's work has pleasure in it, however they may suffer otherwise. It is the lack of this pleasure in daily work which has made our towns and habitations sordid and hideous, insults to the beauty of the earth which they disfigure, and all the accessories of life mean, trivial, ugly—in a word, *vulgar*. Terrible as this is to endure in the present, there is hope in it for the future; for surely it is but just that outward ugliness and disgrace should be the result of the slavery and misery of the people; and that slavery and misery once changed, it is but reasonable to expect that external ugliness will give place to beauty, the sign of free and happy work.

Meantime, be sure that nothing else will produce even a reasonable semblance of art; for think of it! the workers, by means of whose hands the mass of art must be made, are forced by the commercial system to live, even at the best, in places so squalid and hideous that no one could live in them and keep his sanity without losing all sense of beauty, and enjoyment of life. The advance of the industrial army under its 'captains of industry' (save the mark!) is traced, like the advance of other armies, in the ruin of the peace and loveliness of earth's surface, and nature, who will have us live at any cost, compels us to *get used* to our degradation at the expense of losing our manhood, and producing children doomed to live less like men than ourselves. Men living amidst such ugliness cannot conceive of beauty, and, therefore, cannot express it.

Nor is it only the workers who feel this misery (and I rejoice over that, at any rate). The higher or more intellectual arts suffer with the industrial ones. The artists, the aim of whose lives it is to produce beauty and interest, are deprived of the materials for the works in real life, since all around them is ugly and vulgar. They are driven into seeking their materials in the imaginations of past ages, or into giving the lie to their own sense of beauty and knowledge of it by sentimentalizing and falsifying the life which goes on around them; and so, in spite of all their talent, intellect, and enthusiasm, produce little which is not contemptible when matched against the works of the non-commercial ages. Nor must we forget that whatever is produced that is worth anything is the work of men who are in rebellion against the corrupt society of today—rebellion sometimes open, sometimes veiled under cynicism, but by which in any case lives are wasted in a struggle, too often vain, against their fellow-men, which ought to be used for the exercise of special gifts for the benefit of the world.

High and low, therefore, slaveholders and slaves, we lack beauty in our lives, or, in other words, man-like pleasure. This absence of pleasure is the second gift to the world which the development of commercialism has added to its first gift of a propertyless proletariat. Nothing else but the grinding of this iron system could have reduced the civilized world to vulgarity. The theory that art is sick *because* people have turned their attention to science is without foundation. It is true that science is allowed to live because profit can be made of her, and men, who must find some outlet for their energies, turn to her, since she exists, though only as the slave (but now the rebellious slave) of capital; whereas when art is fairly in the clutch of profit-grinding she dies, and leaves behind her but her phantom of *sham art* as the futile slave of the capitalist. . . .

(*Commonweal*, Apr. 1885.)

William Morris, from 'Education Today' (June 1888) IV.22

Just as the capitalists would at once capture education in craftsmanship, seek out what little advantage there is in it, and then throw it away, so they do with all other education. A superstition still remains from the times when 'education' was a rarity that it is a means for earning a superior livelihood; but as soon as it has ceased to be a rarity, competition takes care that education shall not raise wages; that general education shall be worth nothing, and that special education shall be worth just no more than a tolerable return on the money and time spent in acquiring it. . . . As to the pleasure to be derived from education at present by hard-working men, a bookish man is apt to think that even the almighty capitalist can hardly take away from his slave if he has really learned to enjoy reading and to understand books, and that whatever happens he must have an hour in a day (or if it were only half an hour) to indulge himself in this pleasure. But then does the average hard-working man (of any grade) really acquire this capacity by means of the short period of education which he is painfully dragged through? I doubt it. Though even our mechanical school system cannot crush out a natural bent towards literature (with all the pleasures of thought and imagination which that word means) yet certainly its dull round will hardly implant such a taste in anyone's mind. . . . I must say in passing that on the few occasions that I have been inside a Board-school, I have been much depressed by the mechanical drill that was too obviously being applied there to all the varying capacities and moods. My heart sank before Mr M'Choakumchild and his method, and I thought how much luckier I was to have been born well enough off to be sent to a school where I was *taught*—nothing, but *learned* archaeology and romance on the Wiltshire downs.

And then supposing the worker to be really educated, to have acquired both the information and the taste for reading which Mr M'Choakumchild's dole will allow to him under the most favourable circumstances, how will this treasure of knowledge and sympathy accord with his daily life? Will it not make his dull task seem duller? Will it not increase the suffering of the workshop or the factory to him? And if so, may he not strive to forget rather than strive to remember . . . ?

(*Commonweal*, June 1888.)

23 George Bernard Shaw

(a) 'How Handel is Sung' (3 Jan. 1889)

On New Year's night at the Albert Hall, Messiah is the affair of the shilling gallery, and not of the seven-and-sixpenny stalls. Up there you find every chair occupied, and people standing two or three deep behind the chairs. These sitters and standers are the gallery vanguard, consisting of *prima donna* worshippers who are bent on obtaining a bird's-eye view of Madame Albani for their money. At the back are those who are content to hear Handel's music. They sit on the floor against the wall, with their legs converging straight towards the centre of the dome, and terminating in an inner circumference of boot soles in various stages of wear and tear. Between the circle of boots and the circle of sightseers moves a ceaseless procession of promenaders to whom the performance is as the sounding brass and tinkling cymbals of a military band on a pier. The police take this view, and deal with the gallery as with a thoroughfare included in the Trafalgar Square proclamation, calling out, 'Pass along, pass along,' and even going the length of a decisive shove when the promenade is at all narrowed by too many unreasonable persons stopping to listen to the music. The crowd is a motley one, including many mechanics, who have bought Novello's vocal score of the oratorio and are following it diligently; professional men who cannot afford that luxury and are fain to peep enviously over the mechanics' shoulders; musicians in the Bohemian phase of artistic life; masses of 'shilling people' of the ordinary type; the inevitable man with the opera-glass and campstool; and one enthusiast with a blanket on his shoulder, who has apparently been ordered by the police to take up his bed and walk.

(*Star*, 3 Jan. 1889.)

(b) Music in Bow (21 Feb. 1889)

On Monday the editor of The Star summoned me to a private conference. 'The fact is, my dear Corno,' he said, throwing himself back in his chair and arranging his moustache with the diamond which sparkles at the end of his pen-handle, 'I don't believe that music in London is confined to St James's Hall, Covent Garden, and the Albert Hall. People must sing and play elsewhere. Whenever I go down to speak at the big Town Halls at Shoreditch, Hackney, Stratford, Holborn, Kensington, Battersea, and deuce knows where, I always see bills at the door announcing oratorios, organ recitals, concerts by local Philharmonic and Orpheus societies, and all sorts of musical games. Why not criticise these instead of saying the same thing over and over again about Henschel and Richter and Norman

Neruda and the rest?' I replied, as best I could, that my experience as a musical critic had left me entirely unacquainted with these outlandish localities and their barbarous minstrelsy; that I regarded London as bounded on the extreme north-east by Stonecutter Street, on the extreme south-west by Kensington Gore, on the south by the Thames, and on the north by the Strand and Regent-street. He assured me that the places he had mentioned actually existed; but that, as I was evidently hurt by the suggestion that I should condescend to visit them, he would hand the ticket he had just received for a Purcell–Handel performance at Bow, to Musigena. 'What!' I exclaimed, 'Purcell! the greatest of English composers, left to Musigena! to a man whose abnormal gifts in every other direction have blinded him to his utter ignorance of music!' . . . Snatching the tickets from the editor's desk, I hastily ran home to get my revolver as a precaution during my hazardous voyage to the east end. Then I dashed away to Broadstreet, and asked the booking-clerk whether he knew of a place called Bow. He was evidently a man of extraordinary nerve, for he handed me a ticket without any sign of surprise, as if a voyage to Bow were the most commonplace event possible. A little later the train was rushing through the strangest places: Shoreditch, of which I had read in historical novels; Old Ford, which I had supposed to be a character in one of Shakespeare's plays; Homerton, which is somehow associated in my mind with pigeons; and Haggerston, a name perfectly new to me. When I got into the concert-room I was perfectly dazzled by the appearance of the orchestra. Nearly all the desks for the second violins were occupied by ladies: beautiful young ladies. Personal beauty is not the strong point of West-end orchestras, and I thought the change an immense improvement until the performance began, when the fair fiddlers rambled from bar to bar with a certain sweet indecision that had a charm of its own, but was not exactly what Purcell and Handel meant. When I say that the performance began, I do not imply that it began punctually. The musicians began to drop in at about ten minutes past eight, and the audience were inclined to remonstrate; but an occasional apology from the conductor, Mr F. A. W. Docker, kept them in good humor.

Dido and Eneas is 200 years old, and not a bit the worse for wear. I daresay many of the Bowegians thought that the unintentional quaintnesses of the amateurs in the orchestra were Purcellian antiquities. If so, they were never more mistaken in their lives, Henry Purcell was a great composer: a very great composer indeed; and even this little boarding-school opera is full of his spirit, his freshness, his dramatic expression, and his unapproached art of setting English speech to music. The Handel Society did not do him full justice: the work, in fact, is by no means easy; but the choir made up bravely for the distracting dances of the string quartet. . . . Of Alexander's Feast I need only say that I enjoyed it thoroughly, even though I was sitting on a cane-bottomed chair (Thackeray overrated this descrip-

tion of furniture) without adequate room for my knees. The band, rein-
forced by wind and organ, got through with a healthy roughness that
refreshed me; and the choruses were capital. Mr Bantock Pierpoint, the
bass, covered himself with merited glory, and Mr John Probert would
have been satisfactory had he been more consistently careful of his inton-
ation. Miss Fresselle acquitted herself fairly; but her singing is like that of
the society generally: it lacks point and color. Mr Docker must cure his
singers of the notion that choral singing is merely a habit caught in
church, and that it is profane and indecorous to sing Handel's music as if
it meant anything. That, however, is the worst I have to say of them. I am,
on the whole, surprised and delighted with the East end, and shall soon
venture there without my revolver. At the end of the concert, a gentleman,
to my entire stupefaction, came forward and moved a vote of thanks to
the performers. It was passed by acclamation, but without musical
honors.

(*Star*, 21 Feb. 1889.)

(c) **Music and Society (6 Dec. 1889)**

I remember once coming to loggerheads with the late Dr Francis Hueffer,
about fifteen seconds after the opening of our first conversation, on the
subject of musical culture in English society. Whenever the subject arose
between us, I declared that English society did not care about music—did
not know good music from bad. He replied, with great force, that I knew
nothing about it; that nobody had ever seen me in really decent society;
that I moved amidst cranks, Bohemians, unbelievers, agitators, and—
generally speaking—riff-raff of all sorts; and that I was merely theorising
emptily about the people whom I called bloated aristocrats. He described,
by way of example, an evening at Lord Derby's house, where he had
greatly enjoyed some excellent music; and he asked me whether I knew that
such music was, in a quiet way, a constant grace of the best sort of English
social life. I suggested that he should give me an opportunity to judge for
myself by introducing me to these circles, but this he entirely declined to
do; having no confidence whatever in my power of behaving myself in a
seemly manner for five consecutive minutes.

   On the first occasion it so happened, fortunately for me, that a firm of
music publishers, having resolved to venture on the desperate step of publishing six new pianoforte sonatas, had just sent out a circular containing
an appeal *ad misericordiam* that at least a few people would, either in public spirit or charity, take the unprecedented step of buying these compositions. I promptly hurled this at Hueffer's head, and asked whether that
looked like evidence of a constant and enlightened patronage such as the

upper classes accord to racing, millinery, confectionery, and in a minor
degree to literature and painting (for, hang it all! even if the sonatas were
not as good as Beethoven's, they were at any rate no duller than the average
three-volume novel or Academy picture). There the subject dropped, my
method of controversy being at that time crudely unscrupulous and
extravagant. Hueffer, I fancy, regarded me as an unschooled dangerous
character; but once, when I was perched on the gunwale of a wagon in
Hyde Park, filling up some ten minutes of a 'demonstration' with the insuf-
ferable oratorizing which is the only sort feasible on such occasions, I was
astonished to see his long golden beard and massive brow well to the front
among the millions of 'friends and fellow citizens'. He never told me what
he thought about the contrast between the new musical criticism demon-
strating on wagons in the sunlight, and the old, groping in perpetual evening dress from St James's Hall to Covent Garden Opera House and back
again.

One point I might have put to him, but didn't, is that when you get up
a musical entertainment for the exclusive delectation of the nobs, you
must either be content with a very scanty audience, in which case the
nobs will not think it good enough to come again, or else pack the room
with a contingent of musical deadheads, who are not nobs, nor even respectable Philistine snobs, but rank outsiders—though you would be surprised at the costly entertainments, operatic and otherwise, that are run
solely for their sake, and that of the jaded pressmen. Last Friday, happening to have an invitation from the Grosvenor Club to their 'ladies' night'
at the Grosvenor Gallery, I thought I would go and see whether things
were altering at all. For the Grosvenor Club, you must know, is no vulgar free-and-easy; and its concerts, from 9.30 to midnight, are never
wholly nobless.

On entering that Bond Street portal which was brought here bodily all
the way from Italy, and approaching the stairs which I have so often worn
with the weary feet of an art critic, I found on one side a descending stream
of sad and hollow people, and on the other an ascending one, flushed and
swollen. By this I perceived that the refreshments were downstairs; and I
hurried up with all convenient speed. Here I found a nob or two, a dead-
head or two, and a vast majority of solid snobs. No celebrities, no literary
lot, no journalistic lot, no artistic lot, no Bohemian lot, nothing (to speak
of) except plain snobbery, more or less choice. In short, there were—professionally engaged musicians excepted—not above twelve people in the
room known to me; and I should have congratulated Mr Prange on such an
entirely satisfactory result if I had been quite certain that he would have
appreciated the full force of this final proof of the respectability of the gathering, and of the success of his elimination of the great army of 'private
view' people.

I could not get a program; and when Signor Ducci went to the piano, and Mr Radcliffe took his flute, Mr Mann his horn, and the fiddlers four their fiddles, I wondered what was coming. It proved to be resurrection pie of the dustiest flavor. For a long time I was at a loss. I thought vaguely of Clementi, of Dussek, of Field, of all the Sir Arthur Sullivans that existed before Mendelssohn's time. Not until several elegantly empty movements had worn themselves out did I hit on the right man: on Hummel, the genteel, the talented, the tastefully barren. Here are serenades by Mozart, chamber music with wind parts by Schubert, by Weber, by Schumann, by Mendelssohn, by Brahms, all ready to Signor Ducci's hand; and he goes and digs up Jean Nepomuk Hummel! One unfortunate gentleman said to me: 'These things are very nice, of course: but they are very long.' Forgetting that I was for once among respectable people, I morosely expressed an opinion that this particular thing was strongly qualified rubbish. 'Oh' said he 'you are so very critical: I daresay it does not come up to *your* standard. But it was certainly too long for a place like this.' Thus does music get into disrepute. If my friend had heard Beethoven's septet, he would have been delighted. Hearing Hummel instead, he concluded that it was in the nature of classical music to be dull; and he will probably think so to his dying day.

However, the choicer spirits sat in the front of the room and faithfully listened. The others sat at the back and talked. How they talked! One young lady, who must, I should think, be the champion chatterbox of the universe, so outdid with her tongue the most rapid flights of Signor Ducci's fingers that I stole round three times through the east gallery merely to see whether she had stopped from exhaustion: but she was as fresh as an aviary each time. Another lady, who coaches me in the ways of good society, and makes certain prearranged warning signals to me when I eat with my knife or help myself to potatoes with my fingers, was very severe with me because I took sides with the front of the room and listened to the unimpeachable Jean Nepomuk. 'You were a failure there,' she said next day. 'Everybody was noticing your disgraceful behaviour. You will never be a gentleman.' 'What should I have done?' I demanded. 'I say nothing' she replied, 'about your not bringing us down to the refreshment room, and your furtively leaving before you had seen us off in a cab. But you should at least have come and *talked* to us.' 'But that would have disturbed the music' I pleaded. 'Music!' she retorted, with scorn. 'The Grosvenor is a private club where some rather crack people go: not a concert room. People go there to talk. Besides, you *scowled*.' On reflection, I daresay I did. I would suggest to Mr Prange that in future a curtain should shut off the east gallery from the west, and that the fireman should be employed to keep the musical section and the loquacious section in different rooms.

(*Star*, 6 Dec. 1889.)

James Abbott McNeill Whistler, from *The Gentle Art of Making Enemies* (1890)   IV.24

The ATTORNEY-GENERAL complained that no answer was given to a written application by the defendant's solicitors for leave to inspect the pictures which the plaintiff had been called upon to produce at the trial. The WITNESS replied that Mr. Arthur Severn had been to his studio to inspect the paintings, on behalf of the defendant, for the purpose of passing his final judgment upon them and settling that question for ever.

Cross-examination continued: 'What was the subject of the nocturne in blue and silver belonging to Mr. Grahame?'

'A moonlight effect on the river near old Battersea Bridge.'

'What has become of the nocturne in black and gold?'

'I believe it is before you.' (*Laughter.*)

The picture called the nocturne in blue and silver was now produced in Court.

'That is Mr. Grahame's picture. It represents Battersea Bridge by moonlight.'

BARON HUDDLESTON: 'Which part of the picture is the bridge?' (*Laughter*)

His Lordship earnestly rebuked those who laughed. And witness explained to his Lordship the composition of the picture.

'Do you say that this is a correct representation of Battersea Bridge?'

'I did not intend it to be a 'correct' portrait of the bridge. It is only a moonlight scene, and the pier in the centre of the picture may not be like the piers at Battersea Bridge as you know them in broad daylight. As to what the picture represents, that depends upon who looks at it. To some persons it may represent all that is intended; to others it may represent nothing.'

'The prevailing colour is blue?'

'Perhaps.'

'Are those figures on the top of the bridge intended for people?'

'They are just what you like.'

'Is that a barge beneath?'

'Yes. I am very much encouraged at your perceiving that. My whole scheme was only to bring about a certain harmony of colour.'

'What is that gold-coloured mark on the right of the picture like a cascade?'

'The 'cascade of gold' is a firework.'

A second nocturne in blue and silver was then produced.

WITNESS: 'That represents another moonlight scene on the Thames

8. J. A. M. Whistler: *Nocturne in Blue and Gold: Old Battersea Bridge* 1872–5

looking up Battersea Reach. I completed the mass of the picture in one day.' . . .

(The Gentle Art of Making Enemies, 1890, 1919 edn., pp. 7–8.)

George Bernard Shaw, the *Messiah* (21 Jan. 1891)   IV.25

I have long since recognized the impossibility of obtaining justice for that work in a Christian country. Import a choir of heathens, restrained by no considerations of propriety from attacking the choruses with unembarrassed sincerity of dramatic expression, and I would hasten to the performance if only to witness the delight of the public and the discomfiture of the critics. That is, if anything so indecent would be allowed here. We have all had our Handelian training in church, and the perfect church-going mood is one of pure abstract reverence. A mood of active intelligence would be scandalous. Thus we get broken in to the custom of singing Handel as if he meant nothing; and as it happens that he meant a great deal, and was tremendously in earnest about it, we know rather less about him in England than they do in the Andaman Islands, since the Andamans are only unconscious of him, whereas we are misconscious. To hear a thousand respectable young English persons jogging through For He shall purify the sons of Levi as if every group of semiquavers were a whole bar of four crotchets *a capella*, or repeating Let Him deliver Him if He delight in Him with exactly the same subdued and uncovered air as in For with His stripes we are healed, or lumbering along with the Hallelujah as if it were a superior sort of family coach: all this is ludicrous enough; but when the nation proceeds to brag of these unwieldy choral impostures, these attempts to make the brute force of a thousand throats do what can only be done by artistic insight and skill, then I really lose patience. Why, instead of wasting huge sums on the multitudinous dullness of a Handel Festival does not somebody set up a thoroughly rehearsed and exhaustively studied performance of the Messiah in St James's Hall with a chorus of twenty capable artists? Most of us would be glad to hear the work seriously performed once before we die.

(World, 21 Jan. 1891.)

V

The Representation of the People

Harriet Taylor Mill, from 'Enfranchisement of Women' (July 1851) V.1

When a prejudice, which has any hold on the feelings, finds itself reduced to the unpleasant necessity of assigning reasons, it thinks it has done enough when it has re-asserted the very point in dispute, in phrases which appeal to the pre-existing feeling. Thus, many persons think they have sufficiently justified the restrictions on women's field of action, when they have said that the pursuits from which women are excluded are *unfeminine* and that the *proper sphere* of women is not politics or publicity, but private and domestic life.

We deny the right of any portion of the species to decide for another portion, or any individual for another individual, what is and what is not their 'proper sphere.' The proper sphere for all human beings is the largest and highest which they are able to attain to. What this is, cannot be ascertained, without complete liberty of choice. The speakers at the Convention in America have therefore done wisely and right, in refusing to entertain the question of the peculiar aptitudes either of women or of men, or the limits within which this or that occupation may be supposed to be more adapted to the one or to the other. They justly maintain, that these questions can only be satisfactorily answered by perfect freedom. Let every occupation be open to all, without favour or discouragement to any, and employments will fall into the hands of those men or women who are found by experience to be most capable of worthily exercising them. There need be no fear that women will take out of the hands of men any occupation which men perform better than they. Each individual will prove his or her capacities, in the only way in which capacities can be proved—by trial; and the world will have the benefit of the best faculties of all its inhabitants. But to interfere beforehand by an arbitrary limit, and declare that whatever be the genius, talent, energy, or force of mind of an individual of a certain sex or class, those faculties shall not be exerted, or shall be exerted only in some few of the many modes in which others are permitted to use theirs, is not only an injustice to the individual, and a detriment to society, which loses what it can ill spare, but is also the most effectual mode of providing that, in the sex or class so fettered, the qualities which are not permitted to be exercised shall not exist . . .

(*Westminster Review*, July 1851; reprinted in *Essays on Sex Equality*, ed. Alice S. Rossi, 1970, pp. 100–1.)

v.2 Florence Nightingale, from *Cassandra* (1852)

Why have women passion, intellect, moral activity—these three—and a place in society where no one of the three can be exercised? Men say that God punishes for complaining. No, but men are angry with misery. They are irritated with women for not being happy. They take it as a personal offence. To God alone may women complain without insulting Him!

And women, who are afraid, while in words they acknowledge that God's work is good, to say, Thy will be *not* done (declaring another order of society from that which He has made), go about maudling to each other and teaching to their daughters that 'women have no passions.' In the conventional society, which men have made for women, and women have accepted, they *must* have none, they *must* act the farce of hypocrisy, the lie that they are without passion—and therefore what else can they say to their daughters, without giving the lie to themselves?

Suffering, sad 'female humanity!' What are these feelings which they are taught to consider as disgraceful, to deny to themselves? What form do the Chinese feet assume when denied their proper development? If the young girls of the 'higher classes,' who never commit a false step, whose justly earned reputations were never sullied even by the stain which the fruit of mere 'knowledge of good and evil' leaves behind, were to speak, and say what are their thoughts employed upon, their *thoughts*, which alone are free, what would they say?

That, with the phantom companion of their fancy, they talk (not love, they are too innocent, too pure, too full of genius and imagination for that, but) they talk, in fancy, of that which interests them most; they seek a companion for their every thought; the companion they find not in reality they seek in fancy, or, if not that, if not absorbed in endless conversations, they see themselves engaged with him in stirring events, circumstances which call out the interest wanting to them. Yes, fathers, mothers, you who see your daughter proudly rejecting all semblance of flirtation, primly engaged in the duties of the breakfast table, you little think how her fancy compensates itself by endless interviews and sympathies (sympathies either for ideas or events) with the fancy's companion of the hour! And you say, 'She is not susceptible. Women have no passion.' Mothers, who cradle yourselves in visions about the domestic hearth, how many of your sons and daughters are *there*, do you think, while sitting round under your complacent eye? Were you there yourself during your own (now forgotten) girl-hood?

What are the thoughts of these young girls while one is singing Schubert, another is reading the *Review*, and a third is busy embroidering? Is not one fancying herself the nurse of some new friend in sickness; another engaging in romantic dangers with him, such as call out the character and afford more food for sympathy than the monotonous events of domestic society; another undergoing unheard-of trials under the observation of someone whom she has chosen as the companion of her dream; another having a loving and loved companion in the life she is living, which many do not want to change?

And is not this all most natural, inevitable? Are they, who are too much ashamed of it to confess it even to themselves, to be blamed for that which cannot be otherwise, the causes of which stare one in the face, *if one's eyes were not closed*? Many struggle against this as a 'snare.' . . . We fast men-tally, scourge ourselves morally, use the intellectual hair-shirt, in order to subdue that perpetual day-dreaming, which is so dangerous! We resolve 'this day month I will be free from it'; twice a day with prayer and written record of the times when we have indulged in it, we endeavour to combat it. Never, with the slightest success. By mortifying vanity we do ourselves no good. It is the want of interest in our life which produces it; by filling up that want of interest in our life we can alone remedy it. And, did we even see this, how can we make the difference? How obtain the interest which society declares *she* does not want, and *we* cannot want? . . .

Passion, intellect, moral activity—these three have never been satisfied in a woman. In this cold and oppressive conventional atmosphere, they can-not be satisfied. To say more on this subject would be to enter into the whole history of society, of the present state of civilisation.

Look at the poor lives we lead. It is a wonder that we are so good as we are, not that we are so bad. In looking round we are struck with the power of the organisations we see, not with their want of power. Now and then, it is true, we are conscious that *there* is an inferior organisation, but, in general, just the contrary. Mrs A. has the imagination, the poetry of a Mur-illo, and has sufficient power of execution to show that she might have had a great deal more. Why is she not a Murillo? From a material difficulty, not a mental one. If she has a knife and fork in her hand for three hours of the day, she cannot have a pencil or brush. Dinner is the great sacred ceremony of this day, the great sacrament. To be absent from dinner is equivalent to being ill. Nothing else will excuse us from it. Bodily incapacity is the only apology valid. If she has a pen and ink in her hands during other three hours, writing answers for the penny post, again, she cannot have her pen-cil, and so *ad infinitum* through life. People have no type before them in their lives, neither fathers nor mothers, nor the children themselves. They look at things in detail. They say, 'It is very desirable that A., my daughter, should go to such a party, should know such a lady, should sit by such a person.' It is true. But what standard have they before them of the nature and destination of man? The very words are rejected as pedantic. But might they not, at least, have a type in their minds that such an one might be a discoverer through her intellect, such another through her art, a third through her moral power?

Women often try one branch of intellect after another in their youth, *e.g.* mathematics. But that, least of all is compatible with the life of 'society.' It is impossible to follow up anything systematically. Women often long to enter some man's profession where they would find direction, competition (or rather opportunity of measuring the intellect with others) and, above all, time. . . . those institutions which we call monasteries, and which, embracing much that is contrary to the laws of nature, are yet better adapted to the union of the life of action and that of thought than any other mode of life with which we are acquainted; in many such, four and a half hours, at least, are daily set aside for thought, rules are given for thought, training and opportunity afforded. Among us there is *no* time appointed for this purpose, and the difficulty is that, in our social life, we must be always doubtful whether we ought not to be with somebody else or be doing something else.

Are men better off than women in this?

If one calls upon a friend in London and sees her son in the drawing-room, it strikes one as odd to find a young man sitting idle in his mother's drawing-room in the morning. For men, who are seen much in those haunts, there is no end of the epithets we have: 'knights of the carpet,' 'drawing-room heroes,' 'ladies' men.' But suppose we were to see a number of men in the morning sitting round a table in the drawing-room, looking at prints, doing worsted work, and reading little books, how we should laugh! . . .

Now, why is it more ridiculous for a man than for a woman to do worsted work and drive out every day in the carriage? Why should we laugh if we were to see a parcel of men sitting round a drawing-room table in the morning, and think it all right if they were women?

Is man's time more valuable than woman's? or is the difference between man and woman this, that woman has confessedly nothing to do?

Women are never supposed to have any occupation of sufficient import-ance *not* to be interrupted, except 'suckling their fools'; and women them-selves have accepted this, have written books to support it, and have trained themselves so as to consider whatever they do as *not* of such value to the world or to others, but that they can throw it up at the first 'claim of social life.' They have accustomed themselves to consider intellectual occu-pation as a merely selfish amusement, which it is their 'duty' to give up for every trifler more selfish than themselves. . . .

Then as to solitary opportunities. Women never have an half-hour in all their lives (excepting before or after anybody is up in the house) that they can call their own, without fear of offending or of hurting someone. Why do people sit up so late, or, more rarely, get up so early? Not because the day is not long enough, but because they have 'no time in the day to themselves.'

If we do attempt to do anything in company, what is the system of literary exercise which we pursue? Everybody reads aloud out of their own book or newspaper—or, every five minutes, something is said. And what is it to be 'read aloud to'? The most miserable exercise of the human intellect. Or rather, is it any exercise at all? It is like lying on one's back, with one's hands tied and having liquid poured down one's throat. Worse than that, because suffocation would immediately ensue and put a stop to this operation. But no suffocation would stop the other. . . .

It is a thing *so* accepted among women that they have nothing to do, that one woman has not the least scruple in saying to another, 'I will come and spend the morning with you.' And you would be thought quite surly and absurd, if you were to refuse it on the plea of occupation. Nay, it is thought a mark of amiability and affection, if you are 'on such terms' that you can 'come in' 'any morning you please.'

In a country house, if there is a large party of young people, 'You will spend the morning with us,' they say to the neighbours, 'we will drive together in the afternoon,' 'to-morrow we will make an expedition, and we will spend the evening together.' And this is thought friendly and spending time in a pleasant manner. So women play through life. Yet time is the most valuable of all things. If they had come every morning and afternoon and robbed us of half-a-crown we should have had redress from the police. But it is laid down, that our time is of no value. If you offer a morning visit to a professional man, and say, 'I will just stay an hour with you, if you will allow me, till so and so comes back to fetch me'; it costs him the earnings of an hour, and therefore he has a right to complain. But women have no right, because it is '*only* their time.'

Women have no means given them, whereby they *can* resist the 'claims of social life.' They are taught from their infancy upwards that it is a wrong, ill-tempered, and a misunderstanding of 'woman's mission' (with a great M) if they do not allow themselves *willingly* to be interrupted at all hours. If a woman has once put in a claim to be treated as a man by some work of science or art or literature, which she can *show* as the 'fruit of her leisure,' then she will be considered justified in *having* leisure (hardly, perhaps, even then). But if not, not. If she has nothing to show, she must resign herself to her fate. . . .

Women often strive to live by intellect. The clear, brilliant sharp radiance of intellect's moonlight rising upon such an expanse of snow is dreary, it is true, but some love its solemn desolation, its silence, its solitude—if they are but *allowed* to live in it; if they are not perpetually baulked or disappointed. But a woman cannot live in the light of intellect. Society forbids it. Those conventional frivolities, which are called her 'duties,' forbid it. Her 'domestic duties,' high-sounding words, which, for the most part, are bad habits (which she has not the courage to enfranchise herself from, the strength to break through) forbid it. What are these duties (or bad habits)?—Answering a multitude of letters which lead to nothing, from her so-called friends, keeping herself up to the level of the world that she may furnish her quota of amusement at the breakfast-table; driving out her company in the carriage. And all these things are exacted from her by her family which, if she is good and affectionate, will have more influence with her than the world.

What wonder, if, wearied out, sick at heart with hope deferred, the springs of will broken, not seeing clearly *where* her duty lies, she abandons intellect as a vocation and takes it only, as we use the moon, by glimpses through her tight-closed window shutters?

The family? It is too narrow a field for the development of an immortal spirit, be that spirit male or female. The chances are a thousand to one that, in that small sphere, the task for which that immortal spirit is destined by the qualities and the gifts which its Creator has placed within it, will not be found.

The family uses people, *not* for what they are, nor for what they are intended to be, but for what it wants them for—its own uses. It thinks of them not as what God has made them, but as the something which it has arranged that they shall be. If it wants someone to sit in the drawing-room, *that* someone is supplied by the family, though that member may be destined for science, or for education, or for active superintendence by God, *i.e.* by the gifts within.

This system dooms some minds to incurable infancy, other to silent misery.

And family boasts that it has performed its mission well, in as far as it has enabled the individual to say, 'I have *no* peculiar work, nothing but what the moment brings me, nothing that I cannot throw up at once at anybody's claim'; in as far, that is, as it has *destroyed* the individual life. And the individual thinks that a great victory has been accomplished, when, at last, she is able to say that she has 'no personal desires or plans.' What is this but throwing the gifts of God aside as worthless, and substituting for them those of the world?

Marriage is the only chance (and it is but a chance) offered to women for escape from this death; and how eagerly and how ignorantly it is embraced!

At present we live to impede each other's satisfactions; competition, domestic life, society, what is it all but this? We go somewhere where we are not wanted and where we don't want to go. What else is conventional life? *Passivity* when we want to be active. So many hours spent every day in passively doing what conventional life tells us, when we would so gladly be at work.

And is it a wonder that all individual life is extinguished?

Women dream of a great sphere of steady, not sketchy benevolence, of moral activity, for which they would fain be trained and fitted, instead of working in the dark, neither knowing nor registering whither their steps lead, whether farther from or nearer to the aim. . . .

Women long for an education to teach them *to teach*, to teach them the laws of the human mind and how to apply them—and knowing how imperfect, in the present state of the world, such an education must be, they long for experience, not patch-work experience, but experience followed up and systematised, to enable them to know what they are about and *where* they are 'casting their bread', and whether it is '*bread*' or a stone.

How should we learn a language if we were to give it an hour a week? A fortnight's steady application would make more way in it than a year of such patch-work. A 'lady' can hardly go to 'her school' two days running. She cannot leave the breakfast-table—or she must be fulfilling some little frivolous 'duty,' which others ought not to exact, or which might just as well be done some other time.

Dreaming always—never accomplishing; thus women live—too much ashamed of their dreams, which they think 'romantic', to tell them where they will be laughed at, even if not considered wrong. . . .

If a man were to follow up his profession or occupation at odd times, how would he do it? Would he become skilful in that profession? It is acknowledged by women themselves that they are inferior in every occupation to men. Is it wonderful? *They* do *everything* at 'odd times'.

And if a woman's music and drawing are only used by her as an amusement (a *pass-time*, as it is called), is it wonderful that she tires of them, that she becomes disgusted with them?

In every dream of the life of intelligence or that of activity, women are accompanied by a phantom—the phantom of sympathy guiding, lighting the way—even if they do not marry. Some few sacrifice marriage, because they sacrifice all other life if they accept that. That man and woman have an equality of duties and rights is accepted by woman even less than by man. Behind *his* destiny woman must annihilate herself, must be only his complement. A woman dedicates herself to the vocation of her husband; she fills up and performs the subordinate parts in it. But if she has any destiny, any vocation of her own, she must renounce it, in nine cases out of ten. Some few, like Mrs Somerville, Mrs Chisholm, Mrs Fry, have not done so: but these are exceptions. The fact is that woman has so seldom any vocation of her own, that it does not much signify; she has none to renounce. A man gains everything by marriage: he gains a 'helpmate,' but a woman does not.

But if ever women come into contact with sickness, with poverty, and crime in masses, how the practical reality of life revives them! They are exhausted, like those who live on opium or on novels, all their lives—exhausted with feelings which lead to no action. If they see and enter into a continuous line of action, with a full and interesting life, with training constantly kept up to the occupation, occupation constantly testing the training—it is the *beau-ideal* of practical, not theoretical, education—they are re-tempered, their life is filled, they have found their work, and the means to do it. . . .

To have no food for our heads, no food for our hearts, no food for our activity, is that nothing? If we have no food for the body, how do we cry out, how all the world hears of it, how all the newspapers talk of it, with a paragraph headed in great capital letters, DEATH FROM STARVATION! But suppose one were to put a paragraph in the *Times*, Death of Thought from Starvation or Death of Moral Activity from Starvation, how people would stare, how they would laugh and wonder! One would think we had no heads nor hearts, by the total indifference of the public towards them. Our bodies are the only things of any consequence.

We have nothing to do which raises us, no food which agrees with us. We can never pursue any object for a single two hours, for we can never command any regular leisure or solitude; and in social or domestic life one is bound, under pain of being thought sulky, to make a remark every two minutes. . . . With what labour women have toiled to break down all individual and independent life, in order to fit themselves for this social and domestic existence, thinking it right! And when they have killed themselves to do it, they have awakened (too late) to think it wrong.

For, later in life, women could not make use of leisure and solitude if they had it! Like the Chinese woman, who could not make use of her feet, if she were brought into European life.

Some have an attention like a battering-ram, which, slowly, brought to bear, can work upon a subject for any length of time. They can work ten hours just as well as two upon the same thing. But this age would have men like the musket, which you can load so fast that nothing but its heating in the process puts any limit to the number and frequency of times of firing, and at as many different objects as you please.

So, later in life, people cannot use their battering-ram. Their attention, like society's, goes off in a thousand different directions. They are an hour before they can fix it; and by the time it is fixed, the leisure is gone. They become incapable of consecutive or strenuous work.

What these suffer—even physically—from the want of such work no one can tell. The accumulation of nervous energy, which has had nothing to do during the day, makes them feel every night, when they go to bed, as if they were going mad; and they are obliged to lie long in bed in the morning to let it evaporate and keep it down. At last they suffer at once from disgust of the one and incapacity for the other—from loathing of conventional idleness and powerlessness to do work when they have it. . . .

Moral activity? There is scarcely such a thing possible! Everything is sketchy. The world does nothing but sketch. One Lady Bountiful sketches a school, but it never comes to a finished study; she can hardly work at it two weeks consecutively. Here and there a solitary individual, it is true, makes a really careful study,—as Mrs Chisholm of emigration—as Miss Carpenter of reformatory discipline. But, in general, a 'lady' has too many sketches on hand. She has a sketch of society, a sketch of her children's education, sketches of her 'charities,' sketches of her reading. . . .

When shall we see a woman making a *study* of what she does? Married women cannot; for a man would think, if his wife undertook any great work with the intention of carrying it out,—of making anything but a sham of it—that she would 'suckle his fools and chronicle his small beer' less well for it,—that he would not have so good a dinner—that she would destroy, as it is called, his domestic life.

The intercourse of man and woman—how frivolous, how unworthy it is! Can we call *that* the true vocation of woman—her high career? Look round at the marriages which you know. The true marriage—that noble union, by which a man and woman become together the one perfect being—probably does not exist at present upon earth.

It is not surprising that husbands and wives seem so little part of one another. It is surprising that there is so much love as there is. For there is no food for it. What does it live upon—what nourishes it? Husbands and wives never seem to have anything to say to one another. What do they talk about? Not about any great religious, social, political questions or feelings. They talk about who shall come to dinner, who is to live in this lodge and who in that, about the improvement of the place, or when they shall go to London. If there are children, they form a common subject of some nourishment. But, even then, the case is oftenest thus,—the husband is to think of how they are to get on in life; the wife of bringing them up at home.

But any real communion between husband and wife—any descending into the depths of their being, and drawing out thence what they find and comparing it—do we ever dream of such a thing? Yes, we may dream of it during the season of 'passion,' but we shall not find it afterwards. We even expect it to go off, and lay our account that it will. If the husband has, by chance, gone into the depths of *his* being, and found there anything unorthodox, he, oftenest, conceals it carefully from his wife,—he is afraid of 'unsettling her opinions.'

. . . He cannot impart to her his religious beliefs, if he have any, because she would be 'shocked.' Religious men are and must be heretics now—for we must not pray, except in a 'form' of words, made beforehand—or think of God but with a pre-arranged idea.

With the man's political ideas, if they extend beyond the merest party politics, she has no sympathy.

His social ideas, if they are 'advanced,' she will probably denounce without knowing why, as savouring of 'socialism' (a convenient word, which covers a multitude of new ideas and offences). For woman is 'by birth a Tory',—has often been said,—by education a 'Tory,' we mean.

Woman has nothing but her affections,—and this makes her at once more loving and less loved.

But is it surprising that there should be so little real marriage, when we think what the process is which leads to marriage?

Under the eyes of an always present mother and sisters (of whom even the most refined and intellectual cannot abstain from a jest upon the subject, who think it their *duty* to be anxious, to watch every germ and bud of it) the acquaintance begins. It is fed—upon what?—the gossip of art, musical and pictorial, the party politics of the day, the chit-chat of society, and people marry or sometimes they don't marry, discouraged by the impossibility of knowing any more of one another than this will furnish.

They prefer to marry in *thought*, to hold imaginary conversations with one another in idea, rather than, on such a flimsy pretext of communion, to take the chance (certainty it cannot be) of having more to say to one another in marriage.

Men and women meet now *to be idle*. Is it extraordinary that they do not know each other, and that, in their mutual ignorance, they form no surer friendships? Did they meet to *do* something together, then indeed they might form some real tie.

But, as it is, *they* are not there, it is only a mask which is there—a mouthpiece of ready-made sentences about the 'topics of the day'; and then people rail against men for choosing a woman 'for her face'—why, what else do they see?

It is very well to say 'be prudent, be careful, try to know each other'. But how are you to know each other?

Unless a woman had lost all pride, how is it possible for her under the eyes of all her family, to indulge in long exclusive conversations with a man? 'Such a thing' must not take place till after her 'engagement'. And how is she to make an engagement, if 'such a thing' has not taken place? . . .

There are four ways in which people marry. First, accident or relationship has thrown them together in their childhood, and acquaintance has grown up naturally and unconsciously. Accordingly, in novels, it is generally cousins who marry; and now it seems the only natural thing—the only possible way of making any intimacy. And yet, we know that intermarriage between relations is in direct contravention of the laws of nature for the well-being of the race . . .

The second way, and by far the most general, in which people marry, is this. A woman, thoroughly uninterested at home, and having formed a slight acquaintance with some accidental person, accepts him, if he 'falls in love' with her, as it is technically called, and takes the chance. Hence the vulgar expression of marriage being a lottery, which it most truly is, for that the *right* two should come together has as many chances against it as there are blanks in any lottery.

The third way is, that some person is found sufficiently independent, sufficiently careless of the opinions of others, or sufficiently without modesty to speculate thus: 'It is worth while that I should become acquainted with so and so. I do not care what his or her opinion of me is, if, *after* having become acquainted, to do which can bear no other construction in people's eyes than a desire of marriage, I retreat'. But there is this to be said, that it is doubtful whether, under their unnatural tension, which, to all susceptible characters, such a disregard of the opinions which they care for must be, a healthy or a natural feeling can grow up.

And now they are married—that is to say, two people have received the licence of a man in a white surplice. But they are no more man and wife for that than Louis XIV and the Infanta of Spain, married by proxy, were man and wife. The woman who has sold herself for an establishment, in what is she superior to those we may not name?

Lastly, in a few rare, very rare cases, such as circumstances, always provided in novels, but seldom to be met with in real life, present—whether the accident of parents' neglect, or of parents' unusual skill and wisdom, or of having no parents at all, which is generally the case in novels—or by marrying out of the person's rank of life, by which the usual restraints are removed, and there is room and play left for attraction—or extraordinary events, isolation, misfortunes, which many wish for, even though their imaginations be not tainted by romance-reading; such alternatives as these give food and space for the development of character and mutual sympathies. But a girl, if she has any pride, is so ashamed of having anything she wishes to say out of the hearing of her own family, she thinks it must be something so very wrong, that it is ten to one, if she have the opportunity of saying it, that she will not.

And yet she is spending her life, perhaps, in dreaming of accidental means of unrestrained communion.

And then it is thought pretty to say that 'women have no passion.' If passion is excitement in the daily social intercourse with men, women think about marriage much more than men do; it is the only event of their lives. It ought to be a sacred event, but surely not the only event of a woman's life, as it is now. . . .

Women dream till they have no longer the strength to dream; those dreams against which they so struggle, so honestly, vigorously, and conscientiously, and so in vain, yet which are their life, without which they could not have lived; those dreams go at last. All their plans and visions seem vanished, and they know not where; gone, and they cannot recall them. They do not even remember them. And they are left without the food of reality or of hope.

Later in life, they neither desire nor dream, neither of activity, nor of love, nor of intellect. The last often survives the longest. They wish, if their experiences would benefit anybody, to give them to someone. But they never find an hour free in which to collect their thoughts, and so discouragement becomes ever deeper and deeper, and they less and less capable of undertaking anything.

It seems as if the female spirit of the world were mourning everlastingly over blessings, not *lost*, but which she has never had, and which, in her discouragement she feels that she never will have, they are so far off.

The more complete a woman's organisation, the more she will feel it, till at last there shall arise a woman, who will resume, in her own soul, all the sufferings of her race, and that woman will be the Saviour of her race.

Jesus Christ raised women above the condition of mere slaves, mere ministers to the passions of man, raised them by His sympathy, to be Ministers of God. He gave them moral activity. But the Age, the World, Humanity, must give them the means to exercise this moral activity, must give them intellectual cultivation, sphere of action.

There is perhaps no century where the woman shows so meanly as in this. Because her education seems entirely to have parted company with her vocation; there is no longer unity between the woman as inwardly developed, and as outwardly manifested.

In the last century it was not so. In the succeeding one let us hope that it will no longer be so.

But now she is like the Archangel Michael as he stands upon Saint Angelo at Rome. She has an immense provision of wings, which seem as if they would bear her over earth and heaven; but when she tries to use them, she is petrified into stone, her feet are grown into the earth, chained to the bronze pedestal.

Nothing can well be imagined more painful than the present position of woman, unless, on the one hand, she renounces all outward activity and keeps herself within the magic sphere, the bubble of her dreams; or, on the other, surrendering all aspiration, she gives herself to her real life, soul and body. For those to whom it is possible, the latter is best; for out of activity may come thought, out of mere aspiration can come nothing. . . .

The ideal life is passed in noble schemes of good consecutively followed up, of devotion to a great object, of sympathy given and received for high ideas and generous feelings. The actual life is passed in sympathy given and received for a dinner, a party, a piece of furniture, a house built or a garden laid out well, in devotion to your guests—(a too real devotion, for it implies that of all your time)—in schemes of schooling for the poor, which you follow up perhaps in an odd quarter of an hour, between luncheon and driving out in the carriage—broth and dripping are included in the plan—and the rest of your time goes in ordering the dinner, hunting for a governess for your children, and sending pheasants and apples to your poorer relations. Is there anything in *this* life which can be called an Incarnation of the ideal life within? Is it a wonder that the unhappy woman should prefer to keep them entirely separate? not to take the bloom off her Ideal by mixing it up with her Actual; not to make her Actual still more unpalatable by trying to *inform* it with her Ideal? And then she is blamed, and her own sex unites against her, for not being content with the 'day of small things'. She is told that 'trifles make the sum of human things'; they do indeed. She is contemptuously asked, 'Would she abolish domestic life?' Men are afraid that their houses will not be so comfortable, that their wives will make themselves 'remarkable' women, that they will make themselves distasteful to men; they write books (and very wisely) to teach themselves to dramatise 'little things,' to persuade themselves that 'domestic life is their sphere' and to idealise the 'sacred hearth'. Sacred it is indeed. Sacred from the touch of their sons almost as soon as they are out of childhood—from its dulness and its tyrannous trifling *these* recoil. Sacred from the grasp of their daughters' affections upon which it has so light a hold that they seize the first opportunity of marriage, *their* only chance of emancipaton. The 'sacred hearth'; sacred to their husband's sleep, their sons' absence in the body and their daughters' in mind.

Oh! mothers, who talk about this hearth, how much do you know of your son's real life, how much of your daughter's imaginary one? Awake, ye women, all ye that sleep, awake! If this domestic life were so very good, would your young men wander away from it, your maidens think of something else? . . .

People talk about imitating Christ, and imitate Him in the little trifling formal things, such as washing the feet, saying His prayer, and so on; but if anyone attempts the real imitation of Him, there are no bounds to the outcry with which the presumption of that person is condemned.

For instance, Christ was saying something to the people one day, which interested Him very much, and interested them very much; and Mary and His brothers came in the middle of it, and wanted to interrupt Him, and take Him home to dinner, very likely—(how natural that story is! does it not speak more home than any historic evidences of the Gospel's reality?), and He, instead of being angry with their interruption of Him in such an important work for some trifling thing, answers, 'Who is my mother? and who are my brethren? Whosoever shall do the will of my Father which is in heaven, the same is my brother and sister and mother.' But if *we* were to say that, we should be accused of 'destroying the family tie, of diminishing the obligation of the home duties.'

He might well say, 'Heaven and earth shall pass away, but my words shall not pass away.' His words will never pass away. If He had said, 'Tell them that I am engaged at this moment in something very important; that the instruction of the multitude ought to go before any personal ties; that I will remember to come when I have done,' no one would have been impressed by His words; but how striking is that, 'Behold my mother and my brethren!'

The dying woman to her mourners:—'Oh! if you knew how gladly I leave this life, how much more courage I feel to take the chance of another, than of anything I see before me in this, you would put on your wedding-clothes instead of mourning for me!'

'But,' they say, 'so much talent! so many gifts! such good which you might have done!'

'The world will be put back some little time by my death,' she says; 'you see I estimate my powers at least as highly as you can; but it is by the death which has taken place some years ago in me, not by the death which is about to take place now.' And so is the world put back by the death of every one who has to sacrifice the development of his or her peculiar gifts (which were meant, not for selfish gratification, but for the improvement of that world) to conventionality.

'My people were like children playing on the shore of the eighteenth century. I was their hobby-horse, their plaything; and they drove me to and fro, dear souls! never weary of the play themselves, till I, who had grown to woman's estate and to the ideas of the nineteenth century, lay down exhausted, my mind closed to hope, my heart to strength . . . '

(*Cassandra*, 1852, 1st published 1928; reprinted in R. Strachey, *The Cause*, 1978, Appendix I, pp. 396–418.)

v.3 Speech by Thomas Babington Macaulay at Edinburgh (2 Nov. 1852)

The madness of 1848 did not subvert the British throne. The reaction which followed has not destroyed British liberty.

And why is this? Why has our country, with all the ten plagues raging around her, been a land of Goshen? Everywhere else was the thunder, and the fire running along the ground,—a very grievous storm,—a storm such as there was none like it since man was on the earth; yet everything tranquil here; and then again thick night, darkness that might be felt; and yet light in all our dwellings. We owe this singular happiness, under the blessing of God, to a wise and noble constitution, the work of many generations of great men. Let us profit by experience; and let us be thankful that we profit by the experience of others, and not by our own. Let us prize our constitution: let us purify it: let us amend it; but let us not destroy it. Let us shun extremes, not only because each extreme is in itself a positive evil, but also because each extreme necessarily engenders its opposite. If we love civil and religious freedom, let us in the day of danger uphold law and order. If we are zealous for law and order, let us prize, as the best safeguard of law and order, civil and religious freedom.

Yes, Gentlemen; if I am asked why we are free with servitude all around us, why our Habeas Corpus Act has not been suspended, why our press is still subject to no censor, why we still have the liberty of association, why our representative institutions still abide in all their strength, I answer, It is because in the year of revolutions we stood firmly by our Government in its peril; and, if I am asked why we stood by our Government in its peril, when men all around us were engaged in pulling Governments down, I answer, It was because we knew that though our Government was not a perfect Government, it was a good Government, that its fault admitted of peaceable and legal remedies, that it had never inflexibly opposed just demands, that we had obtained concessions of inestimable value, not by beating the drum, not by ringing the tocsin, not by tearing up the pavement, not by running to the gunsmiths' shops to search for arms, but by the mere force of reason and public opinion. And, Gentlemen, preeminent among those pacific victories of reason and public opinion, the recollection of which chiefly, I believe, carried us safely through the year of revolutions and through the year of counter-revolutions, I would place two great reforms, inseparably associated, one with the memory of an illustrious man, who is now beyond the reach of envy, the other with the name of another illustrious man, who is still, and, I hope, long will be, a living mark for detraction. I speak of the great commercial reform of 1846, the work of Sir Robert Peel, and of the great parliamentary reform of 1832, the work of many eminent statesmen, among whom none was more conspicuous than Lord John Russell.

(*The Nineteenth-Century Constitution*, ed. H. J. Hanham, 1969, pp 12–13.)

John Stuart Mill, from 'Of the Extension of the Suffrage' (1861)   v.4

[1.] Such a representative democracy as has now been sketched, representative of all, and not solely of the majority—in which the interests, the opinions, the grades of intellect which are outnumbered would nevertheless be heard, and would have a chance of obtaining by weight of character and strength of argument, an influence which would not belong to their numerical force—this democracy, which is alone equal, alone impartial, alone the government of all by all, the only true type of democracy—would be free from the greatest evils of the falsely-called democracies which now prevail, and from which the current idea of democracy is exclusively derived. But even in this democracy, absolute power, if they chose to exercise it, would rest with the numerical majority; and these would be

composed exclusively of a single class, alike in biases, prepossessions, and
general modes of thinking, and a class, to say no more, not the most highly
cultivated. The constitution would therefore still be liable to the characteristic evils of class government: in a far less degree, assuredly, than that
exclusive government by a class, which now usurps the name of democracy; but still, under no effective restraint, except what might be found in
the good sense, moderation, and forbearance, of the class itself. If checks of
this description are sufficient, the philosophy of constitutional government
is but solemn trifling. All trust in constitutions is grounded on the assurance they may afford, not that the depositaries of power will not, but that
they cannot, misemploy it. Democracy is not the ideally best form of
government unless this weak side of it can be strengthened; unless it can be
so organized that no class, not even the most numerous, shall be able to
reduce all but itself to political insignificance, and direct the course of legislation and administration by its exclusive class interest. The problem is, to
find the means of preventing this abuse, without sacrificing the characteristic advantages of popular government.

[2.] These twofold requisites are not fulfilled by the expedient of a limitation of the suffrage, involving the compulsory exclusion of any portion of
the citizens from a voice in the representation. Among the foremost benefits of free government is that education of the intelligence and of the sentiments, which is carried down to the very lowest ranks of the people when
they are called to take a part in acts which directly affect the great interests
of their country. On this topic I have already dwelt so emphatically, that I
only return to it, because there are few who seem to attach to this effect of
popular institutions all the importance to which it is entitled. People think
it fanciful to expect so much from what seems so slight a cause—to recognize a potent instrument of mental improvement in the exercise of political
franchises by manual labourers. Yet unless substantial mental cultivation
in the mass of mankind is to be a mere vision, this is the road by which it
must come. If any one supposes that this road will not bring it, I call to witness the entire contents of M. de Tocqueville's great work; and especially
his estimate of the Americans. Almost all travellers are struck by the fact
that every American is in some sense both a patriot, and a person of cultivated intelligence; and M. de Tocqueville has shown how close the connexion is between these qualities and their democratic institutions. No such
wide diffusion of the ideas, tastes, and sentiments of educated minds, has
ever been seen elsewhere, or even conceived as attainable. Yet this is
nothing to what we might look for in a government equally democratic in
its unexclusiveness, but better organized in other important points. For
political life is indeed in America a most valuable school, but it is a school
from which the ablest teachers are excluded; the first minds in the country
being as effectually shut out from the national representation, and from
public functions generally, as if they were under a formal disqualification.

The Demos, too, being in America the one source of power, all the selfish ambition of the country gravitates towards it, as it does in despotic countries towards the monarch: the people, like the despot, is pursued with adulation and sycophancy, and the corrupting effects of power fully keep pace with its improving and ennobling influences. If, even with this alloy, democratic institutions produce so marked a superiority of mental development in the lowest class of Americans, compared with the corresponding classes in England and elsewhere, what would it be if the good portion of the influence could be retained without the bad? And this, to a certain extent, may be done; but not by excluding that portion of the people, who have fewest intellectual stimuli of other kinds, from so inestimable an introduction to large, distant, and complicated interests as is afforded by the attention they may be induced to bestow on political affairs. It is by political discussion that the manual labourer, whose employment is a routine, and whose way of life brings him in contact with no variety of impressions, circumstances, or ideas, is taught that remote causes, and events which take place far off, have a most sensible effect even on his personal interests; and it is from political discussion, and collective political action, that one whose daily occupations concentrate his interests in a small circle round himself, learns to feel for and with his fellow-citizens, and becomes consciously a member of a great community. But political discussions fly over the heads of those who have no votes, and are not endeavouring to acquire them. . . . Whoever, in an otherwise popular government, has no vote, and no prospect of obtaining it, will either be a permanent malcontent, or will feel as one whom the general affairs of society do not concern. . .

[3.] Independently of all these considerations, it is a personal injustice to withhold from any one, unless for the prevention of greater evils, the ordinary privilege of having his voice reckoned in the disposal of affairs in which he has the same interest as other people. If he is compelled to pay, if he may be compelled to fight, if he is required implicitly to obey, he should be legally entitled to be told what for; to have his consent asked, and his opinion counted at its worth, though not at more than its worth. There ought to be no pariahs in a full-grown and civilized nation; no persons disqualified, except through their own default. Every one is degraded, whether aware of it or not, when other people, without consulting him, take upon themselves unlimited power to regulate his destiny. . . . No arrangement of the suffrage, therefore, can be permanently satisfactory, in which any person or class is peremptorily excluded; in which the electoral privilege is not open to all persons of full age who desire to obtain it.

[4.] There are, however, certain exclusions, required by positive reasons, which do not conflict with this principle, and which, though an evil in themselves, are only to be got rid of by the cessation of the state of things which requires them. I regard it as wholly inadmissible that any person should participate in the suffrage, without being able to read, write, and, I will add, perform the common operations of arithmetic. Justice demands, even when the suffrage does not depend on it, that the means of attaining these elementary acquirements should be within the reach of every person, either gratuitously, or at an expense not exceeding what the poorest, who earn their own living, can afford. If this were really the case, people would no more think of giving the suffrage to a man who could not read, than of giving it to a child who could not speak; and it would not be society that would exclude him, but his own laziness. When society has not performed its duty, by rendering this amount of instruction accessible to all, there is some hardship in the case, but it is a hardship that ought to be borne. If society has neglected to discharge two solemn obligations, the more important and more fundamental of the two must be fulfilled first: universal teaching must precede universal enfranchisement. No one but those in whom an *a priori* theory has silenced common sense, will maintain, that power over others, over the whole community, should be imparted to people who have not acquired the commonest and most essential requisites for taking care of themselves; for pursuing intelligently their own interests, and those of the persons most nearly allied to them. . . . It would be easy to require from every one who presented himself for registry, that he should, in the presence of the registrar, copy a sentence from an English book, and perform a sum in the rule of three; and to secure, by fixed rules and complete publicity, the honest application of so very simple a test. This condition, therefore, should in all cases accompany universal suffrage; and it would, after a few years, exclude none but those who cared so little for the privilege, that their vote, if given, would not in general be an indication of any real political opinion.

[5.] It is also important, that the assembly which votes the taxes, either general or local, should be elected exclusively by those who pay something towards the taxes imposed. Those who pay no taxes, disposing by their votes of other people's money, have every motive to be lavish, and none to economize. As far as money matters are concerned, any power of voting possessed by them is a violation of the fundamental principle of free government; a severance of the power of control, from the interest in its beneficial exercise. It amounts to allowing them to put their hands into other people's pockets, for any purpose which they think fit to call a public one; which in some of the great towns of the United States is known to have produced a scale of local taxation onerous beyond example, and wholly borne by the wealthier classes. That representation should be co-extensive with taxation, not stopping short of it, but also not going beyond it, is in accordance with the theory of British institutions. But to reconcile this, as a condition annexed to the representation, with universality, it is essential, as it is on many other accounts desirable, that taxation, in a visible shape, should descend to the poorest class . . . a direct tax, in the simple form of a capitation, should be levied on every grown person in the community; or that every such person should be admitted an elector, on allowing himself to be rated *extra ordinem* to the assessed taxes; or that a small annual payment, rising and falling with the gross expenditure of the country, should be required from every registered elector; that so every one might feel that the money which he assisted in voting was partly his own, and that he was interested in keeping down its amount.

[6.] However this may be, I regard it as required by first principles, that the receipt of parish relief should be a peremptory disqualification for the franchise. He who cannot by his labour suffice for his own support, has no claim to the privilege of helping himself to the money of others. By becoming dependent on the remaining members of the community for actual subsistence, he abdicates his claim to equal rights with them in other respects. Those to whom he is indebted for the continuance of his very existence, may justly claim the exclusive management of those common concerns, to which he now brings nothing, or less than he takes away. As a condition of the franchise, a term should be fixed, say five years previous to the registry, during which the applicant's name has not been on the parish books as a recipient of relief. To be an uncertified bankrupt, or to have taken the benefit of the Insolvent Act, should disqualify for the franchise until the person has paid his debts, or at least proved that he is not now, and has not for some long period been, dependent on eleemosynary support. Non-payment of taxes, when so long persisted in that it cannot have arisen from inadvertence, should disqualify while it lasts. These exclusions are not in their nature permanent. They exact such conditions only as all are able, or ought to be able, to fulfil if they choose. They leave the suffrage accessible to all who are in the normal condition of a human being: and if any one has to forgo it, he either does not care sufficiently for it, to do for its sake what he is already bound to do, or he is in a general condition of depression and degradation in which this slight addition, necessary for the security of others, would be unfelt, and on emerging from which, this mark of inferiority would disappear with the rest.

[7.] In the long run, therefore (supposing no restrictions to exist but those of which we have now treated), we might expect that all, except that (it is to be hoped) progressively diminishing class, the recipients of parish relief, would be in possession of votes, so that the suffrage would be, with that slight abatement, universal. That it should be thus widely expanded, is, as we have seen, absolutely necessary to an enlarged and elevated conception of good government. Yet in this state of things, the great majority of voters, in most countries, and emphatically in this, would be manual labourers; and the twofold danger, that of too low a standard of political intelligence, and that of class legislation, would still exist, in a very perilous degree. It remains to be seen whether any means exist by which these evils can be obviated.

[8.] They are capable of being obviated, if men sincerely wish it; not by any artificial contrivance, but by carrying out the natural order of human life, which recommends itself to every one in things in which he has no interest or traditional opinion running counter to it. In all human affairs, every person directly interested, and not under positive tutelage, has an admitted claim to a voice, and when his exercise of it is not inconsistent with the safety of the whole, cannot justly be excluded from it. But though every one ought to have a voice—that every one should have an equal voice is a totally different proposition. When two persons who have a joint interest in any business, differ in opinion, does justice require that both opinions should be held of exactly equal value? If with equal virtue, one is superior to the other in knowledge and intelligence—or if with equal intelligence, one excels the other in virtue—the opinion, the judgement, of the higher moral or intellectual being, is worth more than that of the inferior; . . .

[9.] Now, national affairs are exactly such a joint concern, with the difference, that no one needs ever be called upon for a complete sacrifice of his own opinion. It can always be taken into the calculation, and counted at a certain figure, a higher figure being assigned to the suffrages of those whose opinion is entitled to greater weight. There is not, in this arrangement, anything necessarily invidious to those to whom it assigns the lower degrees of influence. Entire exclusion from a voice in the common concerns, is one thing: the concession to others of a more potential voice, on the ground of greater capacity for the management of the joint interests, is another. The two things are not merely different, they are incommensurable. Every one has a right to feel insulted by being made a nobody, and stamped as of no account at all. No one but a fool, and only a fool of a peculiar description, feels offended by the acknowledgement that there are others whose opinion, and even whose wish, is entitled to a greater amount of consideration than his. To have no voice in what are partly his own concerns, is a thing which nobody willingly submits to; but when what is partly his concern is also partly another's, and he feels the other to understand the subject better than himself, that the other's opinion should be counted for more than his own, accords with his expectations, and with the course of things which in all other affairs of life he is accustomed to acquiesce in. It is only necessary that this superior influence should be assigned on grounds which he can comprehend, and of which he is able to perceive the justice.

[10.] I hasten to say, that I consider it entirely inadmissible, unless as a temporary makeshift, that the superiority of influence should be conferred in consideration of property. I do not deny that property is a kind of test; education in most countries, though anything but proportional to riches, is on the average better in the richer half of society than in the poorer. But the criterion is so imperfect; accident has so much more to do than merit with enabling men to rise in the world; and it is so impossible for any one by acquiring any amount of instruction, to make sure of the corresponding rise in station, that this foundation of electoral privilege is always, and will continue to be, supremely odious. To connect plurality of votes with any pecuniary qualification would be not only objectionable in itself, but a sure mode of discrediting the principle, and making its permanent maintenance impracticable. The Democracy, at least of this country, are not at present jealous of personal superiority, but they are naturally and most justly so of that which is grounded on mere pecuniary circumstances. The only thing which can justify reckoning one person's opinion as equivalent to more than one, is individual mental superiority; and what is wanted is some approximate means of ascertaining that. . . .

[11.] If it be asked, to what length the principle admits of being carried, or how many votes might be accorded to an individual on the ground of superior qualifications, I answer, that this is not in itself very material, provided the distinctions and gradations are not made arbitrarily, but are such as can be understood and accepted by the general conscience and understanding. But it is an absolute condition, not to overpass the limit prescribed by the fundamental principle laid down in a former chapter as the condition of excellence in the constitution of a representative system. The plurality of votes must on no account be carried so far, that those who are privileged by it, or the class (if any) to which they mainly belong, shall outweigh by means of it all the rest of the community. The distinction in favour of education, right in itself, is further and strongly recommended by its preserving the educated from the class legislation of the uneducated; but it must stop short of enabling them to practise class legislation on their own account. Let me add, that I consider it an absolutely necessary part of the plurality scheme, that it be open to the poorest individual in the community to claim its privileges, if he can prove that, in spite of all difficulties and obstacles, he is, in point of intelligence, entitled to them. There ought to be voluntary examinations at which any person whatever might present himself, might prove that he came up to the standard of knowledge and ability laid down as sufficient, and be admitted, in consequence, to the plurality of votes. A privilege which is not refused to any one who can show that he has realized the conditions on which in theory and principle it is dependent, would not necessarily be repugnant to any one's sentiment of justice: but it would certainly be so, if, while conferred on general presumptions not always infallible, it were denied to direct proof.

[12.] Plural voting, though practised in vestry elections and those of poor-law guardians, is so unfamiliar in elections to Parliament, that it is not likely to be soon or willingly adopted: but as the time will certainly arrive when the only choice will be between this and equal universal suffrage, whoever does not desire the last, cannot too soon begin to reconcile himself to the former. . . .

[13.] Until there shall have been devised, and until opinion is willing to accept, some mode of plural voting which may assign to education, as such, the degree of superior influence due to it, and sufficient as a counterpoise to the numerical weight of the least educated class; for so long, the benefits of completely universal suffrage cannot be obtained without bringing with them, as it appears to me, a chance of more than equivalent evils. . . .

[14.] So much importance do I attach to the emancipation of those who already have votes, but whose votes are useless, because always outnumbered; so much should I hope from the natural influence of truth and reason, if only secured a hearing and a competent advocacy—that I should not despair of the operation even of equal and universal suffrage, if made real by the proportional representation of all minorities, on Mr. Hare's principle. But if the best hopes which can be formed on this subject were certainties, I should still contend for the principle of plural voting. I do not propose the plurality as a thing in itself undesirable, which, like the exclusion of part of the community from the suffrage, may be temporarily tolerated while necessary to prevent greater evils. I do not look upon equal voting as among the things which are good in themselves, provided they can be guarded against inconveniences. I look upon it as only relatively good; less objectionable than inequality of privilege grounded on irrelevant or adventitious circumstances, but in principle wrong, because recognizing a wrong standard, and exercising a bad influence on the voter's mind. It is not useful, but hurtful, that the constitution of the country should declare ignorance to be entitled to as much political power as knowledge. The national institutions should place all things that they are concerned with, before the mind of the citizen in the light in which it is for his good that he should regard them: and as it is for his good that he should think that every one is entitled to some influence, but the better and wiser to more than others, it is important that this conviction should be professed by the State, and embodied in the national institutions. Such things constitute the *spirit* of the institutions of a country: that portion of their influence which is least regarded by common, and especially by English, thinkers; though the institutions of every country, not under great positive oppression, produce more effect by their spirit than by any of their direct provisions, since by it they shape the national character. The American institutions have imprinted strongly on the American mind, that any one man (with a white skin) is as good as any other; and it is felt that this false creed is nearly connected with some of the more unfavourable points in American character. It is not a small mischief that the constitution of any country should sanction this creed; for the belief in it, whether express or tacit, is almost as detrimental to moral and intellectual excellence, as any effect which most forms of government can produce.

[15.] It may, perhaps, be said, that a constitution which gives equal influence, man for man, to the most and to the least instructed, is nevertheless conducive to progress, because the appeals constantly made to the less instructed classes, the exercise given to their mental powers, and the exertions which the more instructed are obliged to make for enlightening their judgement and ridding them of errors and prejudices, are powerful stimulants to their advance in intelligence. That this most desirable effect really attends the admission of the less educated classes to some, and even to a large share of power, I admit, and have already strenuously maintained. But theory and experience alike prove that a counter current sets in when they are made the possessors of all power. Those who are supreme over everything, whether they be One, or Few, or Many, have no longer need of the arms of reason: they can make their mere will prevail; and those who cannot be resisted are usually far too well satisfied with their own opinions to be willing to change them, or listen without impatience to any one who tells them that they are in the wrong. The position which gives the strongest stimulus to the growth of intelligence, is that of rising into power, not that of having achieved it; and of all resting-points, temporary or permanent, in the way to ascendancy, the one which develops the best and highest qualities is the position of those who are strong enough to make reason prevail, but not strong enough to prevail against reason. This is the position in which, according to the principles we have laid down, the rich and the poor, the much and the little educated, and all the other classes and denominations which divide society between them, ought as far as practicable to be placed. And by combining this principle with the otherwise just one of allowing superiority of weight to superiority of mental qualities, a political constitution would realize that kind of relative perfection, which is alone compatible with the complicated nature of human affairs.

[16.] In the preceding argument for universal, but graduated suffrage, I have taken no account of difference of sex. I consider it to be as entirely irrelevant to political rights, as difference in height, or in the colour of the hair. All human beings have the same interest in good government; the welfare of all is alike affected by it, and they have equal need of a voice in it to secure their share of its benefits. If there be any difference, women require it more than men, since, being physically weaker, they are more dependent on law and society for protection. Mankind have long since abandoned the only premises which will support the conclusion that women ought not to have votes. No one now holds that women should be in personal servitude; that they should have no thought, wish, or occupation, but to be the domestic drudges of husbands, fathers, or brothers. It is allowed to unmarried, and wants but little of being conceded to married women, to hold property, and have pecuniary and business interests, in the same manner as men. It is considered suitable and proper that women should think, and write, and be teachers. As soon as these things are admitted, the political disqualification has no principle to rest on. The whole mode of thought of the modern world is, with increasing emphasis, pronouncing against the claim of society to decide for individuals what they are and are not fit for, and what they shall and shall not be allowed to attempt. If the principles of modern politics and political economy are good for anything, it is for proving that these points can only be rightly judged of by the individuals themselves: and that, under complete freedom of choice, wherever there are real diversities of aptitude, the great number will apply themselves to the things for which they are on the average fittest, and the exceptional course will only be taken by the exceptions. Either the whole tendency of modern social improvements has been wrong, or it ought to be carried out to the total abolition of all exclusions and disabilities which close any honest employment to a human being.

[17.] But it is not even necessary to maintain so much, in order to prove that women should have the suffrage. Were it as right, as it is wrong, that they should be a subordinate class, confined to domestic occupations and subject to domestic authority, they would not the less require the protection of the suffrage to secure them from the abuse of that authority. . . .

(*Representative Government*, 1861, Ch VIII.)

v.5 From the Representation of the People Act (1867)

2. This Act shall not apply to *Scotland* or *Ireland*, nor in anywise affect the Election of Members . . . for the Universities of *Oxford* or *Cambridge*.

Part I—Franchises

3. Every Man shall, in and after the Year One thousand eight hundred and sixty-eight, be entitled to be registered as a Voter, and when registered, to vote for a Member or Members to serve in Parliament for a Borough, who is qualified as follows: (that is to say,)
   1. Is of full Age, and not subject to any legal Incapacity; and
   2. Is on the last Day of *July* in any Year, and has during the whole of the preceding Twelve Calendar Months been, an Inhabitant Occupier, as Owner or Tenant, of any Dwelling House within the Borough; and
   3. Has during the Time of such Occupation been rated as an ordinary Occupier in respect of the Premises so occupied by him within the Borough to all Rates (if any) made for the Relief of the Poor in respect of such Premises; and
   4. Has on or before the Twentieth Day of *July* in the same Year *bonâ fide* paid an equal Amount in the Pound to that payable by other ordinary Occupiers in respect of all Poor Rates that have become payable by him in respect of the said Premises up to the preceding Fifth Day of *January*:

Provided that no Man shall under this Section be entitled to be registered as a Voter by reason of his being a joint Occupier of any Dwelling House.

4. Every Man shall, in and after the Year One thousand eight hundred

and sixty-eight, be entitled to be registered as a Voter, and, when registered, to vote for a Member or Members to serve in Parliament for a Borough who is qualified as follows: (that is to say,)

1. Is of full Age and not subject to any legal Incapacity; and

2. As a Lodger has occupied in the same Borough separately and as sole Tenant for the Twelve Months preceding the last Day of *July* in any Year the same Lodgings, such Lodgings being Part of one and the same Dwelling House, and of a clear yearly Value, if let unfurnished, of Ten Pounds or upwards; and

3. Has resided in such Lodgings during the Twelve Months immediately preceding the last Day of *July*, and has claimed to be registered as a Voter at the next ensuing Registration of Voters.

5. Every Man shall, in and after the Year One thousand eight hundred and sixty-eight, be entitled to be registered as a Voter, and, when registered, to vote for a Member or Members to serve in Parliament for a County, who is qualified as follows: (that is to say),

1. Is of full Age, and not subject to any legal Incapacity, and is seised at Law or in Equity of any Lands or Tenements of Freehold, Copyhold, or any other Tenure whatever, for his own Life, or for the Life of another, or for any Lives whatsoever, or for any larger Estate of the clear yearly Value of not less than Five Pounds over and above all Rents and Charges payable out of or in respect of the same, or who is entitled, either as Lessee or Assignee, to any Lands or Tenements of Freehold or of any other Tenure whatever, for the unexpired Residue, whatever it may be of any Term originally created for a Period of not less than Sixty Years (whether determinable on a Life or Lives or not), of the clear yearly Value of not less than Five Pounds over and above all Rents and Charges payable out of or in respect of the same:

Provided that no Person shall be registered as a Voter under this Section unless he has complied with the Provisions of the Twenty-sixth Section of the Act of the Second Year of the Reign of His Majesty *William* the Fourth, Chapter Forty-five. . . .

6. Every Man shall, in and after the Year One thousand eight hundred and sixty-eight, be entitled to be registered as a Voter, and, when registered, to vote for a Member or Members to serve in Parliament for a County, who is qualified as follows: (that is to say,)

1. Is of full Age, and not subject to any legal Incapacity; and

2. Is on the last Day of *July* in any Year, and has during the Twelve Months immediately preceding been, the Occupier as Owner or Tenant, of Lands or Tenements within the County of the rateable Value of Twelve Pounds or upwards; and

3. Has during the Time of such Occupation been rated in respect to the Premises so occupied by him to all Rates (if any) made for the Relief of the Poor in respect of the said Premises; and

4. Has on or before the Twentieth Day of *July* in the same Year paid all Poor Rates that have become payable by him in respect of the said Premises up to the preceding Fifth Day of *January*.

7. Where the Owner is rated at the Time of the passing of this Act to the Poor Rate in respect of a Dwelling House or other Tenement situate in a Parish wholly or partly in a Borough, instead of the Occupier, his Liability to be rated in any future Poor Rate shall cease, and the following Enactments shall take effect with respect to rating in all Boroughs:

1. After the passing of this Act no Owner of any Dwelling House or other Tenement situate in a Parish either wholly or partly within a Borough shall be rated to the Poor Rate instead of the Occupier, except as herein-after mentioned:

2. The full rateable Value of every Dwelling House or other separate Tenement, and the full Rate in the Pound payable by the Occupier, and the Name of the Occupier, shall be entered in the Rate Book:

Where the Dwelling House or Tenement shall be wholly let out in Apartments or Lodgings not separately rated, the Owner of such Dwelling House or Tenement shall be rated in respect thereof to the Poor Rate:

Provided as follows:

(1) That nothing in this Act contained shall affect any Composition existing at the Time of the passing of this Act, so nevertheless that no such Composition shall remain in force beyond the Twenty-ninth Day of *September* next:

(2) That nothing herein contained shall affect any Rate made previously to the passing of this Act, and the Powers conferred by any subsisting Act for the Purpose of collecting and recovering a Poor Rate shall remain and continue in force for the Collection and Recovery of any such Rate or Composition:

(3) That where the Occupier under a Tenancy subsisting at the Time of the passing of this Act of any Dwelling House or other Tenement which has been let to him free from Rates is rated and has paid Rates in pursuance of this Act, he may deduct from any Rent due or accruing due from him in respect of the said Dwelling House or other Tenement any Amount paid by him on account of the Rates to which he may be rendered liable by this Act. . . .

9. At a contested Election for any County or Borough represented by Three Members no Person shall vote for more than Two Candidates.

10. At a contested Election for the City of *London* no Person shall vote for more than Three Candidates.

11. No Elector who within Six Months before or during any Election for any County or Borough shall have been retained, hired, or employed for all or any of the Purposes of the Election for Reward by or on behalf of any Candidate at such Election as Agent, Canvasser, Clerk, Messenger, or

in other like Employment, shall be entitled to vote at such Election, and if he shall so vote he shall be guilty of a Misdemeanor.

(30 & 31 Vict., c. 102; reprinted in *The Law and Working of the Constitution,*
ed. W. C. Costin and J. S. Watson, 1952, vol. 2, pp. 103–7.)

George Eliot, from 'Address to Working Men by Felix Holt' (Jan. 1868)   v.6

Fellow-workmen,

I am not going to take up your time by complimenting you. It has been the fashion to compliment kings and other authorities when they have come into power, and to tell them that, under their wise and beneficent rule, happiness would certainly overflow the land. But the end has not always corresponded to that beginning. If it were true that we who work for wages had more of the wisdom and virtue necessary to the right use of power than has been shown by the aristocratic and mercantile classes, we should not glory much in that fact, or consider that it carried with it any near approach to infallibility.

In my opinion, there has been too much complimenting of that sort; and whenever a speaker, whether he is one of ourselves or not, wastes our time in boasting or flattery, I say, let us hiss him. If we have the beginning of wisdom, which is, to know a little truth about ourselves, we know that as a body we are neither very wise nor very virtuous. And to prove this, I will not point specially to our own habits and doings, but to the general state of the country. Any nation that had within it a majority of men—and we are the majority—possessed of much wisdom and virtue, would not tolerate the bad practices, the commercial lying and swindling, the poisonous adulteration of goods, the retail cheating, and the political bribery, which are carried on boldly in the midst of us. A majority has the power of creating a public opinion. We could groan and hiss before we had the franchise; if we had groaned and hissed in the right place, if we had discerned better between good and evil, if the multitude of us artisans, and factory hands, and miners, and labourers of all sorts, had been skilful, faithful, well-judging, industrious, sober—and I don't see how there can be wisdom and virtue anywhere without those qualities—we should have made an audience that would have shamed the other classes out of their share in the national vices. We should have had better members of Parliament, better religious teachers, honester tradesmen, fewer foolish demagogues, less impudence in infamous and brutal men; and we should not have had among us the abomination of men calling themselves religious while living in splendour on ill-gotten gains. I say, it is not possible for any society in which there is a very large body of wise and virtuous men to be as vicious as our society is—to have as low a standard of right and wrong, to have so much belief in falsehood, or to have so degrading, barbarous a notion of what pleasure is, or of what justly raises a man above his fellows. Therefore, let us have done with this nonsense about our being much better than the rest of our countrymen, or the pretence that that was a reason why we ought to have such an extension of the franchise as has been given to us. The reason for our having the franchise, as I want presently to show, lies somewhere else than in our personal good qualities, and does not in the least lie in any high betting chance that a delegate is a better man than a duke, or that a Sheffield grinder is a better man than any one of the firm he works for.

However, we have got our franchise now. We have been sarcastically called in the House of Commons the future masters of the country; and if that sarcasm contains any truth, it seems to me that the first thing we had better think of is, our heavy responsibility; that is to say, the terrible risk we run of working mischief and missing good, as others have done before us. . . .

But I come back to this: that, in our old society, there are old institutions, and among them the various distinctions and inherited advantages of classes, which have shaped themselves along with all the wonderful slow-growing system of things made up of our laws, our commerce, and our stores of all sorts, whether in material objects, such as buildings and machinery, or in knowledge, such as scientific thought and professional skill. Just as in [the case of] the irrigation of a country, which must absolutely have its water distributed or it will bear no crop; there are the old channels, the old banks, and the old pumps, which must be used as they are until new and better have been prepared, or the structure of the old has been gradually altered. But it would be fool's work to batter down a pump only because a better might be made, when you had no machinery ready for a new one: it would be wicked work, if villages lost their crops by it. Now the only safe way by which society can be steadily improved and our worst evils reduced, is not by any attempt to do away directly with the actually existing class distinctions and advantages, as if everybody could have the same sort of work, or lead the same sort of life (which none of my hearers are stupid enough to suppose), but by the turning of Class Interests into Class Functions or duties. What I mean is, that each class should be urged by the surrounding conditions to perform its particular work under the strong pressure of responsibility to the nation at large; that our public affairs should be got into a state in which there should be no impunity for foolish or faithless conduct. In this way, the public judgment would sift out incapability and dishonesty from posts of high charge, and even personal ambition would necessarily become of a worthier sort, since the desires of the most selfish men must be a good deal shaped by the opinions of those around them; and for one person to put on a cap and bells, or to go about dishonest or paltry ways of getting rich that he may spend a vast sum of money in having more finery than his neighbours, he must be pretty sure of a crowd who will applaud him. Now changes can only be good in proportion as they help to bring about this sort of result: in proportion as they put knowledge in the place of ignorance, and fellow-feeling in the place of selfishness. In the course of that substitution class distinctions must inevitably change their character, and represent the varying Duties of men, not their varying Interests. But this end will not come by impatience. 'Day will not break the sooner because we get up before the twilight.' Still less will it come by mere undoing, or change merely as change. And moreover, if we believed that it would be unconditionally hastened by our getting the franchise, we should be what I call superstitious men, believing in magic, or the production of a result by hocus-pocus. Our getting the franchise will greatly hasten that good end in proportion only as every one of us has the knowledge, the foresight, the conscience, that will make him well-judging and scrupulous in the use of it. The nature of things in this world has been determined for us beforehand, and in such a way that no ship can be expected to sail well on a difficult voyage, and reach the right port, unless it is well manned: the nature of the winds and the waves, of the timbers, the sails and the cordage, will not accommodate itself to drunken, mutinous sailors.

You will not suspect me of wanting to preach any cant to you, or of joining in the pretence that everything is in a fine way, and need not be made better. What I am striving to keep in our minds is the care, the precaution, with which we should go about making things better, so that the public order may not be destroyed, so that no fatal shock may be given to this society of ours, this living body in which our lives are bound up. After the Reform Bill of 1832 I was in an election riot, which showed me clearly, on a small scale, what public disorder must always be; and I have never forgotten that the riot was brought about chiefly by the agency of dishonest men who professed to be on the people's side. Now, the danger hanging over change is great, just in proportion as it tends to produce such disorder by giving any large number of ignorant men, whose notions of what is good are of a low and brutal sort, the belief that they have got power into their hands, and may do pretty much as they like. If any one can look round us and say that he sees no signs of any such danger now, and that our national condition is running along like a clear broadening stream, safe not to get choked with mud, I call him a cheerful man: perhaps he does his own gardening, and seldom takes exercise far away from home. To us who have no gardens, and often walk abroad, it is plain that we can never get into a bit of a crowd but we must rub clothes with a set of Roughs, who have the worst vices of the worst rich—who are gamblers, sots, libertines, knaves, or else mere sensual simpletons and victims. They are the ugly crop that has sprung up while the stewards have been sleeping; they are the multiplying brood begotten by parents who have been left without all teaching save that of a too craving body, without all wellbeing save the fading delusions of drugged beer and gin. They are the hideous margin of society, at one edge drawing towards it the undesigning ignorant poor, at the other darkening imperceptibly into the lowest criminal class. Here is one of the evils which cannot be got rid of quickly, and against which any of us who have got sense, decency, and instruction have need to watch. That these degraded fellow-men could really get the mastery in a persistent disobedience to the laws and in a struggle to subvert order, I do not believe; but wretched calamities would come from the very beginning of such a struggle, and the continuance of it would be a civil war, in which the inspiration on both sides might soon cease to be even a false notion of good, and might become the direct savage impulse of ferocity. We have all to see to it that we do not help to rouse what I may call the savage beast in the breasts of our generation—that we do not help to poison the nation's blood, and make richer provision for bestiality to come. . . .

(*Blackwood's Magazine*, Jan. 1868.)

v.7 From speech by Benjamin Disraeli at Manchester (3 Apr. 1872)

Gentlemen,

The programme of the Conservative party is to maintain the Constitution of the country. I have not come down to Manchester to deliver an essay on the English Constitution; but when the banner of Republicanism is unfurled—when the fundamental principles of our institutions are controverted—I think, perhaps, it may not be inconvenient that I should make some few practical remarks upon the character of our Constitution—upon that monarchy, limited by the co-ordinate authority of Estates of the realm, which, under the title of Queen, Lords and Commons, has contributed so greatly to the prosperity of this country, and with the maintenance of which I believe that prosperity is bound up.

Gentlemen, since the settlement of that Constitution, now nearly two centuries ago, England has never experienced a revolution, though there is no country in which there has been so continuous and such considerable change. How is this? Because the wisdom of your forefathers placed the prize of supreme power without the sphere of human passions. Whatever the struggle of parties, whatever the strife of factions, whatever the excitement and exaltation of the public mind, there has always been something in this country round which all classes and parties could rally, representing the majesty of the law, the administration of justice, and involving, at the same time, the security for every man's rights and the fountain of honour. Now, gentlemen, it is well clearly to comprehend what is meant by a country not having a revolution for two centuries. It means, for that space, the unbroken exercise and enjoyment of the ingenuity of man. It means, for that space, the continuous application of the discoveries of science to his comfort and convenience. It means the accumulation of capital, the elevation of labour, the establishment of those admirable factories which cover your district; the unwearied improvement of the cultivation of the land, which has extracted from a somewhat churlish soil harvests more exuberant than those furnished by lands nearer to the sun. It means the continuous order which is the only parent of personal liberty and political right. And you owe all these, gentlemen, to the Throne.

There is another powerful and most beneficial influence which is also exercised by the Crown. Gentlemen, I am a party man. I believe that, without party, Parliamentary government is impossible. I look upon Parliamentary government as the noblest government in the world, and certainly the one most suited to England. But without the discipline of political connection, animated by the principle of private honour, I feel certain that a popular Assembly would sink before the power or the corruption of a minister. Yet, gentlemen, I am not blind to faults of party government. It has one great defect. Party has a tendency to warp the intelligence. . . . It is, therefore, a great merit in our Constitution that before a minister introduces a measure to Parliament, he must submit it to an intelligence superior to all party, and entirely free from influences of that character.

I know it will be said, gentlemen, that, however beautiful in theory, the personal influence of the Sovereign is now absorbed in the responsibility of the minister. Gentlemen, I think you will find there is great fallacy in this view. The principles of the English Constitution do not contemplate the absence of personal influence on the part of the Sovereign; and if they did, the principles of human nature would prevent the fulfilment of such a theory. . . . From the earliest moment of his accession that Sovereign is placed in constant communication with the most able statesmen of the period, and of all parties. Even with average ability it is impossible not to perceive that such a Sovereign must soon attain a great mass of political information and political experience. Information and experience, gentlemen, whether they are possessed by a Sovereign or by the humblest of his subjects, are irresistible in life. No man with the vast responsibility that devolves upon an English minister can afford to treat with indifference a suggestion that has not occurred to him, or information with which he had not been previously supplied. But, gentlemen, pursue this view of the subject. The longer the reign, the influence of that Sovereign must proportionately increase. All the illustrious statesmen who served his youth disappear. A new generation of public servants rises up. There is a critical conjuncture in affairs—a moment of perplexity and peril. Then it is that the Sovereign can appeal to a similar state of affairs that occurred perhaps thirty years before. When all are in doubt among his servants he can quote the advice that was given by the illustrious men of his early years, and though he may maintain himself within the strictest limits of the Constitution, who can suppose when such information and such suggestions are made by the most exalted person in the country that they can be without effect? No, gentlemen; a minister who could venture to treat such influence with indifference would not be a Constitutional minister, but an arrogant idiot.

Gentlemen, the influence of the Crown is not confined merely to political affairs. England is a domestic country. Here the home is revered and the hearth is sacred. The nation is represented by a family—the Royal Family; and if that family is educated with a sense of responsibility and a sentiment of public duty, it is difficult to exaggerate the salutary influence they may exercise over a nation. It is not merely an influence upon manners; it is not merely that they are a model for refinement and for good taste—they affect the heart as well as the intelligence of the people; and in the hour of public adversity, or in the anxious conjuncture of public affairs, the nation rallies round the Family and the Throne, and its spirit is animated and sustained by the expression of public affection.

(*The Nineteenth-Century Constitution*, ed. H. J. Hanham, 1969, pp. 37–9.)

v.8 Walter Bagehot, from *The English Constitution* (1872)

I can conceive that questions *being* raised which, if continually agitated, would combine the working men as a class together, the higher orders might have to consider whether they would concede the measures that would settle such questions, or whether they would risk the effect of the working men's combination.

No doubt the question cannot be easily discussed in the abstract; much must depend on the nature of the measures in each particular case; on the evil they would cause if conceded; on the attractiveness of their idea to the working classes if refused. But in all cases it must be remembered that a political combination of the lower classes, as such and for their own objects, is an evil of the first magnitude; that a permanent combination of them would make them (now that so many of them have the suffrage) supreme in the country; and that their supremacy, in the state they now are, means the supremacy of ignorance over instruction and of numbers over knowledge. So long as they are not taught to act together, there is a chance of this being averted, and it can only be averted by the greatest wisdom and the greatest foresight in the higher classes. They must avoid, not only every evil, but every appearance of evil; while they have still the power they must remove, not only every actual grievance, but, where it is possible, every seeming grievance too; they must willingly concede every claim which they can safely concede, in order that they may not have to concede unwillingly some claim which would impair the safety of the country.

This advice, too, will be said to be obvious; but I have the greatest fear
that, when the time comes, it will be cast aside as timid and cowardly. So
strong are the combative propensities of man that he would rather fight a
losing battle than not fight at all. It is most difficult to persuade people that
by fighting they may strengthen the enemy, yet that would be so here; since
a losing battle—especially a long and well-fought one—would have thoroughly taught the lower orders to combine, and would have left the higher
orders face to face with an irritated, organised, and superior voting power.
The courage which strengthens an enemy and which so loses, not only the
present battle, but many after battles, is a heavy curse to men and
nations. . . .

The Reform Act of 1867 has, I think, unmistakably completed the effect
which the Act of 1832 began, but left unfinished. The middle class element
has gained greatly by the second change, and the aristocratic element has
lost greatly. If you examine carefully the lists of members, especially of the
most prominent members, of either side of the House, you will not find
that they are in general aristocratic names. Considering the power and
position of the titled aristocracy, you will perhaps be astonished at the
small degree in which it contributes to the active part of our governing
assembly. The spirit of our present House of Commons is plutocratic, not
aristocratic; its most prominent statesmen are not men of ancient descent
or of great hereditary estate; they are men mostly of substantial means, but
they are mostly, too, connected more or less closely with the new trading
wealth. The spirit of the two Assemblies has become far more contrasted
than it ever was. . . .

(The English Constitution, 2nd edn., 1872, Introduction.)

From the Representation of the People Act (1884)   v.9

Extension of the Household and Lodger Franchise

2. A uniform household franchise and a uniform lodger franchise at
elections shall be established in all counties and boroughs throughout the
United Kingdom, and every man possessed of a household qualification or
a lodger qualification shall, if the qualifying premises be situate in a county
in England or Scotland, be entitled to be registered as a voter, and when
registered to vote at an election for such county, and if the qualifying premises be situate in a county or borough in Ireland, be entitled to be registered
as a voter, and when registered to vote at an election for such county or
borough.

3. Where a man himself inhabits any dwelling-house by virtue of any
office, service, or employment, and the dwelling-house is not inhabited by
any person under who such man serves in such office, service, or employ-

ment, he shall be deemed for the purposes of this Act and of the Representation of the People Acts to be an inhabitant occupier of such dwelling-house as a tenant.

[**4.** Restriction of multiplication of votes.]

Assimilation of Occupation Certification

5. Every man occupying any land or tenement in a county or borough in the United Kingdom of a clear yearly value of not less than ten pounds shall be entitled to be registered as a voter and when registered to vote at an election for such county or borough in respect of such occupation subject to the like conditions respectively as a man is, at the passing of this Act, entitled to be registered as a voter and to vote at an election for such county in respect of the county occupation franchise, and at an election for such borough in respect of the borough occupation franchise.

[**§6.** Voter not to vote in a county in respect of occupation of property in a borough.]

Supplemental Provisions

9. . . . (2) In every part of the United Kingdom it shall be the duty of the overseers annually, in the months of April and May, or one of them, to inquire or ascertain with respect to every hereditament which comprises any dwelling-house or dwelling-houses within the meaning of the Representation of the People Acts, whether any man, other than the owner or other person rated or liable to be rated in respect of such hereditament, is entitled to be registered as a voter in respect of his being an inhabitant occupier of any such dwelling-house, and to enter in the rate book the name of every man so entitled, and the situation or description of the dwelling-house in respect of which he is entitled, and for the purposes of such entry a separate column shall be added to the rate book.

(8) Both in England and Ireland where a man inhabits any dwelling-house by virtue of any office, service, or employment, and is deemed for the purposes of this Act and of the Representation of the People Acts to be an inhabitant occupier of such dwelling-house as a tenant, and another person is rated or liable to be rated for such dwelling-house, the rating of such other person shall for the purposes of this Act and of the Representation of the People Acts be deemed to be that of the inhabitant occupier; and the several enactments of the Poor Rate Assessment and Collection Act, 1869, and other Acts amending the same referred to in the First Schedule to this Act shall for those purposes apply to such inhabitant occupier, and in the construction of those enactments the word 'owner' shall be deemed to include a person actually rated or liable to be rated as aforesaid.

10. Nothing in this Act shall deprive any person (who at the date of the passing of this Act is registered in respect of any qualification to vote for any county or borough,) of his right to be from time to time registered and to vote for such county or borough in respect of such qualification in like manner as if this Act had not passed.

Provided that where a man is so registered in respect of the county or borough occupation franchise by virtue of a qualification which also qualifies him for the franchise under this Act, he shall be entitled to be registered in respect of such latter franchise only.

Nothing in this Act shall confer on any man who is subject to any legal incapacity to be registered as a voter or to vote, any right to be registered as a voter or to vote, . . .

(48 Vict., c.3; reprinted in *The Law and Working of the Constitution*, ed. W. C. Costin and J. S. Watson, 1952, vol. 2, pp. 126–8.)

Letter from William Ewart Gladstone to Queen Victoria (25 Feb. 1886)

V.10

Mr. Gladstone reports to Your Majesty with his humble duty that the Cabinet today further considered the Crofters' Bill and the very peculiar circumstances with which it has to deal. They agreed upon the leading proposals of the Bill, which may lead to a good deal of debate.

The Cabinet were of opinion that it would be desirable to treat the question of the Woman's Suffrage Bill, which is expected to come on next week, as what is termed an open question. The Ministers generally however are as individuals disinclined to the Bill, & disposed to vote accordingly.

The question of Sir D. Wolff's mission to the East, which stands for early decision on the vote for the expences, was also considered by the Cabinet. The Government will support this vote, but will reserve their judgment on the policy and effect of the mission, until they are in possession of fuller information. They do not desire to disturb it if this can be avoided.

The Chancellor of the Exchequer informed the Cabinet that although the demands of the Military and Naval Departments had by careful effort been much reduced, there still remained an increase of a million more or less. This increase the Cabinet had no option but to accept, as unavoidable under the circumstances, although sensible that the great and frequent augmentations of these Estimates has now brought them to a point highly inconvenient in many points of view.

(*The Nineteenth-Century Constitution*, ed. H. J. Hanham, 1969, pp. 82–3)

VI

Town and Country

Friedrich Engels, from *The Condition of the Working Class in England* VI.1
(1845)

The whole of this built-up area is commonly called Manchester, and contains about 400,000 people. This is probably an underestimate rather than
an exaggeration. Owing to the curious lay-out of the town it is quite possible for someone to live for years in Manchester and to travel daily to and
from his work without ever seeing a working-class quarter or coming into
contact with an artisan. He who visits Manchester simply on business or
for pleasure need never see the slums, mainly because the working-class
districts and the middle-class districts are quite distinct. This division is due
partly to deliberate policy and partly to instinctive and tacit agreement
between the two social groups. In those areas where the two social groups
happen to come into contact with each other the middle classes sanctimon-
iously ignore the existence of their less fortunate neighbours. In the centre
of Manchester there is a fairly large commercial district, which is about
half a mile long and half a mile broad. This district is almost entirely given
over to offices and warehouses. Nearly the whole of this district has no permanent residents and is deserted at night, when only policemen patrol its
dark, narrow thoroughfares with their bull's eye lanterns. This district is
intersected by certain main streets which carry an enormous volume of
traffic. The lower floors of the buildings are occupied by shops of dazzling
splendour. A few of the upper stories on these premises are used as dwellings and the streets present a relatively busy appearance until late in the
evening. Around this commercial quarter there is a belt of built up areas on
the average one and a half miles in width, which is occupied entirely by
working-class dwellings. . . . Beyond this belt of working-class houses or
dwellings lie the districts inhabited by the middle classes and the upper
classes. The former are to be found in regularly laid out streets near the
working-class districts—in Chorlton and in the remoter parts of Cheetham
Hill. The villas of the upper classes are surrounded by gardens and lie in the
higher and remoter parts of Chorlton and Ardwick or on the breezy heights
of Cheetham Hill, Broughton and Pendleton. The upper classes enjoy

healthy country air and live in luxurious and comfortable dwellings which are linked to the centre of Manchester by omnibuses which run every fifteen or thirty minutes. To such an extent has the convenience of the rich been considered in the planning of Manchester that these plutocrats can travel from their houses to their places of business in the centre of the town by the shortest routes, which run entirely through working-class districts, without even realising how close they are to the misery and filth which lie on both sides of the road. This is because the main streets which run from the Exchange in all directions out of the town are occupied almost uninterruptedly on both sides by shops, which are kept by members of the lower middle classes. In their own interests these shopkeepers should keep the outsides of their shops in a clean and respectable condition, and in fact they do so. These shops have naturally been greatly influenced by the character of the population in the area which lies behind them. Those shops which are situated in the vicinity of commercial or middle class residential districts are more elegant than those which serve as a facade for the workers' grimy cottages. Nevertheless, even the less pretentious shops adequately serve their purpose of hiding from the eyes of wealthy ladies and gentlemen with strong stomachs and weak nerves the misery and squalor which are part and parcel of their own riches and luxury. . . .

This sketch will be sufficient to illustrate the crazy layout of the whole district lying near the River Irk. There is a very sharp drop of some 15 to 30 feet down to the south bank of the Irk at this point. As many as three rows of houses have generally been squeezed on to this precipitous slope. The lowest row of houses stands directly on the bank of the river while the front walls of the highest row stand on the crest of the ridge in Long Millgate. Moreover, factory buildings are also to be found on the banks of the river. In short the layout of the upper part of Long Millgate at the top of the rise is just as disorderly and congested as the lower part of the street. To the right and left a number of covered passages from Long Millgate give access to several courts. On reaching them one meets with a degree of dirt and revolting filth, the like of which is not to be found elsewhere. The worst courts are those leading down to the Irk, which contain unquestionably the most dreadful dwellings I have ever seen. In one of these courts, just at the entrance where the covered passage ends there is a privy without a door. This privy is so dirty that the inhabitants of the court can only enter or leave the court if they are prepared to wade through puddles of stale urine and excrement. . . .

It is pertinent at this stage to make some general observations on the normal lay-out of working-class quarters and the normal plan of constructing artisans' dwellings in Manchester. . . . Here the spaces between the blocks of dwellings consist of regular—generally square—courts, from which there is access to the streets by a covered passage. From the point of view of the health of the workers cooped up in these dwellings, this type of regular layout with wholly inadequate ventilation, is even worse than the unplanned streets of the Old Town. The air simply cannot escape and it is only up the chimneys of the houses—when fires happen to be burning—that any draught is provided to help the foul air from the courts to escape. Moreover, the houses surrounding such courts are usually built back to back, with a common rear wall, and this alone is sufficient to hinder any adequate circulation of the air, and since the police do not concern themselves with the state of these courts everything thrown into the courts is allowed to lie there undisturbed, so that it is not surprising that dirt and heaps of ashes and filth are to be found there.

. . . Workers' cottages are now hardly ever built singly, but always in larger numbers—a dozen or even sixty at a time. A single contractor will build one or two whole streets at a time. . . .

This method of construction is adopted partly in order to save materials and partly because the builder is never the owner of the land on which the cottages are put up. The English practice is to lease building land for twenty, thirty, forty, fifty or ninety-nine years. When the lease falls in, possession of the land and the buildings on it reverts to the ground landlord, who does not have to pay any compensation for unexhausted improvements. The builder, therefore, constructs the cottages of a type unlikely to survive beyond the period of the lease. Since some leases are as short as twenty or thirty years it is easy to understand that builders are not likely to sink much capital into cottages built on such land. Moreover, the owners of the houses who are either bricklayers, joiners and carpenters or factory owners, are generally not prepared to spend very much money on repairing and maintaining their property. This is partly because they are not prepared to sacrifice any part of their profits, and partly owing to the system of short leases to which we have referred. . . .

(*The Condition of the Working Class in England*, 1845, trans. and
ed. W. O. Henderson and W. H. Chaloner, 1958, pp. 54–69.)

Reverend Francis Kilvert's Diary (6 May 1870)   VI.2

The mare seemed about the same this morning, perhaps a trifle better, and her cheeks and jaws terribly swollen from the blisters. Went to see Cooper and found him a good deal better and just come in from a slow easy walk round the garden. A letter from Mr Venables urging me to put off my visit to Langley for a week, that I may meet Perch there. So I had to set off for Newchurch again, my second visit there this week. Visited Marianne Price on the Pitch on the way.

In the dingle gardens between the Dulas and Clyro Churchyard, I saw the first rose-coloured and peach-tinted apple blooms. Oh, the orchards, the orchards! Sat on the stile a field above the Tall Trees and the ruined cottage to hear the country sounds, the noises about the farms: dogs barking, cattle lowing, birds singing, children's voices, and the cuckoo calling over all.

Beyond Tynessa I saw the figure of a woman dark against the sky, walking over the Vicar's Hill among the gorse tufts and dead rusty fern. It proved to be Mrs Prothero of Pant-y-ci. She came down into the road which she was going to cross to get to her own house, when I came up. She had a huge root and plant of primroses in her hand, covered with fine blossoms with which she was going to adorn her house. Whilst I was talking to her, old Mrs Gwillim of Tynessa, whom I had seen as I passed fumbling about her garden, deaf and newly blind, came maundering along the road to the spring with a pitcher. I spoke to her but could not make her hear a single word, and all I could get out of her was that she had a great many diseases.

Further on, some boys sitting under the wall were minding half a dozen red and white cattle belonging to Cwm Ithel which were grazing along the road sides. To amuse themselves and pass the time the boys had been making 'a play house', that is, a ground plan of a house with flat stones laid singly on the green turf. Within this plan of a house the boys sat grinning with great content. A hundred yards further on three girls were sitting on the turf under the wall, minding the same cattle and keeping them from straying the other way. One of the girls was my little friend Selina Evans of Cwm Ithel, another was Hannah Parton of Newgate and the third Polly Davies of Tymawr. The girls also were sitting happily in their 'play house' within which they had made a table of stones. They laughed when I asked them what they would give me to eat from their table, and I tried hard to persuade them, and half succeeded, that if they put some 'cuckoo's bread and cheese' on the table and hid behind the wall, they might possibly see the cuckoo come and eat his bread and cheese.

Selina Evans remembered Maria Lake and spoke very kindly and feelingly about her, telling me how often Maria had tried to coax her (Selina's) drunken father away home from the public house when he was getting tipsy. I am sorry to see they have cut down the fir that grew by Tynessa and the bent larch that used to bow over the house. Since Maria's death that larch has always seemed to me to be mourning for her.

I took to Crowther's Pool an order for Charles Williams of Crowther to be an out patient at Brecon Infirmary, which I got from Tom Williams of Llowes for him. The old woman was at home alone but pretty little Selina came up to the door as I went away.

By the Caeau the gold bushes of gorse were creeping down and clothing the old worked-out deserted quarry sides. People had been attempting to burn the gorse trees but had only succeeded in burning the underbrush and charring the long straggling stems of the old gorse trees which still stood up black and naked, crowned with dry withered tufts which the fire had not reached. The fire had, however, had the effect of blackening with scorch and smoke the beautiful silvery bark of some of the lovely birches which form a row down the lane, dividing it from the gorsy field. On one favourite and beautiful silver birch I was almost tempted to carve my name.

When I got out on to the open of the Little Mountain the lapwings were wheeling about the hill by scores, hurtling and rustling with their wings, squirling and wailing, tumbling and lurching on every side, very much disturbed, anxious and jealous about their nests. As I entered the fold of Gilfach-yr-heol, Janet issued from the house door and rushed across the yard, and turning the corner of the wain house I found the two younger ladies assisting at the castration of the lambs, catching and holding the poor little beasts and standing by whilst the operation was performed, seeming to enjoy the spectacle. It was the first time I had seen clergymen's daughters helping to castrate lambs or witnessing that operation and it rather gave me a turn of disgust at first. But I made allowance for them and considered in how rough a way the poor children have been brought up so that they thought no harm of it, and I forgave them. I am glad however that Emmeline was not present, and Sarah was of course out of the way. Matilda was struggling in a pen with a large stout white lamb, and when she had mastered him and got him well between her legs and knees, I ventured to ask where her father was. She signified by a nod and a word that he was advancing behind me, and turning, I saw him crossing the yard with his usual outstretched hand and cordial welcome. I don't think the elder members of the family quite expected that the young ladies would be caught by a morning caller castrating lambs, and probably they would have selected some other occupation for them had they foreseen the coming of a guest. However they carried it off uncommonly well.

We went indoors and settled about the Sunday and Bettws Chapel where the good parson is to attend on May 22nd and until further notice. Then we had tea. Sarah laid the cloth as usual and she and Emmeline as usual sat opposite me, both looking very pretty, Sarah in her blue shirt and Emmeline in her russet-brown dress.

After tea Sarah and Emmeline were to take to Blaencerde some medicine for a sick parishioner which the good curate had concocted, and he walked with them as far as the village. Emmeline looked very bewitching in her little black hat perched on the top of her fair long curls. We parted at the door and Janet and Matilda, having finished their labours with the lambs, were sitting on a trunk of a tree in the fold, but came to say 'Goodbye'. Certainly these are and will be four as fine handsome girls as we would see in a family in a day's march.

Near a copse between the Caeau and Crowther's Pool, I stopped to listen to a cuckoo. He was so near that his strong deep liquid voice shook the whole air. I never heard a cuckoo so close before.

Found the mare no better. Price went to bed and I agreed to stay up all

283

night with Richard Williams, Jim Rogers and William Morgan, the boy.
Rutter came in the night about eleven. Then Price went home and we began
our watch, with a good fire in the saddle room.

(*Kilvert's Diary*, ed. W. Plomer, 1938, vol. 1.)

VI.3 J. T. Emmet, from 'The State of English Architecture' (Apr. 1872)

[1.] For several years past the public mind has been prepared for an earnest endeavour to obtain a decent building for our courts of law. The
attempt has now been strenuously made; time, money, abundant zeal, and
superabundant counsel, have been lavishly expended. Never, perhaps, in
the history of art has so much general intelligence been brought to the preparation for a single work; never has there been a more unanimous desire
that the best thing possible, or even impossible, should be discovered and
achieved; and yet the main result has been dissatisfaction and elaborate
failure. Our most conspicuous Gothic architects sent in designs, whose
exhibition served as a severe but salutary lesson to the art-loving public. . . . The exhibition was melancholy and hopeless, almost without
exception—an artistic *inferno* and a national disgrace.

[2.] In Mr. Street's design, which has been finally selected, the façade or
elevation on the frontage towards the Strand is some five hundred feet long,
which is about the length of St. Paul's and other of our large cathedrals,
there is, consequently, no difficulty on the score of dimensions; the rooms
are not of any special importance, and there is no apparent reason why the
front should not have been treated in a simple and dignified manner. The
roof, however, is broken into fourteen distinct compartments, with as
many angles in the line of wall; producing an infirmity of outline that has
given the front a feeble, dislocated look. The windows also are pretentious,
mean, and ugly, the large pinnacles are useless and absurd, and the tower is
not worth the cost of its foundations.

[3.] Here, then, there is obvious failure; but although simplicity and dignity and power have thus been diligently wasted, they would be regained if
all the lines of roof and wall were made continuous except where they are
interrupted by the gable of the central hall, which might be brought well
forward to the front, and by the angle tower. The octagon staircases could
be changed in form with no loss of convenience; a range of dormer windows might decorate the roof, and an arcade of shops would enliven the
ground-floor frontage abutting on the Strand; the pinnacles and carved
bands might be omitted with advantage in every way; and if Mr. Street is
unable to design windows and tracery in the graceful manner of the fourteenth century, an advertisement in 'The Builder' will discover plenty of
help for him in this rather important branch of Gothic art . . .

9. The Law Courts, London (architect G. E. Street), perspective from the south-west 1872

[4.] Now, what we have proposed for Mr. Street's design is, in fact, extinction; but there is small blame to Mr. Street for this necessity. He, like the rest of his class, has to please or satisfy a public who concerning building art are lamentably ignorant. Accustomed throughout life to the most hideous extent of building that the world ever saw, regarding any knowledge of the house in which he lives as vulgar, fit only for low builders and for fellows of the baser sort, the average Londoner, in presence of the art that most affects his comfort and his life, is supercilious, conceited, and debased. Of the architectural aspect of the streets he has no intelligent opinion, nor even any clear perception; but with Wigmore-street he feels at home: the Regent's-park and Grosvenor-place he thinks are 'fine', and the Museum in Great Russell-street, he is instructed, 'is a masterpiece'.

[5.] This, then, is the quality of mind that an architect who would be successful must attempt to satisfy; and, if he has experience and knowledge of the world, he naturally adopts the most direct and easiest method to command success. Prettiness is, of course, essential; what else is architecture for, if not to be pretty? Of the shortcoming and offensiveness of his design he may be perfectly, or possibly imperfectly, aware; but he overlays it with ornament, and encrusts it with carving, until the whole is pronounced to be beautiful. In this great requisite of modern architecture Mr. Street fails; he has no sense of prettiness, and he substitutes confusion; he was afraid of simple expressiveness, and he has become incoherent. He has grievously erred, not, however, from negligence or want of will, but merely from natural incapacity. Every man is not a born confectioner; and if his work fails through subjection to the influence of a depraved and vulgar 'public taste', which yet he is unable to satisfy, Mr. Street can hardly be reproached for this unfortunate result.

[6.] But there is also the class of *dilettanti* who have to be appeased. These are the people that know all about styles and dates; travelled men, sketchers, ecclesiologists, and the like. Among these Mr. Street appears to have fallen, and to have found their patronage to be as damaging by its priggishness, as the demands of the public are from their ignorance. The influence of this class is occasionally useful, but many a well-meaning architect must have found himself grievously burdened by their equivocal patronage, which becomes a weight quite as often as a support; and Mr. Street has been much injured by their awkward advocacy. The knowing talk about 'skylines' and 'fenestration', and all the cant of the literary amateur, is the adopted language of a certain class of newspapers and magazines. Such 'knowingness' is, however, only that half-knowledge 'that puffeth up'; and its effect is evident in Mr. Street's more public buildings, which seem either to be paralysed by some intrusive clerical infirmity, or to be designed expressly for some sacerdotal epicene. Mr. Street is not the only sufferer from this cause; a large number of our recent churches evince the pernicious influence of this emasculated tone of criticism, and are made mere specimens of the transient ecclesiastical fashion, instead of permanent monuments of art.

[7.] The true artist, however, rejects all these influences, and works to please or satisfy himself, regardless of the public or of patrons. That such is the only sound method of practice may be clearly shown by multiplied examples of success and failure due to the observance or neglect of this distinctly fundamental law of good design.

[8.] In the remarks which we think it our duty to make on the present state of English architecture, we are influenced by no personal or professional prejudice or feeling; and, to avoid at first all questions about styles and schools, we will begin by noticing the works of modern engineers. Rennie and Telford had little or no need to regard the opinion of the public; they had the intelligent support and generous confidence of a few men of influence and good sense; and, as the result, the Menai and London bridges are two of the most simple, dignified, and noble buildings in the world.

[9.] ... About the Midland Railway Terminus, however, there are not two opinions; here the 'public taste' has been exactly suited, and every kind of architectural decoration has been made thoroughly common and unclean; the building, inside and out, is covered with ornament, and there is polished marble enough to furnish a Cathedral; the very parapet of the cab road is panelled and perforated, at a cost that would have supplied foot-warmers to all trains for years to come. This monument of confectionery is a fair specimen of the result of competition among architects for the approval of judges whom they know to be incompetent. The 'Midland' directors are able administrators of the railway business, and probably of their own; but there is little evidence that they were qualified in any way to decide upon the respective merits of the competitors, or to select a design to be built in an important Metropolitan thoroughfare. Were any of these gentlemen completely furnished with the necessary knowledge? and if not, how could their ignorance become efficient in its stead?—are questions that, in the interests of the 'art', about which they are so very careful when their own interests are specially involved, the competing architects ought, as a condition precedent, to have had satisfactorily answered. Judging by the building, however, we imagine that a very different course was taken; and, in the successful design at any rate, the noble art of building has been treated as a mere trade advertisement; showy and expensive, it will, for the present, be a striking contrast with its adjoining neighbour. The Great Northern Terminus is not graceful, but it is simple, characteristic, and true, no one would mistake its nature or its use. The Midland front is inconsistent in its style, and meretricious in detail, a piece of common art manufacture, that makes the Great Northern front appear by contrast almost charming. There is no relief or quiet in any part of the work; the eye is constantly troubled and tormented, and the mechanical patterns follow one another with such rapidity and perseverance, that the mind becomes irritated where it ought to be gratified, and goaded to criticism where it should be led calmly to approve. There is here a complete travesty of noble associations, and not the slightest care to save these from a sordid contact; an elaboration that might be suitable for a Chapter-house, or a Cathedral choir, is used as an 'advertising medium' for bagmen's bedrooms and the costly discomforts of a terminus hotel; and the architect is thus a mere expensive rival of the company's head cook in catering for the low enjoyments of the travelling crowd. To be consistent, the directors should not confine their expressions of artistic feeling to their station buildings only; all their porters might be dressed as javelin men, their guards as beefeaters, and their station-masters might assume the picturesque attire of Garter-king-at-arms; their carriages might be copied from the Lord Mayor's show, and even their large locomotive wheels might imitate the Gothic window near their terminus at York. These things, however, will eventually come; the water tank is moulded in the Gothic style.

[10.] Yet who is to blame for all this? In all this demonstration the directors meant, no doubt, extremely well; they were but in a state of childish and presumptuous ignorance: and if the architect were held responsible, he would most probably refer to the accepted system. Of course the work is mechanical and unimaginative; but is anything superior to this required? How many of the public are there who can judge efficiently of work, or who could with discerning sympathy appreciate artistic workmen? . . .

[11.] The fact is that we have at present no true building art; it is entirely lost; but in its stead we have what is absurdly called the profession of architecture, which, as it pretends to the practice of art, is in the nature of an imposture. The essence of art is handiwork; not the preparations for work, such as the 'designs' and drawings compiled by the architect, his 'assistant', or his numerous 'staff', any more than is the scaffolding erected by the Irish labourer. It is not the painstaking of an imitator, the dull labour of a draughtsman, nor the drudgery of an artisan; but, wholly different, it is the grateful practice of instructed, free, self-guided working men: the conjoint operation of both head and hand. There is no neglect of due subordination or of proper leadership, nor a refusal of mechanical assistance or of any worthy tools, but there is constant play and freedom for the intellect and the imagination, for the well-trained hand and thoroughly instructed mind. The best buildings of all ages have been made, not by professional 'designers' and their drawing clerks, but by the labouring handicraftsmen. The chief buildings of the last three centuries in Europe have been designed by pseudo-architects. They are sometimes scholarly, imposing, and expensive; and of late they have been pretty, vulgar, childish, or grim, as the prevailing fashion, and as individual fancy have required.

[12.] At present there is no help for this substitution of the imposture for the reality. In old times, people built on their own freeholds, modestly, with honest intention, and with the prospect of endurance; they employed free workmen whose delight was in the product of their own skill, and with whom the employer was in constant and familiar intercourse. The style of work was national, and as well understood by the people as their own language; people no more thought of building in 'styles' than of talking in 'tongues'. The master-mason could build simply for a cottage, or gloriously for a cathedral; his perfect familiarity with his work, his good sense and cultivated imagination, were his only guides, his sole assistants were his perfectly instructed fellow craftsmen; and to these plain workmen, whom our modern architects are very proud to imitate, we are indebted for the chief remaining glories of the middle ages.

[13.] But now instead of a class of noble working-men, we have the 'architectural profession,' a number of soft-handed 'gentlemen' who may or may not be able to make sketches, or 'plans and elevations,' but who at any rate can get them made—who prepare what are called 'designs' in any 'style,' and submit them to people ignorant of every style for their approval and acceptance . . .

[14.] The interiors of most of the high ritual churches are marked by the latter peculiarity, and some clear evidence of mental weakness is, in these 'impressive' places, seldom wanting. The font at St. Alban's, Holborn, for instance, which has been 'designed' with much care, would be beneath the genius of a manufacturer of Tonbridge ware; and the speckled and spotted coloured brick patterns on the walls, here and at All-Saints', Margaret Street, are precise reminiscences of a favourite nursery toy. The degradation is, however, more particularly manifested in the 'reredos,' not the old eastern choir-screens, which are sometimes so called, but a comparatively recent importation from abroad, an un-English innovation, favoured as giving an opportunity for a much-desired patch of prettiness, or the exhibition of such superfluous folly as is not entirely used up in other details of the church, and which gives the communion table the appearance of a quasi-medieval sideboard.

[15.] . . . Whether [our modern churches] are 'high' or 'low,' correct or impure, 'original' or eclectic, there is in them a constant straining for effect; it seems as if each architect thought that he would have no other opportunity, and must seize the present chance to make his mark, and light his pound of candles all at once. There is a want of dignity and repose about the work, a consciousness that it will be looked at, and a vain hope that it will be admired, leading to a sort of architectural posture-making and display, that no affectation of propriety, and even of asceticism, will save from a charge of meretricious vanity. Now all this is very unbecoming and inconsistent; a church requires nothing of the kind; it is in fact a very ordinary, common-place building, and only particularly remarkable now because domestic architecture is so excessively debased.

[16.] ... Of public buildings, churches are the most numerous, unless indeed public-houses are included in the category; and as there is so little necessary difference in their plans, there need be none of that agonizing superfluity of contrivance and detail that we are compelled to observe and painfully to regret. We know all about the sacred character of the building, the superlativeness of its requirements, and the 'Lamp of Sacrifice;' but we say that the sanctity of its dedication, and the dignity of its character, would be best demonstrated and maintained by the abandonment of all the frippery and excess of detail that architects find it to be their business to display. There is no 'sacrifice' in this elaboration; its removal would in fact be a purification; the real sacrifice is the offering, genuine, hearty, intelligent, and refined, of the simple working man. . . .

[17.] The church of St. James the Less, at Westminster, has been greatly praised for its decorative work, though it really is but a baby-house. Its particoloured tower is built with polished marbles up amongst the clouds, and of ungainly brickwork level with the eye. Its preposterous ironwork, designed by an architect and manufactured by a mechanic, is so disproportioned as to be absurd, and is quite incongruous with the mean walling that it screens. The interior, chequered all over with bits of colour, is not the serious effort of a man, but mere effeminacy and child's play, giving the same wide-mouthed pleasure as a trick of sleight of hand. The decorations of the roof are for the most part invisible. The mental debasement which we have already referred to has in this and many other churches shown itself by making them what children call 'a place for bogies.' There is a great deal of nonsensical scorn of those who object to Gothic work that it is dark and gloomy; but these childish church architects are the cause, and their works are a justification of this at first sight very reasonable objection. At St. James's the aisle windows are mere slits in the wall, not to admit daylight, evidently, but to show small panels of indifferent stained glass, which cause this dismal darkness and which serve to mystify the weakheaded persons for whom such work is sympathetically designed. . . .

[18.] The buildings we have quoted are public property, or ecclesiastical, and are therefore under very superior control. As we go further from the central government in Church and State we may fare worse. The architectural gibberish of St. James's Club is cognate with similar discordant and incoherent utterances at Manchester. Then there is the whimsical variety at the Gaiety theatre in the Strand and at Keble College; and the childish, half exotic work at the new Museum buildings at Oxford, all which show how desperate are the designers' fears lest they should not be personally recognized and professionally distinguishable: the architect being, in fact, the chief end of the building. In churches we have endless variety of affectation and conceit, from the ritual and grim, and the high and correct, to the Evangelical and dull. And the neo-Gothic Renaissance is at last developed into the elaborate meanness of the Dissenting chapel, and the staring vulgarity of the Marine Hotel.

[19.] The reason of all this aberration and decline is easily explained. The work of design, as it is called, being in comparatively few hands, there is a great loss of artistic power which would be saved and properly employed were each building designed by its own working men. Builders are of the nature of poets: they are born, not made; and it is therefore true policy to secure and utilize as large a number of artistic and poetic minds as can be possibly employed. To ignore these, and to concentrate the work in the hands of a comparatively few, is an abandoned folly, manifest on its mere statement; it prevents the spread of intelligence and cultivation among the working builders, and from them among the masses of the people; and it breeds a class of 'architects,' gamblers in competitions, draughtsmen and surveyors, whose productions are a curse to the nation, and, in various degrees of vileness, a travesty of art. . . .

[20.] The greater part of the house property of London and our large towns belongs to no one in particular; there is great division of property, but in the worst possible way, horizontally, we may say, instead of vertically. First, there is the freeholder, who has a ground rent; then, secondly, a leaseholder, with an improved ground rent; and third, the nominal proprietor, with the rack-rent; fourth, the first mortgagee; and probably, fifth, the second mortgagee; and sixth, the tenant, or leaseholder, with, perhaps, a sub-tenant, yearly, and probably some lodgers by the week or month. Besides these 'interests' there are the lawyers, with their bills of costs, collecting agents, repairing builders, water rates, and insurance charges. This, or something like this, may be taken as the probable condition of three-quarters of the house property of London; the whole metropolis is, in fact, under a curse of law, which has in our great towns destroyed domestic building as an art. Its decadence can be historically traced in proportion to the extension of leasehold tenure. This tenure breeds the class of 'surveyors,' who gradually engross all power, and simultaneously abandon all care, except for the freeholder. These men are, in fact, the spurious successors of the old builders, the ruck of the profession, a mass of struggling impotence, to whom we owe the travesties of Grecian, Gothic, and Venetian 'styles' that speculating builders use to decorate their ill-conditioned works and satisfy the 'public taste' for ornament and 'art.' Their patrons are the lawyers, the solicitors of the 'estates,' who are the chief contrivers and manipulators of this inartistic and demoralizing system; and to whose 'deeds' the degradation of domestic building work is principally due. . . .

[21.] When art becomes securely and intelligently founded in our common practice and experience, it will grow and fructify as in the middle ages,

291

when the workmen ruled; in perfect contrast to its moribund condition while oppressed by Connoisseurs. For the last three hundred years these leaders of opinion have directed public ignorance. They began with the extinction of the pointed style, and they have brought us down to the new buildings at the Kensington Museum, where the eye is pained, and all artistic judgment is offended by the obtrusive colour, uncouth outline, and abundant ugliness of the new buildings; the nursery, home, and illustration, of what is called 'art manufacture.' It is, in fact, neither 'art' nor in any sense true handicraftsman's work, but mere machine and copy work, heartless, senseless, and absurd, false in principle, and paralysing eventually to the artistic skill of any working man who practises it. The decorations on the columns are expensive; but they have neither ideal beauty nor practical fitness. Were one column placed like the central pier of a chapter-house, there might be some excuse for the design; the Trajan column, and the 'apprentice pier,' also, have some similar justification; but these foolish things, placed so high that their enrichment cannot be seen from a distance, and on the edge of a platform, so that they can only be seen on one side, the enrichment being continuous and varied round the column, are to be taken not merely as a specimen of 'art manufacture,' but of the imbecility to which such practice inevitably leads.

[22.] In the Museum are some large wrought-iron gates that have been removed from Hampton Court, with a very proper sense of their value, and of the impossibility of making good the loss should they unhappily be damaged or destroyed. They are not exquisite, but very bold, manly, and effective works, made, and certainly designed, by a thorough workman; and are as good and gratifying a specimen of out-of-door hand-wrought iron-work as can easily be met with. Close by is a gate from Berlin, the smooth and lifeless composition of a draughtsman, whose design was handed over to a manufacturing metal-worker to be carried out. Nothing can be baser than this work, which is thought worthy of a distinguished place in the Kensington Museum. The cost must have been great, and as the work is done with perfect care and nicety the labour was no doubt far greater here than on the older gates; but in all the genius of handicraft, it is the brain of a caterpillar against the intellect of a man; mechanical tool-work, dead as a door-nail or a screw; a piece of stupid luxury of expense; in fact, 'art manufacture.'

[23.] We have endeavoured to describe the forlorn condition in which we are left in all that concerns our public as well as private building-works. Having neither artists to build, nor critics to discuss, nor a public worthy to approve of any work, it is time to institute an architectural reform, to start again in the old genuine practice of artistic work. . . .

(*Quarterly Review*, Apr. 1872.)

Thomas Hardy, from *Under the Greenwood Tree* (1872)   VI.4

It was a satisfaction to walk into the keeper's house, even as a stranger, on a fine spring morning like the present. A curl of wood-smoke came from the chimney and drooped over the roof like a blue feather in a lady's hat; and the sun shone obliquely upon the patch of grass in front, which reflected its brightness through the open doorway and up the stair-case opposite, lighting up each riser with a shiny green radiance and leaving the top of each step in shade.

The window-sill of the front room was between four and five feet from the floor, dropping inwardly to a broad low bench, over which, as well as over the whole surface of the wall beneath, there always hung a deep shade, which was considered objectionable on every ground save one, namely, that the perpetual sprinkling of seeds and water by the caged canary above was not noticed as an eyesore by visitors. The window was set with thickly-leaded diamond glazing, formed, especially in the lower panes, of knotty glass of various shades of green. Nothing was better known to Fancy than the extravagant manner in which these circular knots or eyes distorted everything seen through them from the outside—lifting hats from heads, shoulders from bodies; scattering the spokes of cart-wheels, and bending the straight fir-trunks into semicircles. The ceiling was carried by a beam traversing its midst, from the side of which projected a large nail, used solely and constantly as a peg for Geoffrey's hat; the nail was arched by a rainbow-shaped stain, imprinted by the brim of the said hat when it was hung there dripping wet.

The most striking point about the room was the furniture. This was a repetition upon inanimate objects of the old principle introduced by Noah, consisting for the most part of two articles of every sort. The duplicate system of furnishing owed its existence to the forethought of Fancy's mother, exercised from the date of Fancy's birthday onwards. The arrangement spoke for itself: nobody who knew the tone of the household could look at the goods without being aware that the second set was a provision for Fancy when she should marry and have a house of her own. The most noticeable instance was a pair of green-faced eight-day clocks ticking alternately, which were severally two-and-a-half minutes and three minutes striking the hour of twelve, one proclaiming, in Italian flourishes, Thomas Wood as the name of its maker, and the other—arched at the top, and altogether of more cynical appearance—that of Ezekiel Saunders. They were two departed clockmakers of Casterbridge, whose desperate rivalry throughout their lives was nowhere more emphatically perpetuated than here at Geoffrey's. These chief specimens of the marriage provision were supported on the right by a couple of kitchen dressers, each fitted complete with their cups, dishes, and plates, in their turn followed by two dumb-waiters, two family Bibles, two warming-pans, and two intermixed sets of chairs.

But the position last reached—the chimney-corner—was, after all, the most attractive side of the parallelogram. It was large enough to admit, in addition to Geoffrey himself, Geoffrey's wife, her chair, and her work-table, entirely within the line of the mantel, without danger or even inconvenience from the heat of the fire; and was spacious enough overhead to allow of the insertion of wood poles for the hanging of bacon, which were cloaked with long shreds of soot floating on the draught like the tattered banners on the walls of ancient aisles.

These points were common to most chimney-corners of the neighbourhood; but one feature there was which made Geoffrey's fireside not only an object of interest to casual aristocratic visitors—to whom every cottage fireside was more or less a curiosity—but the admiration of friends who were accustomed to fireplaces of the ordinary hamlet model. This peculiarity was a little window in the chimney-back, almost over the fire, around which the smoke crept caressingly when it left the perpendicular course. The window-board was curiously stamped with black circles, burnt thereon by the heated bottoms of drinking-cups which had rested there after previously standing on the hot ashes of the hearth for the purpose of warming their contents, the result giving to the ledge the look of an envelope which has passed through innumerable post-offices. . . .

(*Under the Greenwood Tree*, 1872, Ch. VI.)

VI.5 **From speech of Joseph Chamberlain as Mayor of Birmingham (13 Jan. 1874)**

In the first place, he would endeavour to carry the Council with him in two principles on which he thought these negotiations should proceed. He distinctly held that all monopolies which were sustained in any way by the State ought to be in the hands of the representatives of the people—by the representative authority should they be administered, and to them should their profits go, and not to private speculators. Moreover . . . he was always inclined to magnify his office; he was inclined to increase the duties and responsibilities of the local authority, in whom he had himself so great a confidence, and would do everything in his power to constitute these local authorities real local parliaments, supreme in their special jurisdiction. He was aware it had been said that these undertakings . . . should be left to private enterprise and energy; but he would say . . . that John Stuart Mill, the greatest political thinker of his age, always asserted . . . that such undertakings . . . should be excluded from the rule . . . and should be placed in the hands of the local authority.

He had been struck with the inadequate means of the Council for the responsible work placed upon them. If they proposed to recompense the faithful service of an officer of the Corporation, and if they proposed to increase their own duties and responsibilities, they were met with a chorus of opposition from the ratepayers . . . and this difficulty was continually increasing, because every day new duties were being imposed upon the Corporation. For instance, there was the great business of the sewage at Saltley. . . . Then very recently they were called upon to take advantage of the Sanitary Act. That again had already involved the Council in a very largely increased expenditure, and must involve it in a still larger expenditure in the future. . . . Birmingham had unfortunately fallen from its high position, and was no longer the healthiest town in the kingdom; it had become one of the most unhealthy of the large cities and boroughs in the country. Under these circumstances it was absolutely necessary that they should devote their attention to the sanitary condition of the town. He need not allude to other matters except to remind them that at the last meeting of the Council a new duty was thrown upon them of protecting property from fire. All these duties involved a largely increased expenditure, and he believed that the pressure of the rates would become intolerable unless some compensation could be found by some new proposal, such as the one he now laid before them. That compensation was secured in the case of other large towns. . . . In Manchester the Corporation possessed the gas and water works, and they secured from the profits of these undertakings an enormous capital. He was told that at present the amount was something like a million sterling, with which they were able to erect those corporate buildings which were the glory of the town.

(Reported in *Birmingham Daily Post* (14 Jan. 1874); reprinted in
The Nineteenth-Century Constitution, ed. H. J. Hanham, 1969, pp. 381–2.)

Richard Jefferies, from *Hodge and his Masters* (1880)   VI.6

There exists at the present day a class that is morally apathetic. In every village, in every hamlet, every detached group of cottages, there are numbers of labouring men who are simply indifferent to church and to chapel alike. They neither deny nor affirm the primary truths taught in all places of worship; they are simply indifferent. Sunday comes and sees them lounging about the cottage door. They do not drink to excess, they are not more given to swearing than others, they are equally honest, and are not of ill-repute. But the moral sense seems extinct—the very idea of anything beyond gross earthly advantages never occurs to them. The days go past, the wages are paid, the food is eaten, and there is all.

Looking at it from the purely philosophic point of view there is something sad in this dull apathy. The most pronounced materialist has a faith in some form of beauty—matter itself is capable of ideal shapes in his conception. These people know no ideal. It seems impossible to reach them because there is no chord that will respond to the most skilful touch. This class is very numerous now—a disheartening fact. Yet perhaps the activity and energy of the clergyman may be ultimately destined to find its reaction, to produce its effect among these very people. They may slowly learn to appreciate tangible, practical work, though utterly insensible to direct moral teaching and the finest eloquence of the pulpit. Finding by degrees that he is really endeavouring to improve their material existence, they may in time awake to a sense of something higher.

What is wanted is a perception of the truth that progress and civilisation ought not to end with mere material—mechanical—comfort or wealth. A cottager ought to learn that when the highest wages of the best paid artisan are reached it is *not* the greatest privilege of the man to throw mutton chops to dogs and make piles of empty champagne bottles. It might almost be said that one cause of the former extravagance and the recent distress and turbulence of the working classes is the absence of an ideal from their minds.

Besides this moral apathy, the cottager too often assumes an attitude distinctly antagonistic to every species of authority, and particularly to that *prestige* hitherto attached to property. Each man is a law to himself, and does that which seems good in his own eyes. He does not pause to ask himself, What will my neighbour think of this? He simply thinks of no one but himself, takes counsel of no one, and cares not what the result may be. It is the same in little things as great. Respect for authority is extinct. The modern progressive cottager is perfectly certain that he knows as much as his immediate employer, the squire, and the parson put together with the experience of the world at their back. He is now the judge—the infallible authority himself. He is wiser far than all the learned and the thoughtful, wiser than the prophets themselves. Priest, politician, and philosopher must bow their heads and listen to the dictum of the ploughman!

This feeling shows itself most strikingly in the disregard of property. There used to be a certain tacit agreement among all men that those who possessed capital, rank, or reputation should be treated with courtesy. The courtesy did not imply that the landowner, the capitalist, or the minister of religion, was necessarily in himself superior. But it did imply that those who administered property really represented the general order in which all were interested. So in a court of justice, all who enter remove their hats, not out of servile adulation of the person in authority, but from respect for the majesty of the law, which it is every individual's interest to uphold. But now, metaphorically speaking, the labourer removes his hat for no man. Whether in the case of a manufacturer or of a tenant of a thousand-acre farm the thing is the same. The cottager can scarcely nod his employer a common greeting in the morning. Courtesy is no longer practised. The idea in the man's mind appears to be to express contempt for his employer's property. It is an unpleasant symptom. . . .

These two characteristics, moral apathy and contempt of property—i.e. of social order—are probably exercising considerable influence in shaping the labourer's future. Free of mental restraint, his own will must work its way for good or evil. It is true that the rise or fall of wages may check or hasten the development of that future. In either case it is not, however, probable that he will return to the old grooves: indeed, the grooves themselves are gone, and the logic of events must force him to move onwards. That motion, in its turn, must affect the rest of the community. Let the mind's eye glance for a moment over the country at large. The villages among the hills, the villages on the plains, in the valleys, and beside the streams represent in the aggregate an enormous power. Separately such hamlets seem small and feeble—unable to impress their will upon the world. But together they contain a vast crowd, which, united, may shoulder itself an irresistible course, pushing aside all obstacles by mere physical weight.

The effect of education has been, and seems likely to be, to supply a certain unity of thought, if not of action, among these people. The solid common sense—the law-abiding character of the majority—is sufficient security against any violent movement. But how important it becomes that that common sense should be strengthened against the assaults of an insidious Socialism! A man's education does not come to an end when he leaves school. He then just begins to form his opinions, and in nine cases out of ten thinks what he hears and what he reads. Here, in the agricultural labourer class, are many hundred thousand young men exactly in this stage, educating themselves in moral, social, and political opinion.

In short, the future literature of the labourer becomes a serious question. He will think what he reads; and what he reads at the present moment is of anything but an elevating character. He will think, too, what he hears; and he hears much of an enticing but subversive political creed, and little of any other. There are busy tongues earnestly teaching him to despise property and social order, to suggest the overthrow of existing institutions; there is scarcely any one to instruct him in the true lesson of history. Who calls together an audience of agricultural labourers to explain to and interest them in the story of their own country? There are many who are only too anxious to use the agricultural labourer as the means to effect ends which he scarcely understands. But there are few, indeed, who are anxious to instruct him in science or literature for his own sake.

(*Hodge and his Masters*, 1880, Ch. xxv.)

vi.7 Thomas Hardy, from 'The Dorsetshire Labourer' (July 1883)

[1.] The hiring-fair of recent years presents an appearance unlike that of former times. A glance up the high street of the town on a Candlemas-fair day twenty or thirty years ago revealed a crowd whose general colour was whity-brown flecked with white. Black was almost absent, the few farmers who wore that shade hardly discernible. Now the crowd is as dark as a London crowd. This change is owing to the rage for cloth clothes which possesses the labourers of to-day. Formerly they came in smock-frocks and gaiters, the shepherds with their crooks, the carters with a zone of whipcord round their hats, thatchers with a straw tucked into the brim, and so on. Now, with the exception of the crook in the hands of an occasional old shepherd, there is no mark of speciality in the groups, who might be tailors or undertakers' men, for what they exhibit externally. . . .

[2.] That peculiarity of the English urban poor (which M. Taine ridicules, and unfavorably contrasts with the taste of the Continental working-people)—their preference for the cast-off clothes of a richer class to a special attire of their own—has, in fact, reached the Dorset farm folk. Like the men, the women are, pictorially, less interesting than they used to be. Instead of the wing bonnet like the tilt of a waggon, cotton gown, bright-hued neckerchief, and strong flat boots and shoes, they (the younger ones at least) wear shabby millinery bonnets and hats with beads and feathers, 'material' dresses, and boot-heels almost as foolishly shaped as those of ladies of highest education.

[3.] Having 'agreed for a place,' as it is called, either at the fair, or (occasionally) by private intelligence, or (with growing frequency) by advertisement in the penny local papers, the terms are usually reduced to writing: though formerly a written agreement was unknown, and is now, as a rule, avoided by the farmer if the labourer does not insist upon one. It is signed by both, and a shilling is passed to bind the bargain. The business is then settled, and the man returns to his place of work, to do no more in the matter till Lady Day, Old Style—April 6.

[4.] Of all the days in the year, people who love the rural poor of the south-west should pray for a fine day then. Dwellers near the highways of the country are reminded of the anniversary surely enough. They are conscious of a disturbance of their night's rest by noises beginning in the small hours of darkness, and intermittently continuing till daylight—noises as certain to recur on that particular night of the month as the voice of the cuckoo on the third or fourth week of the same. The day of fulfilment has come, and the labourers are on the point of being fetched from the old farm by the carters of the new. For it is always by the waggon and horses of the farmer who requires his services that the hired man is conveyed to his destination; and that this may be accomplished within the day is the reason that

10. Sir George Clausen: *The Stone Pickers* 1886–7

the noises begin so soon after midnight. Suppose the distance to be an ordinary one of a dozen or fifteen miles. The carter at the prospective place rises 'when Charles's Wain is over the new chimney,' harnesses his team of three horses by lantern light, and proceeds to the present home of his coming comrade. It is the passing of these empty waggons in all directions that is heard breaking the stillness of the hours before dawn. The aim is usually to be at the door of the removing household by six o'clock, when the loading of goods at once begins; and at nine or ten the start to the new home is made. From this hour till one or two in the day, when the other family arrives at the old house, the cottage is empty, and it is only in that short interval that the interior can be in any way cleaned and lime-whitened for the new comers, however dirty it may have become, or whatever sickness may have prevailed among members of the departed family. . . .

[5.] Ten or a dozen of these families, with their goods, may be seen halting simultaneously at an out-of-the-way inn, and it is not possible to walk a mile on any of the high roads this day without meeting several. This annual migration from farm to farm is much in excess of what it was formerly. For example, on a particular farm where, a generation ago, not more than one cottage on an average changed occupants yearly, and where the majority remained all their lifetime, the whole number of tenants were changed at Lady Day just past, and this though nearly all of them had been new arrivals on the previous Lady Day. Dorset labourers now look upon an annual removal as the most natural thing in the world, and it becomes with the younger families a pleasant excitement. Change is also a certain sort of education. Many advantages accrue to the labourers from the varied experience it brings, apart from the discovery of the best market for their abilities. They have become shrewder and sharper men of the world, and have learnt how to hold their own with firmness and judgment. Whenever the habitually-removing man comes into contact with one of the old-fashioned stationary sort, who are still to be found, it is impossible not to perceive that the former is much more wide awake than his fellow-worker, astonishing him with stories of the wide world comprised in a twenty-mile radius from their homes.

[6.] They are also losing their peculiarities as a class; hence the humorous simplicity which formerly characterised the men and the unsophisticated modesty of the women are rapidly disappearing or lessening, under the constant attrition of lives mildly approximating to those of workers in a manufacturing town. It is the common remark of villagers above the labouring class, who know the latter well as personal acquaintances, that 'there are no nice homely workfolk now as there used to be.' There may be, and is, some exaggeration in this, but it is only natural that, now different districts of them are shaken together once a year and redistributed, like a shuffled pack of cards, they have ceased to be so local in feeling or manner as formerly, and have entered on the condition of inter-social citizens,

'whose city stretches the whole county over.' Their brains are less frequently than they once were 'as dry as the remainder biscuit after a
voyage,' and they vent less often the result of their own observations than
what they have heard to be the current ideas of smart chaps in towns. The
women have, in many districts, acquired the rollicking air of factory hands.
That seclusion and immutability, which was so bad for their pockets, was
an unrivalled fosterer of their personal charm in the eyes of those whose
experiences had been less limited. But the artistic merit of their old condition is scarcely a reason why they should have continued in it when other
communities were marching on so vigorously towards uniformity and
mental equality. It is only the old story that progress and picturesqueness
do not harmonise. They are losing their individuality, but they are widening the range of their ideas, and gaining in freedom. It is too much to expect
them to remain stagnant and old-fashioned for the pleasure of romantic
spectators.

[7.] But, picturesqueness apart, a result of this increasing nomadic habit
of the labourer is naturally a less intimate and kindly relation with the land
he tills than existed before enlightenment enabled him to rise above the
condition of a serf who lived and died on a particular plot, like a tree. During the centuries of serfdom, of copyholding tenants, and down to twenty
or thirty years ago, before the power of unlimited migration had been
clearly realised, the husbandman of either class had the interest of long personal association with his farm. The fields were those he had ploughed and
sown from boyhood, and it was impossible for him, in such circumstances,
to sink altogether the character of natural guardian in that of hireling. Not
so very many years ago, the landowner, if he were good for anything, stood
as a court of final appeal in cases of the harsh dismissal of a man by the
farmer. 'I'll go to my lord' was a threat which overbearing farmers respected, for 'my lord' had often personally known the labourer long before
he knew the labourer's master. But such arbitrament is rarely practicable
now. The landlord does not know by sight, if even by name, half the men
who preserve his acres from the curse of Eden. They come and go yearly,
like birds of passage, nobody thinks whence or whither. This dissociation is
favoured by the customary system of letting the cottages with the land, so
that, far from having a guarantee of a holding to keep him fixed, the
labourer has not even the stability of a landlord's tenant; he is only tenant
of a tenant, the latter possibly a new comer, who takes strictly commercial
views of his man and cannot afford to waste a penny on sentimental considerations.

[8.] Thus, while their pecuniary condition in the prime of life is bet-
tered, and their freedom enlarged, they have lost touch with their environ-
ment, and that sense of long local participancy which is one of the
pleasures of age. The old *casus conscientiae* of those in power—whether
the weak tillage of an enfeebled hand ought not to be put up with in fields

which have had the benefit of that hand's strength—arises less frequently now that the strength has often been expended elsewhere. The sojourning existence of the town masses is more and more the existence of the rural masses, with its corresponding benefits and disadvantages. With uncertainty of residence often comes a laxer morality, and more cynical views of the duties of life. Domestic stability is a factor in conduct which nothing else can equal. On the other hand, new varieties of happiness evolve themselves like new varieties of plants, and new charms may have arisen among the classes who have been driven to adopt the remedy of locomotion for the evils of oppression and poverty—charms which compensate in some measure for the lost sense of home. . . .

[9.] That the labourers of the country are more independent since their awakening to the sense of an outer world cannot be disputed. It was once common enough on inferior farms to hear a farmer, as he sat on horseback amid a field of workers, address them with a contemptuousness which could not have been greatly exceeded in the days when the thralls of Cedric wore their collars of brass. Usually no answer was returned to these tirades; they were received as an accident of the land on which the listeners had happened to be born, calling for no more resentment than the blows of the wind and rain. But now, no longer fearing to avail himself of his privilege of flitting, these acts of contumely have ceased to be regarded as inevitable by the peasant. And while men do not of their own accord leave a farm without a grievance, very little faultfinding is often deemed a sufficient one among the younger and stronger. Such ticklish relations are the natural result of generations of unfairness on one side, and on the other an increase of knowledge, which has been kindled into activity by the exertions of Mr. Joseph Arch.

[10.] Nobody who saw and heard Mr. Arch in his early tours through Dorsetshire will ever forget him and the influence his presence exercised over the crowds he drew. He hailed from Shakespeare's county, where the humours of the peasantry have a marked family relationship with those of Dorset men; and it was this touch of nature, as much as his logic, which afforded him such ready access to the minds and hearts of the labourers here. It was impossible to hear and observe the speaker for more than a few minutes without perceiving that he was a humourist—moreover, a man by no means carried away by an idea beyond the bounds of common sense. Like his renowned fellow-dalesman Corin, he virtually confessed that he was never in court, and might, with that eminent shepherd, have truly described himself as a 'natural philosopher,' who had discovered that 'he that wants money, means, and content, is without three good friends.'

[11.] 'Content' may for a moment seem a word not exactly explanatory of Mr. Arch's views; but on the single occasion, several years ago, on which the present writer numbered himself among those who assembled to listen to that agitator, there was a remarkable moderation in his tone, and an exhortation to contentment with a reasonable amelioration, which, to an impartial auditor, went a long way in the argument. His views showed him to be rather the social evolutionist . . . than the anarchic irreconcilable. The picture he drew of a comfortable cottage life as it should be, was so cosy, so well within the grasp of his listeners' imagination, that an old labourer in the crowd held up a coin between his finger and thumb exclaiming, 'Here's zixpence towards that, please God!' 'Towards what?' said a bystander. 'Faith, I don't know that I can spak the name o't, but I know 'tis a good thing,' he replied.

[12.] The result of the agitation, so far, upon the income of the labourers, has been testified by independent witnesses with a unanimity which leaves no reasonable doubt of its accuracy. It amounts to an average rise of three shillings a week in wages nearly all over the county. The absolute number of added shillings seems small; but the increase is considerable when we remember that it is three shillings on eight or nine—i.e., between thirty and forty per cent. And the reflection is forced upon everyone who thinks of the matter, that if a farmer can afford to pay thirty per cent more wages in times of agricultural depression than he paid in times of agricultural prosperity, and yet live, and keep a carriage, while the landlord still thrives on the reduced rent which has resulted, the labourer must have been greatly wronged in those prosperous times. That the maximum of wage has been reached for the present is, however, pretty clear; and indeed it should be added that on several farms the labourers have submitted to a slight reduction during the past year, under stress of representations which have appeared reasonable.

[13.] It is hardly necessary to observe that the quoted wages never represent the labourer's actual income. Beyond the weekly payment—now standing at eleven or twelve shillings—he invariably receives a lump sum of 2l. or 3l. for harvest work. A cottage and garden is almost as invariably provided, free of rent, with, sometimes, an extra piece of ground for potatoes in some field near at hand. Fuel, too, is frequently furnished, in the form of wood faggots. At springtime, on good farms, the shepherd receives a shilling for every twin reared, while a carter gets what is called journey-money, that is, a small sum, mostly a shilling, for every journey taken beyond the bounds of the farm. Where all these supplementary trifles are enjoyed together, the weekly wage in no case exceeds eleven shillings at the present time . . .

[14.] Women's labour, too, is highly in request, for a woman who, like a boy, fills the place of a man at half the wages, can be better depended on for steadiness. Thus where a boy is useful in driving a cart or a plough, a woman is invaluable in work which, though somewhat lighter, demands thought. In winter and spring a farmwoman's occupation is often 'turnip-hacking'—that is, picking out from the land the stumps of turnips which have been eaten off by the sheep—or feeding the threshing-machine, clearing away straw from the same, and standing on the rick to hand forward the sheaves. In mid-spring and early summer her services are required for weeding wheat and barley (cutting up thistles and other noxious plants with a spud), and clearing weeds from pasture-land in like manner. In later summer her time is entirely engrossed by haymaking—quite a science, though it appears the easiest thing in the world to toss hay about in the sun. The length to which a skilful raker will work and retain command over her rake without moving her feet is dependent largely upon practice, and quite astonishing to the uninitiated.

[15.] Haymaking is no sooner over than the women are hurried off to the harvest-field. . . . The dust, the din, the sustained exertion demanded to keep up with the steam tyrant, are distasteful to all women but the coarsest. I am not sure whether, at the present time, women are employed to feed the machine, but some years ago a woman had frequently to stand just above the whizzing wire drum, and feed from morning to night—a performance for which she was quite unfitted, and many were the manoeuvres to escape that responsible position. A thin saucer-eyed woman of fifty-five, who had been feeding the machine all day, declared on one occasion that in crossing a field on her way home in the fog after dusk, she was so dizzy from the work as to be unable to find the opposite gate, and there she walked round and round the field, bewildered and terrified, till three o'clock in the morning, before she could get out. The farmer said that the ale had got into her head, but she maintained that it was the spinning of the machine. The point was never clearly settled between them; and the poor woman is now dead and buried. . . .

(*Longman's Magazine*, July 1883.)

VI.8 General William Booth, from *In Darkest England and the Way Out* (1890)

The Scheme I have to offer consists in the formation of these people into self-helping and self-sustaining communities, each being a kind of co-operative society, or patriarchal family, governed and disciplined on the principles which have already proved so effective in the Salvation Army.

These communities we will call, for want of a better term, Colonies. There will be—

          (1) The City Colony.
          (2) The Farm Colony.
          (3) The Over-Sea Colony.

The City Colony

By the City Colony is meant the establishment, in the very centre of the ocean of misery of which we have been speaking, of a number of Institutions to act as Harbours of Refuge for all and any who have been ship-wrecked in life, character, or circumstances. These Harbours will gather up the poor destitute creatures, supply their immediate pressing necessities, furnish temporary employment, inspire them with hope for the future, and commence at once a course of regeneration by moral and religious influences.

From these Institutions, which are hereafter described, numbers would, after a short time, be floated off to permanent employment, or sent home to friends happy to receive them on hearing of their reformation. All who remain on our hands would, by varied means, be tested as to their sincerity, industry, and honesty, and as soon as satisfaction was created, be passed on to the Colony of the second class.

The Farm Colony

This would consist of a settlement of the Colonists on an estate in the provinces, in the culture of which they would find employment and obtain support. As the race from the Country to the City has been the cause of much of the distress we have to battle with, we propose to find a substantial part of our remedy by transferring these same people back to the country, that is back again to 'the Garden!'

Here the process of reformation of character would be carried forward by the same industrial, moral, and religious methods as have already been commenced in the City, especially including those forms of labour and that knowledge of agriculture which, should the Colonist not obtain employment in this country, will qualify him for pursuing his fortunes under more favourable circumstances in some other land.

From the Farm, as from the City, there can be no question that large numbers, resuscitated in health and character, would be restored to friends up and down the country. Some would find employment in their own callings, others would settle in cottages on a small piece of land that we should provide, or on Co-operative Farms which we intend to promote; while the great bulk, after trial and training, would be passed on to the Foreign Settlement, which would constitute our third class, namely The Over-Sea Colony.

The Over-Sea Colony

All who have given attention to the subject are agreed that in our Colonies in South Africa, Canada, Western Australia and elsewhere, there are millions of acres of useful land to be obtained almost for the asking, capable of supporting our surplus population in health and comfort, were it a thousand times greater than it is. We propose to secure a tract of land in one of these countries, prepare it for settlement, establish in it authority, govern it by equitable laws, assist it in times of necessity, settling it gradually with a prepared people, and so create a home for these destitute multitudes.

The Scheme, in its entirety, may aptly be compared to A Great Machine, foundationed in the lowest slums and purlieus of our great towns and cities, drawing up into its embrace the depraved and destitute of all classes; receiving thieves, harlots, paupers, drunkards, prodigals, all alike, on the simple conditions of their being willing to work and to conform to discipline. Drawing up these poor outcasts, reforming them, and creating in them habits of industry, honesty, and truth; teaching them methods by which alike the bread that perishes and that which endures to Everlasting Life can be won. Forwarding them from the City to the Country, and there continuing the process of regeneration, and then pouring them forth on to the virgin soils that await their coming in other lands, keeping hold of them with a strong government, and yet making them free men and women; and so laying the foundations, perchance, of another Empire to swell to vast proportions in later times. Why not?

(*In Darkest England and the Way Out*, 1890, 1970 edn., Section 2, 'My Scheme', pp. 90–3.)

vi.9 William Morris, from *News From Nowhere* (1890)

After a pause, I said: 'Your big towns, now; how about them? London, which—which I have read about as the modern Babylon of civilization, seems to have disappeared.'

'Well, well' said old Hammond, 'perhaps after all it is more like ancient Babylon now than the "modern Babylon" of the nineteenth century was. But let that pass. After all, there is a good deal of population in places between here and Hammersmith; nor have you seen the most populous part of the town yet.'

'Tell me, then,' said I, 'how is it towards the east?'

Said he: 'Time was when if you mounted a good horse and rode straight away from my door here at a round trot for an hour and a half, you would still be in the thick of London, and the greater part of that would be "slums", as they were called; that is to say, places of torture for innocent men and women; or worse, stews for rearing and breeding men and women in such degradation that that torture should seem to them mere ordinary and natural life.'

'I know, I know,' I said, rather impatiently. 'That was what was; tell me something of what is. Is any of that left?'

'Not an inch,' said he; 'but some memory of it abides with us, and I am glad of it. Once a year, on May-day, we hold a solemn feast in those easterly communes of London to commemorate The Clearing of Misery, as it is called. On that day we have music and dancing, and merry games and happy feasting on the site of some of the worst of the old slums, the traditional memory of which we have kept. On that occasion the custom is for the prettiest girls to sing some of the old revolutionary songs, and those which were the groans of the discontent, once so hopeless, on the very spots where those terrible crimes of class-murder were committed day by day for so many years. To a man like me, who has studied the past so diligently, it is a curious and touching sight to see some beautiful girl, daintily clad, and crowned with flowers from the neighbouring meadows, standing amongst the happy people, on some mound where of old time stood the wretched apology for a house, a den in which men and women lived packed amongst the filth like pilchards in a cask; lived in such a way that they could only have endured it, as I said just now, by being degraded out of humanity—to hear the terrible words of threatening and lamentation coming from her sweet and beautiful lips, and she unconscious of their real meaning: to hear her, for instance, singing Hood's Song of the Shirt, and to think that all the time she does not understand what it is all about—a tragedy grown inconceivable to her and her listeners. Think of that, if you can, and of how glorious life is grown!'

'Indeed,' said I, 'it is difficult for me to think of it.'

And I sat watching how his eyes glittered, and how the fresh life seemed to glow in his face, and I wondered how at his age he should think of the happiness of the world, or indeed anything but his coming dinner.

'Tell me in detail,' said I, 'what lies east of Bloomsbury now?'

Said he: 'There are but few houses between this and the outer part of the old city; but in the city we have a thickly dwelling population. Our forefathers, in the first clearing of the slums were not in a hurry to pull down the houses in what was called at the end of the nineteenth century the business quarter of the town, and what later got to be known as the Swindling Kens. You see, these houses, though they stood hideously thick on the ground, were roomy and fairly solid in building, and clean, because they were not used for living in, but as mere gambling booths; so the poor people from the cleared slums took them for lodgings and dwelt there, till the folk of those days had time to think of something better for them; so the buildings were pulled down so gradually that people got used to living thicker on the ground there than in most places; therefore it remains the most populous part of London, or perhaps of all these islands. But it is very pleasant there, partly because of the splendour of the architecture, which goes further than what you will see elsewhere. However, this crowding, if it may be called so, does not go further than a street called Aldgate, a name which perhaps you may have heard of. Beyond that the houses are scattered wide about the meadows there, which are very beautiful, especially when you get on to the lovely river Lea (where old Isaak Walton used to fish, you know) about the places called Stratford and Old Ford, names which of course you will not have heard of, though the Romans were busy there once upon a time.'

Not heard of them! thought I to myself. How strange! that I who had
seen the very last remnant of the pleasantness of the meadows by the Lea
destroyed, should have heard them spoken of with pleasantness come back
to them in full measure.

Hammond went on: 'When you get down to the Thames side you come
on the Docks, which are works of the nineteenth century, and are still in
use, although not so thronged as they once were, since we discourage
centralization all we can, and we have long ago dropped the pretension to
be the market of the world. About these Docks are a good few houses,
which, however, are not inhabited by many people permanently; I mean,
those who use them come and go a good deal, the place being too low and
marshy for pleasant dwelling. Past the Docks eastward and landward it is
all flat pasture, once marsh, except for a few gardens, and there are very
few permanent dwellings there: scarcely anything but a few sheds, and cots
for the men who come to look after the great herds of cattle pasturing
there. But however, what with the beasts and the men, and the scattered
red-tiled roofs and the big hayricks, it does not make a bad holiday to get a
quiet pony and ride about there on a sunny afternoon of autumn, and look
over the river and the craft passing up and down, and on to Shooters' Hill
and the Kentish uplands, and then turn round to the wide green sea of the
Essex marshland, with the great domed line of the sky, and the sun shining
down in one flood of peaceful light over the long distance. There is a place
called Canning's Town, and further out, Silvertown, where the pleasant
meadows are at their pleasantest: doubtless they were once slums, and
wretched enough.'

The names grated on my ear, but I could not explain why to him. So I
said: 'And south of the river, what is it like?'

He said: 'You would find it much the same as the land about Hammersmith. North, again, the land runs up high, and there is an agreeable and
well-built town called Hampstead, which fitly ends London on that side. It
looks down on the north-western end of the forest you passed through.'

I smiled. 'So much for what was once London,' said I. 'Now tell me
about the other towns of the country.'

He said: 'As to the big murky places which were once, as we know, the
centres of manufacture, they have, like the brick and mortar desert of London, disappeared; only, since they were centres of nothing but "manufacture", and served no purpose but that of the gambling market, they have
left less signs of their existence than London. Of course, the great change in
the use of mechanical force made this an easy matter, and some approach
to their break-up as centres would probably have taken place, even if we
had not changed our habits so much: but they being such as they were, no
sacrifice would have seemed too great a price to pay for getting rid of the
"manufacturing districts", as they used to be called. For the rest, whatever
coal or mineral we need is brought to grass and sent whither it is needed

with as little as possible of dirt, confusion, and the distressing of quiet people's lives. One is tempted to believe from what one has read of the condition of those districts in the nineteenth century, that those who had them under their power worried, befouled, and degraded men out of malice prepense: but it was not so; like the miseducation of which we were talking just now, it came of their dreadful poverty. They were obliged to put up with everything, and even pretend that they liked it; whereas we can now deal with things reasonably, and refuse to be saddled with what we do not want.'

I confess I was not sorry to cut short with a question his glorifications of the age he lived in. Said I: 'How about the smaller towns? I suppose you have swept those away entirely?'

'No, no,' said he, 'it hasn't gone that way. On the contrary, there has been but little clearance, though much rebuilding, in the smaller towns. Their suburbs, indeed, when they had any, have melted away into the general country, and space and elbow-room has been got in their centres: but there are the towns still with their streets and squares and market-places; so that it is by means of these smaller towns that we of today can get some kind of idea of what the towns of the older world were like—I mean to say at their best.'

'Take Oxford, for instance,' said I.

'Yes,' said he, 'I suppose Oxford was beautiful even in the nineteenth century. At present it has the great interest of still preserving a great mass of precommercial building, and is a very beautiful place, yet there are many towns which have become scarcely less beautiful.'

Said I: 'In passing, may I ask if it is still a place of learning?'

'Still?' said he, smiling. 'Well, it has reverted to some of its best traditions; so you may imagine how far it is from its nineteenth-century position. It is real learning, knowledge cultivated for its own sake—the Art of Knowledge, in short—which is followed there, not the Commercial learning of the past. Though perhaps you do not know that in the nineteenth century Oxford and its less interesting sister Cambridge became definitely commercial. They (and especially Oxford) were the breeding places of a peculiar class of parasites, who called themselves cultivated people; they were indeed cynical enough, as the so-called educated classes of the day generally were; but they affected an exaggeration of cynicism in order that they might be thought knowing and worldly-wise. The rich middle classes (they had no relation with the working classes) treated them with the kind of contemptuous toleration with which a mediaeval baron treated his jester; though it must be said that they were by no means so pleasant as the old jesters were, being, in fact, *the* bores of society. They were laughed at, despised—and paid. Which last was what they aimed at.'

Dear me! thought I, how apt history is to reverse contemporary judgements. Surely only the worst of them were as bad as that. But I must admit that they were mostly prigs, and that they *were* commercial. I said aloud, though more to myself than to Hammond, 'Well, how could they be better than the age that made them?'

'True,' he said, 'but their pretensions were higher.'

'Were they?' said I, smiling.

'You drive me from corner to corner,' said he, smiling in turn. 'Let me say at least that they were a poor sequence to the aspirations of Oxford of "the barbarous Middle Ages".'

'Yes, that will do,' said I.

'Also,' said Hammond, 'what I have been saying of them is true in the main. But ask on!'

I said: 'We have heard about London and the manufacturing districts and the ordinary towns: how about the villages?'

Said Hammond: 'You must know that toward the end of the nineteenth century the villages were almost destroyed, unless where they became mere adjuncts to the manufacturing districts, or formed a sort of minor manufacturing district themselves. Houses were allowed to fall into decay and actual ruin; trees were cut down for the sake of the few shillings which the poor sticks would fetch; the building became inexpressibly mean and hideous. Labour was scarce; but wages fell nevertheless. All the small country arts of life which once added to the little pleasures of country people were lost. The country produce which passed through the hands of the husbandman never got so far as their mouths. Incredible shabbiness and niggardly pinching reigned over the fields and acres which, in spite of the rude and careless husbandry of the times, were so kind and bountiful. Had you any inkling of all this?'

'I have heard that it was so,' said I, 'but what followed?'

'The change,' said Hammond, 'which in these matters took place very early in our epoch, was most strangely rapid. People flocked into the country villages, and, so to say, flung themselves upon the freed land like a wild beast upon his prey; and in a very little time the villages of England were more populous than they had been since the fourteenth century, and were still growing fast. Of course, this invasion of the country was awkward to deal with, and would have created much misery, if the folk had still been under the bondage of class monopoly. But as it was, things soon righted themselves. People found out what they were fit for, and gave up attempting to push themselves into occupations in which they must needs fail. The town invaded the country; but the invaders, like the warlike invaders of early days, yielded to the influence of their surroundings, and became country people; and in their turn, as they became more numerous than the townsmen, influenced them also; so that the difference between town and country grew less and less; and it was indeed this world of the country vivified by the thought and briskness of town-bred folk which has produced that happy and leisurely but eager life of which you have had a first taste. Again I say, many blunders were made, but we have had time to set them right. Much was left for the men of my earlier life to deal with. The crude ideas of the first half of the twentieth century, when men were still oppressed by the fear of poverty, and did not look enough to the present pleasure of ordinary daily life, spoilt a great deal of what the commercial age had left us of external beauty: and I admit that it was but slowly that men recovered from the injuries they had inflicted on themselves even after they became free. But slowly as the recovery came, it *did* come; and the more you see of us, the clearer it will be to you that we are happy. That we live amidst beauty without any fear of becoming effeminate; that we have plenty to do, and on the whole enjoy doing it. What more can we ask of life?'

He paused, as if he were seeking for words with which to express his thought. Then he said:

'This is how we stand. England was once a country of clearings amongst the woods and wastes, with a few towns interspersed, which were fortresses for the feudal army, markets for the folk, gathering places for the craftsmen. It then became a country of huge and foul workshops and fouler gambling-dens, surrounded by an ill-kept, poverty-stricken farm, pillaged by the masters of the workshops. It is now a garden, where nothing is wasted and nothing is spoilt, with the necessary dwellings, sheds, and workshops scattered up and down the country, all trim and neat and pretty. For, indeed, we should be too much ashamed of ourselves if we allowed the making of goods, even on a large scale, to carry with it the appearance, even, of desolation and misery. Why, my friend, those housewives we were talking of just now would teach us better than that.'

Said I: 'This side of your change is certainly for the better. But though I shall soon see some of these villages, tell me in a word or two what they are like, just to prepare me.'

'Perhaps,' said he, 'you have seen a tolerable picture of these villages as they were before the end of the nineteenth century. Such things exist.'

'I have seen several of such pictures,' said I.

'Well,' said Hammond, 'our villages are something like the best of such places, with the church or mote-house of the neighbours for their chief building. Only note that there are no tokens of poverty about them: no tumble-down picturesque: which, to tell you the truth, the artist usually availed himself of to veil his incapacity for drawing architecture. Such things do not please us, even when they indicate no misery. Like the mediaevals, we like everything trim and clean, and orderly and bright; as people always do when they have any sense of architectural power; because then they know that they can have what they want, and they won't stand any nonsense from Nature in their dealings with her.'

'Besides the villages, are there any scattered country houses?' said I.

'Yes, plenty' said Hammond; 'in fact, except in the wastes and forests and amongst the sand-hills (like Hindhead in Surrey), it is not easy to be out of sight of a house; and where the houses are thinly scattered they run large, and are more like the old colleges than ordinary houses as they used to be. That is done for the sake of society, for a good many people can dwell in such houses, as the country dwellers are not necessarily husband-men; though they almost all help in such work at times. The life that goes on in these big dwellings in the country is very pleasant, especially as some of the most studious men of our time live in them, and altogether there is a great variety of mind and mood to be found in them which brightens and quickens the society there.'

'I am rather surprised,' said I, 'by all this, for its seems to me that after all the country must be tolerably populous.'

'Certainly,' said he; 'the population is pretty much the same as it was at the end of the nineteenth century; we have spread it, that is all. Of course, also, we have helped to populate other countries—where we were wanted and were called for.'

Said I: 'One thing, it seems to me, does not go with your word of "gar-den" for the country. You have spoken of wastes and forests, and I myself have seen the beginning of your Middlesex and Essex forest. Why do you keep such things in a garden? and isn't it very wasteful to do so?'

'My friend,' he said, 'we like these pieces of wild nature, and can afford them, so we have them; let alone that as to the forests, we need a great deal of timber, and suppose that our sons and sons' sons will do the like. As to the land being a garden, I have heard that they used to have shrubberies and rockeries in gardens once; and though I might not like the artificial ones, I assure you that some of the natural rockeries of our garden are worth seeing. Go north this summer and look at the Cumberland and Westmorland ones—where, by the way, you will see some sheep feeding, so that they are not so wasteful as you think; not so wasteful as forcing-grounds for fruit out of season, I think. Go and have a look at the sheep-walks high up the slopes between Ingleborough and Pen-y-gwent, and tell me if you think we *waste* the land there by not covering it with factories for making things that nobody wants, which was the chief business of the nine-teenth century.'

'I will try to go there,' said I.

'It won't take much trying,' said he.

(William Morris, *News from Nowhere*, 1890, Ch.x.)

VI.10 Matthew Arnold, 'The Scholar-Gipsy' (1853)

Go, for they call you, shepherd, from the hill;
　　Go, shepherd, and untie the wattled cotes!
　　　No longer leave thy wistful flock unfed,
　　　Nor let thy bawling fellows rack their throats,
　　　　Nor the cropp'd herbage shoot another head.　　　　　5
　　　　But when the fields are still,
　　　And the tired men and dogs all gone to rest,
　　　　And only the white sheep are sometimes seen
　　　　Cross and recross the strips of moon-blanch'd green,[1]
Come, shepherd, and again begin the quest!　　　　　　10

Here, where the reaper was at work of late—
　　In this high field's dark corner, where he leaves
　　　His coat, his basket, and his earthen cruse,
　　　And in the sun all morning binds the sheaves,
　　　　Then here, at noon, comes back his stores to use—　15
　　　　Here will I sit and wait,
　　　While to my ear from uplands far away
　　　　The bleating of the folded flocks is borne,
　　　　With distant cries of reapers in the corn—
All the live murmur of a summer's day.　　　　　　　　20

Screen'd is this nook o'er the high, half-reap'd field,
　　And here till sun-down, shepherd! will I be.
　　　Through the thick corn the scarlet poppies peep,
　　　And round green roots and yellowing stalks I see
　　　　Pale pink convolvulus in tendrils creep;　　　　　25
　　　　And air-swept lindens yield
　　　Their scent, and rustle down their perfumed showers
　　　　Of bloom on the bent grass where I am laid,
　　　　And bower me from the August sun with shade;[2]
And the eye travels down to Oxford's towers.　　　　　30

And near me on the grass lies Glanvil's book—[3]
　　Come, let me read the oft-read tale again!
　　　The story of the Oxford scholar poor,
　　　Of pregnant parts and quick inventive brain,
　　　　Who, tired of knocking at preferment's door,　　　35
　　　　One summer-morn forsook
　　　His friends, and went to learn the gipsy-lore,
　　　　And roam'd the world with that wild brotherhood,
　　　　And came, as most men deem'd, to little good,
But came to Oxford and his friends no more.　　　　　40

But once, years after, in the country-lanes,
    Two scholars, whom at college erst he knew,
        Met him, and of his way of life enquired;
    Whereat he answer'd, that the gipsy-crew,
        His mates, had arts to rule as they desired   45
            The workings of men's brains,
    And they can bind them to what thoughts they will.
        'And I,' he said, 'the secret of their art,
            When fully learn'd, will to the world impart;
    But it needs heaven-sent moments for this skill.'   50

This said, he left them, and return'd no more.—
    But rumours hung about the country-side,
        That the lost Scholar long was seen to stray,
    Seen by rare glimpses, pensive and tongue-tied,
        In hat of antique shape, and cloak of grey,   55
            The same the gipsies wore.
    Shepherds had met him on the Hurst in spring;
        At some lone alehouse in the Berkshire moors,
            On the warm ingle-bench, the smock-frock'd boors
    Had found him seated at their entering,   60

But, 'mid their drink and clatter, he would fly.
    And I myself seem half to know thy looks,
        And put the shepherds, wanderer! on thy trace;
    And boys who in lone wheatfields scare the rooks
        I ask if thou hast pass'd their quiet place;   65
            Or in my boat I lie
    Moor'd to the cool bank in the summer-heats,
        'Mid wide grass meadows which the sunshine fills,
            And watch the warm, green-muffled Cumner hills,
    And wonder if thou haunt'st their shy retreats.   70

For most, I know, thou lov'st retired ground!
    Thee at the ferry Oxford riders blithe,
        Returning home on summer-nights, have met
    Crossing the stripling Thames at Bab-lock-hithe,
        Trailing in the cool stream thy fingers wet,   75
            As the punt's rope chops round;
    And leaning backward in a pensive dream,
        And fostering in thy lap a heap of flowers
            Pluck'd in shy fields and distant Wychwood bowers,
    And thine eyes resting on the moonlit stream.   80

And then they land, and thou art seen no more!—
   Maidens, who from the distant hamlets come
     To dance around the Fyfield elm in May,
   Oft through the darkening fields have seen thee roam,
     Or cross a stile into the public way.   85
       Oft thou hast given them store
   Of flowers—the frail-leaf'd, white anemony,
     Dark bluebells drench'd with dews of summer eves,
     And purple orchises with spotted leaves—
   But none hath words she can report of thee.   90

And, above Godstow Bridge, when hay-time's here
   In June, and many a scythe in sunshine flames,
     Men who through those wide fields of breezy grass
   Where black-wing'd swallows haunt the glittering Thames,
     To bathe in the abandon'd lasher pass,   95
       Have often pass'd thee near
   Sitting upon the river bank o'ergrown;
     Mark'd thine outlandish garb, thy figure spare,
     Thy dark vague eyes, and soft abstracted air—
   But, when they came from bathing, thou wast gone!   100

At some lone homestead in the Cumner hills,
   Where at her open door the housewife darns,
     Thou hast been seen, or hanging on a gate
   To watch the threshers in the mossy barns.
     Children, who early range these slopes and late   105
       For cresses from the rills,
   Have known thee eying, all an April-day,
     The springing pastures and the feeding kine;
     And mark'd thee, when the stars come out and shine,
   Through the long dewy grass move slow away.   110

In autumn, on the skirts of Bagley Wood—
   Where most the gipsies by the turf-edged way
     Pitch their smoked tents, and every bush you see
   With scarlet patches tagg'd and shreds of grey,
     Above the forest-ground called Thessaly—   115
       The blackbird, picking food,
   Sees thee, nor stops his meal, nor fears at all;
     So often has he known thee past him stray,
     Rapt, twirling in thy hand a wither'd spray,
   And waiting for the spark from heaven to fall.   120

And once, in winter, on the causeway chill
  Where home through flooded fields foot-travellers go,
    Have I not pass'd thee on the wooden bridge,
  Wrapt in thy cloak and battling with the snow,
    Thy face tow'rd Hinksey and its wintry ridge?   125
      And thou hast climb'd the hill,
  And gain'd the white brow of the Cumner range;
    Turn'd once to watch, while thick the snowflakes fall,
    The line of festal light in Christ-Church hall—
  Then sought thy straw in some sequester'd grange.   130

But what—I dream![4] Two hundred years are flown
  Since first thy story ran through Oxford halls,
    And the grave Glanvil did the tale inscribe
  That thou wert wander'd from the studious walls
    To learn strange arts, and join a gipsy-tribe;   135
      And thou from earth art gone
  Long since, and in some quiet churchyard laid—
    Some country-nook, where o'er thy unknown grave
    Tall grasses and white flowering nettles wave,
  Under a dark, red-fruited yew-tree's shade.[5]   140

—No, no, thou hast not felt the lapse of hours!
  For what wears out the life of mortal men?
    'Tis that from change to change their being rolls;
  'Tis that repeated shocks, again, again,
    Exhaust the energy of strongest souls   145
      And numb the elastic powers.
  Till having used our nerves with bliss and teen,
    And tired upon a thousand schemes our wit,
    To the just-pausing Genius we remit
  Our worn-out life, and are—what we have been.   150

Thou hast not lived, why should'st thou perish, so?
  Thou hadst *one* aim, *one* business, *one* desire;
    Else wert thou long since number'd with the dead!
  Else hadst thou spent, like other men, thy fire!
    The generations of thy peers are fled,   155
      And we ourselves shall go;
  But thou possessest an immortal lot,
    And we imagine thee exempt from age
    And living as thou liv'st on Glanvil's page,
  Because thou hadst—what we, alas! have not.[6]   160

For early didst thou leave the world, with powers
   Fresh, undiverted to the world without,
      Firm to their mark, not spent on other things;
   Free from the sick fatigue, the languid doubt,
      Which much to have tried, in much been baffled, brings.
         O life unlike to ours!   166
   Who fluctuate idly without term or scope,
Of whom each strives, nor knows for what he strives,
      And each half lives a hundred different lives;
   Who wait like thee, but not, like thee, in hope.   170

Thou waitest for the spark from heaven! and we,
   Light half-believers of our casual creeds,
      Who never deeply felt, nor clearly will'd,
   Whose insight never has borne fruit in deeds,
      Whose vague resolves never have been fulfill'd;   175
         For whom each year we see
Breeds new beginnings, disappointments new;
      Who hesitate and falter life away,
      And lose to-morrow the ground won to-day—
Ah! do not we, wanderer! await it too?   180

Yes, we await it!—but it still delays,
   And then we suffer! and amongst us one,[7]
      Who most has suffer'd, takes dejectedly
   His seat upon the intellectual throne;
      And all his store of sad experience he   185
         Lays bare of wretched days;
   Tells us his misery's birth and growth and signs,
      And how the dying spark of hope was fed,
      And how the breast was soothed, and how the head,
And all his hourly varied anodynes.   190

This for our wisest! and we others pine,
   And wish the long unhappy dream would end,
      And waive all claim to bliss, and try to bear;
   With close-lipp'd patience for our only friend,
      Sad patience, too near neighbour to despair—   195
         But none has hope like thine!
Thou through the fields and through the woods dost stray,
   Roaming the country-side, a truant boy,
   Nursing thy project in unclouded joy,
And every doubt long blown by time away.[8]   200

O born in days when wits were fresh and clear,
  And life ran gaily as the sparkling Thames;
    Before this strange disease of modern life,
  With its sick hurry, its divided aims,
    Its heads o'ertax'd, its palsied hearts, was rife—   205
      Fly hence, our contact fear!
Still fly, plunge deeper in the bowering wood!
    Averse, as Dido did with gesture stern
    From her false friend's approach in Hades turn,
Wave us away, and keep thy solitude!⁹   210

Still nursing the unconquerable hope,
  Still clutching the inviolable shade,
    With a free, onward impulse brushing through,
  By night, the silver'd branches of the glade—
    Far on the forest-skirts, where none pursue.   215
      On some mild pastoral slope
Emerge, and resting on the moonlit pales
    Freshen thy flowers as in former years
    With dew, or listen with enchanted ears,
From the dark dingles, to the nightingales!   220

But fly our paths, our feverish contact fly!
  For strong the infection of our mental strife,
    Which, though it gives no bliss, yet spoils for rest;
  And we should win thee from thy own fair life,
    Like us distracted, and like us unblest.   225
      Soon, soon thy cheer would die,
Thy hopes grow timorous, and unfix'd thy powers,
    And thy clear aims be cross and shifting made;
    And then thy glad perennial youth would fade,
Fade, and grow old at last, and die like ours.¹⁰   230

Then fly our greetings, fly our speech and smiles!
  —As some grave Tyrian trader, from the sea,
    Descried at sunrise an emerging prow
  Lifting the cool-hair'd creepers stealthily,
    The fringes of a southward-facing brow   235
      Among the Ægæan isles;
And saw the merry Grecian coaster come,
    Freighted with amber grapes, and Chian wine,
    Green, bursting figs, and tunnies steep'd in brine—
And knew the intruders on his ancient home,   240

The young light-hearted masters of the waves—
And snatch'd his rudder, and shook out more sail;
And day and night held on indignantly
O'er the blue Midland waters with the gale,
Betwixt the Syrtes and soft Sicily,   245
To where the Altantic raves
Outside the western straits; and unbent sails
There, where down cloudy cliffs, through sheets of foam,
Shy traffickers, the dark Iberians come;
And on the beach undid his corded bales.   250

NOTES

1. 'An Elegy written in a Country Church Yard' by Thomas Gray (1716–71) begins,

> The *Curfeu* tolls the Knell of parting Day,
> The lowing Herd winds slowly o'er the Lea,
> The Plow-man homeward plods his weary Way,
> And leaves the World to Darkness, and to me.
>   Now fades the glimmering Landscape on the Sight,
> And all the Air a solemn Stillness holds;
> Save where the Beetle wheels his droning Flight,
> And drowsy Tinklings lull the distant Folds.

2. Consider the language of this stanza and others with that of the Romantic poet John
Keats (1793–1821). In 'To Autumn' Keats addresses Autumn thus:

> Who hath not seen thee oft amid thy store?
>   Sometimes whoever seeks abroad may find
> Thee sitting careless on a granary floor,
>   Thy hair soft-lifted by the winnowing wind;
> Or on a half-reap'd furrow sound asleep,
>   Drows'd with the fume of poppies, while thy hook
>   Spares the next swath and all its twined flowers:
> And sometimes like a gleaner thou dost keep
>   Steady thy laden head across a brook;
>   Or by a cyder-press, with patient look,
>   Thou watchest the last oozings hours by hours.

3. Arnold included the following note to accompany 'The Scholar-Gipsy':

There was very lately a lad in the University of Oxford, who was by his poverty forced to
leave his studies there; and at last to join himself to a company of vagabond gipsies.
Among these extravagant people, by the insinuating subtlety of his carriage, he quickly
got so much of their love and esteem as that they discovered to him their mystery. After
he had been a pretty while well exercised in the trade, there chanced to ride by a couple
of scholars, who had formerly been of his acquaintance. They quickly spied out their old
friend among the gipsies; and he gave them an account of the necessity which drove him
to that kind of life, and told them that the people he went with were not such impostors
as they were taken for, but they had a traditional kind of learning among them, and
could do wonders by the power of imagination, their fancy binding that of others: that
himself had learned much of their art, and when he had compassed the whole secret, he
intended, he said, to leave their company, and give the world an account of what he had
learned.   Glanvil's *Vanity of Dogmatizing*, 1661.

4. 'But what—I dream!' In 'Ode to a Nightingale', where the poet's consciousness returns from its initial longing for escape into reverie, Keats's final lines are:

> Was it a vision, or a waking dream?
> Fled is that music:—Do I wake or sleep?

5. See also the following lines from Gray's 'Elegy';

> Beneath those rugged Elms, that Yew-Tree's Shade,
> Where heaves the Turf in many a mould'ring Heap,
> Each in his narrow Cell for ever laid,
> The rude forefathers of the Hamlet sleep.

6. The comparison of the 'immortal' Scholar-Gipsy with other lives is echoed in Keats's comparisons between his 'immortal' Nightingale and mortal humankind. In stanza 3 he addresses the Nightingale, contemplating how wine might serve as a means of forgetting the sufferings of life. Thus the poet might, he says,

> Fade far away, dissolve, and quite forget
> What thou among the leaves has never known,
> The weariness, the fever, and the fret
> Here, where men sit and hear each other groan;
> Where palsy shakes a few, sad, last gray hairs,
> Where youth grows pale, and spectre-thin, and dies;
> Where but to think is to be full of sorrow
> And leaden-eyed despairs;
> Where beauty cannot keep her lustrous eyes,
> Or new Love pine at them beyond to-morrow.

7. In his annotated edition of Arnold's poems, Kenneth Allott states there is evidence for this reference applying to Goethe, whose autobiographical work *Dichtung und Wahrheit* Arnold had been reading at the time of composing 'The Scholar-Gipsy'. There is also a strong argument to suggest that the reference could apply to Tennyson, who had been appointed poet laureate in 1850.

8. Arnold sets up an image of the Scholar Gipsy as free and child-like in his 'immortality', implicitly contrasting him with the lives of 'modern' mortals. In 'Ode: Intimations of Immortality from Recollections of Early Childhood', Wordsworth makes use of a similar comparison, but within the life of a single man whose growth into maturity brings with it a consciousness of mortality:

> Our birth is but a sleep and a forgetting:
> The Soul that rises with us, our life's Star,
> Hath had elsewhere its setting,
> And cometh from afar:
> Not in entire forgetfulness,
> And not in utter nakedness,
> But trailing clouds of glory do we come
> From God, who is our home:
> Heaven lies about us in our infancy!
> Shades of the prison-house begin to close
> Upon the growing Boy
> But he beholds the light, and whence it flows,
> He sees it in his joy;
> The Youth, who daily farther from the east
> Must travel, still is Nature's Priest,
> And by the vision splendid
> Is on his way attended;

> At length the Man perceives it die away,
> And fade into the light of common day.

9. The reference to Dido and her 'false friend' relates to the meeting between Dido and
Aeneas in Book VI of Virgil's *Aeneid*. Aeneas visits the Underworld, where he meets
Dido, the Carthaginian queen with whom he fell in love during his journey through the
Mediterranean after the Trojan War. Dido killed herself in despair when Aeneas abandoned her for his greater purpose, which, according to Virgil and other Latin poets, was
to be the destined founder of the Roman Empire. When Aeneas meets Dido's shade in
the Underworld, she spurns him.

> In vain he thus attempts her mind to move
> With tears and pray'rs, and late-repenting love.
> Disdainfully she look'd; then turning round,
> She fix'd her eyes unmoved upon the ground,
> And what he says and swears regards no more
> Than the deaf rocks, when the loud billows roar;
> But whirl'd away, to shun his hateful sight,
> Hid in the forest, and the shades of night.

> > (*Aeneid*, Book VI, ll. 631–8)

10. Look again at the echoes between this stanza and that quoted in note 6 from 'Ode to a
Nightingale'.

> > (*Arnold, Poetical Works*, ed. C. B. Tinker and H. F. Lowry, 1949.)

William Barnes, Poems   VI.11

Sound o' Water (1859)

I born in town! oh no, my dawn
O' life broke here bezide theäse lawn;
Not where pent aïr do roll along.
In darkness drough the wall-bound drong,
An' never bring the goo-coo's zong,   5
Nor sweets o' blossoms in the hedge,
Or benden rush, or sheenen zedge,
    Or sounds o' flowen water.

The aïr that I've a-breath'd did sheäke
The draps o' raïn upon the breäke,   10
An' bear aloft the swingen lark,
An' huffle roun' the elem's bark,
In boughy grove, an' woody park,
An' brought us down the dewy dells,
The high-wound zongs o' nightengeäles,   15
    An' sounds o' flowen water.

An' when the zun, wi' vi'ry rim,
'S a-zinken low, an' wearen dim,
Here I, a'most too tired to stand,
Do leäve my work that's under hand   20
In pathless wood or open land,
To rest 'ithin my thatchen oves,
Wi' ruslen win's in leafy groves,
   An' sounds o' flowen water.

Hallowed Pleaces (1859)

At Woodcombe farm, wi' ground an' tree
Hallow'd by times o' youthvul glee,
At Chris'mas time I spent a night
Wi' feäces dearest to my zight;
An' took my wife to tread, woonce mwore,   5
Her maïden hwome's vorseäken vloor;
An' under stars that slowly wheel'd
Aloft, above the keen-aïr'd vield,
While night bedimm'd the rus'len copse,
An' darken'd all the ridges' tops,   10
The hall, a-hung wi' holly, rung
Wi' many a tongue o' wold an' young.

There, on the he'th's well-hetted ground,
Hallow'd by times o' zitten round,
The brimvul mug o' cider stood   15
An' hiss'd avore the bleäzen wood;
An' zome, a-zitten knee by knee,
Did tell their teäles wi' hearty glee,
An' others gamboll'd in a roar
O' laughter on the stwonen vloor;   20
An' while the moss o' winter-tide
Clung chilly roun' the house's zide,
The hall, a-hung wi' holly, rung
Wi' many a tongue o' wold an' young.

There, on the pworches bench o' stwone,   25
Hallow'd by times o' youthvul fun,
We laugh'd an' sigh'd to think o' neämes
That rung there woonce, in evenen geämes;
An' while the swaÿen cypress bow'd,
In chilly wind, his darksome sh'oud,   30
An' honeyzuckles, beäre o' leaves,
Still reach'd the window-sheädèn eaves

Up where the clematis did trim
The stwonen arches mossy rim,
The hall, a-hung wi' holly, rung   35
Wi' many a tongue o' wold an' young.

There, in the geärden's wall-bound square,
Hallow'd by times o' strollen there,
The winter wind, a-hufflen loud,
Did swaÿ the pear-tree's leafless sh'oud,   40
An' beät the bush that woonce did bear
The damask rwose vor Jenny's heäir;
An' there the walk o' peäven stwone
That burn'd below the zummer zun,
Struck icy-cwold drough shoes a-wore   45
By maïdens vrom the hetted vloor
In hall, a-hung wi' holm, where rung
Vull many a tongue o' wold an' young.

There at the geäte that woonce wer blue,
Hallow'd by times o' passen drough,   50
Light strawmotes rose in flaggen flight,
A-floated by the winds o' night,
Where leafy ivy-stems did crawl
In moonlight on the windblown wall,
An' merry maïdens' vaïces vled   55
In echoes sh'ill, vrom wall to shed,
As shiv'ren in their frocks o' white
They come to bid us there 'Good night,'
Vrom hall, a-hung wi' holm, that rung
Wi' many a tongue o' wold an' young.   60

There in the narrow leäne an' drong
Hallow'd by times o' gwaïn along,
The lofty ashes' leafless sh'ouds
Rose dark avore the clear-edged clouds,
The while the moon, at girtest height,   65
Bespread the pooly brook wi' light,
An' as our child, in loose-limb'd rest,
Lay peäle upon her mother's breast,
Her waxen eyelids seal'd her eyes
Vrom darksome trees, an' sheenen skies,   70
An' halls a-hung wi' holm, that rung
Wi' many a tongue, o' wold an' young.

Our Fathers' Works (1859)

Ah! I do think, as I do tread
Theäse path, wi' elems overhead,
A-climen slowly up vrom bridge,
By easy steps, to Broadwoak Ridge,
That all theäse roads that we do bruise   5
Wi' hosses' shoes, or heavy lwoads;
An' hedges' bands, where trees in row
Do rise an' grow aroun' the lands,
Be works that we've a-vound a-wrought
By our vorefathers' ceäre an' thought.   10

They clear'd the groun' vor grass to teäke
The pleäce that bore the bremble breäke,
An' draïn'd the fen, where water spread,
A-lyen dead, a beäne to men;
An' built the mill, where still the wheel   15
Do grind our meal, below the hill;
An' turn'd the bridge, wi' arch a-spread,
Below a road, vor us to tread.

They vound a pleäce, where we mid seek
The gifts o' greäce vrom week to week;   20
An' built wi' stwone, upon the hill,
A tow'r we still do call our own;
With bells to use, an' meäke rejaïce,
Wi' giant vaïce, at our good news:
An' lifted stwones an' beams to keep   25
The raïn an' cwold vrom us asleep.

Zoo now mid nwone ov us vorget
The pattern our vorefathers zet;
But each be faïn to underteäke
Zome work to meäke vor others' gaïn,   30
That we mid leäve mwore good to sheäre,
Less ills to bear, less souls to grieve,
An' when our hands do vall to rest,
It mid be vrom a work a-blest.

(*Hwomely Rhymes, A Second Collection of Poems in the
Dorset Dialect*, 1859.)

VI.12 **William Morris, 'The Message of the March Wind' (1886)**

Fair now is the springtide, now earth lies beholding
  With the eyes of a lover the face of the sun;
Long lasteth the daylight, and hope is enfolding
  The green-growing acres with increase begun.

Now sweet, sweet it is through the land to be straying   5
  Mid the birds and the blossoms and the beasts of the field;
Love mingles with love, and no evil is weighing
  On thy heart or mine, where all sorrow is healed.

From township to township, o'er down and by tillage
  Far, far have we wandered and long was the day,   10
But now cometh eve at the end of the village,
  Where over the grey wall the church riseth grey.

There is wind in the twilight; in the white road before us
  The straw from the ox-yard is blowing about;
The moon's rim is rising, a star glitters o'er us,   15
  And the vane on the spire-top is swinging in doubt.

Down there dips the highway, toward the bridge crossing over
  The brook that runs on to the Thames and the sea.
Draw closer, my sweet, we are lover and lover;
  This eve art thou given to gladness and me.   20

Shall we be glad always? Come closer, and hearken:
  Three fields further on, as they told me down there,
When the young moon has set, if the March sky should darken,
  We might see from the hill-top the great city's glare.

Hark, the wind in the elm-boughs! From London it bloweth,   25
  And telling of gold, and of hope and unrest;
Of power that helps not; of wisdom that knoweth,
  But teacheth not aught of the worst and the best.

Of the rich men it telleth, and strange is the story
  How they have, and they hanker, and grip far and wide;   30
And they live and they die, and the earth and its glory
  Has been but a burden they scarce might abide.

Hark! the March wind again of a people is telling;
  Of the life that they live there, so haggard and grim,
That if we and our love amidst them had been dwelling   35
  My fondness had faltered, thy beauty grown dim.

This land we have loved in our love and our leisure
    For them hangs in heaven, high out of their reach;
The wide hills o'er the sea-plain for them have no pleasure,
    The grey homes of their fathers no story to teach.   40

The singers have sung and the builders have builded,
    The painters have fashioned their tales of delight;
For what and for whom hath the world's book been gilded,
    When all is for these but the blackness of night?

How long and for what is their patience abiding?   45
    How oft and how oft shall their story be told,
While the hope that none seeketh in darkness is hiding
    And in grief and in sorrow the world groweth old?

Come back to the inn, love, and the lights and the fire,
    And the fiddler's old tune and the shuffling of feet;   50
For there in a while shall be rest and desire,
    And there shall the morrow's uprising be sweet.

Yet, love, as we wend the wind bloweth behind us
    And beareth the last tale it telleth to-night,
How here in the spring-tide the message shall find us;   55
    For the hope that none seeketh is coming to light.

Like the seed of midwinter, unheeded, unperished,
    Like the autumn-sown wheat 'neath the snow lying green,
Like the love that o'ertook us, unawares and uncherished,
    Like the babe 'neath thy girdle that groweth unseen,   60

So the hope of the people now buddeth and groweth—
    Rest fadeth before it, and blindness and fear;
It biddeth us learn all the wisdom it knoweth;
    It hath found us and held us, and biddeth us hear:

For it beareth the message: 'Rise up on the morrow   65
    And go on your ways toward the doubt and the strife;
Join hope to our hope and blend sorrow with sorrow,
    And seek for men's love in the short days of life.'

But lo, the old inn, and the lights and the fire,
    And the fiddler's old tune and the shuffling of feet;   70
Soon for us shall be quiet and rest and desire,
    And to-morrow's uprising to deeds shall be sweet.

(*William Morris*, ed. G. D. H. Cole, 1934.)

vi.13 George Meredith, 'Earth's Secret' (1883)

Not solitarily in fields we find
Earth's secret open, though one page is there—
Her plainest, such as children spell, and share
With bird and beast—raised letters for the blind.
Not where the troubled passions toss the mind,   5
In turbid cities, can the key be bare.
It hangs for those who hither thither fare,
Close interthreading nature with our kind.
They, hearing History speak, of what men were,
And have become, are wise. The gain is great   10
In vision and solidity; it lives.
Yet at a thought of life apart from her,
Solidity and vision lose their state,
For Earth, that gives the milk, the spirit gives.

(*The Poetical Works of George Meredith*, ed. B. M. Trevelyan, 1912.)

Thomas Hardy, 'In a Wood' (1887)

Pale beech and pine so blue,
    Set in one clay,
Bough to bough cannot you
    Live out your day?
When the rains skim and skip,   5
Why mar sweet comradeship,
Blighting with poison-drip
    Neighbourly spray?

Heart-halt and spirit-lame,
    City-opprest,   10
Unto this wood I came
    As to a nest;
Dreaming that sylvan peace
Offered the harrowed ease—
Nature a soft release   15
    From men's unrest.

But, having entered in,
    Great growths and small
Show them to men akin—
    Combatants all!   20

Sycamore shoulders oak,
Bines the slim sapling yoke,
Ivy-spun halters choke
    Elms stout and tall.

Touches from ash, O wych,   25
    Sting you like scorn!
You, too, brave hollies, twitch
    Sidelong from thorn.
Even the rank poplars bear
Lothly a rival's air,   30
Cankering in black despair
    If overborne.

Since, then, no grace I find
    Taught me of trees,
Turn I back to my kind,   35
    Worthy of these.
There at least smiles abound,
There discourse trills around,
There, now and then, are found
    Life-loyalties.   40

(*The Collected Poems of Thomas Hardy*, 1930.)

Biographical Notes on Authors

Prince Albert of Saxe-Coburg-Gotha (1819–61) married Queen Victoria in February 1840. Although having no official status in the constitution, Albert was to become an influential adviser to Victoria. Interested in the arts, science, and industry, he was a prime mover in the organization of the Great Exhibition of 1851. He died of typhoid fever at Windsor Castle in December 1861.

Matthew Arnold (1822–88), eldest son of Thomas Arnold, headmaster of Rugby School. In 1851 Matthew was appointed an inspector of schools and he remained in the post for thirty-five years. His first volume of poems appeared in 1849. He was elected Professor of Poetry at Oxford in 1857. In the 1860s he turned increasingly towards writing prose, and *Culture and Anarchy* was first published in 1869.

Walter Bagehot (1826–77), a London banker. Bagehot moved into journalism and in 1855 became joint editor of the *National Review*. In 1860 he was appointed editor of *The Economist*. *The English Constitution* (1867) was orginally written as a series of articles for the *Fortnightly*. It was, and still is, an admirable introduction to the working of British politics. A second edition of the book, with a new introduction and some important revisions, was published in 1872.

William Barnes (1801–86) was born in the county of Dorset and educated in Dorchester. He later became a headmaster of a school in that town. His interest in grammar and language led him to attack the 'classical' and foreign influences in English literature and he began to concentrate on writing in Dorset dialect. In 1844 he produced *Poems of Rural Life in the Dorset Dialect* and this was followed by two more volumes of dialect poetry. A collection of his dialect poems was published in 1879.

Robert Dudley Baxter (1827–75) entered in 1860 his father's firm of parliamentary lawyers based at Westminster. Conservative in politics and interested in statistics (he was a member of the Statistical Society), Baxter wrote a number of books on politics and the state of the nation of which the *National Income* (1868) is perhaps the best known.

Mrs Isabella Beeton (née Isabella Mayson) (1836–65). In 1856 Isabella married Samuel Beeton, publisher of the *Englishwoman's Domestic Magazine*, the most popular of all the increasing number of journals on cookery and domestic management which appeared in the 1850s. *Household Management* (1861), written by Isabella, appeared first in instalments in the *Englishwoman's Domestic Magazine* in the period 1859–61.

General William Booth (1829–1912), founder and first general of the Salvation Army. Booth worked from 1852, as a minister of first the Wesleyan Reformers, and then to 1861 as a minister of the Methodist New Connexion. In 1865, he undertook evangelical work in East London and established the Christian Mission in Whitechapel. The Mission extended its operations beyond London and in 1878 it became known as the Salvation Army.

Ford Madox Brown (1821–93) was born in Calais and studied on the Continent. He was influenced by the Pre-Raphaelites but was never invited to become one of the Brotherhood. In 1852 he started planning two of his greatest paintings, *The Last of England* and *Work*, the latter of which took him thirteen years to complete.

Elizabeth Barrett Browning (1806–61). A partial invalid, Elizabeth attained success with the publication of collections of her poems in 1838 and 1844. Her reputation in 1845, when she first met Robert Browning, was much higher than his, and remained so until her death in 1861. Indeed, in 1850, on the death of Wordsworth, her name was mentioned as an appropriate successor as poet laureate.

Robert Browning (1812–89) achieved his first critical success with *Paracelsus* in 1835. In 1845 he met Elizabeth Barrett and they married in the following year. They spent most of their time in Italy but, on Elizabeth's death in 1861, Browning returned to Britain. It was in the 1860s that Browning became a popular literary figure and this was highlighted with the formation of the Browning Society in 1881.

Joseph Chamberlain (1836–1914) was the son of a wealthy London boot manufacturer. He first worked in his father's business and then moved to Birmingham to work in a screw factory owned by his relatives. He became a partner in the firm and was able to retire at the age of 38 with a substantial fortune. In 1873 he was appointed Mayor of Birmingham and in 1876 became an MP for the city. In 1880 he was given the presidency of the Board of Trade in Gladstone's Liberal administration. He left the Liberals in 1886 over the question of Ireland and in 1895 became Secretary for the Colonies in Salisbury's Conservative ministry.

Sir George Clausen (1852–1944). Born in London, the son of a Danish sculptor. Heavily influenced by the French painter of peasant life Bastien Lepage, Clausen undertook a series of paintings of the lives of agricultural workers of which *The Stone Pickers* (1886–7) is perhaps the most famous.

William Kingdom Clifford (1845–79). Educated at Trinity College, Cambridge, Clifford was a brilliant mathematician and he became professor of applied mathematics at University College London.

Arthur Hugh Clough (1819–61) came under the influence of Thomas Arnold while a pupil at Rugby. He went as an undergraduate to Oxford and became a fellow of Oriel. He resigned this post but later became principal of University Hall, London and then an examiner in the Education Office.

Hannah Cullwick (1833–1909) was born in Shropshire. She started full-time work at the age of 8 and was to remain in domestic service for most of her life. In 1854, soon after meeting Arthur Munby, Hannah started to keep a diary and she maintained it until 1873 when she married Munby.

Charles Robert Darwin (1809–82). Darwin challenged early Victorian notions of the divine origin of plants and animals by proposing, in his *Origin of Species* (1859), a naturalistic theory of evolution by natural selection. He followed it up with *The Descent of Man* (1871), which gave a fully evolutionary account of human origins.

Charles John Huffham Dickens (1812–70), son of a clerk in the Navy pay office who was imprisoned for debt. Dickens started work at the age of 12 in a blacking warehouse. He learnt shorthand and became parliamentary reporter and then a reporter on the *Morning Chronicle*. His first novel, *The Posthumous Papers of the Pickwick Club*, met with acclaim and the publication of a Dickens novel became almost a yearly event. In 1850 Dickens started the weekly periodical *Household Words*. *Hard Times* appeared in 1854.

Benjamin Disraeli (1804–81). Determined on a political career, Disraeli made a number of unsuccessful attempts to enter Parliament before becoming MP for Maidstone in 1837. He was to become leader of the Conservative party and Prime Minister from 1874 to 1880. In 1876 he received a peerage and was known as the Earl of Beaconsfield. Disraeli was also, especially in his early years, a prolific writer and novelist. However, after *Tancred* in 1847, he wrote no other novels until *Lothair* (1870). *Endymion*, his last completed novel, was published in 1880.

William Maw Egley (1826–1916) exhibited at the Royal Academy from 1843 to 1898. A friend of Frith's, Egley started around 1855 to paint scenes of contemporary life, of which *Omnibus Life in London* (1859) is a good example. In the 1860s Egley turned increasingly to painting eighteenth-century costume and historical scenes.

George Eliot (Mary Ann Evans) (1819–80). Born in rural Warwickshire, she lived there until she became assistant editor of the *Westminster Review*. From 1854, until his death in 1878, Eliot lived with the literary critic George Henry Lewes. Her novel *Adam Bede* (1859) established her as a leading novelist. *Middlemarch* appeared in 1871–2 and *Daniel Deronda*, her last great novel, was published in instalments from 1874 to 1876.

John T. Emmett (1828–98) trained as an architect, and practised from the late 1840s to the late 1860s, building in a conventional Gothic style. He was no more than moderately successful until he returned to journalism in the early 1870s, publishing a series of vituperative attacks on the current Gothic style. He continued to attack the architectural establishment, particularly for the disintegration of the creative process and the growth of professionalism.

Friedrich Engels (1820–95). Son of a German textile manufacturer, Engels came to Britain in 1842 to manage his father's factory in Manchester. His book *The Condition of the Working Class in Britain* was published in 1845. In the previous year he had met Karl Marx and they were to become close friends and collaborators. When Marx came and settled in London in 1849, Engels supported him financially and, after Marx's death, he edited the second and third volumes of *Das Kapital*.

Thomas Hay Sweet Escott (1844–1924), a journalist and, from 1866 to 1873, deputy professor of classical literature at King's College, London. Escott edited the *Fortnightly Review* from 1882 to 1886 and wrote many books on politics and contemporary society.

William Ewart Gladstone (1809–98). Although starting his political career as a

Tory, Gladstone left the party with Peel in 1846. In the 1860s he became the leader of the Liberal party and was Prime Minister on four occasions over the period 1868 to 1894.

Mary, Duchess of Gloucester (1776–1857) was Queen Victoria's aunt. A daughter of George III, she had married a cousin, William, Duke of Gloucester (1776–1834).

Thomas Hardy (1840–1928). Born in a village near Dorchester, Dorset, Hardy started work as an architect. But he began to write novels and poetry and, after the success of *Far From the Madding Crowd* (1874), Hardy was able to give up architecture and concentrate solely on writing. His novels are mainly set in and around the area in which he was brought up and in which he lived for much of his life.

Frederic Harrison (1831–1923) was called to the bar in 1858 and from 1877 to 1889 was professor of jurisprudence at the Inns of Court. He was one of the founders of English Positivism and was, for twenty-five years, president of the English Positivist committee. He was a member of the royal commission on trade unions, 1867–1869.

Gerard Manley Hopkins (1844–89). Educated at Highgate School and Balliol College, Oxford, Hopkins was deeply influenced by the Oxford Movement. In 1866 he became a Roman Catholic and two years later a Jesuit. At the same time he stopped writing poetry and devoted his life to the Church. However, in 1876 Hopkins produced his long poem 'The Wreck of the Deutschland' and although this was rejected by a Jesuit paper on the grounds that it was too difficult, Hopkins continued to write. In 1884 he was appointed professor of Greek and Latin at University College, Dublin. He died five years later of typhoid fever. It was not until 1918 that many of his poems were published, through the efforts of his lifetime friend, the poet Robert Bridges.

Leonard Horner (1785–1864). A keen educationalist, Horner founded in Edinburgh in 1821 the School of Arts 'for the instruction of mechanics'. In 1828 he became warden of the new University of London. He left the post in 1831 and two years later was appointed one of the first factory inspectors in the country. In 1853 he was responsible for an area covering Lancashire, the West and North Ridings of Yorkshire, Durham, Cumberland, Northumberland, and Westmorland and in which there were some 1,700 to 1,800 mills. After his retirement in 1856, Horner spent most of his time studying and writing on his first love, geology. He had been made a fellow of the Geological Society in 1806 and in 1846 he became its president.

William Holman Hunt (1827–1919). In 1848 together with Millais, Gabriel and W. M. Rossetti, Collinson, F. G. Stephens, and Thomas Woolner, Hunt formed the Pre-Raphaelite Brotherhood. Of all the Pre-Raphaelites, Hunt was the one who was to remain closest to the original principles of the Brotherhood. Hunt wrote an account of the formation of the Brotherhood in *Pre-Raphaelitism and the Pre-Raphaelite Brotherhood* (1905).

Richard Jefferies (1848–87) was born near Swindon. He was the son of a farmer but became a reporter on the *North Wilts Herald* in 1866 and went on to writing essays and articles, mainly on natural history and agricultural subjects, for a variety of journals and magazines. *Hodge and his Masters* was published in 1880 and influenced Thomas Hardy in his writing of *The Dorsetshire Labourer*, which appeared in 1883.

Robert Kerr (1823–1904), an architect whose chief works included the National Provident Institution and a large country house built for John Walters, the proprietor of the *Times*. Kerr is best known as a writer on architecture and for his advocacy of the training of architects. He was a founder member and first president (1847) of the Architectural Association and, in 1857, he was appointed a fellow of the Royal Institute of British Architects. He was professor of the arts of construction at King's College, London from 1861–1890.

Reverend Francis Kilvert (1840–79). A curate in Wiltshire and then Powys, Kilvert became vicar of Brewardine, Herefordshire in 1877. Kilvert's diary, which he started in 1870, is one of the few existing accounts of life on the Welsh border in this period.

Lord Leighton (Baron Leighton of Stretton) (1830–96). Leighton's first painting to be exhibited at the Royal Academy in 1855 was bought by Queen Victoria for £600. This helped to ensure Leighton's popularity as a painter. He became a pillar of the Victorian art establishment as well as the leader of the Victorian neo-classical school. Leighton was knighted in 1878, made a baronet in 1886, and raised to the peerage in 1896.

George Henry Lewes (1817–78). Writer, philosopher, and critic, Lewes was editor of the *Leader*, 1851–1854. In 1854 he left his wife to live with George Eliot. He did much to encourage Eliot in her writings but she too helped him in his research on his *Life of Goethe* (1855). In 1863 he founded the *Fortnightly Review*.

Henry Parry Liddon (1829–80). A preacher who attracted large congregations with his fervent, intellectual, but often very lengthy sermons. Liddon was ordained in 1852 and was appointed vice-principal of St Edmund's Hall, Oxford in 1859. Eleven years later, he was appointed Dean Ireland Professor of Exegesis at Oxford and canon of St Paul's.

Thomas Babington Macaulay (1800–59) entered Parliament in 1830 as MP for Calne. He spent four years in India from 1834 to 1838 as a member of the Supreme Council of India. On his return to Britain, Macaulay was elected MP for Edinburgh. In 1848 the first two volumes of his *History of England* were published. A further two volumes appeared in 1855. In 1857 Macaulay was made a peer, Lord Macaulay of Rothbury Temple.

Horace Mann (1823–?), called to the bar in 1847 in Lincoln's Inn. He was the assistant commissioner for the census of 1851 and was the author of the reports on Religious Worship and Education in Connection with the Census of 1851. He was appointed registrar and secretary to the Civil Service Commission in 1855.

Karl Marx (1818–83). Born in Germany and educated at the universities of Bonn and Berlin, where he studied philosophy and history. Marx became editor of the *Rhenish Gazette* in 1842 but the paper was suppressed by the authorities and Marx moved to Paris where he met Engels and with whom he drew up, in 1847, the *Communist Manifesto*. During the revolutionary outbreaks of 1848 Marx returned to Germany but he was expelled and, in 1849, he moved to London where he was to spend the rest of his life. It was in London that he wrote *Das Kapital*, the first volume of which appeared in 1867.

Lowell Mason (1792–1872). An American who was largely responsible for introducing the teaching of music in American public schools and for promoting the training of teachers in music education. He first visited Europe in 1837 but made a longer visit from December 1851 to April 1853. His experiences on this visit are recounted in his *Musical Letters from Abroad*.

Henry Mayhew (1812–87). A playwright and journalist, Mayhew was the first editor of *Punch*. Mayhew became increasingly absorbed in his social investigation and interviewing of the workers and poor living in London, and *London Labour and the London Poor*, which first appeared in articles in the *Morning Chronicle*, was published in book form over the period 1851–62.

George Meredith (1828–1909). Poet and novelist, Meredith's career spanned a long period during which he became a revered figure in the literary world. Meredith's first major novel *The Ordeal of Richard Feverel* was published in 1859. Meredith always regarded himself as a poet first and a novelist second.

Edward Miall (1809–81), MP for Rochdale 1852–67, Bradford 1868–74. An Independent (i.e. congregationalist) minister, he started in 1840 a campaign attacking the established church and in the following year he founded a weekly newspaper, *The Nonconformist*, which he edited until his death in 1881.

John Stuart Mill (1806–73) was the son of the philosopher James Mill. John was influenced strongly in his early years by Bentham. In 1843 he published his *System of Logic*. This was followed in 1848 by *Principles of Political Economy*. He married Harriet Taylor in 1851. Deeply interested in some aspects of political reform, Mill became MP for Westminster from 1865 to 1868 and attempted, unsuccessfully, to secure a Bill giving women the right to vote. His *Subjection of Women* was published in 1869.

Harriet Taylor Mill (1807–58). In 1826 Harriet Hardy married John Taylor, a druggist. Four years later, however, she met John Stuart Mill and from 1833 they met regularly. Harriet had a marked influence on Mill, especially in his thinking on women's rights. In 1851, two years after the death of Taylor, she and Mill married, although Mill protested formally against the existing laws of marriage and renounced all marital rights over Harriet.

John Everett Millais (1829–96) exhibited his first work at the Royal Academy at the age of 16. A leading member of the Pre-Raphaelites, his work in the 1850s was attacked by many critics, although he found a solid defender in John Ruskin. From the 1860s onwards Millais adopted a more popular style. 'Bubbles', 'Cherry Ripe', and 'The Boyhood of Raleigh' are just a few of the paintings which earned him not only popular success but great wealth. By the 1880s it was estimated that he was earning around £30,000 per year. In 1885 Millais became the first English painter to be awarded a baronetcy.

John Duguid Milne a graduate of Aberdeen University and practising lawyer in that city. Milne published his book *The Industrial and Social Position of Women* anonymously in 1857. However, when the book was republished thirteen years later, he added his name. In the note to the 1870 edition, Milne wrote that he had not made many changes to the text but, he added, 'I could not omit to notice the remarkable advance that has taken place during these years, in public opinion and in legislation, on the relative position of the sexes—an advance that has surpassed my expectation.'

William Morris (1834–96). While at Oxford, Morris and Edward Burne-Jones were leading figures in a group cultivating Pre-Raphaelitism. In 1856 Morris was prominent in launching the *Oxford and Cambridge Magazine* for which he wrote essays and poems. In 1858 *The Defence of Guenevere* was published. The following year he married Jane Burden and in 1860 they moved to the Red House which had been specially designed for them by Philip Webb. Morris, together with friends, formed 'The Firm', producing furniture, tapestries, and wallpapers, and they exhibited some of their products at the 1862 London International Exhibition of Art and Industry. In the 1870s Morris turned increasingly towards politics and in 1883 he joined the Democratic Federation. The following year he helped found the Socialist League and he contributed regularly to its journal *Commonweal*.

Florence Nightingale (1820–1910). Daughter of a wealthy middle-class family, her decision in 1845 to take up nursing alienated her from her family who thought such a vocation quite unsuitable. In charge of a group of nurses sent out to the Crimea during the War, she was horrified at the conditions and set about a complete reorganization of military nursing. On her return to Britain she worked tirelessly on a Royal Commission reporting on the Sanitary State of the Army and then in attempting to implement the Commission's recommendations. She did much to establish nursing as a respectable profession for women. Although sympathizing with the women's suffrage movement, Nightingale argued that there were many greater injustices under which women laboured than the lack of the vote.

Walter Horatio Pater (1839–94) became a fellow of Brasenose College, Oxford in 1864 and he spent most of his life in Oxford. The first of the 'aesthetes', his book *The Renaissance* (1873) influenced many undergraduates of the time including Oscar Wilde. In 1885 *Marius the Epicurean* was published. It was to be regarded as an apologia for hedonism and the pursuit of beauty.

Emma Paterson (1848–86) devoted much of her life to the setting up of women's trade unions. In 1874 she established the Women's Provident and Protective League which attempted to form unions amongst lowly paid women workers, but her efforts met with little success. She continued to travel the country and lecture on women's rights and in 1876 she became editor of the *Women's Union Journal*. In 1875 she was one of the first women to be admitted to the Trade Union Congress.

Alexander Redgrave (1818–94). Entered the Home Office at the age of 16. He was transferred to the Office of Factory Inspectors and became an inspector in 1852. He became chief inspector in the 1880s and retired in 1891 at the age of 73.

James Ewing Ritchie (1820–96). A journalist who, as well as contributing numerous articles to magazines and journals, wrote a number of books on political and social themes. They include: *Modern Statesmen, or Sketches from the Strangers' Gallery of the House of Commons* (1861), *Life of Richard Cobden* (1865), *The Religious Life of London* (1870), and *Days and Nights in London* (1880).

Christina Georgina Rossetti (1830–94), a younger sister of Dante Gabriel Rossetti, published a large amount of both prose and poetry. 'A Birthday' and 'A Better Resurrection' appeared in her collection *Goblin Market and other Poems* (1862) and 'If Only' in *The Prince's Progress and other Poems* (1866).

John Ruskin (1819–1900). His five volumes of *Modern Painters*, together with *The Seven Lamps of Architecture* and *The Stones of Venice*, established Ruskin as the leading art critic of the period. In the early 1850s Ruskin defended Millais and other Pre-Raphaelites in the face of furious attacks from other critics. In 1854 his wife divorced him and shortly afterwards married Millais. From the 1860s onwards, Ruskin wrote increasingly on social and economic questions. In 1870 he was made first Slade professor of art at Oxford.

Lord John Russell (1792–1878). A son of the sixth Duke of Bedford, Russell entered the House of Commons at the age of 21 as a member for the family-controlled borough of Tavistock. A member of Lord Grey's Whig administration in 1832, Russell was largely responsible for pushing the 1832 reform legislation through the Commons. He was Prime Minister in 1846–52 and again in 1865–6.

George Bernard Shaw (1856–1950). Born in Dublin, Shaw moved to London in 1876. During his first ten years in London he wrote five novels, none of which met with much critical acclaim, and he attempted to supplement his income by writing music criticisms. By the mid-1880s he was a successful reviewer for the *Pall Mall Gazette* and *Dramatic Review*. In 1886 he became art and music critic for the *World* and he also wrote music reviews for the *Star* under the name 'Corno di Bassetto'. Shaw joined the Fabian Society and edited and contributed two essays to *Fabian Essays in Socialism* (1889). Best known as a dramatist, Shaw's first play *Widowers' Houses* was published in 1893.

Samuel Smiles (1812–1904). Although qualified as a doctor, Smiles took up journalism and became editor of the *Leeds Times*. He later became the secretary of a railway company in Leeds and then London but he continued writing. His major success came with the publication of *Self-Help* in 1859 which sold over 250,000 copies during his lifetime. It was the most popular of all 'success' literature and dealt with the benefits of thrift, temperance, work, and good character.

Arthur Penrhyn Stanley (1815–81). A distinguished scholar, Stanley was educated at Rugby and Balliol College, Oxford. He was ordained in 1856 and became professor of ecclesiastical history at Oxford. In 1864 he was appointed dean of Westminster.

Algernon Charles Swinburne (1837–1909) became known as one of the leaders of the aesthetic movement. His *Atalanta in Calydon*, published in 1865, brought him success. His first series of *Poems and Ballads* appeared in 1866. 'A Forsaken Garden' was printed in the second series of *Poems and Ballads* published in 1878.

Alfred Tennyson (1809–92). Son of a clergyman, he was educated at Trinity College, Cambridge, where he met Arthur Henry Hallam, the son of the historian. The sudden death of Hallam in 1833 was a great shock to him and he started *In Memoriam* which was published in 1850. In the same year, Tennyson was appointed poet laureate in succession to Wordsworth. Tennyson was raised to the peerage in 1884.

Anthony Trollope (1815–82) began work in 1834 as a junior clerk in the General Post Office in London and rose to be a high-ranking official in the Post Office. While there, he was responsible for the introduction of pillar boxes for the dispatch of letters. Trollope resigned from the Post Office in 1867 but by then he was also a well-known and prolific novel writer (47 novels in all). His most popular works were the Barchester series, starting with *The Warden* (1855) and concluding with *The Last Chronicle of Barset* (1867). At the General Election of 1868 Trollope stood unsuccessfully as Liberal candidate for Beverley. Trollope wrote his *Autobiography* in 1875–6 and it was published posthumously a year after his death.

Queen Victoria (1819–1901). Daughter of Edward, Duke of Kent and Victoria, Princess of Saxe-Coburg, Victoria became queen in 1837 on the death of William IV. An inveterate letter writer, Victoria also kept diaries and journals and filled over 100 volumes between the age of 13 and her death.

James Abbott McNeill Whistler (1834–1903) was born in the United States but emigrated to Europe in 1855. A central figure in the Aesthetic Movement, Whistler's work was attacked by Ruskin who accused him of 'flinging a pot of paint in the public's face'. Whistler took Ruskin to court, won and obtained damages of one farthing. Shortly afterwards Whistler went bankrupt. He took his revenge on Ruskin in a series of pamphlets and letters which were later collected and published in *The Gentle Art of Making Enemies* (1890).

Samuel Wilberforce (1805–73). Son of the evangelical, William Wilberforce, who had fought so hard for the abolition of slavery. Samuel was ordained into the Church of England in 1828. In 1845 he became Bishop of Oxford. Known as 'Soapy Sam' he was an eloquent and witty speaker as well as being an able administrator.

Thomas Wright often wrote under the name of the 'Journeyman Engineer'. As well as writing novels Wright wrote his memoirs and books detailing working-class life. Most of his examples were drawn from working life in London.

Index

References in **bold type** indicate quoted extracts.